A John Wesley Reader On Eschatology

Edited By
Mark K. Olson

Truth In Heart
Hayden, Idaho
2011

Olson, Mark K., 1957-

John Wesley, 1703-1791

ISBN: 10: 1-932370-25-0
       13: 978-1-932370-25-6

Library of Congress Control Number: 2011938870

Copyright © 2011
Mark K. Olson
All Rights Reserved

The works of John Wesley in this *Reader* are public domain:

The Sermons & Hymns are from
The Bicentennial Edition of the Works of John Wesley

The title page wood cut is:
"Four Horsemen of the Apocalypse"
By Albrecht Dürer, ca. 1497

Unless otherwise noted
all scripture quotations are from
The Holy Bible, The King James Version

To order more copies of this book:

Truth In Heart
10183 N Aero Dr. Ste. 3.
Hayden, ID 83835
(208) 772-4514

A John Wesley Reader On
Eschatology

Edited By

Mark K. Olson

Truth In Heart
Hayden, Idaho
2011

ALSO BY
MARK K. OLSON

The John Wesley
Christian Perfection Library

VOLUME ONE
JOHN WESLEY'S 'A PLAIN ACCOUNT OF CHRISTIAN PERFECTION'
THE ANNOTATED EDITION

VOLUME TWO
JOHN WESLEY'S THEOLOGY OF CHRISTIAN PERFECTION
DEVELOPMENTS IN DOCTRINE & THEOLOGICAL SYSTEM

VOLUME THREE
THE JOHN WESLEY READER ON CHRISTIAN PERFECTION
1725 – 1791

TRUTHINHEART.COM

Table of Contents

Introduction	vii

Part One: John Wesley's Evangelical Eschatology

1. Millennial Aspirations and the Problem of Religious Nominalism	2
2. The Revival and Methodist Self-Understanding	15
3. From Heaven Above to New Creation Below	26
4. Survey of Major Themes	39
5. The Order of Eschatological Events	47
6. Selections, Text, and Sources	54

Part Two: John Wesley's Sermons on Eschatology

The Great Assize	62
The Mystery of Iniquity	79
The General Spread of the Gospel	96
The Signs of the Times	109
The General Deliverance	119
The New Creation	132
Of Hell	141
On Faith, Hebrews 11:1	153

Part Three: John Wesley's Explanatory Notes on Eschatology

The Teachings of Jesus

The Kingdom of God: Matthew 3:1-2, 13:1-52; Mark 4:21-29; Luke 17:20-37	166
Hymn 72: 2 Corinthians 5:1-9	177
The Fall of Jerusalem and the Parousia of Christ: Matthew 24:1-51; Mark 13:1-37; Luke 21:5-36	178
Hymn 61	191

The Epistles of Paul

Groaning for the New Creation: Romans 8:18-23	192
The Conversion of the Jews: Romans 11:7-32	194
The Resurrection Body: 1 Corinthians 15:22-58	198
Hymn 57	204
The Gathering of Believers: 1 Thessalonians 4:13-5:11	205
Apostasy and the Man of Sin: 2 Thessalonians 2:1-12	206

Marks of the Apostasy: 2 Timothy 3:1-5	209
Hymn 54: 2 Corinthians 5:10	210
The General Epistles	
The Conflagration of the Present Cosmos: 2 Peter 3:1-14	211
Hymn 522	215
The Spirit of Antichrist: 1 John 2:18-29	216
The Book of Revelation	219
The Book of Daniel 2, 7-12	349
Bibliography	374

Introduction

John Wesley (1703-91) is widely recognized as a leader of the eighteenth-century Evangelical Revival and the founder of Methodism. Wesley popularized Arminian theology along with a special emphasis on the doctrine of Christian perfection. Today, scholarship on Wesley is flourishing and this has led to the publication of numerous studies on his life and thought. Still, a neglected area is a good introduction to his views on last things. The purpose of this *Reader* is to help fill this gap. As in other areas of theology or church practice, Wesley was not an innovator in the field of Christian eschatology. He did not introduce any new system, a new school of interpretation, or a new eschatological model. What he did do was to take the views then held by many Protestants and weave them into a vision of his own, an evangelical eschatology centered on the growth of Methodism and of the Revival.

So why study Wesley's eschatology if he was no innovator on the subject? First, Wesley's eschatology informed his overall theology in significant ways, including his views on salvation, Christian discipleship, and holiness. Wesley often taught from a teleological angle, with the end in mind. So a grasp of his eschatology is necessary to fully appreciate other aspects of his theology. Second, his views on last things deeply influenced his vision of Methodism and the Revival. Wesley believed Methodism to be an end-times movement that would one day usher in the millennial reign of Christ. Along with other evangelicals, Wesley's eschatological vision anticipated the birth of the modern missionary movement of the nineteenth and twentieth centuries, which has spread the evangelical faith around the world. Third, and possibly even more significant today, Wesley held that the future eschaton will include the present material cosmos. The implications this has on Christian stewardship still needs to be considered in all of its ramifications, including a whole range of issues from environmental protection and animal rights to questions of theodicy and ultimate cosmological purpose. Finally, a study of Wesley's eschatology offers important insights into his own self-image. With his belief that the Revival was a return of apostolic Christianity, a precursor to the 'latter-day glory,' Wesley saw himself as an evangelical prophet, chosen by God to herald the gospel of *real* Christianity to a nominal Christian world. So, whether one's interest in Wesley is theological, ecclesial, philosophical, historical, biographical, missional, or some other field, a study of his eschatology is necessary to properly evaluate and engage his thought in these other areas.

The *Reader* is organized into three sections. Part One is introductory and provides explanation and historical context for the reader to critically engage Wesley's views. The reader will find that the editor does not critique Wesley or his positions. Instead, Part One empowers the reader to examine Wesley's views on eschatology and to draw conclusions regarding its strengths and weaknesses. For such assessment, Wesley must be read against the backdrop of his own times. Therefore, the first three chapters present the broader historical context that informed the eschatological character of the times and shaped the development of Wesley's views over his long career. Following his Anglican heritage, Wesley first held to the amillennial position. But with his evangelical conversion in 1738, Wesley soon gravitated to a robust postmillennialism. Wesley's views on the eschaton went through an even more radical turn in the 1770s and 80s as he sought to incorporate the latest thought in the sciences to the eschatological hope of a new heavens and new earth. Yet, the one constant in his eschatology after 1738 was the motif of real Christianity. For this reason the opening chapters of Part One highlight the problem of religious nominalism that in large measure drove eschatological speculation in early modern England and fueled the Revival and Wesley's eschatological vision. The next two chapters focus on the major themes that informed Wesley's eschatology and chart the specifics of eschatological fulfillment through the centuries. It is concluded that by the 1780s Wesley should be considered a postmillennial new creationist. The final chapter of Part One explains the editorial decisions that guided the selection of writings included in this *Reader*.

Parts Two and Three include Wesley's sermons and commentary notes (and a few hymns). This *Reader* brings together for the first time all of Wesley's primary writings on eschatology to be studied and compared. In this way the broad contours of Wesley's eschatology become readily apparent and the specifics of his thought can be furthered explored as the reader has interest. In regard to Wesley's *Explanatory Notes*, too little attention has been given to his commentary on the Book of Revelation. It is the hope of this editor that this *Reader* will encourage more interest in this lengthy work. The tendency has been to ignore it because it is believed that Wesley simply abridged the work of Albrecht Bengel and provided no original ideas of his own. But this argument is quite misleading since it can be made against other areas in Wesley's theology and ecclesiology. As was already mentioned above, Wesley's strength was not as an originator, but as an editor; not as an innovator, but as one who takes the ideas of others and harnesses them for his own purposes. This is what Wesley accomplished with his core conviction of real Christianity in his commentary on Revelation. Like a subplot, the motif of real Christianity is woven throughout his entire commentary, from the opening chapters on Christ and the seven churches to the closing chapters on the new creation. The message of evangelical holiness not only guided Wesley's soteriology and sense of mission, but his eschatology as well. Therefore, Wesley's eschatology must be labeled as evangelical.

On a personal note, I want to express appreciation to my former professor, Dr. Andy Johnson, who supported my study of Wesley's commentary in the course on Revelation. From this study I gained fresh appreciation of the significance of Wesley's eschatology in his overall theology, and realized the important role that the motif of real Christianity plays in his commentary and in his eschatology in general. I further want to thank Dr. Geordan Hammond for taking the time to read over the manuscript and to offer many positive and constructive comments. Geordan's friendship has encouraged me to be even more thorough in my scholarship of Wesley. Another Wesley scholar who has always been helpful is Dr. Randy Maddox. As always, Randy responded timely to emails about specific questions. I also want to recognize my fellow PhD student, David Stark. David's knowledge of early Methodism saved me from several historical inaccuracies. Last, I want to thank Rick Friedrich and Truth in Heart publishers for releasing another volume from my pen. I have appreciated Rick's support for each of my publishing endeavors.

Part One

John Wesley's Evangelical Eschatology

Chapter One
Millennial Aspirations and the Problem of Religious Nominalism

Methodism was born in an age when many Protestants believed they were living on the precipice of human history. The roots of this eschatological expectation reach back to the Reformation in the sixteenth century. The great struggle between Roman Catholicism and Protestantism that dominated European politics for over three centuries also served as the lens through which Protestants read biblical prophecy, especially the Book of Revelation. While differing over details of interpretation, Protestants of nearly all stripes agreed the Papacy was the Antichrist, the Church of Rome the harlot Babylon, and that Revelation describes in historical detail the triumph of the true faith over all false faiths in the not-to-distant future. Therefore, Protestants early on developed a unique philosophy of salvation history that centered on the problem of religious nominalism.[1]

To justify their rift with Rome, Protestants turned to the prophetic texts of Holy Scripture. When Martin Luther (1483-1546) published his first German translation of the New Testament in 1522, he had little esteem for the Book of Revelation. His failure to see Christ in its "visions and figures" led Luther to reject outright the book's apostolic and prophetic authority. "First and foremost," wrote Luther, "the apostles do not deal with visions, but prophesy in clear, plain words."[2] By 1545, when his second preface appeared, his views had dramatically shifted. Luther now believed Revelation to reveal in detail the future of the church. By looking at church history, and aligning specific historical events to the narrative of Revelation, Luther concluded that a "sure" and "unobjectionable interpretation" of the book could be maintained. From his own calculations, Luther believed the Papacy was the Antichrist, the sack of Rome in 1527 (by Charles V) the beginning of the destruction of "Babylon the Great," and the Turkish invasion of Europe the

---

[1] In this study religious nominalism is a broad label which refers to a Christian faith deemed false, unscriptural, as mere profession or ritual, or lacking the transformative power of the gospel. Religious nominalism was a fundamental concern of Protestants (ch. 1), of early evangelicals and Methodists (ch. 2), and its antidote, real Christianity, was a major theme in Wesley's eschatology (ch. 4).

[2] Avihu Zakai, *Exile and Kingdom: History and Apocalypse in the Puritan Migration to America.* Cambridge: Cambridge University Press, 1992, 20.

fulfillment of John's vision of "Gog and Magog." No wonder Luther saw the Reformation as the "final years of history."[3]

Across the English Channel similar developments were taking shape. Though the Henrician Reformation left the nation largely unchanged in its religious sympathies, for only a minority was Protestant at the time, the historical method of interpretation (historicism) began to be used by English Protestants to address the problem of religious nominalism. John Bale (1495-1563) borrowed Augustine's analogy of two cities, the heavenly and earthly, but applied the imagery to the struggle between the two churches, Protestant and Catholic. According to Bale, the English church was founded by apostolic commission long before Rome sent her corrupting emissaries in the sixth century. Consequently, ecclesiastical history confirmed to Bale and his readers that Rome was the Great Harlot (Rev. 17) and this justified her expulsion by King Henry VIII.[4]

The merging of religious reformation with the English monarchy found its strongest proponent in John Foxe (1516-87). In his *Acts and Monuments* (later known as *Foxes Book of Martyrs*) Foxe presented an ecclesiastical history in which the English "Babylonish captivity" was nearing its end with the ascension of Queen Elizabeth. Comparing the Protestant Queen to Constantine the Great, who in effect made Christianity the religion of the Roman Empire, Foxe held that England was an "elect nation," chosen by God to overthrow the papal beast. The Reformation "signaled the final battle" in which the true faith, the Protestant religion, would overcome the apostate church of Rome. Like Bale before him, Foxe taught that the chief instrument in this battle was the "Godly Prince," the English monarchy. With the ascension of Elizabeth in 1558, Foxe believed the final stage of providential history was at hand, which would culminate in the final overthrow of the Roman Antichrist.[5] The influence of Foxe's work on the English people is confirmed by James Thompson, "'It became almost the Bible of Protestant England, and was ordered by Convocation to be placed in churches where everyone might have access to it.'"[6] Foxe's *Acts and Monuments* played a powerful role in altering the religious sympathies of the English people, drawing them away from Rome to the Protestant cause.

Nevertheless, not everyone was satisfied with the Elizabethan settlement. Though the Acts of Supremacy and Uniformity formally severed ties with the Church of Rome, the early Puritans felt the Queen had not gone far enough to

---

[3] Ibid., 20-21.
[4] Ibid., 26-31.
[5] Ibid., 31-37.
[6] James Thompson, "A History of Historical Writing," 2 vols. New York, 1942, 1:615, in Avahu Zakai, *Exile,* 33.

reform the nation of popish influence. In light of current events, their concern appeared justified. During Elizabeth's reign, the Pope recruited young English sympathizers to infiltrate the nation and convert the masses. At the same time, Rome agitated political challenges to the young Queen's legitimacy to the throne by supporting her archrival, pro-Catholic Mary Queen of Scots. The Pope's meddling in English affairs did not stop there. By the 1580s, Rome was supporting a massive military invasion known as the Great Spanish Armada. Though the English fended off this invasion (and again in 1596 and 1597), handing the pro-Catholic forces a devastating blow, the Counter-Reformation continued to gain ground on the continent and in the new world through Spanish missions.

The situation in England was aggravated in the sixteenth century by the reigns of James I (1603-25) and Charles I (1625-49). Their dogmatic belief in divine right, that kings receive their authority solely from God and not the people, eventually pushed the Puritans and other republican radicals toward open defiance. This led to civil war in the 1640s and the execution of Charles in 1649. Fear that the nation might slip back under Rome's control reached a feverish pitch. In this volatile climate, revolutionary ideas began to find fertile soil in the hearts of many Englishmen through a more radical reading of the Book of Revelation.

One of the prominent apocalyptic writers of the era was Thomas Brightman (1562-1607). What made his celebrated book *Apocalypsis Apocalypseos, or Revelation of the Revelation* (1609) so influential to the Puritan cause was his radical revision of Foxe and Bale. Whereas the latter writers retained Augustine's dualism of heaven and earth, placing the millennium beyond human history in a heavenly ethereal realm, Brightman located the millennium and the New Jerusalem squarely within human history:

> But as touching this *new-Jerusalem* . . . it is not that *Citie* which the Saintes shall enjoy in the Heaven . . . but that *Church*, that is to be looked upon the earth, the most noble and pure of all other, that ever have been to that tyme.[7]

This blending of the millennium with the eternal state (New Jerusalem) was a common feature of post-Reformation English eschatologies. Besides the postmillennial flavor of Brightman's system, his exegesis stands out for endorsing a double millennium. Holding that the first millennium stretched

---

[7] Avihu Zakai, "Thomas Brightman and English Apocalyptic Tradition," in *Menasseh Ben Israel and His World*. eds. Yoset Kaplan, Richard H. Popkin, and Henry Mechoulan. Leiden: E. J. Brill, 1989, 39.

from the reign of Constantine the Great (AD 304) to the scourge of the Turks in AD 1300, the second millennium would reach from 1300 and culminate in the final triumph of the Reformed faith over the Roman Antichrist.

Brightman's exegesis went even further. He asserted the seventh trumpet, when the "mystery of God should be finished" and the "kingdoms of this world are become *the kingdoms* of our Lord" (Rev. 10:7; 11:15), had already sounded with the ascension of Queen Elizabeth. Therefore, Brightman believed his generation was already living in the "last ages" when God will judge the nations and reward his saints (Rev. 11:18). Three of the vials (bowls) had already been poured out and Brightman expected the fourth (revival of Gospel truth) and the fifth (fall of Rome) to transpire by the 1650s. The great ingathering of the Jews would be the sixth vial. He looked for the Euphrates River to dry up so the lost tribes of Israel in the east could return to their homeland and battle the Turks. With the sack of Rome, the forces of the Antichrist and the Turks would crumble by the 1690s. A stronger chord of imminence could not be struck.

The linchpin for the Puritan revolution was found in Brightman's exegesis of the seven churches. Agreeing that these letters were written to seven historical churches in the first century, Brightman argued they "comprehend the ages following" up to his own day.[8] Identifying the first four churches with prior epochs of church history, Brightman taught that godly Philadelphia and sinful Laodicea point to the current situation in England.[9] This was where his interpretation took a radical turn from Bale and Foxe. Writing nearly a half century later, Brightman had witnessed how Queen Elizabeth became unwilling to push for further reforms. He therefore identified godly Philadelphia with the Reformed churches of Geneva, and soon-to-be-judged Laodicea with the Church of England. The message was clear: the Puritans should not expect significant reform from the "Godly Prince" and instead seek to usher in the kingdom themselves. Brightman's interpretation poured explosive fuel on the Puritan cause. Convinced the nation was on the brink of divine judgment, many Puritans and Separatists fled to the new world in the 1630s,[10] while others decided to stay and fight for the establishment of God's kingdom in the nation. The Puritan revolution reveals a shift in the battle-line over religious nominalism. Whereas in the sixteenth century the line was drawn between two churches, Protestant and

---

[8] Zakai, *Exile*, 48.
[9] Brightman believed Sardis pointed to the German Lutheran church.
[10] Rebecca Fraser estimates up to 5,000 per year immigrated to the Massachusetts colony (Rebecca Fraser, *The Story of Britain: From the Romans to the Present: A Narrative History*. New York: W. W. Norton & Company, 2003, 325).

Roman, now the line was drawn between two Protestant factions, Puritan and Anglican, with many Puritans linking the Anglicans to the Antichrist.[11]

Brightman was not the only voice sounding the alarm that the day of the Lord was at hand. The 1640s saw a burst of millennial frenzy after Archbishop Laud's hold on authority broke down. Radical splinter groups sprung up everywhere anticipating the end-times. Many, like Puritan Thomas Goodwin, mathematician William Oughtred, Fifth Monarchians John Rogers and John Tillinghast,[12] Independent Peter Sterry and others looked to 1656, or there about, as the year when the Antichrist would fall and the great ingathering of the Jews begin.[13] Even the great commentator Joseph Mede looked to the 1650s as the beginning of the messianic age. Using the standard practice of prophetic years, Mede calculated the 1260 days of Revelation 12:6 to represent the Pope's reign of 1260 years (395-1655). Others looked to later dates in the seventeenth century. Sabbatians looked to 1666 when the Messianic age would begin.[14] John Napier, inventor of logarithms, became convinced the end would arrive before the end of the seventeenth century.[15]

Many expected Oliver Cromwell (1599-1658) to inaugurate the millennium. George Fox, the founder of Quakerism and later a pacifist, swept up in the fervor chastised Cromwell in 1657 for not fulfilling the prophecy of Rome's destruction (Rev. 18) by leading an attack on the city.[16] Even the great John Owen (1616-83) saw the rise of Cromwell as the beginning of a new era. Preaching before Cromwell and Parliament only three months after King Charles' execution, Owen took for his text Hebrews 12:26-27, which refers to the shaking of heaven and earth.[17] Interpreting the text to refer to political powers (heaven) and the people (earth), Owen proclaimed that God was now overthrowing governments that support Catholicism and establishing rulers that would serve the interests of the true faith, the Reformed religion. Owen based his thesis on a unique reading of Revelation 17:12-16. The ten kings that give their power to the beast refer to the nations

---

[11] Zakai, *Exile*, 60.

[12] The Fifth Monarchy took their name from the Book of Daniel and the five kingdoms (Babylon, Persia, Greece, Rome, and God's kingdom).

[13] Christopher Hill, "Till the Conversion of the Jews," in *Millenarianism and Messianism in English Literature and Thought 1650-1800*. ed. Richard N. Popkin, Leiden: E. J. Brill, 1988, 14-15.

[14] Harry M. Bracken, "Bishop Berkeley's Messianism," in Popkin, ed. *Millenarianism and Messianism*, 72.

[15] Hill, "Till the Conversion of the Jews," 14-18.

[16] William F. Burns, "The Whig Apocalypse: Astrology, Millenarianism, and Politics in England during the Restoration Crisis, 1678-1683," in *Millenarianism and Messianism in Early Modern European Culture: The Millennial Turn*. eds. James E. Force and Richard H. Popkin. Dordrecht: Kluwer Academic Publishers, 2001, 29.

[17] John Owen, *The Works of John Owen*. Carlisle: Banner of Truth, 1967, 8:247-79.

that have been subservient to papal control (vv. 12-13). The apocalyptic war in which the Lord gains the victory (v. 14) refers to the shaking of western governments since the Reformation. God was now raising up leaders to overthrow the Pope's political power so the true faith could flourish in the world. In simple terms, Owen believed God was shaking the western nations to free the gospel to Christianize the world. This vision of an evangelical gospel unfettered by civil government to convert the world was finding fertile soil in a rising movement on the continent. That movement was Pietism.[18]

The Thirty Years War (1618-48) left German society in shambles, divided into more than three hundred territories and states. As in England, the German Reformers initially looked to political rulers to underwrite their separation from Rome and implement the needed reforms in the church. However, in character with the times, these rulers asserted divine right, which led to state control of the churches. Even though the struggle was at first between Lutherans and Roman Catholics, by the early decades of the seventeenth century the Reformed church made strategic inroads into Lutheran territories. This sparked bitter resentment between both groups, making it impossible for Protestants to present a united front against Rome's Counter-Reformation. Compounding the situation were German rulers who saw the political advantage of maintaining religious uniformity in their territories, thereby encouraging intolerance toward any confession but their own. As a result, the three main confessions hardened in their doctrinal and ecclesiastical positions producing a stale spirit within the life of the churches:

> People attended church partly because they were required to do so by law, and attendance was sometimes thought of as a good work whose performance gave them credit in God's sight. Even more was participation in the Lord's Supper regarded as an act which had a mechanical effect on one's relation to God, and most people were regular communicants, whether once a year, once a quarter, or (occasionally) once a month.[19]

---

[18] Wesley makes the same positive point about the new American government, "The total indifference of the government there whether there be any religion or none leaves room for the propagation of true scriptural religion without the least let or hindrance" ("Of Former Times" §20, *The Works of John Wesley*. 34 projected vols. Nashville: Abingdon Press, 1984-Present, 3:452. Hereafter: *Works*). Albert Outler comments, "An interesting recognition of the positive effects of the principle of the separation of church and state."

[19] Theodore G. Tappert, ed. *Pia Desideria*. Fortress Press, 1964, 7-8. The *Pia Desideria* was published in 1675, 1676, 1678 (fuller edition), with three more German editions by 1712. First published as an introduction to a new collection of Arndt's sermons, Spener's introduction became so popular that it was released six months later as a book.

Although its roots reach back to Johann Arndt (1555-1621) and his influential work *True Christianity*, Pietism began as a movement with the publication of *Pia Desideria* in 1675 by Philip Jacob Spener (1635-1705). Whereas Orthodox Lutherans stressed the more objective *Christus pro nobis* ("Christ for us"), justification by faith alone, Pietists emphasized the more subjective *Christus in nobis* ("Christ in us"), regeneration and sanctification.[20] This meant that having a correct creedal faith was not enough for Pietists; the real need was for a living faith that brings new birth and transformation of life.

Spener was appalled at the spiritual and moral laxity in German society. Like Brightman, Spener compared the German church to lukewarm Laodicea and confessed the Reformation remained incomplete, "We are stuck fast in Babel as much as the Roman church is, and therefore we cannot boast of our withdrawal from it."[21] Though "anti-Christian Rome" had received a "decided jolt" by Luther, its "spiritual power" had not yet been broken. Spener felt the prophecy of Rome's "great fall" in Revelation 18 had not yet been "completely fulfilled."[22] Yet his diagnosis went further. The present spiritual condition of the Protestant church could be compared to the Jews returning from the Babylonian captivity in the sixth century BC. At the time, God's people had been delivered from exile and returned to their homeland, but they failed to "restore the temple and its beautiful services."[23] In a manner quite similar, the German church had failed to complete her deliverance from Rome by reforming the church of her spiritual deadness. Using the mark "love for one another" (Jn. 13:35), Spener concluded, "How difficult it will be to find even a small number of real and true disciples of Christ among the great mass of nominal Christians!"[24]

However, all was not lost. With the same millennial spirit that fueled the Puritan revolution in England, Spener's postmillennialism affirmed that God "promised his church here on earth a better state than this."[25] In agreement with other Christians, Spener anticipated the defeat of the Counter-Reformation, the national conversion of the Jews, and a global Christian faith through evangelism, religious tolerance, and compassionate ministries. At its heart, Spener's message was a call for revival, but a revival infused with an evangelical eschatological hope. Spener saw that the millennium would never

---

[20] K. James Stein, "Philipp Jakob Spener," in *The Pietist Theologians*. Carter Lindberg ed. Malden: Blackwell Publishing, 2005, 89.
[21] Tappert, 69, 84.
[22] Ibid., 77.
[23] Ibid., 73.
[24] Ibid., 57.
[25] Ibid., 76.

be realized unless the level of holiness in the church could be raised. In a manner similar to Brightman, Spener called for true believers to work proactively to revive and reform both church and society, but with an evangelical focus that set his agenda apart from his predecessors. His six-prong program called for the use of Scripture, the engagement of laity in the ministry, the prioritization of Christian practice, the promotion of Christian love in confronting heresy, the training of ministers in holy living as well as in learning ("study without piety is worthless"[26]), and the need for preaching that spiritually edifies its hearers. Spener's program was put into practice through his *collegia pietatis*, small groups for the promotion of personal holiness, which later informed Count Nicholas Zinzendorf's concept of *ecclesiola in ecclesia*, the true church within the nominal church. The line between a true and false faith, first drawn between Protestant and Catholic, then between Puritan and Anglican, was now being drawn between Pietists and nominal Christians.

Across the English Channel apocalyptic expectations continued to flourish despite setbacks. With Cromwell's death in 1658, the Commonwealth soon collapsed leading to the Restoration of the Stuarts in 1660. While Royalists celebrated with a "flood of royalist poems and pamphlets hailing Charles II as a messianic king,"[27] two thousand Dissenting clergy were expelled from their parishes because they would not subscribe to the Church of England's liturgy and episcopal order.[28] The Puritan revolution was essentially over. Yet, with the fading of old hopes new ones began to take root. Tensions continued to rub between the pro-Catholic Stuart monarchy and the deeply committed pro-Protestant Parliament. When James II abdicated the throne in 1688, commentators celebrated the Glorious Revolution of Protestant William and Mary with apocalyptic exuberance.

One of these was Hanserd Knollys (1598-1691), a Baptist by profession, who wrote extensively on biblical prophecy. In his *Exposition of the Whole Book of the Revelation* (1689), Knollys suggested the millennial kingdom had dawned with the Glorious Revolution.[29] Using the Protestant hermeneutic of prophetic years, Knolleys dated the rise of the Antichrist at AD 428, when Celestine I (422-32) attempted to expand the power of the Roman see into North Africa and the East.[30] Maneuvering to find historical events that fit the

---

[26] Ibid., 104.
[27] Bernard Capp, "The Political Dimension of Apocalyptic Thought," in *The Apocalypse in English Renaissance Thought and Literature*. eds. C. A. Patrides and Joseph Wittreich. Manchester: Manchester University Press, 1984, 117.
[28] Fraser, 363.
[29] Kenneth G. C. Newport, *Apocalypse & Millennium: Studies in Biblical Eisegesis.* Cambridge: Cambridge University Press, 2000, 28.
[30] Newport, 29. From 428 to 1688 is 1260 years.

prophetic calendar was a common feature of commentators who leaned on historicism to guide their exposition. Knollys was not the only commentator to see the Glorious Revolution as the fulfillment of biblical prophecy. Benjamin Keach (1640-1704) also believed he was living on the edge of prophetic history.[31] Moving along similar lines as Knollys, Keach proposed the slaying of the two witnesses in Revelation 11:7-10 to represent the sufferings of Dissenters between the Restoration and the Glorious Revolution. This meant the blowing of the seventh trumpet and the turning point of prophetic history was at hand. Leading up to 1688, when pro-Catholic Stuarts sat on the throne, the Antichrist reigned supreme in the nation. Now, with the ascension of William and Mary, the first blow against the papal beast had been struck, Protestantism was now secure in Britain and would soon defeat the beast elsewhere.

These two commentators illustrate the millennial fervor that pervaded the final decades of the seventeenth century. Paul Korshin notes, "Religious writers of every kind mention the beginning of Christ's thousand-year reign."[32] This included Dissenters, more radical groups, like the French Prophets, and even Anglican churchmen. Korshin informs us the early Boyle lectures "often dealt quite thoroughly with expectations of the millennium,"[33] though he notes that by the second decade of the eighteenth century Anglicans became more conservative and less inclined to engage in millennial expectations.[34] Millennial fervor attracted the most prominent scientists of the era. Isaac Newton (1643-1727) spent much energy pouring over the sacred text. Endorsing several Protestant tenets, like historicism, the conversion of the Jews, their restoration to the homeland, and the identity of the Pope as the Antichrist, Newton parted paths with the majority by advocating premillennialism and a literal rebuilding of the Jewish temple. The one who followed Newton as Professor of Mathematics at Cambridge was William Whiston (1657-1752). Best remembered for his translation of the works of Jewish historian Flavius Josephus, Whiston gained notoriety in 1696 with his book *A New Theory of the Earth* (which Wesley read in 1725). Utilizing the new science of Newton, Whiston proposed that the Genesis deluge was caused by cometary catastrophism. Walking in the footsteps of his mentor at Cambridge, Whiston endorsed premillennialism but based his

---

[31] Ibid., 39.

[32] Paul J. Korshin, "Queuing and Waiting: The Apocalypse in England, 1660-1750," in *The Apocalypse in English Renaissance Thought and Literature*. eds. C. A. Patrides and Joseph Wittreich. Manchester: Manchester University Press, 1984, 242.

[33] Korshin, 240. The Boyle Lectures began in 1692 and became a platform for Anglican discourse on matters of religion and science.

[34] Korshin, 249.

eschatology on the idea that the present creation will last six thousand years before the millennial age breaks forth in the eighteenth century.[35]

These intellectuals were heavily influenced by the greatest English commentator on Revelation in the seventeenth century, Joseph Mede (1586-1638). Born in Essex and educated at Christ's College, Cambridge, Mede served as professor of Greek at Cambridge. Since Protestants espoused a historicist reading of Revelation, questions of chronology and synchronism played a significant role in their discussions. Mede presented his breakthrough on synchronization in his *Clavis Apocalyptica* (*The Key to the Revelation*). First published in 1627 and again in 1632, the *Clavis* was released in English posthumously in 1643 by order of the Long Parliament. The "key," of course, was Mede's system of synchronization: "I call a synchronism of the prophecies a concurrence of events predicted therein within the same time; which may be called a contemporary or coetaneous period; for prophecies of contemporary things synchronize."[36] Through a series of fourteen synchronisms, Mede demonstrated that much of Revelation describes people and events that run concurrent to each other. He further advanced what many considered were new ideas on Revelation 20. In contrast to those who espoused a postmillennial vision (e.g. Brightman), Mede advanced a premillennial reading with Christ's physical return inaugurating the millennium. Mede's influence was widespread, stretched well into the eighteenth century, and, as we will see, influenced the eschatologies of both Wesley brothers (especially Charles) and that of Thomas Hartley (whom Wesley read in 1764).

Tensions over Catholicism continued to reverberate throughout the seventeenth and eighteenth centuries with France replacing Spain as Britain's main nemesis.[37] The opening of colonial markets throughout the seventeenth and eighteenth centuries expanded the struggle from one of political conquest to include that of wealth and commerce. In the new global theater, trade became as important as military victory to defeating the Counter-Reformation. Millennial hopes now became intertwined with the expanding

---

[35] This idea goes back to the first-century Christian writing *The Epistle of Barnabas*. It is based on the 7 days of Genesis 1 and Peter's comment that "one day *is* with the Lord as a thousand years" (2 Pet 3:8). The world will last 6,000 years followed by the 1,000 year reign of Christ.

[36] Joseph Mede, *Clavis Apocalyptica, or A Key to the Revelation*. Translated by R. Bransby Cooper. London: J. G. & F. Rivington, 1833, 1.

[37] In 1707 England, Scotland, and Wales were united to form Great Britain, with the Union Jack as the national flag. In 1801 Ireland was incorporated to form the United Kingdom.

British Empire.³⁸ Still, before the mid-1750s, when Wesley penned his commentary on Revelation, several geopolitical events would transpire that alarmed English fears and confirmed once again to British Protestants that Rome was the Antichrist and the harlot Babylon in Revelation.

Even though William (1689-1702) and Mary (1689-1694) and Anne (1702-1714) were Protestant, segments of the nation continued to support the line of James II. Known as Jacobites, support for James III (known as the Old Pretender) broke out in open rebellion in Scotland, leading to a major battle and defeat by government forces in November 1715. The promised French troops never materialized, and though James III arrived in December, the rebellion melted away and the Pretender fled back to France. The '15 rebellion was followed thirty years later by a more serious threat to the Hanoverian line. By 1744 rumors of an imminent French invasion were floating around the British Isles, leading officials to order all Roman Catholics to leave London. In 1745, Prince Charles Stuart (the Young Pretender), landed in Scotland and began his march toward London. Panic struck the nation as the rebellion gained steam with one victory after another, leading the rebel forces as far south as Derby, within striking distance of London. Due to events that many saw as nothing less than divine providence, the '45 rebellion unraveled in the spring of 1746 forcing the Young Pretender to retreat to France, ending any hope of the Catholic Stuarts regaining the throne.³⁹

With Great Britain secure from Jacobite threats, a larger global conflict was brewing between France and Great Britain, and their respective allies. Wesley was just putting the finishing touches on his *Explanatory Notes Upon the New Testament* when the two European super-powers collided over global colonial supremacy. The Seven Years War (1756-1763) was fought on four continents and proved a great victory for the British; her spoils included large sections of territory in North America, expanded control in India, Grenada, and Senegal. Great Britain was now an "empire encircling the globe,"⁴⁰ and with military success came wealth and prosperity. The Industrial Revolution was reshaping British society and produced an expanding market economy for an ever-growing population.⁴¹ By the last third of the eighteenth century, a noticeable rise in affluence became evident

---

³⁸ Hill, 22-23; A. H. Williamson, "Britain and the Beast: The Apocalypse and the Seventeenth-Century Debate About the Creation of the British State," in *Millenarianism and Messianism*, 22.

³⁹ On the '15 and '45 rebellions, see Fraser, 414-17, 432-36. For Wesley's comments on the '45 rebellion in his *Journal*, see *Works* 20:90-94.

⁴⁰ Fraser, 437.

⁴¹ Roy Porter, *English Society in the 18ᵗʰ Century*. Revised Edition. London: Penguin Books, 1990, 185-213.

in British society, leading Wesley to lament the rising standard of living among Methodists.[42]

What constituted a nominal faith now began to shift. As the threat of the Counter-Reformation dissipated in Britain, the transformative effects due to the Industrial Revolution and the Enlightenment left many evangelicals, like Wesley, to reflect on the dangers of wealth, materialism, and natural reason to an authentic faith. Simply stated, the "spirit of antichrist" was now seen as more sinister and pervasive. No longer was the divide between a true and false faith demarcated along confessional lines, even within Protestantism. The impact of the Evangelical Revival carried with it a subtle reshaping of standard Protestant eschatology by infusing it with evangelical priorities. This became evident in Wesley's later life. A preoccupation with the dangers of wealth and materialism was, in Wesley's eyes, "an offence before God and man, an urgent and dire peril to any Christian's profession and hope of salvation."[43] Riches lead to atheism and idolatry, stirring within the human heart pride, self-will, and "every temper that is contrary to the love of God."[44] Framed in eschatological terms, the divide between a true and false faith, the "spirit of truth" and the "spirit of antichrist" (1 Jn. 4:3-6), primarily lies within the human heart. Thomas Hartley (1708-84) made this point explicit, "Mystical *Babel* is in the root of our fallen nature, and born into the world with us all, which the spirit of Christ alone can cast out."[45] Hartley then applied his evangelical hermeneutic to the problem of religious nominalism, clothed in eschatological categories:

> Most of us are apt to look towards Rome only for the signs of the times, as if that were the sole residence of Anti-Christ…But look around thee, spectator, and thou shalt see Anti-Christ and his retinue also behind thee and on each hand of thee, and beware lest he be not also within thee…He is the *beast* in the natural, sensual man, and the *red dragon* in the man of persecution, he is the *serpent* in the sly deceiver and subtle hypocrite, the *false prophet* in the lying lip of interpreting the Scriptures, he is the *whore* in those that commit

---

[42] This was a common concern of Wesley's; see "The Danger of Riches" (1780), *Works* 3:227-46; "On Riches" (1788), *Works* 3:518-28. In this *Reader* see "The Mystery of Iniquity."

[43] Albert C. Outler, Introduction, Wesley's sermon "The Danger of Riches," *Works* 3:227-28.

[44] "On Riches" II.1-7, *Works* 3:519-28.

[45] Thomas Hartley, *Paradise Restored: Or, A Testimony to the Doctrine of the Blessed Millennium*. Leeds: Binns and Brown, 1799, 211, emphasis his. Wesley read his work soon after it was published in 1764. Hartley would later become a follower of Emmanuel Swedenborg.

fornication with the civil powers and great ones of the earth for filthy lucre-sake.[46]

The eighteenth-century Revival led evangelicals, like Wesley, to *interiorize* their eschatology when it came to the problem of religious nominalism, because they saw the fundamental concern to be spiritual and transformative, not creedal. Without denying that Catholicism was the great enemy of God in the Book of Revelation, Wesley and other evangelicals believed Protestantism to be plagued with the same disease: creedal profession apart from living faith in Christ.[47] The central aim of the Revival was to change this reality among the masses. The Revival's message began with the Reformation's emphasis on justification by faith alone, but reemphasized that this faith is the "work of God in us, which changes us and brings us to birth anew from God."[48] This much is widely known and studied. What is lesser known is how the Revival was carried forth by a powerful impulse of eschatological fervor, profoundly shaping early Methodist self-understanding as a movement. As we will see in the next chapter, John Wesley's evangelical eschatology was formed in the crucible of the Evangelical Revival.

---

[46] Ibid,. 210, emphasis mine.
[47] This theme is fully developed in Wesley's sermon "The Mystery of Iniquity."
[48] Martin Luther, *Preface to the Letter of St. Paul to the Romans*. trans. by Andrew Thorton, OSB. Saint Anselm Abbey, 1983. Web: www.ccel.org/l/luther/romans/pref_romans.html. No doubt these words were part of what Wesley heard on the evening of May 24, 1738, which led to his evangelical conversion.

Chapter Two
The Revival and Methodist Self-Understanding

In his classic work on societal awakenings, William McLoughlin repeatedly links the great revivals of the past to millennial aspirations.[1] Even though his focus is on the American scene and its five epochal awakenings,[2] his principles equally apply to the British context since the revivals on both sides of the Atlantic cross-fertilized each other. Great awakenings, says McLoughlin, are "not periods of neurosis (though they begin in times of cultural confusion)" but are "therapeutic and cathartic." They restore "cultural verve" and empower the people to "overcome the roadblocks" of their "millennial mission."[3]

McLoughlin's analysis is important because it points out the organic bond between awakenings, millennial expectations, and group identity. We saw in the last chapter how millennial expectations fueled Puritan and Pietistic reforms in the seventeenth century. The Evangelical Revival was no exception, for it too was bathed with millennial aspirations and infused with eschatological significance. As we will see below, John Wesley and the early Methodists accomplished this infusion of eschatological significance in two ways. First, they linked the Revival to the sacred narrative of Christ's first advent and the birth of the Christian faith.[4] Second, they looked to God's promises of the future and Christ's millennial reign.[5] In other words, early Methodists believed they were living in historic times, even epochal in God's redemptive plan, because they linked their *present* experience to the *past* narrative of the apostolic era (Gospels and Acts) and to the *future* hope of

---

[1] William G. McLoughlin, *Revivals, Awakenings, and Reform*. Chicago: University of Chicago Press, 1978, 3-23.

[2] Ibid., Puritan Awakening 1610-1640; First Great Awakening 1730-1760; Second Great Awakening 1800-1830; Third Great Awakening 1890-1920; Fourth Great Awakening 1960-1990(?). Since McLoughlin was writing in the late seventies, he identified the end of the present awakening in keeping with the thirty-year cycle of the prior ones.

[3] Ibid., 2.

[4] Besides the examples given below, Charles Wesley placed great stress on the fact his evangelical conversion happened on Pentecost Sunday (*The Journal of Charles Wesley*, 2 vols. Grand Rapids: Baker Book House, 1980, I:90).

[5] At times converts used second advent language to express their experience in the new birth (*Works* 19:26). For example, Charles Wesley's 1738 sermon on the three states incorporated language of the resurrection state with the emotions of conversion (Kenneth G. C. Newport, *The Sermons of Charles Wesley*. Oxford: Oxford University Press, 139).

Christ's millennial reign (Revelation). In this way they developed the identity of an *eschatological movement*.[6]

To see how this identity developed we begin with Wesley's 1739 *Journal*, which in large part reads like the Book of Acts. The linking of the Revival to the sacred narrative is intentional by Wesley, for it serves not only to vindicate his ministry, but also demonstrates the eschatological character of the awakening. Beginning with the Fetter Lane Pentecost on January 1, Wesley records over the next several months that "signs and wonders" followed his ministry as it did in apostolic times.[7] Convulsions, cries of anguish, sighs, and groanings were a common sight wherever Wesley ministered. He tells stories of healings, deliverances, even exorcisms; all meant to infuse the Revival with eschatological significance.[8] To give an example, on April 17 Wesley records that he expounded on Acts 4, the second Pentecostal outpouring of the Spirit, at the Baldwin Street Society. When he finished, the group "called upon God to confirm his word." Suddenly, one after another were seized with pain and cried out as if in the "agonies of death," some as if they were in the "belly of hell"—an obvious allusion to the prophet Jonah. Wesley concluded by paraphrasing Acts 4:30 with the accent on the present time: "So many living witnesses hath God given that 'his hand is *still* stretched out to heal, and that signs and wonders are even *now* wrought by his holy child Jesus.'"[9] According to Wesley, the apostolic ministry of signs and wonders had returned. The great promise of Joel[10] was now being fulfilled, evidenced by visions, dreams, and the sudden work of sovereign grace.[11]

Even stronger links to the apostolic era are made by the portrayal of Wesley in the Revival narrative. At Baldwin Street the sound of groans and cries could be heard through the audience as Wesley proclaimed "him that is mighty to save."[12] A Quaker, taken back by all that was happening, suddenly

---

[6] "The General Spread of the Gospel" §16, *Works* 2:493; "The Signs of the Times" II.1, *Works* 2:525.

[7] See Romans 15:18-19, where Paul appeals to signs and wonders to confirm his apostolic ministry.

[8] For healings and deliverances, see *Journal*: January 21, February 9-17, April 26, 30, May 16, 19, June 15, 24, 25. For exorcisms: May 2 and 21. On June 30 Wesley includes a letter in his *Journal* from Scottish minister Ralph Erskine, who defends these manifestations as a supernatural work of God overthrowing Satan's kingdom, and links then to stories in the Gospels (*Works* 19:76).

[9] *Works* 19:49; emphasis his.

[10] "And it shall come to pass afterward, *that* I will pour out my spirit upon all flesh; and your sons and your daughters shall prophesy, your old men shall dream dreams, your young men shall see visions" (2:28).

[11] "Journal" *Works* 19:59-60.

[12] Is. 63:1; *Works* 19:53.

"dropped down as thunderstruck." Wesley gathered around the man and began to intercede. After the man found relief, he cried out to Wesley before the people, "'Now I know, thou art a prophet of the Lord.'" Wesley is here portrayed as an evangelical prophet with apostolic authority.[13] On April 2, Wesley went a step further and applied Luke 4:18-19, a clear messianic text, to himself and other revival ministers.[14] For Wesley's readership, the message could not be more clear: the Revival was a new Pentecost, a fresh outpouring of the eschatological Spirit, the same Spirit that worked in Jesus and the apostles. Wesley summed it up many years later, "No 'former time' since the apostles left the earth has been 'better than the present'. None has been comparable to it in several respects. We are not born out of due time, but in the day of his power, a day of glorious salvation, wherein he is hastening to renew the whole race of mankind in righteousness and true holiness."[15] For John Wesley and the early Methodists, the "day of the Lord" had begun. God was once again "visiting and redeeming his people."[16]

Across the Atlantic, evangelicals were convinced the awakening had millennial overtones. Jonathan Edwards (1703-58) believed the "days of the apostles" had returned.[17] The signs and wonders witnessed in America paralleled those on British soil. As did Wesley, Edwards interpreted the physical manifestations to be a "great struggle" in which "Satan the old inhabitant seems to exert himself like a serpent disturbed and enraged," only to have his kingdom overthrown by a greater power.[18] The Revival was the "dawning" of millennial glory.[19] His generation was living on the precipice of human history, located between the fifth and sixth vials in God's timetable. Accordingly, Edwards anticipated the destruction of the papal Antichrist by 1866, after the forces of the Antichrist, Islam, and Heathenism join for one last-ditch effort to overthrow Christ's rule through his church.

---

[13] "Evangelical prophet" is the label Wesley gives Isaiah on April 8, but his use of the term connotes its application to himself.

[14] *Works* 19:46. In a manner similar to the apostles in Acts 4, Wesley was asked by what authority he exercised his open-air ministry. Wesley's response mirrors Peter's, "By the authority of Jesus Christ, conveyed to me by the Archbishop of Canterbury, when he laid his hands upon me and said, 'Take thou authority to preach the gospel'" (*Works* 19:64). Since Wesley was a staunch believer in apostolic procession, he no doubt understood his ordination included apostolic authority.

[15] "Of Former Times" §23, *Works* 3:453.

[16] "An Earnest Appeal to Men of Reason and Religion" §99, *Works* 11:89.

[17] "Some Thoughts Concerning the Present Revival of Religion" (1742), in C. C. Goen, ed. *The Great Awakening, The Works of Jonathan Edwards,* vol. 4. New Haven: Yale University Press, 1972, 319.

[18] "A Faithful Narrative" (1738), "Distinguishing Marks" (1741), *Works* 4:163, 230. Wesley takes the same position as Edwards on the revival manifestations.

[19] Ibid., 324.

Yet, before this final battle, Edwards believed God would pour out his Spirit in an extraordinary fashion leading to the expansion of the evangelical gospel. This end-time revival will convert the masses of nominal Christians, draw in the Jewish people, overthrow the powers of Islam and Heathenism, and finally destroy "Satan's visible kingdom on earth," the Papacy.[20]

Evangelicals of all stripes saw themselves as the true eschatological community, the restorers of the apostolic faith, the custodians of the Reformation, and the heralds of God's final act to inaugurate Christ's millennial kingdom. By common consensus evangelicals held to the basic contours of Protestant eschatology: historicism, the papal Antichrist, the conversion of the Jews, and the hope of a global evangelical faith. Where they began to part paths with one another was over the question of pre- or post-millennialism. While the latter position still dominated, the premillennial views of Joseph Mede were influencing a greater number of evangelicals, including leading Methodists like Charles Wesley, John Fletcher, and Joseph Benson. While John Wesley's writings are consistently postmillennial, he did flirt with premillennialism for a short period.[21] It should be remembered that during the eighteenth century the two models were not so far apart as in the nineteenth and twentieth centuries when premillennialism took on a dispensational flavor.

One of the most significant documents in the early years of the Revival is Wesley's university sermon *Scriptural Christianity*, preached at St. Mary's, Oxford, in 1744. It should be noted at the outset, Wesley's purpose is not to lay out his millennial views; instead, his aim is to castigate the university and city for its nominal religious faith, "Is this city a Christian city? Is Christianity, scriptural Christianity, found here?" (IV.3). But this is what makes the sermon so insightful for our purposes. The fact that *Scriptural Christianity* embodies a robust millennialism in its core argument is telling about early Methodist self-understanding. Using Acts 4:31 as his text, Wesley describes the transformative power of the Gospel working in individual believers, spreading from person to person, and becoming a global faith.[22] As he did in his 1739 *Journal*, Wesley links the Revival to the great redemptive moments of the *past* and to the *future*, for in this way he infuses the *present* with eschatological significance. The Revival is a return of apostolic Christianity, the dawn of millennial glory, the forerunner of a global evangelical faith, in holiness as well as in creed. In the end, *Scriptural*

---

[20] See chs 22-27 of "A History of the Work of Redemption" (1739); for his eschatology see John F. Wilson, ed. *The Works of Jonathan Edwards*, vol. IX. New Haven: Yale University Press, 1989.

[21] This topic is addressed in the next chapter.

[22] The reader might want to read the sermon at this point; *Works* 1:159-80.

Christianity is more than a critique of nominal Christianity found in the institutions of church and state, its salvo opens a window into the self-understanding of early Methodists, and of Wesley himself.[23]

This self-understanding permeated early Methodism to a degree that is often not realized by contemporary Wesleyans. Since Wesley was reticent to endorse specific eschatologies and timetables, it is often assumed that early Methodists had little interest in eschatology. Nothing could be further from the truth. Early Methodists, including Wesley, were immersed in the culture of the Revival, and that culture was eschatological at its core. In an important study, Kenneth Newport catalogues the millennial fervor of many early Methodists.[24] One example given by Newport concerns a new Methodist convert, John Brown of Tanfield Lea. Having been converted the day before, apparently by a dream, Brown, caught up with eschatological fervor, rode through town "hollowing and shouting and driving all the people before him, telling them God had told him he should be a king, and should tread all his enemies under his feet."[25]

One of the factors that aroused Methodist interest in the 1740s was the geopolitical tensions between pro-Catholic France and pro-Protestant Britain. The '45 Rebellion filled the nation with panic as the Young Pretender came close to entering London. It was during this period that Charles Wesley (1707-1788) began to take personal interest in biblical prophecy. In an exchange of letters, John Robertson shared with Charles that according to his calculations the millennium would begin in 1836.[26] Over the next several years, Charles applied himself to the study of Daniel and Revelation. It appears that Methodists were proclaiming the end may be near because one of the public criticisms leveled against Wesley (and the Methodists) was that he taught the Revival signaled the arrival of the Day of the Lord.[27] Apocalyptic panic struck London in 1750 when the city was battered by a series of earthquakes. Luke Tyerman describes the fear that captured the hearts of many when a soldier, carried away by enthusiasm, prophesied that

---

[23] Another example of Wesley's millennialism influencing his views of the Revival, see his preface to his third *Journal* extract, written in 1742 (*Works* 19:4, par. 8). Wesley quotes Rev. 6:2 ("ride on, conquering and to conquer") in a doxology praising God for the spread of the Revival till the evangelical gospel becomes a global faith.
[24] Newport, *Apocalypse & Millennium: Studies in Biblical Eisegesis*.
[25] *Works* 19:304.
[26] Newport, 97.
[27] Newport, 93. George Lavington, *The Enthusiasm of Methodists and Papists Compared*. London: J. & P. Knapton, 1754, §30, 61-62. Lavington pulled most of his quotations from Wesley's "Earnest Appeal to Men of Reason and Religion." For example, see Wesley's comment on the Day of the Lord in "An Earnest Appeal to Men of Reason and Religion" §99, *Works* 11:89.

half of London and Westminster would be destroyed by another quake in April.[28] The churches and Methodist chapels were filled to overflowing as thousands fled the city to await the apocalypse. Charles preached several times *The Cause and Cure of Earthquakes*, published that spring (and again in 1756), pointing out that these mighty shakings are God's judgment on human sin.[29]

The 1750s saw the flowering of Methodist interest in eschatology. Vincent Perronet (1693-1785) wrote to his son in the early fifties that the "beginning of alarming providences" could now be seen, if only a "sinking world" could see that "the end of all things is at hand."[30] Critic Richard Hardy pointed out in 1753 that one of Methodism's chief errors was "'confidently asserting, that the millennium is at hand.'"[31] By the middle of the decade, Europe exploded into war when the two titans, Britain and France, fought over global colonial supremacy.[32] The opening of hostilities in June 1755 was followed by poor harvests, a severe cattle plague, and the great Lisbon earthquake on November 1. In a matter of minutes over 60,000 souls were engulfed as the shocks were felt throughout much of Europe. Fear struck many hearts as people wondered if the world would soon end. Seeing an evangelistic opportunity, Wesley quickly published *Some Thoughts Occasioned by the Late Earthquake at Lisbon*.[33] He rebuts the idea that earthquakes are caused by natural forces and instead attributes them to God's sovereign judgment on human sin. The tract turns apocalyptic when Wesley includes a somewhat lengthy exposition on Edmond Halley's prediction that the return of the great comet in 1758 (now named after him) could bring apocalyptic destruction upon the earth. Early in 1756 Charles published a collection of seventeen hymns for a National Fast Day on February 6th.[34] In these hymns Charles' premillennial aspirations become evident as the signs of war, earthquake, famine, plague, and national confusion point to the Lord's soon return. Believing the seventh trumpet is soon to sound, Charles anticipates the Lord to descend from heaven, meeting his rising bride in the

---

[28] Luke Tyerman, *The Life and Times of the Rev. John Wesley*. 3 vols. Stoke-on-Trent: Tentmaker Publications, 2003, 2:71-74.

[29] Located in John Wesley's *Works* (Jackson) 7:386-99 (though was written and preached by Charles).

[30] Newport, 96. Randy Maddox confirms that Imrie published the letter in 1755 (*A Letter from the Reverend Mr. David Imrie, Minister of the Gospel at St Mungo, in Annandale; To a Gentleman in the City of Edinburgh*. Edinburgh: s.n., 1755.)

[31] Ibid., 99.

[32] See chapter one.

[33] *Works* (Jackson) 11:1-13; Tyerman, 2:223-25; see *Works* 7:153, footnote Hymn 59.

[34] *Works* 7:153, introductory note.

clouds, to begin the "grand millennial reign."[35] He firmly believed Christians must "watch and pray" to be "counted worthy to escape all the judgments coming on the world, and to stand before the Son of Man."[36]

Another early Methodist who expected Christ's soon return was John Fletcher (1729-85). Like Charles, Fletcher was a premillennialist and studiously poured over prophetic numbers to decipher the chronology of end-times events. He too looked for Rome's fall, along with every form of "antichristianism." Fletcher believed "the greatest wonders and signs shall attend these revolutions, insomuch that Turks and Jews, heathens and savages, will know the hand of the Lord." However, Fletcher differed from standard premillennialism by espousing a third coming of Christ at the end of the millennium. His letter to John Wesley in late 1755 confirms the deep interest Methodists took in trying to decipher the prophecies of Daniel and Revelation.[37] Fletcher closes with a strong appeal to not judge rashly, nor to "utter vain predictions in the name of the Lord." Instead, Methodists were admonished to remain "watchful," "rousing people out of their sleep, of confirming the weak brethren, and building up in our most holy faith those who know in whom they have believed." Like Charles, Fletcher called Methodists to fervent prayer to hasten Christ's return, when the "saints raised from the dead shall converse with living saints."

Methodism's identity as an eschatological movement exploded into apocalyptic enthusiasm in early 1762 when George Bell taught that the millennium was already breaking forth. A new wave of revival was sweeping through the societies with hundreds professing the experience of Christian perfection. The revival, which began in Yorkshire, spread far and wide. Against this backdrop of charged emotions, Bell and his loyal followers began to entertain visions in which they saw Satan bound and cast into the bottomless pit, with the angel placing a seal on him to keep him from deceiving the nations (Rev. 20:2-3).[38] Wesley later recorded in his *Plain Account of Christian Perfection* that Bell and his supporters taught they would never die, they could not be tempted, nor could they feel pain or grief anymore. Believing the charismata of the Spirit had returned, Bell and other perfectionists claimed the gifts of prophecy, discerning of spirits, and gifts of

---

[35] Ibid., 7:155-57. In 1754 Charles copied a lengthy letter by the Rev. David Imrie outlining a robust premillennial expectation of the Lord's return by 1794 (Newport, 124ff.). Randy Maddox confirms that Imrie published the letter in 1755 (*A Letter from the Reverend Mr. David Imrie, Minister of the Gospel at St Mungo, in Annandale; To a Gentleman in the City of Edinburgh*. Edinburgh: s.n., 1755.)
[36] Newport, 123.
[37] Ibid., 94-95. Fletcher's letter can be found in Wesley's *Works* 26:613-16.
[38] Newport, 97.

healing.[39] They professed the gift of Adamic perfection: being already one with God, having died and risen with Christ, seated with him in the heavenly realm, taken up into his heavenly throne, now living in the New Jerusalem, free from all works (i.e. the means of grace).[40] To promote their gospel of millennial perfectionism, Bell began to hold meetings for only their supporters. This led to the infection of schism, which spread like gangrene through the societies and frustrated any attempt by Wesley to bring correction or balance. Towards the end of 1762, Bell's fanaticism reached its peak when he prophesied the world would end in a great apocalyptic conflagration on February 28, 1763. How he arrived at this date remains a mystery. As the day approached, Bell gave a solemn farewell to William Briggs, "'Farewell – I shall see your face no more before we hear the last trumpet'!"[41] On that fateful night, Wesley remarked that he went to bed at his usual time and enjoyed a peaceful sleep.

Though Bell was shown to be an apocalyptic fanatic, Methodists continued to show an interest in the end-times. Joseph Benson (1748-1821), one of the most successful circuit riders, preached the soon coming of Christ, even within his lifetime. At a Methodist chapel in Colchester in 1797, John Stevens told his audience that the Antichrist (Rome) was soon to fall and the fields were "white unto harvest" (Jn 4:35). Stevens felt the church must make great haste to evangelize before the end arrives.[42] David Simpson, before his death in 1799, published a detailed work on biblical prophecy. He too believed the Roman Antichrist and the "Mahomentans" would fall in the near future, followed by the conversion of the Jews. "It is not very improbable," writes Simpson, "that this generation shall not pass away before most of these things be fulfilled."[43]

In 1780 James Kershaw (d. 1797), a personal acquaintance of Wesley, published a two-volume work on the Book of Revelation. Newport points out that Kershaw was a premillennialist, though, like Fletcher, he endorsed a third coming of Christ after the millennium.[44] Kershaw furthered agreed with the position of William Whiston by advocating the return of Christ around the year 2,000. Since Genesis states that God created the world in six days,

---

[39] Mark K. Olson, *John Wesley's 'A Plain Account of Christian Perfection': The Annotated Edition*. Fenwick: Truth in Heart, 2005, ch 20. Wesley had first stated these things in the 1762 tract *Cautions and Directions Given to the Greatest Professors in The Methodist Societies* in Albert Outler, *John Wesley*. Oxford: Oxford University Press, 1964, 305.
[40] Ibid., 214. See Outler, *John Wesley*, 301.
[41] Newport, 97; the last trump refers to 1 Th. 4:16.
[42] Ibid., 98. It is questionable whether Stevens himself was a Methodist, but the general point remains relevant since he was preaching in a Methodist chapel.
[43] Ibid., 113.
[44] Ibid., 109. See Newport for a summary of Kershaw's complex views.

and 2 Peter 3:8 teaches that "one day *is* with the Lord as a thousand years, and a thousand years as one day," Kershaw concluded that with a 4000 BC creation date the end of this present age must happen around AD 2000.[45] Although Kershaw held the end would not fully arrive until many years later, he remained confident the world was advancing according to a definite timetable, with Methodists called by God to prepare people for the end.

Another Methodist deeply concerned with prophetic events was Thomas Taylor (1738-1816). Wesley spoke well of his work in Ireland and in 1796 he was elected president of the Wesleyan conference. Taylor, who leaned more toward postmillennialism, published fifteen sermons on the subject in 1789. Believing his generation was close to the eschatological renewal, Taylor looked for the destruction of the Antichrist, the binding of Satan, the cessation of strife, the universal spread of the gospel, the ingathering of the Jewish people, and the conversion of the nations. After these conditions are met, wrote Taylor, the Lord Jesus will establish his kingdom on the earth. Significant to our study was Taylor's belief that the Antichrist will be defeated by the preaching of the "pure gospel of Christ." This began in the twelfth century with the Waldenses and Albigenses, symbolized by the first vial in Revelation 16, and continued up to the present time. Taylor saw himself (and Methodism) as more than a preacher, but as an "instrument in God's hands, a divine weapon used by the Almighty to deliver another withering, perhaps the last, blow against Antichrist."[46]

John Wesley believed that God had chosen Methodism to "spread scriptural holiness over the land,"[47] and thereby prepare the way for the Lord's millennial reign. Along with other evangelicals, he held that his generation was living on the precipice of human history: God was now doing a new work; the eschatological Spirit had been poured out; the gospel was going forth into all the world; the Day of the Lord was at hand. Although Luther once stated that revivals do not last beyond a generation (thirty years), Wesley testified that this revival had prospered for above five decades and was still gaining momentum. In light of God's promises to his church, what could this mean but the "dawn of 'the latter day glory'"?[48] Wesley concluded that the Revival was the greatest work of God since apostolic times.[49]

---

[45] See ch. 1 n 34.
[46] Newport, 111.
[47] "Minutes of Several Conversations Between the Rev. Mr. Wesley and Others: From the Year 1744, to the Year 1789" Q. 3, *Works* (Jackson) 8:299; see his 1790 letter to Robert Brackenbury stating the same purpose, *Works* (Jackson) 13:9.
[48] "The General Spread of the Gospel" §16, *Works* 2:492-93; "The Signs of the Times" II.1, *Works* 2:525.
[49] "Of Former Times" §23, *Works* 3:453; "On God's Vineyard" IV.4, *Works* 3:514.

Through the centuries, Christians have often looked back to a golden era when the church was pure and her doctrine and holiness were pristine. Protestants, by definition, hold that the church became corrupt and needed reform and renewal. As Wesley surveyed church history, cognizant as he was of the great movements and workings of God in the past, he often noted how religious nominalism continued to sap the life out of the church and her witness. Applying the words of the Apostle Paul—"the mystery of iniquity doth already work"—Wesley recognized that even the great Protestant communions were not immune to this sinister disease. Had not the "reformers themselves complained that the Reformation was not carried far enough?" quipped Wesley.[50] Focusing on the "circumstantials of religion," the "reformation of opinions and rites and ceremonies," these great churches had left out the "essentials of religion," the "entire change of men's tempers and lives."[51]

This is where Methodism shined as a beacon of light. Wesley repeatedly proclaimed that Methodism was nothing more than a recovery of the primitive faith, "plain, old Christianity" as he called it. What marks a Methodist is not his or her opinion regarding "this or that scheme of religion," nor matters of custom and tradition, but the "common, fundamental principles of Christianity."[52] Accordingly, Wesley never applied any denominational or doctrinal test for people to join a Methodist society. The only requirement was "a desire to flee from the wrath to come, to be saved from their sins,"[53] and a willingness to participate in the Methodist plan of intentional discipleship.[54] Here was the secret of Methodism's self-understanding as an eschatological movement. When Wesley declared those now famous words—"the world is my parish"[55]—he was announcing more than a personal mission; he was defining the mission of the Methodist movement that would emerge under his leadership. Given his belief that the Revival was a restoration of apostolic Christianity and that Methodism's vocation was to "spread scriptural holiness over the land," Wesley definitely saw Methodism as an eschatological movement to usher in that glorious day. The "time is at hand," Wesley announced, for God to "set up his kingdom over all the earth"[56] and for the "whole race of mankind" to be renewed in

---

[50] "The Mystery of Iniquity" §29, *Works* 2:465.
[51] Ibid.
[52] "The Character of a Methodist," *Works* 9:33, 34, 41.
[53] "General Rules of the United Societies," *Works* 9:70.
[54] Specifically, keeping the General Rules and participating in a society and class.
[55] *Works* 19:67.
[56] "The Signs of the Times" II.1, 10, *Works* 2:525, 531. See "The Mystery of Iniquity" §36, *Works* 2:470.

"righteousness and true holiness."[57] John Wesley's millennial aspirations could not be stated any clearer.[58]

---

[57] "Of Former Times" §23, *Works* 3:453.
[58] Russell Richey makes a similar argument as made in this chapter regarding nineteenth-century American Methodists. This confirms the eschatological character of early Methodism on both sides of the Atlantic. See his "Methodism as New Creation: An Historical Theological Enquiry," in Douglas Meeks, ed. *Wesleyan Perspectives on the New Creation*, Nashville: Kingswood Press, 2004, 73-92.

Chapter Three
From Heaven Above to New Creation Below

In the first two chapters, we learned that millennial aspirations helped shape the political and religious culture of early modern England, including the Evangelical Revival and Methodist self-understanding. We now take a closer look at the development of Wesley's eschatology from his early days at Oxford to its mature articulation in the 1780s. Randy Maddox has shown that at different times Wesley was swayed by each of the three main positions on the millennial reign of Christ.[1] He explains the Christian concept of a millennium is rooted in second temple Judaism:

> It emerged in pre-Christian Judaism as a way of handling the alternative models of the future hope offered in Isaiah (long life in this world) and Daniel (eternal life in a reconstituted world). As an option to forcing a choice between these two models, it was proposed that Isaiah was describing a still-future thousand-year golden age in this world, while Daniel was describing the final state after this age. Within Judaism this left three options: affirming Isaiah's vision of shalom in this world as the ultimate hope, affirming instead Daniel's vision of shalom coming fully only in a future world, or combining these with a millennium as an intermediate expression of the final hope.[2]

It was the last option that found expression in Revelation 20, which led many early church fathers to espouse a premillennial hope when the entire created order, including plants and animals, enjoy the bountiful blessing of God as a prelude to the new heavens and new earth.[3] For example, Irenaeus (ca. 202) taught the millennium is necessary for the fulfillment of certain promises that declare God's future reign over the present created order. He also maintained that deceased believers do not enter directly into God's heavenly presence, but reside in Hades until the general resurrection. God's

---

[1] See his *Responsible Grace*. Nashville: Kingswood Press, 1994, 231-35; and "Nurturing the New Creation: Reflections on a Wesleyan Trajectory" in Meeks, *Wesleyan Perspectives on the New Creation*, 21-52. Much of the main points in this chapter rely on Maddox's work in the above two books.

[2] "Nurturing the New Creation," 35-36.

[3] Stanley J. Grenz, *The Millennial Maze: Sorting Out Evangelical Options*. Downers Grove: InterVarsity Press, 1992, 39.

purpose is for believers to attain further growth in preparation for the new creation.

By contrast, other Christians embraced a more spiritualized Christian hope. Clement of Alexandria (ca. 215) and Origen (d. 255) cast aside the chiliast vision of an earthly millennium and its material pleasures, arguing instead for an ethereal heavenly state. Seeing no need for an earthly millennium, these church fathers spiritualized God's eternal rule by elevating it above the material creation. Diverging from Irenaeus, they affirmed that at death Christians enter directly into God's heavenly presence. The ablest proponent of what became known as amillennialism was Saint Augustine (354-430). Though his thought on last things developed over time, his mature position rejected outright the premillennialism of the early church fathers, including the belief that deceased believers wait in Hades until the resurrection. Augustine did affirm that the Scriptures teach a future reembodiment of believers at the general resurrection (though he did not see plants and animals participating in this future redemption). Glorified believers will dwell eternally in ethereal bodies, basking in the fullness and contemplation of the Triune God. As the Christian hope moved more and more toward a spiritualized state, little room remained for any concept of a renewed material creation. The present reign of Christ became associated with existing church structures and church order, with the focus of salvation on the human soul. The goal of every believer was to save one's soul through deliverance from this "probationary world" and to "ascend into the 'rest' of the timeless and ethereal heavenly realm."[4]

Even though the Reformers broke with Rome over several issues, they continued to embrace Augustine's transcendental eschatology. Maddox informs us that the transcendental model of eschatology dominated Wesley's studies at Oxford and continued to inform his eschatology for quite some time.[5] In his earliest manuscript sermons, "Death and Deliverance" (1725) and "Seek First the Kingdom" (1725), salvation is presented as deliverance from this life's troubles, including human infirmities and sin, into a kingdom that is "not of this world," where there is perfect happiness in the heavenly city of God. Wesley is even more explicit in his first university sermon, "The Image of God" (1730). After the "seeds of spiritual death" are finally expelled when this "earthly tabernacle is dissolved," the same body will be "rebuilt 'eternal in the heavens.'"[6] Wesley was emphatic that God will use the same elements of the earthly body to recreate the new glorified body. In a sermon by Joseph Calamy that Wesley transcribed and preached (1732-34),

---

[4] Maddox, "Nurturing the New Creation," 25.
[5] Ibid., 38, 45.
[6] "The Image of God" III, *Works* 4:299.

he belabors the point that God will use the same dusty remains of the dissolved body to rebuild one that is immortal, incorruptible, glorious, spiritual, and angelic.[7] At the time, Wesley's eschatology was quite elementary: Christ will descend in the clouds, the dead will be raised, the judgment will be set, and the righteous will shine as stars in heaven where they will forever gaze upon Him who is eternal.[8] Regarding the intermediate state, Wesley follows Irenaeus by suggesting the soul of the believer waits in Hades to be reunited with their body at the resurrection.[9] It should be noted that Wesley was exposed to alternative views while at Oxford. Maddox notes that one of Wesley's early lectures addressed the question of whether animals have souls. He also read the writings of premillennialists William Whiston and Thomas Burnet.[10]

The amillennial transcendental model not only defined Wesley's eschatology, it governed his early soteriology. Since the model emphasized personal salvation in a heavenly ethereal realm, Wesley naturally focused on preparing himself for death and justification at the final judgment. Holiness became the great pursuit of his life, which, in turn, led him to develop a regimen of disciplines for the formation of holy tempers. A radical reversal took place in Wesley's soteriology when he embraced the Moravian gospel of salvation by faith alone. Whereas before he pursued holiness to prepare for justification before God, he now realized justification is a gift to be received by faith in the present. The message of present salvation meant that God's eschatological kingdom was already *present* in the work of the eschatological Spirit. No longer was the kingdom seen as something outside of this world, only as an ethereal heavenly state; the kingdom is present, active, powerful, and transforming—ready to sweep across the entire world:

> May 'he who hath the keys of the house of David, who openeth and no man shutteth', open 'a great and effectual door' by whom it pleaseth him, for his everlasting gospel! May he 'send by whom he will send', so it may 'run and be glorified' more and more! May he 'ride on, conquering and to conquer', until 'the fullness of the

---

[7] "On the Resurrection of the Dead," *Works* (Jackson) 7:474-85. Joseph Calamy was Vicar of St. Lawrence, Jewry, London.

[8] "The Image of God" III.2, *Works* 4:303; "The Circumcision of the Heart" P.3, *Works* 1:402; "The Promise of Understanding" III.3, *Works* 4:289. At the time Wesley never stated what he expected to transpire before Christ's return.

[9] "Death and Deliverance" §17, *Works* 4:214. Wesley explicitly says "hell" but he must have meant Hades since the AV inappropriately has the word "hell" in Luke 16:23.

[10] "Nurturing the New Creation," 39, n. 53; 46, n. 68.

Gentiles be come in', and 'the earth be full of the knowledge of the glory of the Lord, as the waters cover the sea'![11]

The Revival convinced Wesley that not only a new day had begun in God's redemptive plan, but a new understanding of this plan now opened up to him. As we saw in the last chapter, the Revival's inherent worldview was eschatological, even apocalyptic. Early Methodists, including Wesley, believed they were living on the edge of human history. This vision of a mighty work of divine grace sweeping across the globe in the last days is what moved Wesley toward the postmillennial position. While not fully rejecting the amillennial transcendental model, in the 1740s Wesley grasped the eschatological significance of the Revival as a new "day of the Lord." God was once again restoring primitive, apostolic Christianity for the express purpose of renewing the "face of the earth."[12] Nevertheless, Wesley still affirmed an ethereal heaven above when he spoke of himself as a "spirit come from God and returning to God." Soon, Wesley told his readership, he would drop out of sight into an "unchangeable eternity."[13]

Both aspects of Wesley's eschatology were further clarified in his discourse on the Lord's Prayer.[14] The *kingdom of grace* is "set up in the believer's heart" when the person repents and believes in Christ. Drawing on the imagery of Revelation 6:2 (the rider on the white horse goes forth "conquering, and to conquer"), Christ reigns to subdue all things in the *soul* to himself. One day this kingdom of grace will be established across the world. The fullness of the Gentiles will come into it and all Israel will be saved. On that day, Christ will appear to "every soul of man as King of kings, and Lord of lords." The kingdom of grace will "swallow up all the kingdoms of the earth," with the entire human race "filled with righteousness and peace and joy, with holiness and happiness." Then will come the *kingdom of glory*. This is the "grand event," says Wesley, when God finally renovates all things by "putting an end to misery and sin, to infirmity and death...setting up the kingdom which endureth throughout all ages."[15]

In the 1750s the same eschatological paradigm shows up in his *Explanatory Notes Upon the New Testament*.[16] Wesley described the kingdom of glory as "wholly spiritual," and the resurrection body as

---

[11] "Preface to Journal 3" (1742) §8, *Works* 19:4.
[12] "An Earnest Appeal to Men of Reason and Religion" (1743) §§98, 99, *Works* 11:88-89.
[13] "Preface to Sermons" (1746) §5, *Works* 1:104-05.
[14] "Upon our Lord's Sermon on the Mount: Discourse the Sixth" (1748) III.8, *Works* 1:581-82.
[15] In this *Reader* the two phases of the kingdom are addressed in the parables (Matt. 13).
[16] First edition was published in 1755, second edition in 1757, and a third expanded edition in 1762.

"spiritual," "clothed with robes of light," "like the angels of God," and "heavenly."[17] When Christ appears in the air the "wicked will remain beneath, while the righteous, being absolved, shall be assessors with their Lord in the judgment."[18] Turning to the Book of Revelation, Wesley states the present cosmos will be "wholly dissolved" and "were no more."[19] The New Jerusalem does not belong to this world, yet believers inherit real bodies, but they are spiritual in nature.[20] Nevertheless, Wesley begins to question the underlying premises of this transcendental model in his comments on Romans 8:20-22. In response to Paul's hope that the "creation itself shall be delivered from the bondage of corruption," Wesley's presents the fundamental argument that will later inform his new creation eschatology, "Destruction is not deliverance; therefore whatsoever is destroyed, or ceases to be, is not delivered at all. Will, then, any part of the creation be destroyed?" This last question represents the beginning of a monumental shift in Wesley's eschatology.

This incipient new creation model was rooted in a natural philosophy that reached back to Plato and Aristotle, and came to dominate the worldview of medieval and Renaissance cultures, including eighteenth-century England. Known as the "Chain of Being," Maddox summarizes its basic contours:

> This model conceived of nature as a hierarchy of beings organized by relative excellence of abilities. Fish were higher in the chain than plants, dogs higher than fish, humans higher than dogs, and celestial beings higher than humans. A central assumption of the model was that the only type of cosmos fitting for a Perfect Being to produce was one in which every conceivable niche was occupied by its appropriate type of being.[21]

---

[17] 1 Corinthians 15:43-51.

[18] 1 Thessalonians 4:17.

[19] Revelation 20:11; cf. 2 Peter 3:10-11. Yet, compare with Charles Wesley's 1747 hymn where the new creation resurrects out of the ashes of the present cosmos (*Works* 7:716-17). This hymn points to an earlier date when the Wesley's began to enunciate the permanence of the created order.

[20] Revelation 21:2, 17.

[21] "Wesley's Engagement in the Natural Sciences," in *The Cambridge Companion to John Wesley*. eds. Randy L. Maddox and Jason E. Vickers. Cambridge: Cambridge University Press, 2010, 171. The classic studies on the Chain of Being are Arthur O. Lovejoy, *The Great Chain of Being: A Study of the History of an Idea*. New York: Harper & Brothers, 1936; and E. M. W. Tillyard, *The Elizabethan World Picture*. New York: Vintage Books, 1959. Also the website by Dr. L. Kip Wheeler: http://web.cn.edu.kwheeler/Tillyard01.html (last viewed: 3/2/11).

Referred to as divine plentitude, this central assumption further implied that God created every type of being at the original creation. The Chain carried another assumption: the permanence of the created order. That is, once created the heavens, world, and its creatures will continue to exist in some form. Years later Wesley summarized the creation's permanence this way:

> All matter indeed is continually changing, and that into ten thousand forms. But that it is changeable does in no wise imply that it is perishable. The substance may remain one and the same, though under innumerable forms. It is very possible any portion of matter may be resolved into the atoms of which it was originally composed. But what reason have we to believe that one of these atoms ever was or ever will be annihilated? It never can, unless by the uncontrollable power of its almighty Creator…Yea, by this (fire) 'the heavens' themselves 'will be dissolved; the elements shall melt with fervent heat.' But they will be only dissolved, not destroyed: they will melt, but they will not perish. Though they lose their present form, yet not a particle of them will ever lose its existence; but every atom of them will remain under one form or other to all eternity.[22]

Wesley was first exposed to the "Chain of Being" model at Oxford,[23] and the assumption regarding the permanence of creation probably informed his early argument that the resurrection body will be made out of the exact same "dust" (atoms) of the dissolved mortal body.[24] Yet it would not be until the 1770s that Wesley began to integrate more thoroughly this model into his eschatology through his reading of Thomas Burnet's *The Sacred Theory of the Earth*,[25] James Knight's *A Discourse on the Conflagration and Renovation of the World*,[26] and especially Charles Bonnet's *La palingénésie philosophique*.[27] Not only will the new heavens and new earth rise from the

---

[22] "On Eternity" (1775) §7, *Works* 2:362-63.
[23] For example, in the early thirties Wesley read John Ray's *The Wisdom of God Manifested in the Works of the Creation* (Tenth Edition, London: Innys & Manby, 1735). Ray was a Fellow of the Royal Society and utilized the chain in his study of the natural order.
[24] See note 7 above. Cf. Outler's comments on this sermon in *Works* 4:528-30.
[25] London: Walter Kettilby, 1684-1690. Burnet was a premillennialist and was an early leader at explaining creation, fall, the present world and its renewal through the use of modern science. See Book IV, Ch. 1 for his bold declaration that the present cosmos will be dissolved but not destroyed or annihilated. Wesley first read Burnet in 1734. His rereading of Burnet signifies a renewed interest by Wesley in the subject of creation's permanence.
[26] London: J. Cox, 1736.
[27] Second edition; Munster: Philip Henry Perrenon, 1770. Bonnet was an avid exponent of animal salvation and, as we will soon see, informed Wesley's sermon "General Deliverance"

ashes (i.e. atoms) of the exiting cosmos,[28] Wesley began to consider the minority opinion that animals have souls and thereby are recipients of Christ's cosmic redemption.[29] This trajectory will be addressed below but first other shifts in Wesley's eschatology need to be noted.

Wesley published his *Explanatory Notes Upon the New Testament* in late 1755 just when the Seven Years War was heating up, along with wide-spread fears of the world's demise.[30] In his preface he acknowledged several sources, including Anglican John Heylyn (d. 1759),[31] and Dissenters John Guyse (1680-1761)[32] and Philip Doddridge (1702-1751),[33] both avowed postmillennialists. From his *Notes* we know Wesley relied on other authors, like first-century Jewish historian Flavius Josephus.[34] Wesley felt that Josephus' *History of the Jewish War* was the "best commentary" on Jesus' prophecy of Jerusalem's destruction in AD 70 (Matt. 24:14; Lk. 21:11). What is less known was his reliance on Catholic historian Bartolomeo Platina (1421-81), who's *Lives of the Popes* (pub. 1479) informed many of Wesley's historical notes regarding the papal beast in Revelation 13. Surprisingly, Wesley never mentioned in his *Notes* Joseph Mede, the great expositor of English eschatology, or his supporters Isaac Newton and William Whiston, all premillennialists. The fact John relied on only postmillennial expositors for his commentary is telling, to say the least.

(1781). For a general overview of Bonnet's system, see Arthur McCalla, *A Romantic Historiosophy: The Philosophy of History of Pierre-Simon Ballanche*. Boston: Brill, 1998.

[28] Wesley's most explicit statement on the permanence of the creation is found in his sermon "On Eternity" §7, *Works* 2:362-63.

[29] For example, see the sermon "On the Trinity" (1775) §11, *Works* 2:382.

[30] See chapter two. A second edition was published two years later, followed by an expanded third edition in 1762.

[31] Wesley first read Heylyn's writings while at Oxford and later in America. Wesley went to hear him preach on the eve of his Aldersgate conversion and was deeply impressed (*Works* 18:241). Heylyn's first volume of *Theological Lectures* was published in 1749. In this work Heylyn mirrors Wesley's views on the kingdom of God, referring to both God's present reign in the heart and his future reign in the world.

[32] Wesley used his *An Exposition of the New Testament in the Form of a Paraphrase*. 3 vols., 1739-52.

[33] Doddridge was a Reformed theologian, a prolific author and hymn writer, and a supporter of the revival (esp. George Whitefield's ministry). His most influential work was *The Rise and Progress of Religion in the Soul* (1745). His commentary *Family Expositor* (6 vols., 1736-56) reflects a preterist postmillennial interpretation of Jesus' Olivet Discourse, where the heavenly signs represent Jerusalem's destruction (Matt. 24:29) and the angels are messengers of the gospel until all nations acknowledge the Lordship of Jesus Christ (Matt. 24:30-31).

[34] Translated into English by William Whiston in 1737.

The person Wesley relied on the most for his *Notes* was that "great light of the Christian world"[35] New Testament scholar and Pietist Johann Albrecht Bengel (1687-1752).[36] Bengel pioneered a system that identified variant readings of the Greek text. His Greek text appeared in 1734 and was followed up eight years later with his critical commentary *Gnomon Novi Testamenti*. Besides his interest in textual criticism and biblical exegesis, Bengel was drawn to the study of salvation history (*Heilsgeschichte*). In 1741 he published *Ordo Temporum*, a treatise on the chronology of Scripture, in which he enters into speculations about the end of the world. Then four years later he published his thoughts on the orbital periods of the planets (*Cyclus*). From these two studies, Bengel developed his concept of time as chronos (1111 1/9 years) and tempus (222 2/9 years). Along with the hermeneutic of historicism, these two units of time guided his interpretation of the numbers in Revelation and therefore show up in Wesley's commentary (Rev. 6:11; 11:13; 12:11, 14). Given Bengel's esteemed reputation as a scholar, Wesley's admiration of him is understandable.

The one area Bengel is probably most remembered for is his concept of dual millenniums. We saw in chapter one that the concept of dual millenniums was espoused by Thomas Brightman. Yet contrary to Brightman, Bengel proposed that both millenniums were still future. Since Wesley's commentary on Revelation was primarily an abridgement of Bengel's work, the question arises if Wesley ever really supported Bengel's interpretation given his reticence toward speculation. The question becomes pertinent in light of Wesley's letter to Christopher Hopper in 1788:

> I said nothing, less or more, in Bradford church, concerning the end of the world, neither concerning my own opinion, but what follows: That Bengelius had given it as his opinion, not that the world would then end, but that the millennial reign of Christ would begin in the year 1836. I have no opinion at all upon the head: I can determine nothing at all about it. These calculations are far above, out of my sight. I have only one thing to do, — to save my soul, and those that hear me.[37]

---

[35] John Wesley, "Preface" §7, *Explanatory Notes Upon the New Testament*. 2 vols. Grand Rapids: Baker Book House, 1983 Reprint.

[36] For an overview of Bengel's life and work, see Carter Lindberg, ed. *The Pietist Theologians*. Malden: Blackwell Publishing, 2005.

[37] *Works* (Jackson) 12:319. Wesley communicated the same sentiments in a letter to Walter Churchey on June 26, 1788: "What I spoke was a citation from Bengelius, who thought, not that the world would end, but that the Millennium would begin, about the year 1836. Not that I affirmed this myself, nor ever did. I do not determine any of these things: They are too high for me. I only desire to creep on in the vale of humble love." *Works* (Jackson) 12:437.

This letter confirms Wesley's reserve toward speculation, but also reveals the level of confidence he had in Bengel, even after thirty years. For why would he quote Bengel if he had little confidence in his views? Wesley's esteem of Bengel was confirmed in a letter written eleven years earlier to Joseph Benson (whom we saw was a premillennialist):

> But there is no comparison, either as to sense, learning, or piety, between Bishop Newton and Bengelius. The former is a mere child to the latter. I advise you to give another serious and careful reading to that extract from his Comment on the Revelation, which concludes the Notes. There you have one uniform consistent [view], far beyond any I ever saw. And I verily believe, the more deeply you consider it, the more you will admire it.[38]

Both letters show that not withstanding his reticence toward prophetic speculation, Wesley did maintain a high regard for Bengel's work. Though he entertained doubts about some of the particulars, and this might have included the idea of two millenniums, Wesley did not question the core principles of Bengel's eschatology: historicism, the papal Antichrist, the national conversion of the Jews, and Christ's postmillennial reign on earth. One point remains to be made. Wesley refers to the importance of having a living faith in Christ. As we will see in the next chapter, real Christianity is one of the leitmotifs of Wesley's eschatology. A careful reading of his *Notes* on Revelation bears this out. As he worked with the text and its message, utilizing Bengel's insightful exegesis that linked text to present historical realities and beyond, Wesley saw with greater clarity that the Revival and its message of real Christianity was ordained by God to usher in the end-times. This was a momentous step for Wesley, though imperceptible at first. For from this insight he later developed the belief that Methodism was an eschatological movement.

The eschatology of Wesley's *Notes* is visible in his sermon on the final judgment. Preached at St. Paul's, Bedford, on March 10, 1758, before the presiding Judge of Common Pleas, Sir Edward Clive, *The Great Assize* is one of his best summaries on the second coming, final judgment, conflagration,

---

[38] *Works* (Jackson) 12:427. Thomas Newton D.D. (1704-1782) was Bishop of Bristol and later Dean of St. Paul's Cathedral in London until his death. He published a annotated edition of Milton's *Paradise Lost* in 1749 and wrote *Dissertations on the Prophecies* in 1754. Like Dr. Doddridge, Newton embraced a postmillennial preterist position on Jesus' Olivet discourse (Matthew 24 concerns the destruction of Jerusalem in AD 70, and verses 30-31 refer not to the second coming but to the spread of Christianity until all nations acknowledge Christ).

and the new heavens and new earth. The sermon assumes a postmillennial vision of last things since he leaves out all the signs that premillennialists anticipate. Instead, Wesley follows his exegesis on Matthew 24:29-31 by identifying natural and cosmic phenomenon as signs heralding the second coming. He affirms the permanence of the created order at the atomic level—"no atom in the universe will be totally or finally destroyed" (III.3)—reminding us that the Chain of Being was percolating in his eschatology, only later would its ramifications be fully worked out. The strangest part of this sermon, though, was Wesley's speculations about the duration of the final judgment. In the second section, he proposes that the judgment will last a thousand years, possibly thousands of years! Then he quickly retreats to safety, "But God shall reveal this also in its season" (II.2). Wesley was simply not given to speculation when it came to date-setting or applying real numbers to prophetic events, unless those events were already fulfilled in the past.[39]

Soon after publishing his *Notes* Wesley received a letter from John Fletcher encouraging him to consider the premillennial option. With Fletcher, his brother Charles, and other Methodists ardent support, and in light of current geopolitical events, we should not be surprised that John would at some point consider the premillennial position. That end-time scenarios were probably on John's mind is confirmed by a journal comment in December 1762.[40] In early 1764 Wesley read Thomas Hartley's *Paradise Restored*, which contains a lengthy argument for the premillennial position.[41] Wesley's letter to Hartley has been quoted many times:

> Your book on the Millennium and the Mystic writers was lately put into my hands. I cannot but thank you for your strong and seasonable confirmation of that comfortable doctrine, of which I cannot entertain the least doubt as long as I believe the Bible.[42]

---

[39] Take special note of Wesley's comment in his *Journal*, "Monday 6 and the following days, I corrected the Notes upon the Revelation. O how little do we *know* of this deep book! At least, how little do *I* know! I can barely conjecture, nor affirm any one point, concerning that part of it which is yet unfulfilled" (12/6/62, *Works* 21:400, emphasis his). The implication is clear: he can affirm those parts already fulfilled. This includes the first 14 chapters of the Revelation.

[40] See note 39 above. That Wesley was working on his *Notes* on Revelation does imply he would have been thinking on the subject at the time.

[41] Thomas Hartley, *Paradise Restored*. Leeds: Binns and Brown, 1799.

[42] John Telford, *The Letters of John Wesley*. London: Epworth Press, 1931, 4:234 (March 27, 1764).

Luke Tyerman concludes from this comment that Wesley was a premillennialist.[43] Maddox points out that Hartley probably influenced Wesley to interpret the messianic promise of peace in Isaiah 60:18 along premillennial lines.[44] Yet in light of Wesley's other comments on this section of Isaiah (chs 60-66), this note can be made to fit a postmillennial reading. It must be remembered that prior to the nineteenth century premillennialism and postmillennialism shared many of the same end-time beliefs: historicism, the Roman Antichrist, the Turkish threat from the east, the eschatological character of the Revival, the national conversion of the Jews, and the saints' future reign over the nations. Whereas postmillennialists understood this last point as an extension of the present kingdom of grace, with Christ reigning through the gospel, premillennialists linked this glorious period to the future kingdom of glory, with the New Jerusalem present in the millennium (Rev. 20:9) and the new creation (Rev. 21:2).[45] The central issue was in how both camps envisioned the end of this present age: premillennialists saw the present age unraveling into chaos followed by Christ's glorious return, whereas postmillennialists looked for an imperceptible transition when Christ's spiritual reign introduces a golden era of universal peace before the final apostasy transpires (Rev. 20:7-10). Maddox is certainly correct that the gradualism of postmillennialism resonated with Wesley's soteriological interests.[46] He moreover appropriately notes that one of the elements in Hartley's exposition, which especially appealed to Wesley, was that all creation, not just humanity, will participate in God's redemptive work.[47]

Early in the 1780s Wesley published a bold statement on Romans 8:19-22 and animal redemption, based on an essay by John Hildrop.[48] Whereas before (in his *Notes*) Wesley questioned the assumption that the present creation will ever be destroyed, he now asserted in *The General Deliverance* that God's wisdom and goodness called for the redemption of the animal kingdom.

---

[43] Luke Tyerman, *The Life and Times of the Rev. John Wesley*. 3 vols. Stoke-on-Trent: Tentmaker Publications, 2003, 2:523.

[44] The comment Maddox refers to is "'the thousand years wherein Christ shall reign upon the earth.'" (*Responsible Grace*, 238).

[45] E.g. Thomas Hartley, *Paradise Restored*, 78, 189. It should be understood that many commentators of the era tended to merge or blend the millennium with the eternal state.

[46] "Nurturing the New Creation," 40-41.

[47] *Responsible Grace*, 239. Cf. Hartley, *Paradise Restored*, 64, 78. It should be noted that Wesley agreed with Hartley on many points, including the two phases of the kingdom (grace & glory), Christian perfection, free-will, the nature of true faith, the Roman Antichrist, the millennium did not begin under Constantine, the eschatological character of the revival, the national conversion of the Jews, Edenic restoration, and degrees of glory.

[48] *Free Thoughts upon the Brute Creation*, 2 vols. London: R. Minors, 1742-43. Wesley published an abridgment of Hildrop's work in the *Arminian Magazine* (1783). For his preface see *Works* (Jackson) 14:290.

"Nothing is more sure than that as 'the Lord is loving to every man', so 'his mercy is over all his works'—all that have sense, all that are capable of pleasure or pain, of happiness or misery."[49] Like a great chain, the human race and the animal kingdom (and the rest of creation) are inseparably connected so each link can fulfill its divine purpose. Just as animals were created to love and serve the human race, so Adam and Eve were created to love and serve the Creator—and to communicate the blessings of God to the lower creation. With Adam's fall came the plight of the animal kingdom: beast preying on beast, the strong killing the weak, with humanity as their common enemy. Wesley now proclaimed that God will deliver the "brute creation" from this bondage, elevate them on the scale of being, and most likely endow them with a capacity that humans now enjoy to know and love God. Maddox points out that this "sermon was unusual for its time and is often cited today as a pioneer effort at reaffirming the doctrine of animal salvation in the Western church."[50]

Four years later Wesley followed up *The General Deliverance* with an even bolder affirmation of a restored heaven and earth, bringing his new creation eschatology to full maturity. In *The New Creation*, the reader will find Wesley's description of a transformed solar system, atmosphere, and biosphere both fascinating and insightful. The organization of the sermon around the four elements (fire, air, water, earth), once again, alerts the reader of Wesley's dependence on the Chain of Being for his new creation eschatology. Still, what should grab the reader's attention is the sheer *physicality* of Wesley's description. The eternal state is no longer located in "heaven above," in some kind of ethereal state, but consists of a renewed material earth inhabited with every kind of being that make up the great Chain of Being.[51] Thus, we see the shift in Wesley's eschatology was largely due to his understanding of natural philosophy.

In the 1780s Wesley presented his eschatology in a series of sermons. In *The Mystery of Iniquity* (1783), he rehearses church history and concludes the great apostasy predicted by the Apostle Paul (2 Th. 2:3) was the religious nominalism plaguing the national churches, both Catholic and Protestant. It must be remembered that Protestant eschatology in the eighteenth century

---

[49] "The General Deliverance," *Works* 2:437.
[50] "Nurturing the Creation," 47.
[51] One aspect of this natural philosophy was the idea of plenitude, which means that in the original creation no link in the chain was missing, every kind of being that comprises the chain was made by God. When the idea of plenitude is conjoined with the idea of permanence (the creation will never be destroyed or annihilated), then the conclusion must be drawn that in the eternal state every kind of being (link in the chain) will continue to exist. Therefore, the new heavens and earth will be physical and contain every link in the chain. See note 22 above.

was largely governed by the geopolitical tensions between these two factions. With Britain's resounding victory in the Seven Years War, and the demotion of papal political influence on the Italian Peninsula, Wesley lived to see the twilight of the Catholic Counter-Reformation. Writing to Joseph Benson in 1777 on Bishop Newton's views of the Papacy:

> But with regard to the passage you mention I cannot agree with him (Newton) at all. I believe the Romish antichrist is already so fallen that he will not again lift up his head in any considerable degree. The Bishop of Rome has little more power now than any other of the Italian Princes. I therefore concur with you in believing his tyranny is past never to return.[52]

Wesley is here echoing what was considered by most Protestants as a major sign of the end-times, pointing to the dawn of the millennial age. Methodism was now seen by Wesley as "one of the landmark events in the whole of church history."[53] To any sensible person, Wesley asserted, "the signs of the times" are evident for all to see. The "great work of God" that began in the 1730s will continue to spread until the latter-day glory breaks forth, and the evangelical gospel becomes a global faith. Behind Wesley's historicism and postmillennial optimism lay his belief that the *past is the key to the future*. Since "God is one, so the work of God is uniform in all ages. May we not then conceive how he *will* work on the souls of men in times to come by considering how he *does* work *now*? And how he *has* wrought in times past?"[54] This quote reveals the inner logic of Wesley's eschatological vision. Over the decades Wesleyans have debated long and hard whether John Wesley was a premillennialist or a postmillennialist.[55] When we consider all that he wrote on the subject in the 1770s and 80s, we must conclude that the late Wesley was a postmillennial new creationist.

---

[52] Telford, 6:291 (12/8/77).
[53] Albert Outler, Introduction to "The Signs of the Times," *Works* 2:521. On Methodism's special vocation see "On Laying the Foundation of the New Chapel" (1777), *Works* 3:577-93; "The Wisdom of God's Counsels" (1784), *Works* 2:551-66; "Of Former Times" (1787), *Works* 3:440-53; "On God's Vineyard" (1787), *Works* 3:502-17.
[54] "The General Spread of the Gospel" §10, *Works* 2:489 (emphasis his).
[55] See Kenneth O. Brown, "John Wesley - Post Or Premillennialist?" *Methodist History*, 28:1 (October 1989); H. Ray Dunning, ed. *The Second Coming: A Wesleyan Approach to the Doctrine of Last Things,* 139-40; Randy Maddox, *Responsible Grace*, 238-39.

Chapter Four
Survey of Major Themes

John Wesley's evangelical eschatology must be understood against the backdrop of the eighteenth century. For the most part, English Protestants were keenly sensitive to Rome's political clout and the advances made by the Counter-Reformation in the recent past. The outcome of the Thirty Years War (1618-48) and the epochal events of the seventeenth century in England were not forgotten in light of repeated Jacobite threats to Hanoverian rule. The Seven Years War only heightened these fears. When we add the powerful earthquakes that struck London (1750) and Lisbon (1755), the widespread crop failures, unusual weather patterns, and severe cattle plague in the mid-fifties, and Edmond Halley's prediction of possible apocalyptic destruction due to cometary collision, there is little wonder that many people, including Methodists, believed the "signs" were at hand.[1] This explains the rise of interest in end-times during the 1750s.

The Evangelical Revival

Besides these signs, early evangelicals, like Wesley, understood the Revival to be a new Pentecost, a prelude to Christ's millennial reign (whether pre- or post-), and God's final antidote to religious nominalism. The leitmotif of real versus nominal Christianity[2] not only pervaded Wesley's ministry, it runs as a thread through every aspect of his eschatology. Every tract, sermon, letter, and commentary note on the subject is driven by the same evangelical heartbeat that pulsated through the rest of his ministry. This partially explains Wesley's attraction to postmillennialism. Of the three basic millennial paradigms, the postmillennial vision best captured the core message of the Revival. This message appealed primarily to the "almost Christian," that person who lacked a dynamic life-changing faith in Christ.[3] A good example of how the theme of real versus nominal Christianity informed Wesley's eschatology is found in his commentary on Revelation. The great conflict

---

[1] See John Wesley's tract "Serious Thoughts Occasioned by the Late Earthquake at Lisbon," *Works* (Jackson), 11:1-12.
[2] Kenneth Collins has contributed much to highlight this theme in Wesley's theology. For example, see his *John Wesley: A Theological Journey*. Nashville: Abingdon Press, 2003, 243-47.
[3] This excellent point was made by Ronald Knox, *Enthusiasm: A Chapter in the History of Religion*. New York: Oxford University Press, 438.

between real versus nominal Christianity serves as the sub-plot for the entire commentary,[4] including his discussion of the seven churches, the throne room, the seals and trumpets, the great conflict between the papal beast and "real, inward Christians" (13:15), and in his vision of the new heavens and new earth. Wesley continually uses the adjectives "true" and "real" to distinguish between those who are authentic and those who are "dead, unholy Christians" (8:7). Though the great villain in Revelation is the Papacy, in *The Mystery of Iniquity* and *The General Spread of the Gospel* Wesley diagnoses Protestantism to have caught the same fatal disease. He saw religious nominalism as the great apostasy predicted by the Apostle Paul (2 Th. 2:3).

The Kingdom of God

Wesley's hope rests on the kingdom of God. This kingdom is the one rule of God that unfolds in two phases. In his commentary on the kingdom parables (Matt. 13), Wesley distinguishes between these two phases and defines their purpose. The *kingdom of grace* is Christ reigning in the heart. It encompasses both "inward religion" (v. 24), which is the "life of Christ in the soul" (v. 32),[5] and the "gospel dispensation" (v. 24), aimed to "leaven the world, and grace the Christian" (v. 33). Here, Wesley conjoins his postmillennialism to his doctrine of Christian perfection. On a structural level, Wesley never severs his soteriology from his theology of holiness, and both deeply inform his eschatology. This is equally true of the future *kingdom of glory*. At times Wesley refers to this dimension of the kingdom as the *immediate* reign of the Father, to distinguish it from the *mediate* reign of the Son (1 Cor. 15:24). This phase of the kingdom comes after Satan, sin, and death are vanquished and God makes all things new (1 Cor. 15:26; Rev. 21:5). Then, the Three-One God will be all in all (1 Cor. 15:28) when all creation enjoys "a deep, an intimate, an uninterrupted union with God" in an "unmixed state of holiness and happiness far superior to that which Adam enjoyed in paradise."[6] For Wesley, God's reign is salvific and transformative, reaching from the first creation to the new creation, revealing his love and holiness in all his works.

---

[4] On the surface, the plot is to expose Rome as the great enemy of God (heathen and papal). A closer reading reveals a deeper sub-plot, real vs. nominal religion and the identification of Methodists and other evangelicals as God's elect.

[5] This phrase is an obvious allusion to devotional classic *The Life of God in the Soul of Man* by Henry Scougal. Wesley read Scougal while at Oxford. This book led to George Whitefield's evangelical conversion in 1735.

[6] "The New Creation" §18.

Salvation History

The plan of God to fulfill his kingdom purposes is the subject of salvation history. As we saw in chapter one, most Protestants in Wesley's day believed the Book of Revelation to map out in detail the church age from the first century to the end of the age. Wesley endorsed this historical school of interpretation and asserted that biblical prophecy consists of "one complete chain" (Rev. 1:3), reaching back through the church age (Revelation) to the prophecies of Christ concerning the Jewish state (Gospels), to the five kingdoms outlined in Daniel. In other words, the prophecies in these books present one continuous narrative of salvation history that weaves through second temple Judaism to the destruction of Jerusalem (AD 70), followed by the church age and the millennial reign of Christ. Most significant about this history was what it implied in regard to God's kingdom rule: *the past is the key to the future.*[7] In other words, how God worked in the past reveals how he will work in the future. This explains Wesley's confidence that Christ's millennial reign will build on his present reign of grace. The lasting power of the Revival convinced Wesley that the kingdom of grace would reach the "remotest parts, not only of Europe, but of Asia, Africa, and America."[8] Therefore, Wesley's postmillennialism was grounded on his understanding of salvation history.

Another implication of Wesley's historicism was his outright rejection of Calvinism, with its emphasis on God's absolute sovereignty. Instead, Wesley's eschatology reflects the same Arminian concepts that characterize his soteriology. It is interesting to see how he weaves eschatological themes, which tend to stress God's sovereign action, with exhortations for authentic human agency in the fulfillment of God's end-time purposes. Since God in the past accomplished his redemptive purposes by working in and through human agency, with real people exercising authentic human freedom, then surely the same principle applies in the fulfillment of future prophecies. Consequently, Wesley stated on more than one occasion the transition from this present age to the millennial kingdom will not be recognized on earth. The reason is that in both eras the synergism of human freedom and divine sovereignty function in the same manner. Only at the second coming of Christ, which includes the conflagration, final judgment, and reconstitution, will God's sovereign action temporarily set aside the kind of synergism that has operated throughout salvation history under the kingdom of grace. In the kingdom of glory a new synergism will emerge when the redeemed actively

---

[7] To see how this principle guides Wesley's argument, see "The General Spread of the Gospel."
[8] "The General Spread of the Gospel" §18.

worship and commune with the Three-One God and enjoy eternal peace and harmony with every other link on the Great Chain of Being.[9]

The Chain of Being

We have seen that Wesley's eschatology was influenced by his natural philosophy (science). We saw in the last chapter that one of the implications of the Chain of Being was that matter will not be ultimately destroyed. Wesley believed the present heavens and earth will one day be dissolved down to their atomic level, to be recreated to form a new heavens and a new earth, far better than the one Adam enjoyed in the garden. No link in the great chain will be lost. The kingdom of glory will be the reconstitution of the present physical cosmos, with a real material heavens and earth. In this new order, all creation, at least all sentient beings, will be lifted higher on the chain to enjoy even more the richness of God's grace. Humanity will be lifted to the level of the angels, the animal kingdom to the level of humanity. The order, plenitude, and perfection of the chain remain intact. But this means that Wesley's eschatology leaves no room for any kind of annihilationism. Early on Wesley taught the resurrection body will be recreated out of the very same atoms that composed the earthly mortal body.[10]

The Chain of Being reached into other aspects of Wesley's eschatology. The concept of humanity as a channel of divine blessing or judgment to lower links on the chain fits into Wesley's views of humanity ruling over the creation (i.e. the political image) and of God's intention to recreate the material cosmos and give the animal kingdom a share in the general resurrection.[11] Since the idea of plenitude meant that God created every link on the chain at the original creation, Wesley refused to believe that stars were older than the earth, as some in his day began to expostulate,[12] and he read Genesis 1 in a straightforward manner—a recent creation in six literal days.[13] In keeping with the Chain, Wesley understood the four elements of fire, air, water, and earth to be the constituent parts of the present creation.[14] These

---

[9] See "The New Creation" §18.

[10] See "On the Resurrection of the Dead" (1732), *Works* (Jackson) 7:474-85. See Outler's remarks on this sermon by Benjamin Calamy that Wesley transcribed and preached, *Works* 4:528-530.

[11] "The General Deliverance;" *Notes* Gen. 1:26-28.

[12] See *Notes* 2 Peter 3:11.

[13] Creation in six literal days, see "God's Approbation of His Works" I.7-11, *Works* 2:391-395; creation six thousand years ago, see "On the Fall of Man" II.4, *Works* 2:407.

[14] "God's Approbation of His Works" I.1-6, *Works* 2:388-91. E.M. W. Tillyard explains, "Now just as God, source of all existence, to the medieval mind was first of all one and after was divided in this way or that; so matter was one, and the elements far from being ultimate

elements will constitute the basic building blocks of the new creation[15] and will remain untouched by the conflagration.[16] The four elements feature in Wesley's eschatology at points not expected, like in his description of the signs immediately preceding the second coming: tumultuous earthquakes (earth), giant tsunamis (water), tempest storms from pole to pole (air), along with stars and heavenly bodies "thrown out of their orbits" (fire).[17]

Imminence

How close did Wesley believe the end to be? We have already seen that he did see Methodism as an eschatological movement called to prepare the way for the latter-day glory.[18] He further asserted the Roman beast to be in political decline.[19] Following Bengel, Wesley made a distinction between the beast rising out of the sea from the beast rising out of the abyss. The first beast is the "Papacy of many ages," the second the eschatological Pope.[20] It was this last personage that Wesley stated in 1755 will be destroyed "soon" by the Lord's power (2 Th. 2:8). Moving to Revelation, he made numerous comments that reflect his belief the end was imminent. When the Apostle John encouraged his audience to hear and keep the words of this prophecy, Wesley responded, "Especially at this time, when so considerable a part of them is on the point of being fulfilled" (1:3). To John's phrase, "the time is near," Wesley added, "Even when St. John wrote. How much nearer to us is even the full accomplishment of this weighty prophecy!" He then followed up that chapters 15-19 are to be "fulfilled shortly" (4:1). When we consider his other comments, we can conclude that Wesley did believe he was living close to the end of Antichrist's rule (Rev. 12:12; 13:1; 17:10; 19:7; 20:3). It should be remembered what the demise of the Antichrist meant to Wesley. What he anticipated was not necessarily the demise of the Roman Catholic Church, but the end of the Pope's *political* power.[21] From the vantage point where he stood, Wesley expected the Counter-Reformation to dissipate

---

and different indivisibles were primarily certain qualities attributable to all matter" (*The Elizabethan World Picture*. New York: Vintage Books, 1959, 61).

[15] "The New Creation" §10-13.
[16] *Notes* 2 Peter 3:10.
[17] "The Great Assize" I.1.
[18] See chapter two.
[19] Telford, 6:291 (12/8/77).
[20] Revelation 11:7; 13:1, Obs. 16; 17:8.
[21] On this point the reader needs to examine Wesley's notes on Revelation 13 and 17. Wesley also looked for the destruction of the city of Rome (Rev. 18). The nineteenth century did witness the eroding loss of political power by the Pope that culminated under Pius IX (1846-78) in 1870.

further, opening an opportunity for the Revival to spread throughout Christendom until real, authentic Christianity rules over the nations, leading to a golden era of universal peace and holiness in the world.

The Millennium

By now the reader is aware that Wesley's notes on Revelation 20 are an abridgment of Bengel's concept of a *dual millennium*. Apart from the commentary, we have no record of Wesley ever espousing this idea. His one sermon that deals with the subject at length never mentions a second thousand years. Nevertheless, the main point of *The General Spread of the Gospel* is to proclaim the hope that the Revival will usher in the (first) millennium. Apart from his commentary, written in the mid-fifties, Wesley has not left us any sermon or tract dealing with Revelation 20:7-10. We simply do not know his later position on these verses. Bengel and Wesley were correct that vv. 7-10 follow the (first) thousand years. Whether we assign a thousand years to these verses or a shorter period, the narrative does place the final apostasy *after* the thousand years are completed. So the basic idea Bengel and Wesley propose is not as far fetched as some might assume. Another question concerns the armies of Gog and Magog, the second coming, and the conflagration. All three events are chronologically connected by Wesley in Revelation 20:9-11, with each involving the element of fire. It is possible that Wesley believed the fire, which devours the armies of Gog and Magog, will be the same fire that marks the return of Christ and dissolves the cosmos.[22]

The Second Coming

Wesley's depiction of the events surrounding the Lord's coming is cosmic, cataclysmic, eschatological, and graphic: the earth reels with horrific earthquakes; giant tsunamis wash over its face; "ten thousand" lightning storms terrify from "pole to pole;" planets and stars are "thrown out of their orbits." Then the angels give a loud shout, as the graves are opened and the elect are gathered from the four corners of the earth. The Lord personally descends on the clouds. After these things, the final judgment is set, while the material cosmos is dissolved in the flames. Wesley did envision living saints being "raptured" (to use a contemporary term), but he would not have had any concept of a pre-, mid- or post- scenario since these ideas did not come into vogue until the nineteenth and twentieth centuries. In 1755 he simply

---

[22] Consider *Notes* 2 Peter 3:10-11, Revelation 20:7-11; "The Great Assize."

states living believers will be "absolved" (1 Th 4:17) at the Lord's coming and the resurrection body will be "so changed in its properties as we cannot now conceive."[23] Given his new creation eschatology, Wesley did look for real material bodies in the resurrection, but bodies no longer bound by the remains of the Adamic curse.

The Eternal States

The *new creation* will be recreated from of the same atoms that constituted the old creation. Wesley's depiction emphasizes the materiality of the restored cosmos, minus the defects caused by Adam's fall. He assumes the earth will be roughly the same size, with everything restored to its pristine purity and order. His speculations are fascinating and reflect the level of scientific knowledge available in the eighteenth century. To offer one example, Wesley states there will be no comets in the new creation. The common assumption in the eighteenth century was that comets were "blazing stars," potentially destructive to the earth. Dr. Halley had warned that if the fiery tail of the "great comet" brushed the earth "it will set the earth on fire, and burn it to a coal."[24] Today we know comets to be comprised of rock, dust, ice, and frozen gas. They are not "blazing stars." A comet's tail would certainly not cause the earth's surface to burn.

Drawing on the scholastic distinction between *poena damni* (punishment of loss) and *poena sensus* (punishment of the senses), Wesley describes the final state of the damned as conscious and unredeemable. Once again, Wesley emphasizes the materiality of the place of punishment. The fire will be physical and the suffering both physical[25] and mental, in proportion to the guilt each person bears before the great tribunal. To the argument that a physical fire cannot burn forever, Wesley responds that at the great renovation, present physical laws no longer apply. Under the new constitution, a physical fire will burn forever since material existence endures forever. Therefore, Wesley did anticipate the unredeemed to be physically raised at the general resurrection.

---

[23] "The Great Assize" I.1.
[24] The quotations are from Wesley, but he is summarizing Halley's views. See Wesley's "Serious Thoughts Occasioned by the Late Earthquake at Lisbon," *Works* (Jackson) 11:9. This tract is a good example how Wesley played on the fears of the populace for evangelistic purposes.
[25] The general resurrection includes both the righteous and the unrighteous. So the inhabitants of hell will have bodies by which to experience real pain.

The Intermediate State

When Wesley addresses the intermediate state, he moves from the material to the ethereal. Hades is located in the "invisible world," where disembodied immortal spirits of good and evil dwell. He leans heavily on the story of the rich man and Lazarus (Lk.16:19-31) to decipher what transpires in this state.[26] He rejects outright any notion of a purgatory, which offers a second chance to the deceased. The unholy dead cannot cross over to the paradise of the righteous. The righteous experience bliss while the unholy suffer loss and pain. But the inhabitants of Hades are not idle. The unholy dead serve alongside demons by inflicting evil and harm on this world, including storms, earthquakes, disease, and mental illness. The righteous spirits are active in withstanding these evils by "preventing our being hurt by men, or beasts, or inanimate creatures."[27] So Wesley definitely believed in guardian angels or spirits, both good and bad, and speculated that departed humans remain engaged in the affairs of this present age. The disembodied "traverse the whole universe" at the speed of thought and experience dramatic increase in knowledge, but only the righteous will "advance in holiness, in the whole image of God wherein they were created."[28] Therefore, Wesley envisioned the deceased to be still engaged in the great eschatological struggle between good and evil, with the field of battle located on this planet.

---

[26] See Wesley's sermon on this story, "Dives and Lazarus" (1788), *Works* 4:5-18.
[27] "On Faith" (Heb. 11:1) §12, *Works* 4:197. Compare with Wesley's early sermon "On Guardian Angels" (1726), *Works* 4:225-35, and his 1783 sermons "Of Good Angels" and "Of Evil Angels," *Works* 3:3-29.
[28] "On Faith" (Heb. 11:1) §11, *Works* 4:196.

Chapter Five
The Order of Eschatological Events

Below are three outlines. The first one is by the editor and the last two come from Wesley's commentary on Revelation. A good understanding of these outlines will help the reader to piece together into a coherent whole Wesley's writings on eschatology and salvation history. The two outlines on Revelation are important to understand how Wesley correlates the prophecy to salvation history: past, present, and future.

John Wesley's Order of Events

The following detailed outline is John Wesley's order of eschatological events according to the sermons and commentary notes found in this *Reader*. When the exact chronological order is in question, the editor followed the order in the sermons and let the commentary fill in the details. The references to the right identify where the subjects are addressed in this *Reader*.

Eschatological Events	References
The Five Kingdoms	Daniel 2, 7-12
Babylon	
Persia	
Greece	
Alexander the Great	
Four realms	
Ptolemies & Seleucids	Daniel 10-11
Antiochus Epiphanies	Daniel 8
Rome	
Heathen	Revelation 6:11; 8:7-12
Papal	2 Thessalonians 2:3-10
Kingdom of God	
Son of man receives kingdom	Daniel 7:13
70 weeks of years	Daniel 9:24-27
Finish transgression	
End sin	
Make reconciliation	

Jesus Christ's Kingdom
   Life & ministry

His death ends ceremonial law	Daniel 9:27
Resurrection as Second Adam	1 Corinthians 15:23
Ascension & royal investiture	Daniel 7:13; Revelation 5
Given all authority	
Protects true church	
Defeats God's enemies	
Restores divine rule	
Phases of the Kingdom	
Kingdom of grace	Matthew 13; Mark 4
Kingdom of glory	Luke 17:20-37

Destruction of Jerusalem AD 70

	Matthew 24, Mark 13, Luke 21
Religious deception	Daniel 9:26
War & rumors of war	
Famine & plagues	
Persecution	
Gospel to all nations	
Abomination of desolation	
Great tribulation	
God preserves his people	
Religious deception	
Heavenly signs	
City/temple destroyed	
The times of the Gentiles	Luke 21:24

The Church Age

Real vs. nominal religion	Revelation 2-3, 6-19
True believers persecuted	
Christ preserves his people	
Apostasy of nominal religion	The Mystery of Iniquity
Apostolic era	2 Timothy 3:1-5
Early church	1 John 2:18-28
Constantine the Great	
Catholicism	2 Thessalonians 2:1-12
Protestantism	
The rise & fall of Antichrist's Kingdom	Revelation 13-19
Pope's rise in 11th century	
Pope's fall is at hand	
Present revival of true Christianity	The Signs of the Times
Extraordinary work of God	
Latter-day glory at hand	

First Millennium

	Revelation 20:1-3, 7a
Satan is bound	The General Spread
Nations no longer deceived	of the Gospel

The Order of Eschatological Events

Christendom converted
    Protestant nations
    Catholic nations
Jewish conversion   Romans 11:7-32
Islamic conversion
Heathen conversion
Global evangelical faith
    No violence
    Universal salvation
    Universal holiness & happiness
    Christ's universal reign

Second Millennium   Revelation 20:4-10
    Satan is loosed
    Saints reign in heaven
    Nations on earth deceived
    Gog & Magog attack Gentile church
    Fire of God destroys his enemies[1]

Christ's Parousia[2]   The Great Assize
Cosmic signs   Matthew 24:29
    Violent earthquakes
    Giant tsunamis
    Thunder & Lightning storms
    Heavenly chaos: sun, moon, stars
Angelic herald   1 Thessalonians 4:13-18
    Shout of heavenly company
    Voice of archangel
    Trumpet of God
General resurrection
    Graves open
    Sea gives up dead
    Bodily resurrection
Gathering of saints

---

[1] Wesley gives no comment regarding the fire that destroys the armies of Gog and Magog. But two factors might link this fire to the cosmic signs that precede the second coming: first, he locates the second coming between verses 10 and 11 in Rev. 20 (20:3 note), which immediately follows the story of God's fire falling on his enemies. Second, he believes the cosmic signs and other upheavals that immediately precede the second coming include the element of fire (Matt 24:29-30; "The Great Assize"). Therefore, in Wesley's order of eschatological events the fire that destroys the armies of Gog and Magog is possibly linked to the cosmic signs that precede the second coming of Christ. This fire is probably linked to the conflagration since the cosmic signs preceding the second coming are the same sources of the fire that dissolves the present heavens and earth.

[2] This section follows the order in "The Great Assize."

Son sends forth his angels	Matthew 24:31
Dead saints raised first	
Living saints caught up	1 Thessalonians 4:17
Meet in the clouds	
Second Coming	
Sign	Matthew 24:30
In the clouds	
Sits in judgment	
Final Judgment	Revelation 20:11-15
All people gathered	
Saints rewarded	
Sinners condemned	
Hell	Of Hell
Sinners turned into hell	
Everlasting destruction	
Eternal torment	
Conflagration	2 Peter 3:10-12
Heaven/earth dissolved	
Source of the fire: volcanoes,	The Great Assize
comets, ethereal fire (i.e. electricity)	

The Kingdom of Glory

Son gives Father the kingdom	1 Corinthians 15:24-28
God is all in all	
New heavens & new earth	The New Creation
Animal redemption	The General Deliverance
Harmonious cosmos	Romans 8:18-27
No sea; only gentle rivers	Revelation 21-22
No pain, death, sorrow	
Perfect communion with God	

John Wesley's Outlines on Revelation

The following two outlines are located at the end of Wesley's commentary on Revelation. They come from Johann Bengel's introduction to Revelation.[3] The brief introductory comments are from Wesley's pen. The editor did make some changes to aid clarity: (1) scripture references are made more specific or added to show how Wesley and Bengel collate Revelation to history; (2) clarifying comments are added

---

[3] *Bengelius's Introduction to His Exposition of the Apocalypse*, London: J. Ryall and R. Withy, 1757, 235-42. Bengal adds in his remarks on this outline that he offers it with "*Caution,* that I by no means pretend to have adapted the years to every article with *equal* certainty" (240, emphasis his).

in parentheses. In the second outline, the roman numerals on the left represent each century of the church age from the second century to Wesley's time (eighteenth century).

First Outline

It may be proper to subjoin here a short view of the whole contents of this book. In the year of the world, A.D. 3940, Jesus Christ is born, three years before the common computation. In that which is vulgarly called, the thirtieth year of our Lord, Jesus Christ dies; rises; ascends.

Year (A.D.)	Event As Described In Revelation	Chapter/Verse
96	The Revelation is given; the coming of our Lord is declared to the seven churches in Asia, and their angels	1-3
97, 98	The seven seals are opened, and under the fifth (seal) the chronos[4] is declared	4-6
	Seven trumpets are given to the seven angels	7-8
2nd-5th Cen.	The trumpet of the 1st, 2nd, 3rd, 4th angel	8:7-12
510-589	The first woe (Persians)	9:1-11
589-634	The interval after the first woe	9:12
634-840	The second woe (Saracens)	9:13-19
800	The beginning of the non-chronos,[5] many (Christian) kings (10:6 note)	9-10
840-947	The interval after the second woe	9:20-10
847-1521	The twelve hundred and sixty days of the woman (true Christianity preserved	

---

[4] Chronos ("time") refers to a specific period of 1111 years; see Rev 6:11 note (see Johann Bengel, *Bengelius's Introduction,* 174-186).
[5] Non-chronos refers to the angel's statement in Rev 10:6, "there shall be no more time." So this unspecified period of time is referred to by Wesley/Bengel as non-chronos.

	from papal oppression), after she hath brought forth the man child	12:6
947-1836	The third woe (Papacy)	12:12
1058-1836	The time, times, and half a time,[6] and within that period, the beast, his forty-two months, his number 666	13:5
1209	War with the saints; the end of the chronos (i.e. the *end* of heathen Rome's persecution, 6:11 note)	13:7
1614	An everlasting gospel promulgated	14:6
1810	The end of the forty-two months of the Beast; after which, and the pouring out of the phials, he (beast) is not, and Babylon (city of Rome) reigns queen (i.e. over the beast/papacy)	15-16
1832	The beast ascends from the bottomless pit (this is the eschatological Pope who rules for 3 1/2 years)	17-18
1836	(The first millennium): The end of the non-chronos and of the many kings (8:6 n); the fulfilling of the word and of the mystery of God (10:7); the repentance of the (Jewish) survivors in the great city (11:13); the end of the "little time" (12:12), and of the three times and a half (12:14) – the destruction of the beast (19:12); the imprisonment of Satan	19-20:3
(2836)	Afterward, (the second millennium): The loosing of Satan for a small time (20:3, 7); the beginning of the thousand years' reign of the saints; the end of the small time	20:4-10

---

[6] Bengel proposed a "time" to be 222 years based on his calculations of the orbital periods of the planets (see chapter 3). The "time, times, and half a time" equals 777 years (222+222+222+111=777), and according to Bengel runs from 1058 to 1836, when the eschatological beast (pope) is destroyed and the first millennium begins.

| (3836) | The end of the world (including the second coming); all things new | 20:11-22:6 |

Second Outline

The several ages, from the time of St. John's being in Patmos, down to the present time, may, according to the chief incidents mentioned in the Revelation, be distinguished thus:

Age[7]	Event As Described In Revelation	Chapter/Verse
II.	The destruction of the Jews by Adrian	8:7
III.	The inroads of the barbarous nations	8:8
IV.	The Arian bitterness	8:10
V.	The end of the western empire	8:12
VI.	The Jews tormented in Persia	9:1
VII.	The Saracen (Moslem) cavalry	9:13
VIII.	Many (Christian) kings	10:11
IX.	The ruler of the nations born	12:5
X.	The third woe	12:12
XI.	The ascent of the beast out of the pen	13:1
XII.	Power given to the beast	13:5
XIII.	War with the saints	13:7
XIV.	The middle of the third woe	
XV.	The beast in the midst of his strength	13:8
XVI.	The Reformation; the woman better fed	13:9
XVII.	An everlasting gospel promulgated	14:6
XVIII.	The worship of the beast and of his image	14:9

O God, whatsoever stands or falls,
stands or falls by thy judgment.
Defend thy own truth!
Have mercy on me and my readers!
To thee be glory for ever!

---

[7] That is centuries. Therefore, II means the second century, III the third century, etc.

Chapter Six
Selections, Text & Sources

Selections

A work of this nature requires the editor to make some tough decisions to keep the book manageable in size, yet comprehensive enough for the reader to gain a broad understanding of Wesley's eschatology. Since the main contours of Wesley's eschatology are found in his sermons and commentary notes, the bulk of the selections were taken from these two sources. The introductions alert the reader of significant themes and other relevant material in the Wesley corpus for further study. A couple of priorities guided the selection of sermons. First, the editor decided to include sermons that reflect Wesley's mature thought. All the sermons in this *Reader* come from the 1780s, except *The Great Assize*. The other priority was to make sure the broad themes of Wesley's eschatology are covered. In a few cases, more than one sermon in the Wesley corpus addresses the same theme. In these cases, the editor chose a single representative sermon and informs the reader of the other sermons in the introduction. For those interested, Albert Outler's introductions are referenced in the sermon introductions. The sermon texts are taken from *The Bicentennial Edition of the Works of John Wesley* (Abingdon Press). The footnotes are an abridgement of Outler's edition. The reader can look up Outler's edition of the sermons for further study of his notes. In all, eight sermons are included in this *Reader* and are topically arranged:

The Great Assize (1758)	Second Coming
The Mystery of Iniquity (1783)	Great Apostasy
The General Spread of the Gospel (1783)	Millennium
The Signs of the Times (1787)	Revival & Millennium
General Deliverance (1781)	Animal Redemption
The New Creation (1785)	New Heavens & Earth
Of Hell (1788)	Final Punishment
On Faith, Heb. 11:1 (1791)	Intermediate State

Wesley's *Explanatory Notes Upon the New Testament* was originally published in late 1755. A second edition was released two years later and a third fuller edition in 1763 (with the help of Charles).[1] The edition in this *Reader* comes from the first edition. *Explanatory Notes Upon the Old Testament* followed in 1765. The following passages were selected for this *Reader*, including the entire Book of Revelation:

Matthew 3:1-2	Kingdom of God
Matthew 13, Mark 4:21-29	Kingdoms of Grace & Glory
Luke 17:20-37	Kingdom's Arrival
Matthew 24, Mark 13, Luke 21	Fall of Jerusalem
Romans 8:18-23	Groanings for the New Age
Romans 11:7-32	Conversion of the Jews
1 Corinthians 15:22-58	Resurrection Body
1 Thessalonians 4:13-5:11	Gathering of Believers
2 Thessalonians 2:1-12	Apostasy and the Man of Sin
2 Timothy 3:1-5	Marks of the Apostasy
2 Peter 3:1-14	Conflagration
1 John 2:18-29	Spirit of Antichrist
Revelation 1-22	Salvation History: Church Age
Daniel 2, 7-12	Salvation History: Jewish Age

The 1780 *Collection of Hymns* includes three sections of hymns on judgment (second coming), heaven, and hell.[2] Though Charles authored these hymns and did not agree with every aspect of his brother's eschatology, the fact John included these hymns in the collection means they passed his editorial approval. Of course, this does not mean he felt obligated to agree with every sentiment his brother expressed.[3] All the same, it is striking how most of the hymns on judgment agree with Wesley's postmillennialism. In these hymns the rapture, conflagration, final judgment, and renovation are linked to the second coming of Christ. The sole exception is Hymn #60, which is an explicit statement of Charles' premillennialism. None of the hymns on heaven agree with Wesley's new creation eschatology found in his later sermons. The reader can ponder why John included no hymns that agree with his mature position. Possibly, Charles never embraced John's views on the new creation. The editor selected five hymns as a representative sample. They are included at appropriate places in the commentary section (one on heaven; four on the second coming and related events).[4]

---

[1] John Wesley refers to himself correcting the Notes on Revelation in his Journal on December 6, 1762 (*Works* 21:400).
[2] Hymns #53-64 are on judgment (second coming), Hymns #65-77 on heaven, and hymn #78 describes hell (*Works* 7:146-77).
[3] *Works* 7:2.
[4] Hymns 54, 57, 61, 72, 522 (see *Works*, vol. 7).

Scripture Text

Wesley's New Testament text was largely taken from Bengal's *Gnomon Novi Testamenti* and represents thousands of changes from the King James Version (abbreviated AV in this *Reader*). The characteristic changes Wesley employed were simplified wording, removing excessive words, or changing word order. He updated spelling (e.g. names) and on occasion added words. Rarer still were significant word changes. At times he changed tenses, like changing a past to present or a present to a past. The more significant changes are found in the Epistles and Revelation over the Gospels. Here are some examples from this *Reader*:

Romans 8:20-22
- Wesley changed "creature" to the more inclusive "creation."
- In v. 22 he removed "in pain" from the phrase "creation groaneth and travaileth in pain together."
- At the end of v. 20 the AV has "subjected it in hope, because the creature..." Wesley moved the comma and clarified the passage, "subjected it, in hope that the creation..."

First Thessalonians 4:13
- Wesley changed the singular to a plural. The AV "But I would not..." becomes "Now we would not..." with Paul speaking on behalf of his ministry team, Silas and Timothy, who were co-authors of the letter (1:1).

Second Thessalonians 2:1-11
- In v. 1 the AV "coming" becomes "appearing," which is a better translation of the Greek word *parousia*.
- In v. 2 Wesley intensified the language by changing the AV "troubled" to "terrified"— "That ye be not soon shaken in mind or terrified..."
- Better clarity is given in v. 7 by changing the AV "he that letteth will let" to "he that restraineth will restrain..."
- At v. 11 a subtle change is made in the article for emphasis. The AV "a lie" is changed to "the lie," meaning a specific lie is being referred to.

Second Timothy 3:1
- The meaning is somewhat altered by changing the AV "in the last days *perilous* times shall come" to "in the last days *grievous* times will come."

Second Peter 3:7-11
- In v. 7 better clarity is given by changing the AV "perdition of ungodly men" to "destruction of ungodly men."

- At v. 9 Wesley improved on the AV "The Lord is not slack concerning his promise" to "The Lord is not slow concerning his promise."
- Then in v. 11 Wesley made a significant change in the tense of the verb. The AV "Seeing then that all these things shall be dissolved" is altered to "Seeing then all these things are dissolved." The present tense makes the promise more certain, as if it is already accomplished.

Revelation contains the most significant changes. Here are a few examples:
- In the seven beatitudes (e.g. 1:3) Wesley consistently changed the AV "blessed" to "happy."
- Throughout Revelation the AV "kindreds" is changed to "tribes" to reflect Wesley's interpretation that the word always refers to the Jewish people (see 1:7).
- At 13:1 and elsewhere the AV "beast" is changed to "wild beast."
- Speaking of the second wild beast in 13:15, the AV "he had power to give life unto the image" is altered to "it was given him to give breath to the image." The passive tense reflects the role of divine sovereignty in the false prophet's actions.
- At 17:15 Wesley strengthened the fact that the enemies of Rome are accomplishing God's will. The AV "God hath put in their hearts to fulfill his will" became "God hath put it into their hearts to execute his sentence."

Whether the changes are small or large, significant or trivial, the reader should be alert to the fact that Wesley's views are found not only in the commentary notes, but in the changes he made to the text itself. The reader will be rewarded if he or she remembers this insight. In this *Reader*, the editor has noted any change that could possibly affect interpretation by underlining the word(s) in the text and listing in the commentary section below what the AV contains in Ariel font.

Sources

Wesley was a prolific reader and many sources informed his eschatology in all its particulars. The following is a topical listing of the major sources that influenced his eschatology. The fact Wesley read or quoted a source does not mean he agreed with the author on all points and at times with very little.

<u>Animal Souls & Salvation</u>
John Hildrop, *Free Thoughts upon the Brute Creation,* 2 vol. (1742).

Humphrey Ditton, *A Discourse Concerning the Resurrection of Christ...with an appendix concerning...the nature of human souls and of the brutes* (1712).

John Locke, *Essay Concerning Human Understanding* (1690).

Apostasy
George Fox, *Journal* (1694).

Thomas Hartley, *Paradise Restored* (1764).

Chain of Being
Charles Bonnet, *La Palingenesie philosophique* (2nd edn., 1770).

John Hildrop, *Free Thoughts upon the Brute Creation*, 2 vol. (1742).

John Ray, *The Wisdom of God Manifested in the Work of the Creation*, 2 vols. (10th edn., 1735).

Church Fathers
Augustine, Barnabas, Cyprian, Irenaeus, Justin Martyr, Lanctantius, Melito, Methodius, Origen, Papias, Tertullian.

Classical Authors
Cicero, Homer, Juvenal, Ovid, Virgil.

Conflagration
James Knight, *A Discourse on the Conflagration and Renovation of the World* (1736).

Constantine the Great
Thomas Newton, *Dissertations on the Prophecies, which have remarkably been fulfilled, and at this time are fulfilling the world* (2nd edn., 1760. Note: Wesley sharply disagreed with Newton).

Destruction of Jerusalem, AD 70
Flavius Josephus, *History of the Jewish War* (1st Century).

Natural Phenomenon (Earthquakes, etc.)
Thomas Burnet, *The Sacred Theory of the Earth*, 2 vols. (1684-1690).

Thomas Hartley, *Paradise Restored* (1764).

John Ray, *The Wisdom of God Manifested in the Work of the Creation*, 2 vols. (10th edn., 1735).

William Whiston, *New Theory of the Earth* (1691).

Intermediate State
Archibald Campbell, *The Doctrines of a Middle State Between death and the Resurrection* (1721).

John Flavell, *Husbandry Spiritualized* (1740).

Thomas Deacon, *Compleat Collection of Devotions* (1734).

Papacy
Bartolomeo Platina, *Lives of the Popes* (1479).

Papal Inquisition
Samuel Chandler, *The History of Persecution* (1736).

Michael Geddes, *A View of the Inquisition of Portugal; with a list of the Prisoners which came out of the Inquisition of Lisbon* (1682, 1730).

Plurality of Inhabitable Worlds[5]
Louis Dutens, *Inquiry into the Origin of the Discoveries Attributed to the Moderns* (1769).

Bovier de Fontenelle, *Conversations On the Plurality of Worlds* (4 English translations: 1688-1760).

Poetry & Quotes
John Milton, *Paradise Lost* (1667).

Punishments in Hell
Thomas Boston, *Human Nature in Its Fourfold State* (1720).

Postmillennialism
Johann Bengel, *Gnomon Novi Testamenti* (1742).[6]

Philip Doddridge, *The Family Expositor*, 6 vols. (1736-56).

---

[5] This subject comes up in "The New Creation."
[6] Wesley read several of Bengel's works. See his Introduction to Revelation.

John Guyse, *A Practical Exposition of the Four Evangelists, in the Form of a Paraphrase, with Occasional Notes*, 3 vols. (1739-42).

Premillennialism & Restoration of Paradise on Earth
Thomas Burnet, *The Sacred Theory of the Earth*, 2 vols. (1684-1690).

Thomas Hartley, *Paradise Restored* (1764).

William Whiston, *New Theory of the Earth* (1691).

State of the Nations in the World[7]
Edward Brerewood, *Enquiries Touching the Diversities of Languages and Religions Through the Chief Parts of the Earth* (1614).

Lady Mary Wortley Montagu, *Letters* (1763).

Bartholomew Ziegenbalg, *The Propagation of the Gospel in the East* (1718).

---

[7] See "The General Spread of the Gospel."

Part Two

John Wesley's Sermons on Eschatology

The Great Assize
1758

This is the fullest statement by Wesley on the events surrounding the Lord's parousia: the second coming, final judgment, and the conflagration of the present heavens and earth. Though written and preached in 1758, when Wesley's eschatology was still in its adolescence, he would later remark in 1778, "I cannot write a better sermon on the Great Assize than I did twenty years ago" (Journal, Sept. 1), thus reflecting that his views did not materially change over time. The signs of the Lord's return described therein clearly fit a postmillennial scheme, since there is no mention of the kind of signs that premillennialists anticipate (e.g. war, the conversion of the Jews, the defeat of the Antichrist). Instead, the signs consist of cataclysmic natural phenomenon ushering in the standard eschatological earmarks found in several passages of Holy Writ. Wesley draws his inspiration from such passages as Matthew 24:29-31, 1 Thessalonians 4:13-17, 2 Peter 3:10-12, *and* Revelation 20:7-21:5 *(Wesley located the second coming at 20:11). The reader should compare his commentary on these passages with this sermon. For another brief statement by Wesley on the second coming and final judgment, see* On the Discoveries of Faith §10 *(Works 4:33). In* The Great Assize *the reader will find of interest Wesley's order of events, the length of time for the final judgment as well as its location. Note how the Chain of Being shapes his understanding of the conflagration and new creation. Finally, the last section reflects his evangelical priorities. Sprinkled throughout the sermon are several remarks of imminence. For Albert Outler's introduction, see Works 1:354.*

We shall all stand before the judgment seat of Christ.

Romans 14:10

1. How many circumstances concur to raise the awfulness of the present solemnity! The general concourse of people of every age, sex, rank, and condition of life, willingly or unwillingly gathered together, not only from the neighbouring, but from distant parts: *criminals*, speedily to be brought forth,

and having no way to escape; *officers*, waiting in their various posts to execute the orders which shall be given; and the *representative* of our gracious Sovereign, whom we so highly reverence and honour. The *occasion* likewise of this assembly adds not a little to the solemnity of it: to hear and determine causes of every kind, some of which are of the most important nature; on which depends no less than life or death—death, that uncovers the face of eternity! It was doubtless in order to increase the serious sense of these things, and not in the minds of the vulgar only, that the wisdom of our forefathers did not disdain to appoint even several minute circumstances of this solemnity. For these also, by means of the eye or ear, may more deeply affect the heart. And when viewed in this light, trumpets, staves, apparel, are no longer trifling or insignificant, but subservient in their kind and degree to the most valuable ends of society.

2. But as awful as this solemnity is, one far more awful is at hand. For yet a little while and 'we shall all stand before the judgment seat of Christ. For, As I live, saith the Lord, every knee shall bow to me, and every tongue shall confess to God.' And in that day 'every one of us shall give account of himself to God.'[1]

3. Had all men a deep sense of this, how effectually would it secure the interests of society! For what more forcible motive can be conceived to the practice of genuine morality? To a steady pursuit of solid virtue, an uniform walking in justice, mercy, and truth? What could strengthen our hands in all that is good, and deter us from all evil, like a strong conviction of this—'The judge standeth at the door,'[2] and we are shortly to *stand before* him?

4. It may not therefore be improper, or unsuitable to the design of the present assembly, to consider,

I. The chief circumstances which will precede our standing before the judgment seat of Christ.
II. The judgment itself, and
III. A few of the circumstances which will follow it.

I. Let us, in the first place, consider the chief circumstances which will precede our standing before the judgment seat of Christ.

---

[1] Rom. 14:10-12.
[2] Ja. 5:9.

And first, 1. 'God will show signs in the earth beneath:'[3] particularly, he will 'arise to shake terribly the earth'.[4] 'The earth shall reel to and fro like a drunkard, and shall be removed like a cottage.'[5] 'There shall be earthquakes' *kata topous* (not in divers only, but) 'in all places'[6]—not in one only, or a few, but in every part of the habitable world—even 'such as were not since men were upon the earth, so mighty earthquakes and so great'.[7] In one of these 'every island shall flee away, and the mountains will not be found.'[8] Meantime all the waters of the terraqueous globe will feel the violence of those concussions: 'the sea and waves roaring',[9] with such an agitation as had never been known before since the hour that 'the fountains of the great deep were broken up,'[10] to destroy the earth which then 'stood out of the water and in the water'.[11] The air will be all storm and tempest, full of dark 'vapours and pillars of smoke';[12] resounding with thunder from pole to pole, and torn with ten thousand lightnings. But the commotion will not stop in the region of the air: 'The powers of heaven also shall be shaken.' 'There shall be signs in the sun and in the moon and in the stars'[13]—those fixed as well as those that move round them. 'The sun shall be turned into darkness and the moon into blood, before the great and terrible day of the Lord come.'[14] 'The stars shall withdraw their shining,'[15] yea and 'fall from heaven',[16] being thrown out of their orbits. And then shall be heard the universal 'shout' from all the companies of heaven, followed by 'the voice of the archangel' proclaiming the approach of the Son of God and man, 'and the trumpet of God'[17] sounding an alarm to all 'that sleep in the dust of the earth'.[18] In consequence of this all the graves shall open, and the bodies of men arise.[19] 'The sea also shall give up the dead which are therein,'[20] and everyone shall rise with his

---

[3] Acts 2:19.
[4] Is. 2:19.
[5] Is. 24:20.
[6] Lk. 21:11.
[7] Rev. 16:18.
[8] Rev. 16:20.
[9] Lk. 21:25.
[10] Gen. 7:11.
[11] 2 Pet. 3:5.
[12] Joel 2:30.
[13] Lk. 21:25, 26.
[14] Joel 2:31.
[15] Joel 3:15.
[16] Matt. 24:29.
[17] 1 Th. 4:16.
[18] Dan. 12:2.
[19] Cf. Eze. 37:12-13; Matt. 27:52-53.
[20] Rev. 20:13.

own body—his own in substance, although so changed in its properties as we cannot now conceive. For 'this corruptible will then put on incorruption, and this mortal put on immortality.'[21] Yea, 'death and Hades', the invisible world, shall 'deliver up the dead that are in them';[22] so that all who ever lived and died since God created man shall be raised incorruptible and immortal.

2. At the same time 'the Son of man shall send forth his angels' over all the earth, 'and they shall gather his elect from the four winds, from one end of heaven to the other.'[23] And the Lord himself shall 'come with clouds, in his own glory and the glory of his Father, with ten thousand of his saints, even myriads of angels',[24] and 'shall sit upon the throne of his glory. And before him shall be gathered all nations, and he shall separate them one from another, and shall set the sheep' (the good) 'on his right hand, and the goats' (the wicked) 'upon the left.'[25] Concerning this general assembly it is that the beloved disciple speaks thus: 'I saw the dead' (all that had been dead) 'small and great, stand before God. And the books were opened (a figurative expression, plainly referring to the manner of proceeding among men), and the dead were judged out of those things which were written in the books according to their works.'[26]

II. These are the chief circumstances which are recorded in the oracles of God as preceding the general judgment. We are, secondly, to consider the judgment itself, so far as it hath pleased God to reveal it.

1. The person by whom God 'will judge the world'[27] is his only-begotten Son, whose 'goings forth are from everlasting',[28] 'who is God over all, blessed for ever'.[29] Unto him, 'being the out-beaming of his Father's glory, the express image of his person',[30] the Father 'hath committed all judgment, [. . .] because he is the Son of man';[31] because, though he was 'in the form of God, and thought it not robbery to be equal with God, yet he emptied himself,

---

[21] 1 Cor. 15:53.
[22] Rev. 20:13.
[23] Matt. 24:31.
[24] Cf. Matt. 24:30; Lk. 9:26; Jude 14; Heb. 12:22.
[25] Matt. 25:31-33.
[26] Rev. 20:12.
[27] Cf. Rom. 3:6; 1 Cor. 6:2.
[28] Mic. 5:2.
[29] Rom. 9:5.
[30] Heb. 1:3.
[31] Jn. 5:22, 27.

taking upon him the form of a servant, being made in the likeness of men'.[32] Yea, because 'being found in fashion as a man, he humbled himself' yet farther, 'becoming obedient unto death, even the death of the cross. Wherefore God hath highly exalted him,'[33] even in his human nature, and 'ordained him'[34] as man to try the children of men, to be the 'judge both of the quick and dead';[35] both of those who shall be found alive at his coming, and of those who were before 'gathered to their fathers'.[36]

2. The time termed by the prophet 'the great and the terrible day'[37] is usually in Scripture styled 'the day of the Lord'.[38] The space from the creation of man upon the earth to the end of all things is the day of the sons of men. The time that is now passing over us is properly our day. When this is ended, the day of the Lord will begin. But who can say how long it will continue? 'With the Lord one day is as a thousand years, and a thousand years as one day.'[39] And from this very expression some of the ancient Fathers drew that inference, that what is commonly called 'the day of judgment'[40] would be indeed a thousand years. And it seems they did not go beyond the truth; nay, probably they did not come up to it. For if we consider the number of persons who are to be judged, and of actions which are to be inquired into, it does not appear that a thousand years will suffice for the transactions of that day. So that it may not improbably comprise several thousand years. But God shall reveal this also in its season.

3. With regard to the place where mankind will be judged we have no explicit account in Scripture. An eminent writer (but not he alone; many have been of the same opinion) supposes it will be on earth, where the works were done according to which they shall be judged, and that God will in order thereto employ the angels of his strength,

> To smooth and lengthen out the boundless space,
> And spread an area for all human race.[41]

---

[32] Phil. 2:6-7.
[33] Phil. 2:8-9.
[34] Acts 17:31.
[35] 1 Pet. 4:5.
[36] Jdg. 2:10.
[37] Joel 2:31.
[38] Joel 1:15.
[39] 2 Pet. 3:8.
[40] Matt. 10:15.
[41] Young, *Last Day,* ii.19-20; cf. Wesley, *Collection of Moral and Sacred Poems* (1744), II.76.

But perhaps it is more agreeable to our Lord's own account of his 'coming in the clouds'[42] to suppose it will be above the earth, if not 'twice a planetary height'.[42] And this supposition is not a little favoured by what St. Paul writes to the Thessalonians. 'The dead in Christ shall rise first. Then we who remain alive shall be caught up together with them, in the clouds, to meet the Lord in the air.'[43] So that it seems most probable the 'great white throne'[44] will be high exalted above the earth.

4. The persons to be judged who can count, any more than the drops of rain or the sands of the sea? I beheld, saith St. John, 'a great multitude which no man can number, clothed with white robes, and palms in their hands'.[45] How immense then must be the total multitude of all nations, and kindreds, and people, and tongues! Of all that have sprung from the loins of Adam since the world began, till time shall be no more! If we admit the common supposition, which seems noways absurd, that the earth bears at any one time no less than four hundred millions of living souls—men, women, and children—what a congregation must all those generations make who have succeeded each other for seven thousand years!

> Great Xerxes' world in arms, proud Cannae's host, . . .
>   They all are here, and here they all are lost:
>   Their numbers swell to be discerned in vain;
>   Lost as a drop in the unbounded main.[46]

Every man, every woman, every infant of days that ever breathed the vital air will then hear the voice of the Son of God, and start into life, and appear before him. And this seems to be the natural import of that expression, 'the dead, small and great':[47] all universally, all without exception, all of every age, sex, or degree; all that ever lived and died, or underwent such a change as will be equivalent with death. For long before that day the phantom of human greatness disappears and sinks into nothing. Even in the moment of death that vanishes away. Who is rich or great in the grave?

---

[42] Matt. 24:30; Mk. 13:26.
[42] Young, *Last Day,* ii.274; cf. Wesley, *Collection of Moral and Sacred Poems,* II.82.
[43] 1 Th. 4:16-17.
[44] Rev. 20:11.
[45] Rev. 7:9.
[46] Young, *Last Day,* ii.189, 194-96.
[47] Rev. 20:12.

5. And every man shall there 'give an account of his own works',[48] yea, a full and true account of all that he ever did while in the body, whether it was good or evil. O what a scene will then be disclosed in the sight of angels and men! While not the fabled Rhadamanthus, but the Lord God Almighty, who knoweth all things in heaven and earth,

> *Castigatque, auditque dolos; subigitque fateri*
> *Quae quis apud superos, furto laetatus inani,*
> *Distulit in seram commissa piacula mortem.*[49]

Nor will all the actions alone of every child of man be then brought to open view, but all their words, seeing 'every idle word which men shall speak, they shall give account thereof in the day of judgment.' So that, 'By thy words' (as well as works) 'thou shalt be justified; or by thy words thou shalt be condemned'.[50] Will not God then bring to light every circumstance also that accompanied every word or action, and if not altered the nature, yet lessened or increased the goodness or badness of them? And how easy is this to him who is 'about our bed and about our path, and spieth out all our ways'![51] We know 'the darkness is no darkness to him, but the night shineth as the day.'[52]

6. Yea, he 'will bring to light' not 'the hidden works of darkness'[53] only, but the very 'thoughts and intents of the heart'.[54] And what marvel? For he 'searcheth the reins',[55] and 'understandeth all our thoughts'.[56] 'All things are

---

[48] Lk. 16:2; Rom. 14:12; Rev. 20:12.

[49] Virgil, *Aeneid*, vi.567-69. Outler explains, "Wesley offers no translation, but in the 'Explanation of the latin Sentences' added to Vol. 32 of his *Works* (1774) Wesley prefixed the preceding line, '*Haec Rhadamanthus habet durissima regna*', and furnished his own translation of the quatrain:

> O'er these drear realms stern Rhadamanthus reigns,
> Detects each artful villain, and constrains
> To own the crimes, long veiled from human sight:
> In vain! Now all stand forth in hated light."

Outler adds that "Wesley continued to read Virgil 'for peasure', even into his old age. Thus he may have had a copy of the *Aeneid* at hand, which would explain this rare verbatim quotation." (*Works* 1:362, n. 41).

[50] Matt. 12:36-37.

[51] Ps. 139:2 (Book of Common Pray; hereafter BCP).

[52] Ps. 139:11-12 (a conflation of BCP & AV).

[53] 1 Cor. 4:5.

[54] Heb. 4:12.

[55] Rev. 2:23.

naked and open to the eyes of him with whom we have to do.'[57] 'Hell and destruction are before him' without a covering; 'how much more the hearts of the children of men!'[58]

7. And in that day shall be discovered every inward working of every human soul: every appetite, passion, inclination, affection, with the various combinations of them, with every temper and disposition that constitute the whole complex character of each individual. So shall it be clearly and infallibly seen who was righteous, and who unrighteous; and in what degree every action or person or character was either good or evil.

8. 'Then the king will say to them upon his right hand, Come, ye blessed of my Father. For I was hungry and ye gave me meat; thirsty and ye gave me drink; I was a stranger and ye took me in; naked and ye clothed me.'[59] In like manner, all the good they did upon earth will be recited before men and angels: whatsoever they had done either 'in word or deed, in the name', or for the sake 'of the Lord Jesus'.[60] All their good desires, intentions, thoughts, all their holy dispositions, will also be then remembered; and it will appear that though they were unknown or forgotten among men, yet God 'noted' them 'in his book'.[61] All their sufferings likewise for the name of Jesus and for the testimony of a good conscience will be displayed, unto their *praise* from the righteous judge, their *honour* before saints and angels, and the increase of that 'far more exceeding and eternal weight of glory'.[62]

9. But will their evil deeds too—since if we take in his whole life 'there is not a man on earth that liveth and sinneth not'[63]—will these be remembered in that day, and mentioned in the great congregation? Many believe they will not, and ask, 'Would not this imply that their sufferings were not at an end, even when life ended? Seeing they would still have sorrow, and shame, and confusion of face to endure?' They ask farther, 'How can this be reconciled with God's declaration by the Prophet, "If the wicked will turn from all his sins that he hath committed, and keep all my statutes, and do that which is lawful and right; . . . all his transgressions that he hath committed, they shall

---

[56] Ps. 139:2.
[57] Heb. 4:13.
[58] Pr. 15:11.
[59] Matt. 25:34-36.
[60] Col. 3:17.
[61] Is. 30:8.
[62] 2 Cor. 4:17.
[63] Eccl. 7:20.

not be once mentioned unto him"?⁶⁴ How is it consistent with the promise which God has made to all who accept of the gospel covenant, "I will forgive their iniquities, and remember their sin no more"?⁶⁵ Or as the Apostle expresses it, "I will be merciful to their unrighteousness, and their sins and iniquities will I remember no more"?'⁶⁶

10. It may be answered, it is apparently and absolutely necessary, for the full display of the glory of God, for the clear and perfect manifestation of his wisdom, justice, power, and mercy toward the heirs of salvation, that all the circumstances of their life should be placed in open view, together with all their tempers, and all the desires, thoughts, and intents of their hearts. Otherwise how would it appear out of what a depth of sin and misery the grace of God had delivered them? And, indeed, if the whole lives of all the children of men were not manifestly discovered, the whole amazing contexture of divine providence could not be manifested; nor should we yet be able in a thousand instances to 'justify the ways of God to man'.⁶⁷ Unless our Lord's words were fulfilled in their utmost sense, without any restriction or limitation, 'there is nothing covered that shall not be revealed, or hid that shall not be known,'⁶⁸ abundance of God's dispensations under the sun would still appear without their reasons. And then only when God hath brought to light all the hidden things of darkness, whosoever were the actors therein, will it be seen that wise and good were all his ways; that he 'saw through the thick cloud',⁶⁹ and governed all things by the wise 'counsel of his own will';⁷⁰ that nothing was left to chance or the caprice of men, but God disposed all 'strongly and sweetly',⁷¹ and wrought all into one connected chain of justice, mercy, and truth.

11. And in the discovery of the divine perfections the righteous will rejoice with joy unspeakable; far from feeling any painful sorrow or shame for any of those past transgressions which were long since blotted out as a cloud, washed away by the blood of the Lamb. It will be abundantly sufficient for them that 'all the transgressions which they had committed shall not be once mentioned unto them'⁷² to their disadvantage; that 'their sins and

---

⁶⁴ Eze. 18:21-22.
⁶⁵ Jer. 31:34.
⁶⁶ Heb. 8:12.
⁶⁷ Cf. Milton, *Paradise Lost,* 1.26.
⁶⁸ Matt. 10:26.
⁶⁹ A paraphrase of Job 22:12-14.
⁷⁰ Eph. 1:11.
⁷¹ Cf. George Herbert, *The Temple,* 'Providence', ll.1-2 and, especially 29-32.
⁷² Eze. 18:22.

transgressions and iniquities shall be remembered no more'[73] to their condemnation. This is the plain meaning of the promise; and this all the children of God shall find true, to their everlasting comfort.

12. After the righteous are judged, the king will turn to them upon his left hand, and they shall also be judged, every man 'according to his works'.[74] But not only their outward works will be brought into the account, but all the evil words which they have ever spoken; yea, all the evil desires, affections, tempers, which have or have had a place in their souls, and all the evil thoughts or designs which were ever cherished in their hearts. The joyful sentence of acquittal will then be pronounced upon those on the right hand, the dreadful sentence of condemnation upon those on the left—both of which must remain fixed and unmovable as the throne of God.

III.1. We may, in the third place, consider a few of the circumstances which will follow the general judgment. And the first is the execution of the sentence pronounced on the evil and on the good. 'These shall go away into eternal punishment, and the righteous into life eternal.'[75] It should be observed, it is the very same word which is used both in the former and the latter clause: it follows that either the punishment lasts for ever, or the reward too will come to an end. No, never, unless God could come to an end, or his mercy and truth could fail. 'Then shall the righteous shine forth as the sun in the kingdom of their Father,'[76] and shall 'drink of those rivers of pleasure which are at God's right hand for evermore'.[77] But here all description falls short; all human language fails! Only one who is caught up into the third heaven can have a just conception of it. But even such an one cannot express what he hath seen—these things 'it is not possible for man to utter.'[78]

'The wicked', meantime, 'shall be turned into hell,' even 'all the people that forget God'.[79] They will be 'punished with everlasting destruction from the presence of the Lord, and from the glory of his power'.[80] They will be 'cast into the lake of fire burning with brimstone',[81] originally 'prepared for the devil and his angels';[82] where they will 'gnaw their tongues'[83] for anguish

---

[73] Heb. 8:12; 10:17.
[74] Matt. 16:27.
[75] Matt. 25:46.
[76] Matt. 13:43.
[77] Pss. 16:11; 36:8.
[78] 2 Cor. 12:2, 4.
[79] Ps. 9:17 (BCP).
[80] 2 Th. 1:9.
[81] Rev. 19:20.
[82] Matt. 25:41.

and pain; they will 'curse God, and look upward':[84] there the dogs of hell—pride, malice, revenge, rage, horror, despair—continually devour them. There 'they have no rest day or night, but the smoke of their torment ascendeth for ever and ever.'[85] 'For their worm dieth not, and the fire is not quenched.'[86]

2. Then the heavens will be shrivelled up 'as a parchment scroll',[87] and 'pass away with a great noise';[88] they will 'flee from the face of him that sitteth on the throne, and there will be found no place for them'.[89] The very manner of their passing away is disclosed to us by the Apostle Peter: 'In the day of God, the heavens, being on fire, shall be dissolved.'[90] The whole beautiful fabric will be overthrown by that raging element, the connection of all its parts destroyed, and every atom torn asunder from the others. By the same 'the earth also and the works that are therein shall be burnt up.'[91] The enormous works of nature, 'the everlasting hills',[92] mountains that have defied the rage of time, and stood unmoved so many thousand years, will sink down in fiery ruin. How much less will the works of art, though of the most durable kind, the utmost efforts of human industry—tombs, pillars, triumphal arches, castles, pyramids—be able to withstand the flaming conqueror. All, all will die, perish, vanish away, like a dream when one awaketh!

3. It has indeed been imagined by some great and good men that as it requires that same almighty power to annihilate things as to create, to speak into nothing or out of nothing; so no part of, no atom in the universe will be totally or finally destroyed. Rather, they suppose that as the last operation of fire which we have yet been able to observe is to reduce into glass what by a smaller force it had reduced to ashes; so in the day God hath ordained the whole earth, if not the material heavens also, will undergo this change, after which the fire can have no farther power over them. And they believe this is intimated by that expression in the Revelation made to St. John: 'Before the throne there was a sea of glass like unto crystal.'[93] We cannot now either affirm or deny this; but we shall know hereafter.

---

[83] Rev. 16:10.
[84] Is. 8:21.
[85] Rev. 14:11.
[86] Mk. 9:44.
[87] Rev. 6:14.
[88] 2 Pet. 3:10.
[89] Rev. 20:11.
[90] 2 Pet. 3:12.
[91] 2 Pet. 3;10.
[92] Gen. 49:26.
[93] Rev. 4:6.

4. If it be inquired by the scoffers, the minute philosophers: 'How can these things be? Whence should come such an immense quantity of fire as would consume the heavens and the whole terraqueous globe?' we would beg leave, first, to remind them that this difficulty is not peculiar to the Christian system. The same opinion almost universally obtained among the unbigoted heathens. So one of those celebrated 'free-thinkers' speaks according to the generally received sentiment:

> *Esse quoque in fatis reminiscitur, affore tempus,*
> *Quo mare, quo tellus, correptaque regia coeli*
> *Ardeat, et mundi moles operosa laboret.*[94]

But, secondly, it is easy to answer, even from our slight and superficial acquaintance with natural things, that there are abundant magazines of fire ready prepared, and treasured up against the day of the Lord. How soon may a comet, commissioned by him, travel down from the most distant parts of the universe? And were it to fix upon the earth in its return from the sun, when it is some thousand times hotter than a red-hot cannon-ball, who does not see what must be the immediate consequence? But, not to ascend so high as the ethereal heavens, might not the same lightnings which give 'shine to the world',[95] if commanded by the Lord of nature give ruin and utter destruction? Or, to go no farther than the globe itself, who knows what huge reservoirs of liquid fire are from age to age contained in the bowels of the earth? Aetna, Hecla, Vesuvius, and all the other volcanoes that belch out flames and coals of fire, what are they but so many proofs and mouths of those fiery furnaces? And at the same time so many evidences that God hath in readiness wherewith to fulfil his word. Yea, were we to observe no more than the surface of the earth, and the things that surround us on every side, it is most certain (as a thousand experiments prove beyond all possibility of denial) that we ourselves, our whole bodies, are full of fire, as well as everything round about us. Is it not easy to make this ethereal fire visible even to the naked eye? And to produce thereby the very same effects on combustible matter which are produced by culinary fire? Needs there then any more than for God to unloose that secret chain whereby this irresistible agent is now bound down, and lies quiescent in every particle of matter? And

---

[94] Ovid, *Metamorphoses,* i.256-58: "He remembered also that 'twas in the fates that a time would come when sea and land, the unkindled palace of the sky, and the beleaguered structure of the universe, should be destroyed by fire" (Outler, *Works* 1:369, n. 92).

[95] Ps. 97:4 (BCP).

how soon would it tear the universal frame in pieces, and involve all in one common ruin?

5. There is one circumstance more which will follow the judgment that deserves our serious consideration. 'We look', says the Apostle, 'according to his promise, for new heavens and a new earth, wherein dwelleth righteousness.'[96] The promise stands in the prophecy of Isaiah: 'Behold, I create new heavens and a new earth. And the former shall not be remembered';[97] so great shall the glory of the latter be. These St. John did behold in the visions of God. 'I saw', saith he, 'a new heaven and a new earth; for the first heaven and the first earth were passed away.'[98] And only 'righteousness dwelt therein.'[99] Accordingly he adds, 'And I heard a great voice from' the third 'heaven, saying, Behold, the tabernacle of God is with men, and he will dwell with them, and they shall be his people, and God himself shall be with them, and be their God.'[1] Of necessity, therefore, they will all be happy: 'God shall wipe away all tears from their eyes, and there shall be no more death, neither sorrow, nor crying; neither shall there be any more pain.'[2] 'There shall be no more curse; but [. . .] they shall see his face,'[3] shall have the nearest access to, and thence the highest resemblance of him. This is the strongest expression in the language of Scripture to denote the most perfect happiness. 'And his name shall be on their foreheads.'[4] They shall be openly acknowledged as God's own property; and his glorious nature shall most visibly shine forth in them. 'And there shall be no night there; and they need no candle, neither light of the sun; for the Lord God giveth them light, and they shall reign for ever and ever.'[5]

IV. It remains only to apply the preceding considerations to all who are here before God. And are we not directly led so to do by the present solemnity, which so naturally points us to that day when the Lord 'will judge the world in righteousness'?[6] This, therefore, by reminding us of that more awful season, may furnish many lessons of instruction. A few of these I may be permitted just to touch on. May God write them on all our hearts!

---

[96] 2 Pet. 3:13.
[97] Is. 65:17.
[98] Rev. 21:1.
[99] 2 Pet. 3:13.
[1] Rev. 21:3.
[2] Rev. 21:4.
[3] Rev. 22:3, 4.
[4] Rev. 22:4.
[5] Rev. 22:5.
[6] Ps. 9:8.

1. And, first, 'how beautiful are the feet'[7] of those who are sent by the wise and gracious providence of God to execute justice on earth, to defend the injured, and punish the wrongdoer! Are they not 'the ministers of God to us for good',[8] the grand supporters of the public tranquillity, the patrons of innocence and virtue, the great security of all our temporal blessings? And does not every one of these represent not only an earthly prince, but the Judge of the earth; him whose 'name is written upon his thigh, King of Kings, and Lord of Lords'![9] O that all these sons 'of the right hand of the Most High'[10] may be holy as he is holy! Wise with the 'wisdom that sitteth by his throne',[11] like him who is the eternal wisdom of the Father! No respecters of persons, as he is none; but 'rendering to every man according to his works':[12] like him inflexibly, inexorably just, though pitiful and of tender mercy! So shall they be terrible indeed to them that do evil, as 'not bearing the sword in vain'.[13] So shall the laws of our land have their full use and due honour, and the throne of our King be still 'established in righteousness'.[14]

2. Ye truly honourable men, whom God and the King have commissioned in a lower degree to administer justice, may not ye be compared to those ministering spirits who will attend the Judge coming in the clouds? May you, like them, burn with love to God and man! May you love righteousness and hate iniquity! May ye all minister in your several spheres (such honour hath God given you also!) to them that shall be heirs of salvation, and to the glory of your great Sovereign! May ye remain the establishers of peace, the blessing and ornaments of your country, the protectors of a guilty land, the guardian angels of all that are round about you!

3. You whose office it is to execute what is given you in charge by him before whom you stand, how nearly are you concerned to resemble those that stand before the face of the Son of man! Those 'servants of his that do his pleasure',[15] 'and hearken to the voice of his words'.[16] Does it not highly import *you* to be as uncorrupt as *them*? To approve yourselves the servants of

---

[7] Is. 52:7.
[8] Rom. 13:4.
[9] Rev. 19:16.
[10] Ps. 77:10.
[11] Wisd. 9:4.
[12] Pr. 24:12; Matt. 16:27.
[13] Rom. 13:4.
[14] Pr. 25:5.
[15] Ps. 103:21 (BCP).
[16] Ps. 103:20 (BCP).

God? To do justly and love mercy; to do to all as ye would they should do to you? So shall that great Judge, under whose eye you continually stand, say to you also, 'Well done, good and faithful servants: enter ye into the joy of your Lord!'[17]

4. Suffer me to add a few words to all of you who are this day present before the Lord. Should not you bear it in your minds all the day long that a more awful day is coming? A large assembly this! But what is it to that which every eye will then behold—the general assembly of all the children of men that ever lived on the face of the whole earth! A few will stand at the judgment seat this day, to be judged touching what shall be laid to their charge. And they are now reserved in prison, perhaps in chains, till they are brought forth to be tried and sentenced. But we shall all, I that speak and you that hear, 'stand at the judgment seat of Christ'.[18] And we are now reserved on this earth, which is not our home, in this prison of flesh and blood, perhaps many of us in chains of darkness too, till we are ordered to be brought forth. Here a man is questioned concerning one or two facts which he is supposed to have committed. There we are to give an account of all our works, from the cradle to the grave: of all our words; of all our desires and tempers, all the thoughts and intents of our hearts; of all the use we have made of our various talents, whether of mind, body, or fortune, till God said, 'Give an account of thy stewardship; for thou mayest be no longer steward.'[19] In this court it is possible some who are guilty may escape for want of evidence. But there is no want of evidence in that court. All men with whom you had the most secret intercourse, who were privy to all your designs and actions, are ready before your face. So are all the spirits of darkness, who inspired evil designs, and assisted in the execution of them. So are all the angels of God—those 'eyes of the Lord that run to and fro over all the earth'[20]—who watched over your soul, and laboured for your good so far as you would permit. So is your own conscience, a thousand witnesses in one, now no more capable of being either blinded or silenced, but constrained to know and to speak the naked truth touching all your thoughts and words and actions. And is conscience as a thousand witnesses? Yea, but God is as a thousand consciences! O who can stand before the face of 'the great God, even our Saviour, Jesus Christ'![21]

---

[17] Matt. 25:21, 23.
[18] Rom. 14:10.
[19] Lk. 16:2.
[20] Zech. 4:10.
[21] Tit. 2:13.

See, see! He cometh! He maketh the clouds his chariots. He rideth upon the wings of the wind! A devouring fire goeth before him, and after him a flame burneth! See, he sitteth upon his throne, clothed with light as with a garment, arrayed with majesty and honour! Behold his eyes are as a flame of fire, his voice as the sound of many waters!

How will ye escape? Will ye call to the mountains to fall on you, the rocks to cover you? Alas, the mountains themselves, the rocks, the earth, the heavens, are just ready to flee away! Can ye prevent the sentence? Wherewith? With all the substance of thy house, with thousands of gold and silver? Blind wretch! Thou camest naked from thy mother's womb, and shalt move naked into eternity. Hear the Lord, the Judge! 'Come ye blessed of my Father! Inherit the kingdom prepared for you from the foundation of the world.'[22] Joyful sound! How widely different from that voice which echoes through the expanse of heaven, 'Depart, ye cursed, into everlasting fire, prepared for the devil and his angels!'[23] And who is he that can prevent or retard the full execution of either sentence? Vain hope! Lo, 'hell is moved from beneath'[24] to receive those who are ripe for destruction! And the 'everlasting doors lift up their heads' that the heirs of glory may come in![25]

5. 'What manner of persons (then) ought we to be, in all holy conversation and godliness?'[26] We know it cannot be long before the Lord will descend 'with the voice of the archangel, and the trumpet of God';[27] when every one of us shall appear before him and 'give account of his own works'.[28] 'Wherefore, beloved, seeing ye look for these things',[29] seeing ye know he will come and will not tarry, 'be diligent that ye may be found of him in peace, without spot, and blameless.'[30] Why should ye not? Why should one of you be found on the left hand at his appearing? He 'willeth not that any should perish, but that all should come to *repentance*';[31] by repentance to faith in a bleeding Lord; by faith to spotless love, to the full image of God renewed in the heart, and producing all holiness of conversation. Can you doubt of this when you remember the Judge of all is likewise 'the Saviour of

---

[22] Matt. 25:34.
[23] Matt. 25:41.
[24] Is. 14:9.
[25] Ps. 24:7, 9.
[26] 2 Pet. 3:11.
[27] 1 Th. 4:16.
[28] Lk. 16:2; Rev. 20:12.
[29] 2 Pet. 3:14.
[30] 2 Pet. 3:14.
[31] 2 Pet. 3:9.

all'?[32] Hath he not bought you with his own blood, that ye might 'not perish, but have everlasting life'?[33] O make proof of his mercy rather than his justice! Of his love rather than the thunder of his power! 'He is not far from every one of us';[34] and he is now come, 'not to condemn, but to save the world'.[35] He standeth in the midst! Sinner, doth he not now, even now, knock at the door of thy heart? O that thou mayst know, at least *'in this thy day'*, the things that belong unto thy peace![36] O that ye may now give yourselves to him who 'gave himself for you',[37] in humble faith, in holy, active, patient love! So shall ye rejoice with exceeding joy *in his day*, when he cometh in the clouds of heaven.

---

[32] 1 Tim. 4;10.
[33] Jn. 3:16.
[34] Acts. 17:27.
[35] Jn. 3:17.
[36] Lk. 19:42.
[37] Gal. 2:20.

The Mystery of Iniquity
1783

This sermon offers important insights into Wesley's understanding of salvation history. Wesley believed the great apostasy predicted by the Apostle Paul (2 Th. 2:3) was fulfilled in the religious nominalism of Christendom. In his assessment of the Reformation, Wesley parts paths with John Bale, John Foxe, Thomas Brightman, and other Puritans and instead follows the lead of Philip Jacob Spener. Tracing the roots of the disease back to the apostolic age, and even further back to Adam's fall, he finds the cure in the present Evangelical Revival, which will usher in a new age of gospel holiness and happiness (i.e. the millennium). This is the heartbeat of Wesley's evangelical eschatology, which identified the lack of holiness in professed Christians and the increase of wealth as the primary barriers to converting the world. The blame is squarely laid at the feet of Constantine the Great, who opened the floodgate of 'riches, honours, and power' upon the church (§27). By the last third of the eighteenth century, the Industrial Revolution was changing the face of British society and the increase in wealth brought forth incessant warnings from Wesley's pen. For more of Wesley's remarks on Constantine, see Prophets and Priests *§8 (Works 4:77). For sermons addressing similar themes, see* The Danger of Riches *(Works 3:227-46),* On Riches *(Works 3:518-28),* The Causes of the Inefficacy of Christianity *(Works 4:85-96),* On a Single Eye *(Works 4:120-30),* On the Wedding Garment *(Works 4:139-48), and* The Danger of Increasing Riches *(Works 4:177-86). For Albert Outler's introduction, see Works 2:451.*

The mystery of iniquity doth already work.

2 Thessalonians 2:7

1. Without inquiring how far these words refer to any particular event in the Christian church, I would at present take occasion from them to consider that important question—in what manner 'the mystery of iniquity' hath 'wrought' among us till it hath well nigh covered the whole earth.

2. It is certain that God 'made man upright',[1] perfectly holy and perfectly happy. But by rebelling against God he destroyed himself, lost the favour and the image of God, and entailed sin, with its attendant pain, on himself and all his posterity. Yet his merciful Creator did not leave him in this helpless, hopeless state. He immediately appointed his Son, his well-beloved Son, 'who is the brightness of his glory, the express image of his person',[2] to be the Saviour of men, 'the propitiation for the sins of the whole world';[3] the great Physician, who by his almighty Spirit should heal the sickness of their souls, and restore them not only to the favour but to 'the image of God wherein they were created'.[4]

3. This great 'mystery of godliness'[5] began to work from the very time of the original promise. Accordingly the Lamb, being (in the purpose of God) 'slain from the beginning of the world',[6] from the same period his sanctifying Spirit began to renew the souls of men. We have an undeniable instance of this in Abel, who 'obtained a testimony' from God 'that he was righteous'.[7] And from that very time all that were partakers of the same faith were partakers of the same salvation; were not only reinstated in the favour, but likewise restored to the image of God.

4. But how exceeding small was the number of these, even from the earliest ages! No sooner did 'the sons of men multiply upon the face of the earth' than 'God', looking down from heaven, 'saw that the wickedness of man was great upon earth'; so great 'that every imagination of the thoughts of his heart was evil, only evil', and that 'continually'.[8] And so it remained without any intermission till God executed that terrible sentence, 'I will destroy man, whom I have created, from the face of the earth.'[9]

5. 'Only Noah found grace in the eyes of the Lord,' being 'a just man and perfect in his generations.'[10] Him therefore, with his wife, his sons, and their wives, God preserved from the general destruction. And one might have imagined that this small remnant would likewise have been 'perfect in their

---

[1] Eccl. 7:29.
[2] Heb. 1:3.
[3] 1 Jn. 2:2.
[4] Col. 3:10.
[5] 1 Tim. 3:16.
[6] Rev. 13:8.
[7] Heb. 11:6.
[8] Gen. 6:1-5.
[9] Gen. 6:7.
[10] Gen. 6:8-9.

generations'. But how far was this from being the case! Presently after this signal deliverance we find one of them, Ham, involved in sin, and under his father's curse. And how did the mystery of iniquity afterwards work, not only in the posterity of Ham, but in the posterity of Japhet; yea, and of Shem—Abraham and his family only excepted!

6. Yea, how did it work even in the posterity of Abraham, in God's chosen people! Were not these also, down to Moses, to David, to Malachi, to Herod the Great, 'a faithless and stubborn generation'?[11] 'A sinful nation, a people laden with iniquity', continually 'forsaking the Lord, and provoking the Holy One of Israel'?[12] And yet we have no reason to believe that these were worse than the nations that surrounded them, who were universally swallowed up in all manner of wickedness, as well as in damnable idolatries, not having the God of heaven 'in all their thoughts',[13] but working all uncleanness with greediness.

7. In the fullness of time, when iniquity of every kind, when ungodliness and unrighteousness had spread over all nations, and covered the earth as a flood; it pleased God to lift up a standard against it, by 'bringing his first-begotten into the world'.[14] Now, then, one would expect the mystery of godliness would totally prevail over the mystery of iniquity—the Son of God would be 'a light to lighten the Gentiles', as well as 'salvation to his people Israel'.[15] All Israel, one would think, yea, and all the earth, will soon be filled with the glory of the Lord. Nay; the mystery of iniquity prevailed still, wellnigh over the face of the earth. How exceeding small was the number of those whose souls were healed by the Son of God himself! 'When Peter stood up in the midst of them, the number of names was about a hundred and twenty.'[16] And even these were but imperfectly healed; the chief of them being a little before so weak in faith that though they did not, like Peter, forswear their Master, yet 'they all forsook him and fled.'[17] A plain proof that the sanctifying 'Spirit was not' then to 'given', because 'Jesus was not glorified.'[18]

---

[11] Ps. 78:9 (BCP).
[12] Is. 1:4.
[13] Ps. 10:4.
[14] Heb. 1:6.
[15] Lk. 2:32.
[16] Acts. 1:15.
[17] Mk. 14:50.
[18] Jn. 7:39.

8. It was then, when he had 'ascended up on high, and led captivity captive',[19] that 'the promise of the Father' was fulfilled, 'which they had heard from him'.[20] It was then he began to work like himself, showing that 'all power was given to him in heaven and earth.'[21] 'When the day of Pentecost was fully come, suddenly there came a sound from heaven, as of a rushing mighty wind, and there appeared tongues as of fire, and they were all filled with the Holy Ghost.'[22] In consequence of this three thousand souls received 'medicine to heal their sickness',[23] were restored to the favour and the image of God, under one sermon of St. Peter's. 'And the Lord added to them daily' (not 'such as should be saved'—a manifest perversion of the text—but) 'such as were saved.'[24] The expression is peculiar; and so indeed is the position of the words, which run thus, 'And the Lord added those that were saved daily to the church.' First, *they were saved* from the guilt and power of sin; then *they were added* to the assembly of the faithful.

9. In order clearly to see how they were already saved we need only observe the short account of them which is recorded in the latter part of the second and in the fourth chapter. 'They continued steadfastly in the apostles' doctrine, and in the fellowship, and in the breaking of bread, and in the prayers':[25] that is, they were daily taught by the apostles, and had all things common, and received the Lord's Supper, and attended all the public service. 'And all that believed were together, and had all things common; and sold their possessions, and parted them to all men, as every man had need.'[26] And again: 'The multitude of them that believed', now greatly increased, 'were of one heart and of one soul. Neither said any of them that ought of the things which he possessed was his own, but they had all things common.'[27] And yet again: 'Great grace was upon them all; neither was there any among them that lacked. For as many as were possessors of lands or houses sold them, and brought the price of the things that were sold, and laid them at the apostles' feet. And distribution was made unto every man according as he had need.'[28]

---

[19] Eph. 4:8.
[20] Acts 1:4.
[21] Matt. 28:18.
[22] Acts 2:1-4.
[23] Ps. 147:3 (BCP).
[24] Acts 2:47. Wesley's correction of the KJV (cf. *Notes*).
[25] Acts 2:42.
[26] Acts 2:41, 44-45.
[27] Acts 4:31-32.
[28] Acts 4:33-35.

10. But here a question will naturally occur. How came they to act thus, to have all things in common, seeing we do not read of any positive command to do this? I answer, there needed no outward command: the command was written on their hearts. It naturally and necessarily resulted from the degree of love which they enjoyed. Observe! 'They were of one heart and of one soul: and not so much as one' (so the words run) 'said' (they could not, while their hearts so overflowed with love) 'that any of the things which he possessed was his own.' And wheresoever the same cause shall prevail the same effect will naturally follow.

11. Here was the dawn of the proper gospel day. Here was a proper Christian church. It was now 'the Sun of righteousness rose' upon the earth, 'with healing in his wings.'[29] He did now 'save his people from their sins':[30] he 'healed' all 'their sickness'.[31] He not only taught that religion which is the true 'healing of the soul',[32] but effectually planted it in the earth; filling the souls of all that believed in him with *righteousness*, gratitude to God, and goodwill to man, attended with a *peace* that surpassed all understanding, and with *joy* unspeakable and full of glory.

12. But how soon did 'the mystery of iniquity' work again and obscure the glorious prospect! It began to work (not openly indeed, but covertly) in two of the Christians, Ananias and Sapphira. 'They sold their possession' like the rest, and probably for the same motive. But afterwards, giving place to the devil, and reasoning with flesh and blood, they 'kept back part of the price'.[33] See the first Christians that 'made shipwreck of faith and a good conscience'![34] The first that 'drew back to perdition', instead of continuing to 'believe to the' final 'salvation'[35] of the soul. Mark the first plague which infected the Christian church! Namely, the love of money! And will it not be the grand plague in all generations, whenever God shall revive the same work? O ye believers in Christ, take warning! Whether you are yet but 'little children', or 'young men' that 'are strong'[36] in the faith. See the snare! *Your* snare in particular! That which you will be peculiarly exposed to after you have escaped from gross pollutions. 'Love not the world, neither the things of

---

[29] Mal. 4:2.
[30] Matt. 1:21.
[31] Matt. 9:35.
[32] Ps. 41:4.
[33] Acts 5:1-2.
[34] 1 Tim. 1:19.
[35] Heb. 10:39.
[36] 1 Jn. 2:12-14.

the world. If any man love the world', whatever he was in times past, 'the love of the Father is not' now 'in him.'[37]

13. However, this plague was stayed in the first Christian church by instantly cutting off the infected persons. And by that signal judgment of God on the first offenders, 'great fear came upon all',[38] so that for the present at least no one dared to follow their example. Meantime *believers*, men full of faith and love, who rejoiced to have all things in common, 'were the more added to the Lord, multitudes both of men and women.'[39]

14. If we inquire in what manner the mystery of iniquity, the energy of Satan, began to work again in the Christian church, we shall find it wrought in quite a different way, putting on quite another shape. Partiality crept in among the Christian believers. Those by whom the distribution to everyone was made had respect of persons, largely supplying those of their own nation, while the other 'widows' who were not Hebrews 'were neglected in the daily administration'.[40] Distribution was not made to them according as everyone had need. Here was a manifest breach of brotherly love in the Hebrews, a sin both against justice and mercy; seeing the Grecians, as well as the Hebrews, had 'sold all that they had, and laid the price at the apostles' feet'.[41] See the second plague that broke in upon the Christian church—partiality: respect of persons, too much regard for those of our own side, and too little for others, though equally worthy.

15. The infection did not stop here, but one evil produced many more. From partiality in the Hebrews 'there arose in the Grecians a murmuring against them';[42] not only discontent and resentful thoughts, but words suitable thereto; unkind expressions, hard speeches, evil-speaking, and backbiting naturally followed. And by the 'root of bitterness' thus 'springing up', undoubtedly 'many were defiled'.[43] The apostles indeed soon found out a means of removing the occasion of this murmuring; yet so much of the evil root remained that God saw it needful to use a severer remedy. He let loose the world upon them all, if haply by their sufferings, by the spoiling of their goods, by pain, imprisonment, and death itself, he might at once punish and

---

[37] 1 Jn. 2:15.
[38] Acts 5:11.
[39] Acts 5:14.
[40] Acts 6:1.
[41] Acts 4:37.
[42] Acts 6:1.
[43] Heb. 12:15.

amend them. And persecution, God's last remedy for a backsliding people, had the happy effect for which he intended it. Both the partiality of the Hebrews ceased, and the murmuring of the Grecians. And 'then had the churches rest, and were edified,' built up in the love of God and one another. 'And walking in the fear of the Lord, and in the comforts of the Holy Ghost, were multiplied.'[44]

16. It seems to have been some time after this that the mystery of iniquity began to work in the form of *zeal*. Great troubles arose by means of some who zealously contended for circumcision and the rest of the ceremonial law, till the apostles and elders put an end to the spreading evil by that final determination: 'It seemed good unto the Holy Ghost, and to us, to lay on you no greater burden than these necessary things, that ye abstain from meats offered to idols, and from blood, and from things strangled, and from fornication.'[45] Yet was not this evil so thoroughly suppressed but that it frequently broke out again, as we learn from various parts of St. Paul's epistles, particularly that to the Galatians.

17. Nearly allied to this was another grievous evil which at the same time sprang up in the church: want of mutual forbearance, and of consequence anger, strife, contention, variance. One very remarkable instance of this we find in this very chapter. When 'Paul said to Barnabas, Let us visit the brethren where we have preached the word, Barnabas determined to take with him John,'[46] because he was 'his sister's son'.[47] 'But Paul thought it not good to take him who had deserted them before.'[48] And he had certainly reason on his side. But Barnabas resolved to have his own way. *Kai egeneto paroxusmos*, 'And there was a fit of anger.'[49] It does not say on St. Paul's side. Barnabas only had passion, to supply the want of reason. Accordingly he departed from the work, and went home, while St. Paul 'went' forward 'through Syria and Cilicia, confirming the churches'.[50]

18. The very first society of Christians at Rome were not altogether free from this evil leaven. There were 'divisions and offences'[51] among them also,

---

[44] Acts 9:31.
[45] Acts 15:28-29.
[46] Acts 15:36-37.
[47] Col. 4:10.
[48] Acts 15:38.
[49] Acts 15:39.
[50] Acts 16:41.
[51] Rom. 16:17.

although in general they seem to have 'walked in love'.[52] But how early did the mystery of iniquity work, and how powerfully, in the church at Corinth! Not only 'schisms' and 'heresies',[53] animosities, fierce and bitter contentions were among them, but open, actual sins; yea, 'such fornication as was not named among the heathens'.[54] Nay, there was need to remind them that 'neither adulterers, nor thieves, nor drunkards' could 'enter into the kingdom of heaven'.[55] And in all St. Paul's epistles we meet with abundant proof that tares grew up with the wheat in all the churches, and that the mystery of iniquity did everywhere in a thousand forms counterwork the mystery of godliness.

19. When St. James wrote his Epistle, directed more immediately 'to the twelve tribes scattered abroad',[56] to the converted Jews, the tares sown among his wheat had produced a plentiful harvest. That grand pest of Christianity, a faith without works, was spread far and wide, filling the church with a wisdom from beneath which was 'earthly, sensual, devilish';[57] and which gave rise not only to rash judging and evil-speaking but to 'envy, strife, confusion, and every evil work'.[58] Indeed whoever peruses the fourth and fifth chapters of this Epistle with serious attention will be inclined to believe that even in this early period the tares had nigh choked the wheat, and that among most of those to whom St. James wrote no more than the form of godliness, if so much, was left.

20. St. Peter wrote about the same time to 'the strangers', the Christians 'scattered abroad through' all those spacious provinces of 'Pontus, Galatia, Cappadocia, Asia (Minor) and Bithynia'.[59] These probably were some of the most eminent Christians that were then in the world. Yet how exceeding far were even these from being 'without spot and blemish'![60] And what grievous tares were here also growing up with the wheat! Some of them were 'bringing in damnable heresies, even denying the Lord that bought them'.[61] And 'many followed their pernicious ways,' of whom the Apostle gives that terrible character, they 'walk after the flesh, in the lust of uncleanness, [. . .]

---

[52] Eph. 5:2.
[53] 1 Cor. 12:25; 11:19.
[54] 1 Cor. 5:1.
[55] 1 Cor. 6:9-10.
[56] Ja. 1:1.
[57] Ja. 3:15.
[58] Ja. 3:16.
[59] 1 Pet. 1:1.
[60] 1 Pet. 1:19.
[61] 2 Pet. 2:1.

like brute beasts, made to be taken and destroyed.[. . .] Spots they are, and blemishes, while they feast with you' (in the 'feasts of charity'[62] then celebrated throughout the whole church); 'having eyes full of adultery, and that cannot cease from sin.[. . .] These are wells without water, clouds that are carried with a tempest, for whom the mist of darkness is reserved for ever.'[63] And yet these very men were called Christians, and were even then in the bosom of the church! Nor does the Apostle mention them as infesting any one particular church only, but as a general plague, which even then was dispersed far and wide among all the Christians to whom he wrote.

21. Such is the authentic account of the mystery of iniquity, working even in the apostolic churches! An account given, not by the Jews or heathens, but by the apostles themselves. To this we may add the account which is given by the Head and Founder of the church—him 'who holds the stars in his right hand',[64] who is 'the faithful and true witness'.[65] We may easily infer what was the state of the church in general from the state of the seven churches in Asia. One of these, indeed, the Church of Philadelphia, had 'kept his word, and had not denied his name'.[66] The Church of Smyrna was likewise in a flourishing state. But all the rest were corrupted more or less; insomuch that several of them were not a jot better than the present race of Christians; and our Lord then threatened, what he has long since performed, to 'remove the candlestick'[67] from them.

22. Such was the real state of the Christian church, even during the first century, while not only St. John, but most of the apostles, were present with and presided over it. But what a mystery is this! That the all-wise, the all-gracious, the Almighty should suffer it so to be! Not in one only, but as far as we can learn in every Christian society, those of Smyrna and Philadelphia excepted. And how came these to be excepted? Why were these less corrupted (to go no farther) than the other churches of Asia? It seems, because they were less wealthy. The Christians in Philadelphia were not literally 'increased in goods',[68] like those in Ephesus or Laodicea; and if the Christians at Smyrna had acquired more wealth, it was swept away by

---

[62] Jude 12.
[63] 2 Pet. 2:14, 17.
[64] Rev. 2:1.
[65] Rev. 3:14.
[66] Rev. 3:8.
[67] Rev. 2:5.
[68] Rev. 3:17.

persecution. So that these, having less of this world's goods, retained more of the simplicity and purity of the gospel.

23. But how contrary is this scriptural account of the ancient Christians to the ordinary apprehensions of men! We have been apt to imagine that the primitive church was all excellence and perfection! Answerable to that strong description which St. Peter cites from Moses: 'Ye are a chosen generation, a royal priesthood, a holy nation, a peculiar people.'[69] And such, without all doubt, the first Christian church which commenced at the day of Pentecost was. But how soon did the fine gold become dim! How soon was the wine mixed with water! How little time elapsed before the god of this world so far regained his empire that Christians in general were scarce distinguishable from heathens, save by their opinions and modes of worship!

24. And if the state of the church in the very first century was to so bad, we cannot suppose it was any better in the second. Undoubtedly it grew worse and worse. Tertullian, one of the most eminent Christians of that age, has given us an account of it in various parts of his writings, whence we learn that real, internal religion was hardly found; nay, that not only the tempers of the Christians were exactly the same with those of their heathen neighbours (pride, passion, love of the world reigning alike in both), but their lives and manners also. The bearing a faithful testimony against the general corruption of Christians seems to have raised the outcry against Montanus; and against Tertullian himself, when he was convinced that the testimony of Montanus was true. As to the heresies fathered upon Montanus, it is not easy to find what they were. I believe his grand heresy was the maintaining that 'without' inward and outward 'holiness no man shall see the Lord.'[70]

25. Cyprian, Bishop of Carthage, in every respect an unexceptionable witness, who flourished about the middle of the third century, has left us abundance of letters in which he gives a large and particular account of the state of religion in this time. In reading this, one would be apt to imagine he was reading an account of the present century; so totally void of true religion were the generality both of the laity and clergy; so immersed in ambition, envy, covetousness, luxury, and all other vices, that the Christians of Africa were then exactly the same as the Christians of England are now.

26. It is true that during this whole period, during the first three centuries, there were intermixed longer or shorter seasons wherein true Christianity

---

[69] 1 Pet. 2:9.
[70] Heb. 12:14.

revived. In those seasons the justice and mercy of God let loose the heathens upon the Christians. Many of these were then called to resist unto blood. And the blood of the martyrs was the seed of the church. The apostolical spirit returned; and many 'counted not their lives dear unto themselves, so they might finish their course with joy'.[71] Many others were reduced to happy poverty; and being stripped of what they had loved too well, they 'remembered from whence they were fallen, and repented, and did their first works'.[72]

27. Persecution never did, never could give any lasting wound to genuine Christianity. But the greatest it ever received, the grand blow which was struck at the very root of that humble, gentle, patient love, which is the fulfilling of the Christian law, the whole essence of true religion, was struck in the fourth century by Constantine the Great, when he called himself a Christian, and poured in a flood of riches, honours, and power upon the Christians, more especially upon the clergy. Then was fulfilled in the Christian church what Sallust says of the people of Rome: *Sublata imperii aemula, non sensim sed praecipiti cursu, a virtutibus descitum, ad vitia transcursum.*[73] Just so, when the fear of persecution was removed, and wealth and honour attended the Christian profession, the Christians did not gradually sink, but rushed headlong into all manner of vices. Then the mystery of iniquity was no more hid, but stalked abroad in the face of the sun. Then, not the golden, but the iron age of the church commenced: then one might truly say,

> *Protinus irrupit venae peioris in aevum*
> *Omne nefas; fugere pudor, verumque fidesque;*
> *In quorum subiere locum fraudesque, dolusqse,*
> *Insidiaeque, et vis, et amor sceleratus habendi.*[74]

> At once in that unhappy age broke in
> All wickedness and every deadly sin:
> Truth, modesty, and love fled far away,
> And force, and thirst of gold claimed universal sway.

---

[71] Acts 20:24.
[72] Rev. 2:5.
[73] "A lapsed memory here; this is not Sallust but a garbled version, to the same point, of Vellwius Paterculus, *History of Rome,* 'Liber Posterior', II. i. 2-5" (Outler).
[74] Orvid, *Metamorphoses,* 1. 128-31.

28. And this is the event which most Christian expositors mention with such triumph! Yea, which some of them suppose to be typified in the Revelation by the 'New Jerusalem coming down from heaven'![75] Rather say it was the coming of Satan and all his legions from the bottomless pit: seeing from that very time he hath set up his throne over the face of the whole earth, and reigned over the Christian as well as the pagan world with hardly any control. Historians indeed tell us very gravely of nations in every century who were by such and such (*saints*, without doubt!) converted to Christianity. But still these converts practiced all kinds of abominations, exactly as they did before; no way differing either in their tempers or in their lives from the nations that were still called heathens. Such has been the deplorable state of the Christian church from the time of Constantine till the Reformation. A Christian nation, a Christian city (according to the scriptural model) was nowhere to be seen; but every city and country, a few individuals excepted, was plunged in all manner of wickedness.

29. Has the case been altered since the Reformation? Does the mystery of iniquity no longer work in the church? No. The Reformation itself has not extended to above one-third even of the western church. So that two-thirds of this remain as they were; so do the eastern, southern, and northern churches. They are as full of heathenish, or worse than heathenish, abominations as ever they were before. And what is the condition of the reformed churches? It is certain that they were reformed in their opinions as well as their modes of worship. But is not this all? Were either their tempers or lives reformed? Not at all. Indeed many of the reformers themselves complained that the Reformation was not carried far enough. But what did they mean? Why, that they did not sufficiently reform the *rites* and *ceremonies* of the church. Ye fools and blind! To fix your whole attention on the circumstantials of religion! Your complaint ought to have been, the essentials of religion were not carried far enough. You ought vehemently to have insisted on an entire change of men's *tempers* and *lives*; on their showing they had 'the mind that was in Christ',[76] by 'walking as he also walked'.[77] Without this how exquisitely trifling was the reformation of opinions and rites and ceremonies! Now let anyone survey the state of Christianity in the reformed parts of Switzerland; in Germany or France; in Sweden, Denmark, Holland; in Great Britain and Ireland. How little are any of these reformed Christians better than heathen nations! Have they more (I will not say communion with God, although there is no Christianity without it) but have they more justice,

---

[75] Rev. 21:2.
[76] Phil. 2:5.
[77] 1 Jn. 2:6.

mercy, or truth, than the inhabitants of China or Indostan? O no! We must acknowledge with sorrow and shame that we are far beneath them!

> That we, who by thy name are named,
> The heathens unbaptized out-sin![78]

30. Is not this the 'falling away' or 'apostasy' from God foretold by St. Paul in his Second Epistle to the Thessalonians?[79] Indeed I would not dare to say with George Fox that this apostasy was universal; that there never were any real Christians in the world from the days of the apostles till his time. But we may boldly say that wherever Christianity has spread, the apostasy has spread also. Insomuch that although there are now, and always have been, individuals who were real Christians, yet the whole world never did, nor can at this day, show a Christian country or city.

31. I would now refer it to every man of reflection who believes the Scriptures to be of God whether this general apostasy does not imply the necessity of a general reformation? Without allowing this, how can we possibly justify either the wisdom or goodness of God? According to Scripture the Christian religion was designed 'for the healing of the nations';[80] for the saving from sin, by means of the Second Adam, all that were *constituted sinners* by the first. But it does not answer this end: it never did, unless for a short time at Jerusalem. What can we say but that if it *has not* yet, it surely *will* answer it. The time is coming when not only 'all Israel shall be saved,'[81] but 'the fullness of the Gentiles will come in.'[82] The time cometh when 'violence shall no more be heard in the earth, wasting or destruction within our borders'; but every city shall 'call her walls salvation, and her gates praise'; when the people, saith the Lord, 'shall be all righteous; they shall inherit the land for ever, the branch of my planting, the work of my hands, that I may be glorified.'[83]

32. From the preceding considerations we may learn the full answer to one of the grand objections of infidels against Christianity, namely, the *lives of Christians*. Of Christians, do you say? I doubt whether you ever knew a

---

[78] Cf. John and Charles Wesley, *Hymns on the Lord's Supper* (1745), 128.
[79] 2 Th. 2:3.
[80] Rev. 22:2.
[81] Rom 11:26.
[82] Rom 11:25.
[83] Is. 60:18, 21.

Christian in your life. When Tomo Chachi,[84] the Indian chief, keenly replied to those who spoke to him of being a Christian: 'Why, these are Christians at Savannah! These are Christians at Frederica!'—the proper answer was, 'No, they are not; they are no more Christians than you and Sinauky.' 'But are not those Christians in Canterbury, in London, in Westminster?' No, no more than they are angels. None are Christians but they that have the mind which was in Christ, and walk as he walked. 'Why, if these only are Christians', said an eminent wit, 'I never saw a Christian yet.' I believe it: you never did. And perhaps you never will. For you will never find them in the grand or the gay world. The few Christians that are upon the earth are only to be found where *you* never look for them. Never therefore urge this objection more: never object to Christianity the lives or tempers of heathens. Though they are *called* Christians, the name does not imply the thing: they are as far from this as hell from heaven.

33. We may learn from hence, secondly, the extent of the fall, the astonishing spread of original corruption. What! among so many thousands, so many millions, is there none righteous, no not one? Not by nature. But including the grace of God I will not say with the heathen poet,

*Rari quippe boni: numera, vix sunt totidem quot
Thebarum portae vel divitis ostia Nili.*[85]

As if he had allowed too much in supposing there were a hundred good men in the Roman Empire he comes to himself, and affirms there are hardly seven. Nay, surely there were seven thousand! There were so many long ago in one small nation where Elijah supposed there were none at all. But, allowing a few exceptions, we are authorized to say, 'The whole world lieth in wickedness';[86] yea, 'in the wicked one' (as the words properly signify). 'Yes, the whole heathen world.' Yea, and the Christian, too (so called); for where is the difference, save in a few externals? See with your own eyes. Look into that large country, Indostan. There are Christians and heathens too. Which have more justice, mercy, and truth? The Christians or the heathens? Which are most corrupt, infernal, devilish in their tempers and practice? The English or the Indians? Which have desolated whole countries, and clogged the rivers with dead bodies?

---

[84] Cf. JWJ, Feb. 13, 1736; Diary for Easter, 1736; June 29, 1736; April 11, 1737.
[85] Juvenal, *Satires*, xiii. 26-27: 'Good men are rare; scarcely more in number than the gates of Thebes or the mouths of the enriching Nile' (Outler).
[86] 1 Jn. 5:19.

> O sacred name of Christian! how profaned![87]

O earth, earth, earth! How dost thou groan under the villainies of thy *Christian* inhabitants!

34. From many of the preceding circumstances we may learn, thirdly, what is the genuine tendency of riches: what a baleful influence they have had in all ages upon pure and undefiled religion. Not that money is an evil of itself: it is applicable to good as well as bad purposes. But nevertheless it is an undoubted truth that 'the love of money is the root of all evil';[88] and also that the possession of riches naturally breeds the love of them. Accordingly it is an old remark,

> *Crescit amor nummi, quantum ipsa pecunia crescit.*[89]

'As money increases, so does the love of it'—and always will, without a miracle of grace. Although therefore other causes may concur, yet this has been in all ages the principal cause of the decay of true religion in every Christian community. As long as the Christians in any place were poor they were devoted to God. While they had little of the world they did not love the world; but the more they had of it the more they loved it. This constrained the Lover of their souls at various times to unchain their persecutors, who by reducing them to their former poverty reduced them to their former purity. But still remember: riches have in all ages been the bane of genuine Christianity.

35. We may learn hence, fourthly, how great watchfulness they need who desire to be real Christians, considering what a state the world is in! May not each of them well say,

> Into a world of ruffians sent,
> I walk on hostile ground:
> Wild, human bears on slaughter bent,
> And ravening wolves surround.[90]

---

[87] Milton, *Paradise Lost*, iv. 951.
[88] 1 Tim. 6:10.
[89] Juvenal, *Satires*, xiv. 139: 'the love of money grows in proportion as wealth accumulates' (Outler).
[90] Charles Wesley, *Hymns and Sacred Poems* (1749), II. 126.

They are the most dangerous because they commonly appear in sheep's clothing. Even those who do not pretend to religion yet make fair professions of goodwill, of readiness to serve us, and perhaps of truth and honesty. But beware of taking their word. Trust not any man until he fears God. It is a great truth,

> He that fears no God, can love no friend![91]

Therefore stand upon your guard against everyone that is not earnestly seeking to save his soul. We have need to keep both our heart and mouth 'as with a bridle, while the ungodly are in our sight'.[92] Their conversation, their spirit, is infectious, and steals upon us unawares, we know not how. 'Happy is the man that feareth always'[93] in this sense also, lest he should partake of other men's sins! 'O keep thyself pure!'[94] 'Watch and pray, that thou enter not into temptation!'[95]

36. We may learn from hence, lastly, what thankfulness becomes those who have escaped the corruption that is in the world, whom God hath chosen out of the world to be holy and unblameable. 'Who is it that maketh thee to differ? And what hast thou which thou hast not received?'[96] 'Is it not God' alone 'who worketh in thee both to will and to do for his good pleasure?'[97] 'And let those give thanks whom the Lord hath redeemed and delivered from the hand of the enemy.'[98] Let us praise him that he hath given us to see the deplorable state of all that are round about us; to see the wickedness which overflows the earth, and yet not be borne away by the torrent! We see the general, the almost universal contagion; and yet it cannot approach to hurt us! Thanks be unto him 'who hath delivered us from so great a death', and 'doth' *still* 'deliver'![99] And have we not farther ground for thankfulness, yea, and strong consolation, in the blessed hope which God hath given us that the time is at hand when righteousness shall be as universal as unrighteousness is now? Allowing that 'the whole creation now groaneth together'[1] under the

---

[91] Torquato Tasso, *Godfrey of Bulloigne; or the Recoverie of Jerusalem* (tr. By Edward Fairfax, 1600), Bk. IV, st. 65, 1. 5.
[92] Ps. 139:2 (BCP).
[93] Pr. 28:14.
[94] 1 Tim. 5:22.
[95] Matt. 26:41.
[96] 1 Cor. 4:7.
[97] Phil. 2:13.
[98] Ps. 107:2 (BCP).
[99] 2 Cor. 1:10.
[1] Rom. 8:22.

sin of man, our comfort is, it will not always groan: God will arise and maintain his own cause. And the whole creation shall then be delivered both from moral and natural corruption. Sin, and its consequence, pain, shall be no more; holiness and happiness will cover the earth. Then shall all the ends of the world see the salvation of our God. And the whole race of mankind shall know and love and serve God, and reign with him for ever and ever!

The General Spread of the Gospel
1783

Wesley here picks up where The Mystery of Iniquity *ends, with the Evangelical Revival ushering in the postmillennial reign of Christ (the first millennium in Bengel's scheme). Although the present condition of the world is painted quite bleak, the optimism of God's sovereign grace shines through with the binding of Satan (§8), the conversion of the Christian nations (§§17-18), Jews (§20), Moslems (§21), and distant lands (§22). Essential to Wesley's historicism was his belief that the past is the key to the future — how God has worked reveals how he will work. Accordingly, Wesley was confident the present Revival would continue till the evangelical gospel becomes a global faith. Already believing the Antichrist had politically fallen (see Telford, 6:291), Wesley's millennial vision anticipated the Protestant missionary movement of the next century, but he never foresaw the collapse of Christian dominance in the west with an encroaching secularism. This sermon should be read in conjunction with his* Notes *on* Romans 11:7-32 *and* Revelation 20:1-10, *along with his earlier postmillennial sermons* Scriptural Christianity *(Works 1:159-80) and* Upon our Lord's Sermon on the Mount VI III.8 *(Works 1:582). The reader might want to check out Wesley's brief comments on Justin Martyr and his millennial views in a letter to Conyers Middleton (Works, Jackson, 10:31). For Albert Outler's introduction, see* Works 2:485.

---

*The earth shall be full of the knowledge of the Lord,
as the waters cover the sea.*

Isaiah 11:9

1. In what a condition is the world at present! How does darkness, intellectual darkness, ignorance, with vice and misery attendant upon it, cover the face of the earth! From the accurate inquiry made with indefatigable pains by our ingenious countryman, Mr. Brerewood (who travelled himself over a great part of the known world in order to form the more exact judgment), supposing the world to be divided into thirty parts, nineteen of them are

professed heathens, altogether as ignorant of Christ as if he had never come into the world. Six of the remaining parts are professed Mahometans: so that only five in thirty are so much as nominally Christians!

2. And let it be remembered that since this computation was made many new nations have been discovered—numberless islands, particularly in the South Seas, large and well inhabited. But by whom? By heathens of the basest sort, many of them inferior to the beasts of the field. Whether they eat men or no (which indeed I cannot find any sufficient ground to believe) they certainly kill all that fall into their hands. They are therefore more savage than lions, who kill no more creatures than are necessary to satisfy their present hunger. See the real dignity of human nature! Here it appears in its genuine purity; not polluted either by those 'general corrupters, kings', or by the least tincture of religion! What will Abbé Raynal (that determined enemy to monarchy and revelation) say to this?

3. A little, and but a little, above the heathens in religion are the Mahometans. But how far and wide has this miserable delusion spread over the face of the earth! Insomuch that the Mahometans are considerably more in number (as six to five) than Christians. And by all the accounts which have any pretence to authenticity these are also in general as utter strangers to all true religion as their four-footed brethren. As void of mercy as lions and tigers, as much given up to brutal lusts as bulls or goats; so that they are in truth a disgrace to human nature, and a plague to all that are under their iron yoke.

4. It is true, a celebrated writer (Lady Mary Wortley Montagu), gives a very different character of them. With the finest flow of words, in the most elegant language, she labours to wash the Ethiop white. She represents them as many degrees above the Christians, as some of the most amiable people in the world, as possessed of all the social virtues, as some of the most accomplished of men. But I can in no wise receive her report: I cannot rely upon her authority. I believe those round about her had just as much religion as their admirer had when she was admitted into the interior parts of the Grand Signior's seraglio. Notwithstanding therefore all that such a witness does or can say in their favour, I believe the Turks in general are little, if at all, better than the generality of the heathens.

5. And little, if at all, better than the Turks are the Christians in the Turkish dominions, even the best of them, those that live in the Morea,[1] or are

---

[1] "The old designation for the peninsula south of the isthmus of Corinth" (Outler).

scattered up and down in Asia. The more numerous bodies of Georgian, Circassian, Mingrelian[2] Christians, are a proverb of reproach to the Turks themselves; not only for their deplorable ignorance, but for their total, stupid, barbarous irreligion.

6. From the most authentic accounts we can obtain of the southern Christians, those in Abyssinia, and of the northern churches, under the jurisdiction of the Patriarch of Moscow, we have reason to fear they are much in the same condition, both with regard to knowledge and religion, as those in Turkey. Or if those in Abyssinia[3] are more civilized and have a larger share of knowledge, yet they do not appear to have any more religion than either the Mahometans or pagans.

7. The western churches seem to have the pre-eminence over all these in many respects. They have abundantly more knowledge; they have more scriptural and more rational modes of worship. Yet two-thirds of them are still involved in the corruptions of the Church of Rome; and most of these are entirely unacquainted with either the theory or practice of religion. And as to those who are called Protestants or Reformed, what acquaintance with it have they? Put Papists and Protestants, French and English together, the bulk of one and of the other nation; and what manner of Christians are they? Are they 'holy, as he that hath called them is holy'?[4] Are they filled with 'righteousness, and peace, and joy in the Holy Ghost'?[5] Is there 'that mind in them which was also in Christ Jesus'?[6] And do they 'walk as Christ also walked'?[7] Nay, they are as far from it as hell is from heaven.

8. Such is the present state of mankind in all parts of the world! But how astonishing is this, if there is a God in heaven! And if his eyes are over all the earth! Can he despise the work of his own hand? Surely this is one of the greatest mysteries under heaven! How is it possible to reconcile this with either the wisdom or goodness of God? And what can give ease to a thoughtful mind under so melancholy a prospect? What but the consideration that things will not always be so; that another scene will soon be opened. God will be jealous of his honour: he will arise and maintain his own cause. He will judge the prince of this world, and spoil him of his usurped dominion.

---

[2] Regions within on the eastern extremity of the Black Sea (Outler).
[3] That is, Ethiopia (Outler).
[4] 1 Pet. 1:15.
[5] Rom. 14:17.
[6] Phil. 2:5.
[7] 1 Jn. 2:6.

He will 'give' his Son 'the heathen for his inheritance, and the uttermost parts of the earth for his possession'.[8] 'The earth shall be filled with knowledge of the Lord, as the waters cover the sea.'[9] The loving knowledge of God, producing uniform, uninterrupted holiness and happiness, shall cover the earth, shall fill every soul of man.

9. 'Impossible!' will some men say. 'Yea, the greatest of all impossibilities! That we should see a Christian world! Yea, a Christian nation, or city! "How can these things be?"'[10] On one supposition, indeed, not only all impossibility but all difficulty vanishes away. Only suppose the Almighty to act *irresistibly*, and the thing is done; yea, with just the same ease as when 'God said, Let there be light; and there was light.'[11] But then man would be man no longer; his inmost nature would be changed. He would no longer be a moral agent, any more than the sun or the wind, as he would no longer be endued with liberty, a power of choosing or self-determination. Consequently he would no longer be capable of virtue or vice, of reward or punishment.

10. But setting aside this clumsy way of cutting the knot which we are not able to untie, how can all men be made holy and happy while they continue men? While they still enjoy both the understanding, the affections, and the liberty which are essential to a moral agent? There seems to be a plain, simple way of removing this difficulty without entangling ourselves in any subtle, metaphysical disquisitions. As God is one, so the work of God is uniform in all ages. May we not then conceive how he *will* work on the souls of men in times to come by considering how he *does* work *now*? And how he *has* wrought in times past?

11. Take one instance of this, and such an instance as you cannot easily be deceived in. You know how God wrought in your own soul when he first enabled you to say, 'The life I now live, I live by faith in the Son of God, who loved me, and gave himself for me.'[12] He did not take away your understanding, but enlightened and strengthened it. He did not destroy any of your affections; rather they were more vigorous than before. Least of all did he take away your liberty, your power of choosing good or evil; he did not force you; but being *assisted* by his grace you, like Mary, *chose* the better part. Just so has he *assisted* five in one house to make that happy *choice*, fifty

---

[8] Ps. 2:8.
[9] Hab. 2:14.
[10] Jn. 3:9.
[11] Gen. 1:3.
[12] Gal. 2:20.

or five hundred in one city, and many thousands in a nation, without depriving any of them of that liberty which is essential to a moral agent.

12. Not that I deny that there are exempt cases wherein

The o'erwhelming power of saving grace[13]

does, for a time, work as irresistibly as lightning falling from heaven. But I speak of God's general manner of working, of which I have known innumerable instances; perhaps more within fifty years last past than anyone in England or in Europe. And with regard even to these exempt cases: although God does work irresistibly *for the time*, yet I do not believe there is any human soul in which God works irresistibly *at all times*. Nay, I am fully persuaded there is not. I am persuaded there are no men living that have not many times 'resisted the Holy Ghost',[14] and 'made void the counsel of God against themselves'.[15] Yea, I am persuaded every child of God has at some time 'life and death set before him',[16] eternal life and eternal death, and has in himself the casting voice. So true is that well-known saying of St. Austin (one of the noblest he ever uttered), *Qui fecit nos sine nobis, non salvabit nos sine nobis*—he that made us *without ourselves* will not save us *without ourselves*. Now in the same manner as God *has* converted so many to himself without destroying their liberty, he *can* undoubtedly convert whole nations, or the whole world. And it is as easy to him to convert a world as one individual soul.

13. Let us observe what God has done already. Between fifty and sixty years ago God raised up a few young men in the University of Oxford, to testify those grand truths which were then little attended to:

That without holiness no man shall see the Lord;
That this holiness is the work of God, who worketh in us both to will and to do;
That he doth it of his own good pleasure, merely for the merits of Christ;
That this holiness is the mind that was in Christ, enabling us to walk as Christ also walked;
That no man can be thus sanctified till he is justified; and
That we are justified by faith alone.

---

[13] Charles Wesley, 'The Invitation', st. 10, in *Hymns on the Great Festivals* (1746).
[14] Acts 7:51.
[15] Lk. 7:30.
[16] Dt. 30:19.

These great truths they declared on all occasions in private and in public; having no design but to promote the glory of God, and no desire but to save souls from death.

14. From Oxford, where it first appeared, the little leaven spread wider and wider. More and more saw the truth as it is in Jesus, and received it in the love thereof. More and more 'found redemption through the blood of Jesus, even the forgiveness of sins'.[17] They were born again of his Spirit, and filled with righteousness, and peace, and joy in the Holy Ghost. It afterwards spread to every part of the land, and a little one became a thousand. It then spread into north Britain and Ireland, and, a few years after, into New York, Pennsylvania, and many other provinces in America, even as high as Newfoundland and Nova Scotia. So that although at first this 'grain of mustard seed' was 'the least of all the seeds', yet in a few years it grew into a 'large tree, and put forth great branches'.[18]

15. Generally when these truths—justification by faith in particular—were declared in any large town, after a few days or weeks there came suddenly on the great congregation, not in a corner (at London, Bristol, Newcastle upon Tyne in particular) a violent and impetuous power, which

Like mighty wind or torrent fierce,
Did then opposers all o'errun.[19]

And this frequently continued, with shorter or longer intervals, for several weeks or months. But it gradually subsided, and then the work of God was carried on by gentle degrees; while that Spirit, in watering the seed that had been sown, in confirming and strengthening them that had believed,

deigned his influence to infuse,
Secret, refreshing as the silent dews.[20]

And this difference in his usual manner of working was observable not only in Great Britain and Ireland, but in every part of America, from south to north, wherever the word of God came with power.

---

[17] Col. 1:14.
[18] Matt. 13:31-32.
[19] Henry More, 'An Hymn Upon the Descent of the Holy Ghost at the Day of Pentecost', st. 12, in *Theological Works* (London, 1708), p. 826.
[20] Mark Le Pla, *The Song of the Three Children Paraphrased*, st. 16.

16. Is it not then highly probable that God will carry on his work in the same manner as he has begun? That he will carry it on I cannot doubt; however Luther may affirm that a revival of religion never lasts above a generation, that is, thirty years (whereas the present revival has already continued above fifty); or however prophets of evil may say, 'All will be at an end when the first instruments are removed.' There will then very probably be a great shaking; but I cannot induce myself to think that God has wrought so glorious a work to let it sink and die away in a few years. No; I trust this is only the beginning of a far greater work—the dawn of 'the latter day glory'.[21]

17. And is it not probable, I say, that he will carry it on in the same manner as he has begun? At the first breaking out of his work in this or that place there may be a shower, a torrent of grace; and so at some other particular seasons which 'the Father has reserved in his own power'.[22] But in general it seems the kingdom of God will not 'come with observation',[23] but will silently increase wherever it is set up, and spread from heart to heart, from house to house, from town to town, from one kingdom to another. May it not thus spread, first through the remaining provinces, then through the isles of North America? And at the same time from England to Holland, where there is already a blessed work in Utrecht, Harlem, and many other cities? Probably it will spread from these to the Protestants in France, to those in Germany, and those in Switzerland. Then to Sweden, Denmark, Russia, and all the other Protestant nations in Europe.

18. May we not suppose that the same leaven of pure and undefiled religion, of experimental knowledge and love of God, of inward and outward holiness, will afterwards spread to the Roman Catholics, in Great Britain, Ireland, Holland; in Germany, France, Switzerland; and in all other countries where Romanists and Protestants live intermixed and familiarly converse with each other? Will it not then be easy for the wisdom of God to make a way for religion, in the life and power thereof, into those countries that are merely popish, as Italy, Spain, Portugal? And may it not be gradually diffused from thence to all that name the name of Christ in the various provinces of Turkey, in Abyssinia, yea, and in the remotest parts, not only of Europe, but of Asia, Africa, and America?

19. And in every nation under heaven we may reasonably believe God will observe the same order which he hath done from the beginning of

---

[21] Job 19:25.
[22] Acts 1:7.
[23] Lk. 17:20.

Christianity. 'They shall all know me,' saith the Lord, not from the greatest to the least (this is that wisdom of the world which is foolishness with God) but 'from the least to the greatest,'[24] that the praise may not be of men, but of God. Before the end even the rich shall enter into the kingdom of God. Together with them will enter in the great, the noble, the honourable; yea, the rulers, the princes, the kings of the earth. Last of all the wise and learned, the men of genius, the philosophers, will be convinced that they are fools; will 'be converted and become as little children, and enter into the kingdom of God'.[25]

20. Then shall be fully accomplished to 'the house of Israel',[26] the spiritual Israel, of whatever people or nation, that gracious promise: 'I will put my laws in their mind, and write them in their hearts; and I will be to them a God, and they shall be to me a people. And they shall not teach every man his neighbour, and every man his brother, saying, Know the Lord; for they shall all know me, from the least to the greatest. For I will be merciful to their unrighteousness, and their sins and their iniquities will I remember no more.'[27] Then shall 'the times of' universal 'refreshment come from the presence of the Lord'.[28] The grand Pentecost shall 'fully come', and 'devout men in every nation under heaven', however distant in place from each other, shall 'all be filled with the Holy Ghost'.[29] And they will 'continue steadfast in the apostles' doctrine and in the fellowship, and in the breaking of bread, and in prayers'.[30] They will 'eat their meat', and do all that they have to do, 'with gladness and singleness of heart'.[31] 'Great grace' will be 'upon them all'; and they will be all 'of one heart and of one soul'.[32] The natural, necessary consequence of this will be the same as it was in the beginning of the Christian church. 'None of them will say that ought of the things which he possesses is his own, but they will have all things common. Neither will there be any among them that want; for as many as are possessed of lands or houses will sell them, and distribution will be made to every man, according as he has need.'[33] All their desires, meantime, and passions, and tempers will be cast in one mould, while all are doing the will of God on earth as it is done

---

[24] Heb. 8:11.
[25] Matt. 18:3.
[26] Heb. 8:10.
[27] Heb. 8:10-12.
[28] Acts 3:19.
[29] Acts 2:1, 4, 5.
[30] Acts 2:42.
[31] Acts 2:46.
[32] Acts 4:32-33.
[33] Acts 4:32, 34-35.

in heaven. All their 'conversation will be seasoned with salt',[34] and will 'minister grace to the hearers';[35] seeing it will not be so much they that speak 'as the Spirit of their Father that speaketh in them'.[36] And there will be no 'root of bitterness springing up', either to 'defile' or trouble them.[37] There will be no Ananias or Sapphira, to bring back the cursed love of money among them. There will be no partiality; no 'widows neglected in the daily ministration'.[38] Consequently there will be no temptation to any murmuring thought or unkind word of one against another, while

> *They all are of one heart and soul,*
> *And only love informs the whole.*[39]

21. The grand stumbling-block being thus happily removed out of the way, namely, the lives of the Christians, the Mahometans will look upon them with other eyes, and begin to give attention to their words. And as their words will be clothed with divine energy, attended with the demonstration of the Spirit and of power, those of them that fear God will soon take knowledge of the Spirit whereby the Christians speak. They will 'receive with meekness the engrafted word',[40] and will bring forth fruit with patience. From them the leaven will soon spread to those who till then had no fear of God before their eyes. Observing 'the Christian dogs', as they used to term them, to have changed their nature, to be sober, temperate, just, benevolent—and that in spite of all provocations to the contrary—from admiring their lives they will surely be led to consider and embrace their doctrine. And then the Saviour of sinners will say: 'The hour is come. I will glorify my Father. I will seek and save the sheep that were wandering on the dark mountains. Now will I avenge myself of my enemy, and pluck the prey out of the lion's teeth. I will resume my own for ages lost: I will claim the purchase of my blood.' So he will go forth in the greatness of his strength, and all his enemies shall flee before him. All the prophets of lies shall vanish away, and all the nations that had followed them shall acknowledge the great Prophet of the Lord, 'mighty in word and deed';[41] and 'shall honour the Son, even as they honour the Father'.[42]

---

[34] Col. 4:6.
[35] Eph. 4:29.
[36] Matt 10:20.
[37] Heb. 12:15.
[38] Acts 6:1.
[39] Charles Wesley, 'Primitive Christianity', *Hymns and Sacred Poems* (1749), II.333.
[40] Ja. 1:21.
[41] Lk. 24:19.
[42] Jn. 5:23.

22. And then the grand stumbling-block being removed from the heathen nations also, the same spirit will be poured out upon them, even those that remain in the uttermost parts of the sea. The poor American savage will no more ask, 'What, are the Christians better than us?' when they see their steady practice of universal temperance, and of justice, mercy, and truth. The Malabarian heathen will have no more room to say: 'Christian man take my wife; Christian man much drunk; Christian man kill man! *Devil-Christian*! Me no Christian.' Rather, seeing how far the Christians exceed their own countrymen in whatsoever things are lovely and of good report, they will adopt a very different language, and say, '*Angel-Christian*!' The holy lives of the Christians will be an argument they will not know how to resist; seeing the Christians steadily and uniformly practise what is agreeable to the law written in their own hearts, their prejudices will quickly die away, and they will gladly receive 'the truth as it is in Jesus'.[43]

23. We may reasonably believe that the heathen nations which are mingled with the Christians, and those that bordering upon Christian nations have constant and familiar intercourse with them, will be some of the first who learn to worship God in spirit and in truth; those, for instance, that live on the continent of America, or in the islands that have received colonies from Europe. Such are likewise all those inhabitants of the East Indies that adjoin to any of the Christian settlements. To these may be added numerous tribes of Tartars, the heathen parts of the Russias, and the inhabitants of Norway, Finland, and Lapland. Probably these will be followed by those more distant nations with whom the Christians trade; to whom they will impart what is of infinitely more value than earthly pearls, or gold and silver. The God of love will then prepare his messengers and make a way into the polar regions, into the deepest recesses of America, and into the interior parts of Africa; yea, into the heart of China and Japan, with the countries adjoining to them. And 'their sound' will then 'go forth into all lands, and their voice to the ends of the earth'.[44]

24. But one considerable difficulty still remains. There are very many heathen nations in the world that have no intercourse either by trade or any other means with Christians of any kind. Such are the inhabitants of the numerous islands in the South Sea, and probably in all large branches of the ocean. Now what shall be done for these poor outcasts of men? 'How shall they believe', saith the Apostle, 'in him of whom they have not heard? And how shall they hear without a preacher?' You may add, 'And how shall

---

[43] Eph. 4:21.
[44] Rom. 10:18.

preach, unless they be sent?'[45] Yea, but is not God able to send them? Cannot he raise them up, as it were, out of the stones? And can he ever want means of sending them? No: were there no other means, he 'can take them by his Spirit' (as he did Ezekiel),[46] or by 'his angel', as he did Philip,[47] and set them down wheresoever it pleaseth him. Yea, he can find out a thousand ways, to foolish man unknown. And he surely will: for heaven and earth may pass away; but his word shall not pass away. He will 'give his Son the uttermost part of the earth for his possession'.[48]

25. 'And so all Israel' too 'shall be saved.' For 'blindness has happened to Israel' (as the great Apostle observes) 'till the fullness of the Gentiles be come in.' Then 'the Deliverer that cometh out of Zion shall turn away iniquity from Jacob. [. . .] God hath' now 'concluded them all in unbelief, that he may have mercy upon all.'[49] Yea, and he will so have mercy upon all Israel as to give them all temporal with all spiritual blessings. For this is the promise: 'For the Lord thy God will gather thee from all nations, whither the Lord thy God hath scattered thee. [. . .] And the Lord thy God will bring thee into the land which thy fathers possessed, and thou shalt possess it. And the Lord thy God will circumcise thy heart, and the heart of thy seed, to love the Lord thy God with all thy heart, and with all thy soul.'[50] Again: 'I will gather them out of all countries whither I have driven them; and I will bring them again to this place, and I will cause them to dwell safely. [. . .] And I will give them one heart, and one way, that they may fear me forever. I will put my fear into their hearts, that they shall not depart from me. And I will plant them in this land assuredly, with all my heart, and with all my soul.'[51]

Yet again: 'I will take you from among the heathen, and gather you out of all countries, and will bring you into your own land. Then will I sprinkle clean water upon you, and ye shall be clean; from all your filthiness and from all your idols will I cleanse you. [. . .] And ye shall dwell in the land that I gave to your fathers; and ye shall be my people, and I will be your God.'[52]

26. At that time will be accomplished all those glorious promises made to the Christian church, which will not then be confined to this or that nation, but

---

[45] Rom. 10:14-15.
[46] Ezek. 11:24.
[47] Acts 8:26.
[48] Ps. 2:8.
[49] Rom. 11:25-26, 32.
[50] Dt. 30:3, 5-6.
[51] Jer 32:37, 39-41.
[52] Ezek. 36:24-25, 28.

will include all the inhabitants of the earth. 'They shall not hurt nor destroy in all my holy mountain.'[53] 'Violence shall no more be heard in thy land, wasting nor destruction within thy borders; but thou shalt call thy walls, Salvation, and thy gates, Praise.'[54] Thou shalt be encompassed on every side with salvation, and all that go through thy gates shall praise God. 'The sun shall be no more thy light by day; neither for brightness shall the moon give light unto thee; but the Lord shall be unto thee an everlasting light, and thy God thy glory.'[55] The light of the sun and moon shall be swallowed up in the light of his countenance shining upon thee. 'Thy people also shall be all righteous, [. . .] the work of my hands, that I may be glorified.'[56] 'As the earth bringeth forth her bud, and the garden causeth the things that are sown in it to spring forth; so the Lord God will cause righteousness and praise to spring forth before all the nations.'[57]

27. This I apprehend to be the answer, yea, the only full and satisfactory answer that can be given, to the objection against the wisdom and goodness of God, taken from the present state of the world. It will not always be thus: these things are only permitted for a season by the great Governor of the world, that he may draw immense, eternal good out of this temporary evil. This is the very key which the Apostle himself gives us in the words above recited, 'God hath concluded them all under sin, that he might have mercy upon all!'[58] In view of this glorious event how well may be cry out, 'O the depth of the riches both of the wisdom and knowledge of God!' Although for a season 'his judgments were unsearchable, and his ways past finding out.'[59] It is enough we are assured of this one point, that all these transient evils will issue well, will have a happy conclusion, and that 'Mercy first and last will reign.'[60] All unprejudiced persons may see with their eyes that he is already renewing the face of the earth. And we have strong reason to hope that the work he hath begun he will carry on unto the day of his Lord Jesus; that he will never intermit this blessed work of his Spirit until he has fulfilled all his promises; until he hath put a period to sin and misery, and infirmity, and death; and re-established universal holiness and happiness, and caused all the inhabitants of the earth to sing together, 'Hallelujah! The Lord God

---

[53] Is. 11:9.
[54] Is. 60:18.
[55] Is. 60:19.
[56] Is. 60:21.
[57] Is. 61:11.
[58] Rom. 11:32.
[59] Rom. 11:33.
[60] Milton, *Paradise Lost*, iii. 132-34.

omnipotent reigneth!'[61] 'Blessing, and glory, and wisdom, and honour, and power, and might be unto our God for ever and ever!'[62]

---

[61] Rev. 19:6.
[62] Rev. 7:12.

The Signs of the Times
1787

Wesley long held the Evangelical Revival was a restoration of primitive Christianity. Just as skeptics in Jesus' time failed to read the 'signs of the times', so the blind guides of nominal Christianity were failing to read the present signs of the approaching 'latter-day glory'. Therefore, this sermon is a study in Wesley's views on the imminent arrival of the millennium. Once again, this sermon is grounded on a robust postmillennial interpretation of the kingdom as an extension of the present reign of Christ through the Gospel (kingdom of grace). The theme of imminence is sprinkled throughout Wesley's eschatological writings, especially in his Notes *on* Revelation. *For other assessments by Wesley on the eschatological character of the Revival and Methodism, see* The Wisdom of God's Counsels *(Works 2:551-66),* Of Former Times *(Works 3:440-53),* On God's Vineyard *(Works 3:502-17), and* The Late Work of God in North America *(Works 3:594-608). For Albert Outler's introduction, see Works 2:521.*

Ye can discern the face of the sky; but can ye not discern the signs of the times?

Matthew 16:3

1. The entire passage runs thus: 'The Pharisees also, with the Sadducees, came, and tempting, desired him that he would show them a sign from heaven. He answered and said, When it is evening, ye say, It will be fair weather, for the sky is red; and in the morning, It will be foul weather today, for the sky is red and lowering. O ye hypocrites, ye can discern the face of the sky; but can ye not discern the signs of the times?'

2. 'The Pharisees also, with the Sadducees, came.' In general these were quite opposite to each other; but it is no uncommon thing for the children of the world to lay aside their opposition to each other (at least for a season) and cordially to unite in opposing the children of God. 'And tempting', that is, making a trial whether he was indeed sent of God, 'desired him that he would

show them a sign from heaven', which they believed no false prophet was able to do. It is not improbable they imagined this would convince them that he was really sent from God. 'He answered and said unto them, When it is evening, ye say, It will be fair weather, for the sky is red; and in the morning, It will be foul weather today, for the sky is red and lowering.' Probably there were more certain signs of fair and foul weather in their climate than there are in ours. 'O ye hypocrites', making profession of love while you have enmity in your hearts; 'ye can discern the face of the sky,' and judge thereby what the weather will be; 'but can ye not discern the signs of the times,' when God brings his first-begotten Son into the world?

3. Let us more particularly inquire, first, What were 'the times' whereof our Lord speaks? And what were 'the signs' whereby those times were to be distinguished from all others? We may then inquire, secondly, what are 'the times' which we have reason to believe are *now* at hand? And how is it that all who are called Christians do not discern 'the signs of these times'?

I.1. Let us in the first place inquire, What times were those concerning which our Lord is here speaking? It is easy to answer: the times of the Messiah, the times ordained before the foundation of the world wherein it pleased God to give his only-begotten Son to take our nature upon him, to be 'found in fashion as a man', to live a life of sorrow and pain, and at length to be 'obedient unto death, even the death of the cross';[1] to the end 'that whosoever believeth on him should not perish, but have everlasting life'.[2] This was the important time, the signs whereof the Pharisees and Sadducees could not discern. Clear as they were in themselves, yet so thick a veil was upon the heart of these men that they did not discern the tokens of his coming, though foretold so long before.

2. But what were those signs of the coming of that Just One[4] which had been so long and so clearly foretold? And whereby they might easily have discerned those times, had not the veil been on their heart? They are many in number; but it may suffice to mention a few of them. One of the first is that pointed out in the solemn words spoken by Jacob a little before his death: 'The sceptre shall not depart from Judah, nor a lawgiver from between his feet, until Shiloh come.'[3] All, both ancient and modern Jews, agree that by 'Shiloh' we are to understand the Messiah; who was therefore to come, according to the prophecy, 'before the sceptre', that is, the sovereignty,

---

[1] Phil. 2:8.
[2] Jn. 3:16.
[3] Gen. 49:10.

'departed from Judah'. But it did without controversy depart from Judah at this very time; an infallible sign that at this very time 'Shiloh', that is the Messiah, 'came'.

3. A second eminent sign of those times, the times of the coming of the Messiah, is given us in the third chapter of the prophecy of Malachi: 'Behold, I send my messenger, and he shall prepare my way before me; and the Lord whom ye seek shall suddenly come to his temple.'[4] How manifestly was this fulfilled, first, by the coming of John the Baptist; and then by our blessed Lord himself, 'coming suddenly to his temple'! And what sign could be clearer to those that impartially considered the words of the prophet Isaiah: 'The voice of one crying in the wilderness, Prepare ye the way of the Lord, make his paths straight!'[5]

4. But yet clearer signs than these (if any could be clearer) were the mighty works that he wrought. Accordingly he himself declares, 'The works which I do, they testify of me.'[6] And to these he explicitly appeals in his answer to the question of John the Baptist (not proposed, as some have strangely imagined, from any doubt which he had himself; but from a desire of confirming his disciples who might possibly waver when their master was taken from their head): 'Art thou he that should come,' the Messiah? 'Or look we for another?'[7] No bare verbal answer could have been so convincing as what they saw with their own eyes. Jesus therefore referred them to this testimony: 'He answered and said unto them, Go and show John the things which ye hear and see: the blind receive their sight, and the lame walk; the lepers are cleansed, and the deaf hear; the dead are raised up, and the poor have the gospel preached unto them.'[8]

5. But how then came it to pass that those who were so sharp-sighted in other things, who could 'discern the face of the sky', were not able to discern those signs which indicated the coming of the Messiah? They could not discern them, not for want of evidence—this was full and clear—but for want of integrity in themselves; because they were a 'wicked and adulterous generation';[9] because the perverseness of their hearts spread a cloud over their understanding. Therefore although the Sun of righteousness shone

---

[4] Mal. 3:1.
[5] Is. 40:3.
[6] Jn. 5:36 (*NT Notes*).
[7] Lk. 7:19, 20.
[8] Matt. 11:4-5.
[9] Matt. 16:4.

bright, yet they were insensible of it. They were not willing to be convinced; therefore they remained in ignorance. The light was sufficient; but they shut their eyes that they might not see it. So that they were without excuse, till vengeance came upon them to the uttermost.

II.1. We are in the second place to consider, What are 'the times' which we have reason to believe are *now* at hand? And how is it that all who are called Christians do not discern 'the signs of these times'?

'The times' which we have reason to believe are at hand (if they are not already begun) are what many pious men have termed the time of 'the latter-day glory';[10] meaning the time wherein God would gloriously display his power and love in the fulfillment of his gracious promise that 'the knowledge of the Lord shall cover the earth, as the waters cover the sea.'[11]

2. 'But are there in England, or in any part of the world, any *signs* of such a time approaching?' It is not many years since that a person of considerable learning, as well as eminence in the Church (then Bishop of London), in his pastoral letter made this observation: 'I cannot imagine what persons mean by talking of "a great work of God" at this time. I do not see any work of God now, more than has been at any other time.'[12] I believe it. I believe that great man did not see any extraordinary work of God. Neither he nor the generality of Christians, so called, saw any signs of the glorious day that is approaching. But how is this to be accounted for? How is it that those who can now 'discern the face of the sky', who are not only great philosophers, but great divines, as eminent as ever the Sadducees, yea, or the Pharisees, were, do not discern the signs of those glorious times, which if not begun, are nigh, even at the door?

3. We allow indeed that in every age of the Church, 'the kingdom of God came not with observation';[13] not with splendour and pomp, or with any of those outward circumstances which usually attend the kingdoms of this world. We allow this 'kingdom of God is within us';[14] and that consequently when it begins either in an individual or in a nation it 'is like a grain of mustard seed', which at first 'is the least of all seeds'; but nevertheless

---

[10] Jer. 49:39; Hag. 2:9.
[11] Is. 11:9; Hab. 2:14.
[12] "A blurred memory of Bishop Edmund Gibson's general disapproval of the early Methodists" (Outler).
[13] Lk. 17:20.
[14] Lk. 17:21.

gradually increases till 'it becomes a great tree.'[15] Or, to use the other comparison of our Lord, it is like a little 'leaven, which a woman took and hid in three measures of meal, till the whole was leavened'.[16]

4. But may it not be asked, Are there now any signs that the day of God's power is approaching? I appeal to every candid, unprejudiced person, whether we may not at this day discern all those signs (understanding the words in a spiritual sense) to which our Lord referred to John's disciples. 'The blind receive their sight.'[17] Those who were blind from their birth, unable to see their own deplorable state, and much more to see God and the remedy he has prepared for them in the Son of his love, now see themselves, yea, and 'the light of the glory of God in the face of Jesus Christ'.[18] 'The eyes' of their 'understanding' being now 'opened',[19] they see all things clearly. 'The deaf hear.'[20] Those that were before utterly deaf to all the outward and inward calls of God now hear, not only his providential calls, but also the whispers of his grace. 'The lame walk.' Those who never before arose from the earth, or moved one step toward heaven, are now walking in all the ways of God; yea, running the race that is set before them. 'The lepers are cleansed.' The deadly leprosy of sin, which they brought with them into the world, and which no art of man could ever cure, is now clean departed from them. And surely never in any age or nation since the apostles have those words been so eminently fulfilled, 'The poor have the gospel preached unto them,' as it is at this day. At this day the gospel leaven—faith working by love, inward and outward holiness, or (to use the terms of St. Paul) 'righteousness, and peace, and joy in the Holy Ghost'[21]—hath so spread in various parts of Europe, particularly in England, Scotland, Ireland, in the islands, in the north and south, from Georgia to New England and Newfoundland, that sinners have been truly converted to God, thoroughly changed both in heart and in life; not by tens, or by hundreds only, but by thousands, yea, by myriads! The fact cannot be denied: we can point out the persons, with their names and places of abode. And yet the wise men of the world, the men of eminence, the men of learning and renown, 'cannot imagine what we mean by talking of any extraordinary work of God'! They

---

[15] Matt. 13:31-32.
[16] Matt. 13:33.
[17] Matt. 11:5.
[18] 2 Cor. 4:6.
[19] Lk. 24:45; Eph. 1:18.
[20] Matt. 11:5.
[21] Rom. 14:17.

cannot discern the signs of *these times*! They can see no sign at all of God's arising to maintain his own cause and set up his kingdom over the earth!

5. But how may this be accounted for? How is it that they cannot discern the signs of these times? We may account for their want of discernment on the same principle we accounted for that of the Pharisees and Sadducees; namely, that they likewise were what those were, an 'adulterous and sinful generation'.[22] If their eye was single, their whole body would be full of light. But suppose their eye be evil, their whole body must be full of darkness. Every evil temper darkens the soul; every evil passion clouds the understanding. How then can we expect that those should be able to discern the signs of the times who are full of all disorderly passions, and slaves to every evil temper? But this is really the case. They are full of pride; they think of themselves far more highly than they ought to think. They are vain; they 'seek honour one of another, and not the honour that cometh of God only'.[23] They cherish hatred and malice in their hearts: they give place to anger, to envy, to revenge. They return evil for evil, and railing for railing. Instead of overcoming evil with good, they make no scruple of demanding an eye for an eye, and a tooth for a tooth. They 'savour not the things that are of God, but the things that are of men'.[24] They set their affections, not on things above, but on things that are of the earth. They 'love the creature more than the Creator':[25] they are 'lovers of pleasure more than lovers of God'.[26] How then should they discern the signs of the times? The god of this world whom they serve has blinded their hearts, and covered their minds with a veil of thick darkness. Alas! What have these 'souls of flesh and blood' (as one speaks)[27] to do with God or the things of God?

6. St. John assigns this very reason for the Jews not understanding the things of God, namely, that in consequence of their preceding sins and willful rejecting the light, God had now delivered them up to Satan, who had blinded them past recovery. Over and over, when they might have seen they would not; they shut their eyes against the light. And now they cannot see, God having given them up to an undiscerning mind; therefore they do not believe because of the reason given in that saying of Isaiah, 'He hath blinded their eyes, and hardened their hearts; that they should not see with their eyes, nor

---

[22] Mk. 8:38.
[23] Jn. 5:44.
[24] Mk. 8:33.
[25] Rom. 1:25.
[26] 2 Tim. 3:4.
[27] "This may be a garbled echo from Law's *Spirit of Prayer*" (Outler).

understand with their hearts, and be converted, and I should heal them.'[28] The plain meaning is, not that God did this by his own immediate power—it would be flat blasphemy to say that God in this sense hardens any man—but his Spirit strives with them no longer, and then Satan hardens them effectually.

7. And as it was with them in ancient times, so it is with the present generation. Thousands of those who bear the name of Christ are now given up to an undiscerning mind. The god of this world hath so blinded their eyes that the light cannot shine upon them, so that they can no more discern the signs of the times than the Pharisees and Sadducees could of old. A wonderful instance of this spiritual blindness, this total inability to discern the signs of the times mentioned in Scripture, is given us in the very celebrated work of a late eminent writer, who supposes 'the new Jerusalem came down from heaven'[29] when Constantine the Great called himself a Christian. I say, 'called himself a Christian'; for I dare not affirm that *he was one*, any more than Peter the Great. I cannot but believe he would have come nearer the mark if he had said, that was the time when a huge cloud of infernal brimstone and smoke came up from the bottomless pit. For surely there never was a time wherein Satan gained so fatal an advantage over the church of Christ as when such a flood of riches, and honour, and power broke in upon it, particularly on the clergy.

8. By the same rule, what signs would this writer have expected of the approaching conversion of the heathens? He would doubtless have expected a hero, like Charles of Sweden, or Frederick of Prussia, to carry fire, and sword, and Christianity through whole nations at once. And it cannot be denied that since the time of Constantine many nations have been converted in this way. But could it be said concerning such conversions as these, 'The kingdom of heaven cometh not with observation'?[30] Surely everyone must observe a warrior rushing through the land at the head of fifty or sixty thousand men! But is this the way of spreading Christianity which the author of it, the Prince of Peace, has chosen? Nay, it is not in this manner that a grain of mustard seed grows up into a great tree. It is not thus that 'a little leaven leavens the whole lump.'[31] Rather, it spreads by degrees farther and farther, till the whole is leavened. We may form a judgment of what will be hereafter by what we have seen already. And this is the way wherein true

---

[28] Jn. 12:40.
[29] Rev. 21:2, 10.
[30] Lk. 17:20.
[31] Cf. 1 Cor. 5:6; Gal. 5:9.

Christian religion, the faith that worketh by love, has been spreading, particularly through Great Britain and its dependencies, for half a century.

9. In the same manner it continues to spread at the present time also, as may easily appear to all those whose eyes are not blinded. All those that experience in their own hearts the power of God unto salvation will readily perceive how the same religion which they enjoy is still spreading from heart to heart. They take knowledge of the same grace of God, strongly and sweetly working on every side; and rejoice to find another and another sinner, first inquiring, 'What must I do to be saved?'[32] and then testifying, 'My soul doth magnify the Lord, and my spirit doth rejoice in God my Saviour.'[33] Upon a fair and candid inquiry they find more and more, not only of those who had some form of religion, but of those who had no form at all, who were profligate, abandoned sinners, now entirely changed, truly fearing God and working righteousness. They observe more and more, even of these poor outcasts of men, who are inwardly and outwardly changed, loving God and their neighbour; living in the uniform practice of justice, mercy, and truth; as they have time, doing good to all men; easy and happy in their lives, and triumphant in their death.

10. What excuse then have any that believe the Scriptures to be the Word of God for not discerning the signs of these times, as preparatory to the general call of the heathens? What could God have done which he hath not done to convince you that the day is coming, that the time is at hand, when he will fulfill his glorious promises; when he will arise to maintain his own cause, and to set up his kingdom over all the earth? What, indeed, unless he had *forced* you to believe? And this he could not do without destroying the nature which he had given you. For he made you free agents; having an inward power of self-determination, which is essential to your nature. And he deals with you as free agents from first to last. As such, you may shut or open your eyes as you please. You have sufficient light shining all around you; yet you need not see it unless you will. But be assured God is not well-pleased with your shutting your eyes and then saying, 'I cannot see.' I counsel you to bestow an impartial examination upon the whole affair. After a candid inquiry into matter of fact, consider deeply, 'What hath God wrought?'[34] 'Who hath seen such a thing? Who hath heard such a thing? Hath not a nation', as it were, been 'born in a day?'[35] How swift, as well as how deep,

---

[32] Acts 16:30.
[33] Lk. 1:46-47.
[34] Num. 23:23.
[35] Is. 66:8.

and how extensive a work has been wrought in the present age! And certainly, 'not by might, neither by power, but by the Spirit of the Lord'.[36] For how utterly inadequate were the means! How insufficient were the instruments to work any such effect! At least those of which it has pleased God to make use of in the British dominions and in America. By how unlikely instruments has God been pleased to work from the beginning! 'A few, young, raw heads!' said the Bishop of London, 'What can they pretend to do?'[37] They pretended to be *that* in the hand of God that a pen is in the hand of a man. They pretended (and do so at this day) to do the work whereunto they are sent; to do just what the Lord pleases. And if it be his pleasure to throw down the walls of Jericho, the strongholds of Satan, not by the engines of war but by the blasts of rams' horns, who shall say unto him, 'What dost thou?'[38]

11. Meantime, 'Blessed are your eyes, for they see. [. . .] Many prophets and righteous men have desired to see the things you see, and have not seen them, and to hear the things that you hear, and have not heard them.'[39] You see and acknowledge the day of your visitation—such a visitation as neither you nor your fathers had known. You may well say, 'This is the day which the Lord hath made; we will rejoice and be glad therein.'[40] You see the dawn of that glorious day whereof all the prophets have spoken. And how shall you most effectually improve this day of your visitation?

12. The first point is—see that you yourselves receive not the blessing of God in vain. Begin at the root, if you have not already. Now repent and believe the gospel. If you have believed, 'Look to yourselves, that ye lose not what you have wrought, but that ye receive a full reward!'[41] 'Stir up the gift of God that is in you!'[42] 'Walk in the light, as he is in the light.'[43] And while you 'hold fast'[44] 'that which you have attained',[45] 'go on unto perfection.'[46] Yea, and when you are 'made perfect in love',[47] still, 'forgetting the things that are

---

[36] Zech. 4:6.
[37] "Another blurred memory" of Gibson's *Observations* (Outler).
[38] Jn. 6:30.
[39] Matt. 13:16-17.
[40] Ps. 118:24.
[41] 2 Jn. 8.
[42] 2 Tim. 1:6.
[43] 1 Jn. 1:7.
[44] Heb. 3:6.
[45] Phil. 3:12, 16.
[46] Heb. 6:1.
[47] 1 Jn. 4:18.

behind, press on to the mark for the prize of the high calling of God in Christ Jesus.'[48]

13. It behoves you in the next place to help your neighbours. 'Let your light so shine before men that they may see your good works, and glorify your Father which is in heaven.'[49] As you have time, do good unto all men, but especially unto them that are of the household of faith. Proclaim the glad tidings of salvation ready to be revealed, not only to those of your own household, not only to your relations, friends, and acquaintance, but to all whom God providentially delivers into your hands. 'Ye', who already know in whom you have believed, 'are the salt of the earth.'[50] Labour to season, with the knowledge and love of God, all that you have any intercourse with. 'Ye are a city set upon a hill'; ye 'cannot', ye ought not to 'be hid'.[51] 'Ye are the light of the world.' 'Men do not light a candle and put it under a bushel'; how much less the all-wise God. No, let it 'shine to all that are in the house',[52] all that are witnesses of your life and conversation. Above all, continue instant in prayer, both for yourselves, for all the church of God, and for all the children of men, that they may remember themselves and be turned unto our God. That they likewise may enjoy the gospel blessing on earth, and the glory of God in heaven.

---

[48] Phil. 3:13-14.
[49] Matt. 5:16.
[50] Matt. 5:13.
[51] Matt. 5:14.
[52] Matt. 5:14-15.

The General Deliverance
1781

Wesley now moves from the kingdom of grace to the kingdom of glory. The idea that the animal kingdom will participate in the general resurrection was a logical outcome of a natural philosophy that grounds all reality in Platonic and Aristotelian categories (i.e. the Chain of Being). In his Notes *on* Romans 8:22 *Wesley questioned the idea that the creation will ever be destroyed (see* On Eternity §7, Works 2:361-62). *Here, Wesley boldly proclaims the new creation will reverse the effects of Adam's sin and elevate the entire creation to levels of resurrection glory not imagined in the present order. This sermon should be read in conjunction with* On the Fall of Man *(Works 2:400-12),* God's Love for Fallen Man *(Works 2:422-35), and in this Reader* The New Creation. *For Albert Outler's introduction, see Works 2:436.*

The earnest expectation of the creature waiteth for the manifestation of the sons of God. For the creature was made subject to vanity, not willingly, but by reason of him that subjected it. Yet in hope that the creature itself also shall be delivered from the bondage of corruption, into the glorious liberty of the sons of God. For we know that the whole creation groaneth, and travaileth in pain together until now.

Romans 8:19-22

1. Nothing is more sure than that, as 'the Lord is loving to every man', so 'his mercy is over all his works'[1]—all that have sense, all that are capable of pleasure or pain, of happiness or misery. In consequence of this 'he openeth his hand and filleth all things living with plenteousness':[2] 'he prepareth food for cattle,' as well as 'herbs for the children of men.'[3] He provideth for the fowls of the air, 'feeding the young ravens when they cry unto him'.[4] 'He

---

[1] Ps. 145:9 (BCP).
[2] Ps. 145:16 (BCP).
[3] Pss. 104:14; 147:8-9 (BCP).
[4] Ps. 147:9 (BCP).

sendeth the springs into the rivers that run among the hills,' to give drink to every beast of the field, and that even 'the wild asses may quench their thirst.'[5] And suitably to this he directs us to be tender of even the meaner creatures, to show mercy to these also. 'Thou shalt not muzzle the ox that treadeth out the corn'[6]—a custom which is observed in the eastern countries even to this day. And this is by no means contradicted by St. Paul's question, 'Doth God take care for oxen?'[7] Without doubt he does. We cannot deny it without flatly contradicting his word. The plain meaning of the Apostle is— Is this all that is implied in the text? Hath it not a farther meaning? Does it not teach us we are to feed the bodies of those whom we desire to feed our souls? Meantime it is certain God 'giveth grass for the cattle', as well as 'herbs for the use of men'.[8]

2. But how are these Scriptures reconcilable to the present state of things? How are they consistent with what we daily see round about us in every part of the creation? If the Creator and Father of every living thing is rich in mercy towards all; if he does not overlook or despise any of the works of his own hands;[9] if he wills even the meanest of them to be happy according to their degree—how comes it to pass that such a complication of evils oppresses, yea, overwhelms them? How is it that misery of all kinds overspreads the face of the earth? This is a question which has puzzled the wisest philosophers in all ages. And it cannot be answered without having recourse to the oracles of God. But taking these for our guide we may inquire,

      I. What was the original state of the brute creation?
      II. In what state is it at present? And
      III. In what state will it be at the manifestation of the children of God?

I.1. We may inquire, in the first place, What was the original state of the brute creation? And may not we learn this even from the place which was assigned them, namely, the garden of God? All the beasts of the field, and all the fowls of the air, were with Adam in paradise. And there is no question but their state was suited to their place: it was paradisiacal, perfectly happy. Undoubtedly it bore a near resemblance to the state of man himself. By taking therefore a short view of the one we may conceive the other. Now

---

[5] Ps 104:10-11 (BCP).
[6] Dt. 25:4.
[7] 1 Cor. 9:9.
[8] Ps. 147:8-9 (BCP).
[9] Job 10:3.

'man was made in the image of God.'[10] But 'God is a spirit.'[11] So therefore was man. Only that spirit, being designed to dwell on earth, was lodged in an earthly tabernacle.[12] As such he had an innate principle of *self-motion*. And so, it seems, has every spirit in the universe; this being the proper distinguishing difference between spirit and matter, which is totally, essentially passive and inactive, as appears from a thousand experiments. He was, after the likeness of his Creator, endued with *understanding*, a capacity of apprehending whatever objects were brought before it, and of judging concerning them. He was endued with a *will*, exerting itself in various affections and passions; and, lastly, with *liberty*, or freedom of choice, without which all the rest would have been in vain, and he would have been no more capable of serving his Creator than a piece of earth or marble. He would have been as incapable of vice or virtue as any part of the inanimate creation. In these, in the power of self-motion, understanding, will, and liberty, the natural image of God consisted.

2. How far his power of self-motion then extended it is impossible for us to determine. It is probable that he had a far higher degree both of swiftness and strength than any of his posterity ever had, and much less any of the lower creatures. It is certain he had such strength of understanding as no man ever since had. His understanding was perfect in its kind; capable of apprehending all things clearly, and judging concerning them according to truth, without any mixture of error. His will had no wrong bias of any sort, but all his passions and affections were regular, being steadily and uniformly guided by the dictates of his unerring understanding; embracing nothing but good, and every good in proportion to its degree of intrinsic goodness. His liberty likewise was wholly guided by his understanding: he chose or refused according to its direction. Above all (which was his highest excellence, far more valuable than all the rest put together) he was a creature capable of God, capable of knowing, loving, and obeying his Creator. And in fact he did know God, did unfeignedly love and uniformly obey him. This was the supreme perfection of man, as it is of all intelligent beings—the continually seeing and loving and obeying the Father of the spirits of all flesh.[13] From this right state, and right use of all his faculties, his happiness naturally flowed. In this the essence of his happiness consisted; but it was increased by all the things that were round about him. He saw with unspeakable pleasure the order, the beauty, the harmony of all the creatures: of all animated, all

---

[10] Gen. 1:27.
[11] Jn. 4:24.
[12] 2 Cor. 5:1.
[13] Num. 16:22; 27:16.

inanimate nature—the serenity of the skies, the sun walking in brightness,[14] the sweetly variegated clothing of the earth; the trees, the fruits, the flowers,

And liquid lapse of murmuring streams.

Nor was this pleasure interrupted by evil of any kind. It had no alloy of sorrow or pain, whether of body or mind. For while he was innocent he was impassive, incapable of suffering. Nothing could stain his purity of joy. And to crown all, he was immortal.

3. To this creature, endued with all these excellent faculties, thus qualified for his high charge, God said, 'Have thou dominion over the fish of the sea, and over the fowl of the air, and over every living thing that moveth upon the earth'.[15] And so the Psalmist: 'Thou madest him to have dominion over the works of thy hands; thou hast put all things under his feet: all sheep and oxen, yea, and the beasts of the field; the fowl of the air, and the fish of the sea, and whatsoever passeth through the paths of the seas!'[16] So that man was God's vicegerent upon earth, the prince and governor of this lower world; and all the blessings of God flowed through him to the inferior creatures. Man was the channel of conveyance between his Creator and the whole brute creation.

4. But what blessings were those that were then conveyed through man to the lower creatures? What was the original state of the brute creatures when they were first created? This deserves a more attentive consideration than has been usually given it. It is certain these, as well as man, had an innate principle of *self-motion*; and that at least in as high a degree as they enjoy it at this day. Again: they were endued with a degree of *understanding* not less than that they are possessed of now. They had also a *will* including various passions, which likewise they still enjoy. And they had *liberty*, a power of choice, a degree of which is still found in every living creature. Nor can we doubt but their understanding too was in the beginning perfect in its kind. Their passions and affections were regular, and their choice always guided by their understanding.

5. What then makes the barrier between men and brutes? The line which they cannot pass? It was not reason. Set aside that ambiguous term: exchange it for the plain word, understanding, and who can deny that brutes have this? We may as well deny that they have sight or hearing. But it is this: man is

---

[14] Job 31:26.
[15] Gen. 1:28.
[16] Ps. 8:6-8.

capable of God; the inferior creatures are not. We have no ground to believe that they are in any degree capable of knowing, loving, or obeying God. This is the specific difference between man and brute—the great gulf which they cannot pass over. And as a loving obedience to God was the perfection of men, so a loving obedience to man was the perfection of brutes. And as long as they continued in this they were happy after their kind; happy in the right state and the right use of their respective faculties. Yea, and so long they had some shadowy resemblance of even *moral goodness*. For they had gratitude to man for benefits received, and a reverence for him. They had likewise a kind of benevolence to each other, unmixed with any contrary temper. How *beautiful* many of them were we may conjecture from that which still remains; and that not only in the noblest creatures, but in those of the lowest order. And they were all surrounded not only with plenteous food, but with everything that could give them pleasure; pleasure unmixed with pain; for pain was not yet—it had not entered into paradise. And they too were immortal. For 'God made not death: neither hath he pleasure in the death of any living.'[17]

6. How true then is that word, 'God saw everything that he had made: and behold it was very good.'[18] But how far is this from being the case now! In what a condition is the whole lower world! To say nothing of inanimate nature, wherein all the elements seem to be out of course, and by turns to fight against man. Since man rebelled against his Maker, in what a state is all animated nature! Well might the Apostle say of this, 'The whole creation groaneth together, and travaileth together in pain until now.'[19] This directly refers to the brute creation. In what state this is at present we are now to consider.

II.1. As all the blessings of God in paradise flowed through man to the inferior creatures; as man was the great channel of communication between the Creator and the whole brute creation; so when man made himself incapable of transmitting those blessings, that communication was necessarily cut off. The intercourse between God and the inferior creatures being stopped, those blessings could no longer flow in upon them. And then it was that 'the creature', every creature, 'was subject to vanity',[20] to sorrow, to pain of every kind, to all manner of evils. 'Not' indeed 'willingly'; not by its own choice, not by any act or deed of its own; 'but by reason of him that

---

[17] Wisdom 1:13.
[18] Gen. 1:31.
[19] Rom. 8:22.
[20] Rom. 8:20.

subjected it'; by the wise permission of God, determining to draw eternal good out of this temporary evil.

2. But in what respects was 'the creature', every creature, then 'made subject to vanity'? What did the meaner creatures suffer when man rebelled against God? It is probable they sustained much loss even in the lower faculties, their vigour, strength, and swiftness. But undoubtedly they suffered far more in their understanding, more than we can easily conceive. Perhaps insects and worms had then as much understanding as the most intelligent brutes have now; whereas millions of creatures have at present little more understanding than the earth on which they crawl or the rock to which they adhere. They suffered still more in their will, in their passions, which were then variously distorted, and frequently set in flat opposition to the little understanding that was left them. Their liberty likewise was greatly impaired, yea, in many cases totally destroyed. They are still utterly enslaved to irrational appetites which have the full dominion over them. The very foundations of their nature are out of course, are turned upside down. As man is deprived of *his* perfection, his loving obedience to God, so brutes are deprived of *their* perfection, their loving obedience to man. The far greater part of them flee from him, studiously avoid his hated presence. The most of the rest set him at open defiance, yea, destroy him if it be in their power. A few only, those we commonly term domestic animals, retain more or less of their original disposition, and (through the mercy of God) love him still and pay obedience to him.

3. Setting these few aside, how little shadow of good, of gratitude, of benevolence, of any right temper is now to be found in any part of the brute creation! On the contrary, what savage fierceness, what unrelenting cruelty, are invariably observed in thousands of creatures, yea, are inseparable from their natures! Is it only the lion, the tiger, the wolf, among the inhabitants of the forest and plains; the shark and a few more voracious monsters among the inhabitants of the waters; or the eagle among birds; that tears the flesh, sucks the blood, and crushes the bones of their helpless fellow-creatures? Nay, the harmless fly, the laborious ant, the painted butterfly, are treated in the same merciless manner even by the innocent songsters of the grove! The innumerable tribes of poor insects are continually devoured by them. And whereas there is but a small number, comparatively, of beasts of prey on the earth, it is quite otherwise in the liquid element: there are but few inhabitants of the waters, whether of the sea or of the rivers, which do not devour whatsoever they can master. Yea, they exceed herein all the beasts of the

forest, and all the birds of prey. For none of these have been ever observed to prey upon their own species,

> Saevis inter se convenit ursis—[21]
> Even savage bears will not each other tear.

But the water savages swallow up all, even of their own kind, that are smaller and weaker than themselves. Yea, such at present is the miserable constitution of the world, to such 'vanity' is it now 'subjected',[22] that an immense majority of creatures, perhaps a million to one, can no otherwise preserve their own lives than by destroying their fellow-creatures.

4. And is not the very form, the outward appearance of many of the creatures, as horrid as their dispositions? Where is the beauty which was stamped upon them when they came first out of the hands of their Creator? There is not the least trace of it left: so far from it that they are shocking to behold! Nay, they are not only terrible and grisly to look upon, but deformed, and that to a high degree. Yet their features, ugly as they are at best, are frequently made more deformed than usual when they are distorted by pain, which they cannot avoid any more than the wretched sons of men. Pain of various kinds, weakness, sickness, diseases innumerable, come upon them, perhaps from within, perhaps from one another, perhaps from the inclemency of seasons, from fire, hail, snow, or storm, or from a thousand causes which they cannot foresee or prevent.

5. Thus 'as by one man sin entered into the world, and death by sin; even so death passed upon all men.'[23] And not on man only, but on those creatures also that 'did not sin after the similitude of Adam's transgression'.[24] And not death alone came upon them, but all of its train of preparatory evils: pain, and ten thousand sufferings. Nor these only, but likewise all those irregular passions, all those unlovely tempers (which in men are sins, and even in the brutes are sources of misery) 'passed upon all' the inhabitants of the earth, and remain in all, except the children of God.

6. During this season of 'vanity', not only the feebler creatures are continually destroyed by the stronger; not only the strong are frequently destroyed by those that are of equal strength; but both the one and the other

---

[21] Juvenal, *Satires,* xv.164.
[22] Rom. 8:20.
[23] Rom. 5:12.
[24] Rom. 5:14.

are exposed to the violence and cruelty of him that is now their common enemy—man. And if his swiftness or strength is not equal to theirs, yet his art more than supplies that defect. By this he eludes all their force, how great so ever it be; by this he defeats all their swiftness, and notwithstanding their various shifts and contrivances, discovers all their retreats. He pursues them over the widest plains, and through the thickest forests. He overtakes them in the fields of air, he finds them out in the depths of the sea. Nor are the mild and friendly creatures who still own his sway, and are duteous to his commands, secured thereby from more than brutal violence, from outrage and abuse of various kinds. Is the generous horse, that serves his master's necessity or pleasure with unwearied diligence, is the faithful dog, that waits the motion of his hand or his eye, exempt from this? What returns for their long and faithful service do many of these poor creatures find? And what a dreadful difference is there between what they suffer from their fellow brutes and what they suffer from the tyrant, man! The lion, the tiger, or the shark, give them pain from mere necessity, in order to prolong their own life; and put them out of their pain at once. But the human shark, without any such necessity, torments them of his free choice; and perhaps continues their lingering pain till after months or years death signs their release.

III.1. But will *the creature*, will even the brute creation, always remain in this deplorable condition? God forbid that we should affirm this; yea, or even entertain such a thought! While 'the whole creation groaneth together' (whether men attend or not) their groans are not dispersed in idle air, but enter into the ears of him that made them. While his creatures 'travail together in pain', he knoweth all their pain, and is bringing them nearer and nearer to the birth which shall be accomplished in its season. He seeth 'the earnest expectation' wherewith the whole animated creation 'waiteth for' that final 'manifestation of the sons of God': in which 'they themselves also shall be delivered' (not by annihilation: annihilation is not deliverance) 'from the' present 'bondage of corruption, into' a measure of 'the glorious liberty of the children of God.'

2. Nothing can be more express. Away with vulgar prejudices, and let the plain word of God take place. They 'shall be delivered from the bondage of corruption into glorious liberty'; even a measure, according as they are capable, of 'the liberty of the children of God'.

A general view of this is given us in the twenty-first chapter of the Revelation. When he that 'sitteth on the great white throne'[25] hath pronounced, 'Behold I make all things new';[26] when the word is fulfilled, 'The tabernacle of God is with men, [. . .] and they shall be his people, and God himself shall be with them and be their God';[27] then the following blessing shall take place (not only on the children of men—there is no such restriction in the text—but) on every creature according to its capacity: 'God shall wipe away all tears from their eyes. And there shall be no more death, neither sorrow nor crying. Neither shall there be any more pain: for the former things are passed away.'[28]

3. To descend to a few particulars. The whole brute creation will then undoubtedly be restored, not only to the vigour, strength, and swiftness which they had at their creation, but to a far higher degree of each than they ever enjoyed. They will be restored, not only to that measure of understanding which they had in paradise, but to a degree of it as much higher than that as the understanding of an elephant is beyond that of a worm. And whatever affections they had in the garden of God will be restored with vast increase, being exalted and refined in a manner which we ourselves are not now able to comprehend. The liberty they then had will be completely restored, and they will be free in all their motions. They will be delivered from all irregular appetites, from all unruly passions, from every disposition that is either evil in itself or has any tendency to evil. No rage will be found in any creature, no fierceness, no cruelty or thirst for blood. So far from it that 'the wolf shall dwell with the lamb, the leopard shall lie down with the kid, the calf and the young lion together; and a little child shall lead them. The cow and the bear shall feed together, and the lion shall eat straw like the ox.[. . .] They shall not hurt or destroy in all my holy mountain.'[29]

4. Thus in that day all the 'vanity' to which they are now helplessly 'subject' will be abolished; they will suffer no more either from within or without; the days of their groaning are ended. At the same time there can be no reasonable doubt but all the horridness of their appearance, and all the deformity of their aspect, will vanish away, and be exchanged for their primeval beauty. And with their beauty their happiness will return; to which there can then be no obstruction. As there will be nothing within, so there will be nothing without,

---

[25] Rev. 20:11.
[26] Rev. 21:5.
[27] Rev. 21:3.
[28] Rev. 21:4.
[29] Is. 11:6, 7, 9.

to give them any uneasiness—no heat or cold, no storm or tempest, but one perennial spring. In the new earth, as well as in the new heavens, there will be nothing to give pain, but everything that the wisdom and goodness of God can create to give happiness. As a recompense for what they once suffered while under 'the bondage of corruption', when God has 'renewed the face of the earth',[30] and their corruptible body has put on incorruption,[31] they shall enjoy happiness suited to their state, without alloy, without interruption, and without end.

5. But though I doubt not that the Father of all has a tender regard for even his lowest creatures, and that in consequence of this he will make them large amends for all they suffer while under their present bondage, yet I dare not affirm that he has an *equal regard* for them and for the children of men. I do not believe that

> *He sees with equal eyes, as Lord of all,*
> *A hero perish or a sparrow fall!*

By no means. This is exceeding pretty; but it is absolutely false. For though

> *Mercy, with truth and endless grace,*
> *O'er all his works doth reign,*
> *Yet chiefly he delights to bless*
> *His favourite creature, man.*

God regards his meanest creatures much; but he regards man much more. He does not *equally regard* a hero and a sparrow, the best of men, and the lowest of brutes. 'How *much more* does your heavenly Father care for you'![32] says he who is 'in the bosom of the Father'.[33] Those who thus strain the point are clearly confuted by his question, 'Are not ye *much better* than they?'[34] Let it suffice that God regards everything that he hath made in its own order, and in proportion to that measure of his own image which he has stamped upon it.

6. May I be permitted to mention here a conjecture concerning the brute creation? What if it should then please the all-wise, the all-gracious Creator, to raise them higher in the scale of beings? What if it should please him,

---

[30] Ps. 104:30.
[31] 1 Cor. 15:53, 54.
[32] Matt. 7:11.
[33] Jn. 1:18.
[34] Matt. 6:26.

when he makes us 'equal to angels',[35] to make them what we are now? Creatures capable of God? Capable of knowing, and loving, and enjoying the Author of their being? If it should be so, ought our eye to be evil because he is good?[36] However this be, he will certainly do what will be most for his own glory.

7. If it be objected to all this (as very probably it will): 'But of what use will those creatures be in that future state?' I answer this by another question—'What use are they of now?' If there be (as has commonly been supposed) eight thousand species of insects, who is able to inform us of what use seven thousand of them are? If there are four thousand species of fishes, who can tell us of what use are more than three thousand of them? If there are six hundred sorts of birds, who can tell of what use five hundred of those species are? If there be four hundred sorts of beasts, to what use do three hundred of them serve? Consider this; consider how little we know of even the present designs of God; and then you will not wonder that we know still less of what he designs to do in the new heavens and the new earth.[37]

8. 'But what end does it answer to dwell upon this subject which we so imperfectly understand?' To consider so much as we do understand, so much as God has been pleased to reveal to us, may answer that excellent end—to illustrate that mercy of God which is 'over all his works',[38] And it may exceedingly confirm our belief that much more he is 'loving to every man'. For how well may we urge our Lord's word, 'Are not ye much better than they?'[39] If then the Lord takes such care of the fowls of the air and of the beasts of the field, shall he not much more take care of you, creatures of a nobler order? If 'the Lord will save' (as the inspired writer affirms) 'both man and beast' in their several degrees, surely 'the children of men may put their trust under the shadow of his wings'![40]

9. May it not answer another end, namely, furnish us with a full answer to a plausible objection against the justice of God in suffering numberless creatures that never had sinned to be so severely punished? They could not sin, for they were not moral agents. Yet how severely do they suffer! Yea, many of them, beasts of burden in particular, almost the whole time of their

---

[35] Lk. 20:36.
[36] Matt. 20:15.
[37] 2 Pet. 3:13; Rev. 21:1.
[38] Ps. 145:9 (BCP).
[39] Matt. 6:26.
[40] Ps. 36:7 (BCP).

abode on earth. So that they can have no retribution here below. But the objection vanishes away if we consider that something better remains after death for these poor creatures also! That these likewise shall one day be delivered from this bondage of corruption, and shall then receive an ample amends for all their present sufferings.

10. One more excellent end may undoubtedly be answered by the preceding considerations. They may encourage us to imitate him whose mercy is over all his works. They may soften our hearts towards the meaner creatures, knowing that the Lord careth for them. It may enlarge our hearts towards those poor creatures to reflect that, as vile as they appear in our eyes, not one of them is forgotten in the sight of our Father which is in heaven. Through all the vanity to which they are now subjected, let us look to what God hath prepared for them. Yea, let us habituate ourselves to look forward, beyond this present scene of bondage, to the happy time when they will be delivered therefrom into the liberty of the children of God.

11. From what has been said I cannot but draw one inference, which no man of reason can deny. If it is this which distinguishes men from beasts, that they are creatures capable of God, capable of knowing, and loving, and enjoying him; then whoever is 'without God in the world'[41]—whoever does not know, or love, or enjoy God, and is not careful about the matter—does in effect disclaim the nature of man, and degrade himself into a beast. Let such vouchsafe a little attention to those remarkable words of Solomon: 'I said in my heart concerning the estate of the sons of men, . . . they might see that they themselves are beasts.'[42] *These* sons of men are undoubtedly beasts— and that by their own act and deed. For they deliberately and wilfully disclaim the sole characteristic of human nature. It is true they may have a share of reason—they have speech and they walk erect. But they have not the mark, the only mark, which totally separates man from the brute creation. 'That which befalleth beasts, the same thing befalleth them.'[43] They are equally without God in the world, 'so that a man' of this kind 'hath no pre-eminence above a beast.'

12. So much more let all those who are of a nobler turn of mind assert the distinguishing dignity of their nature! Let all who are of a more generous spirit know and maintain their rank in the scale of beings. Rest not till you enjoy the privilege of humanity—the knowledge and love of God. Lift up

---

[41] Eph. 2:12.
[42] Eccl. 3:18.
[43] Eccl. 3:19.

your heads, ye creatures capable of God. Lift up your hearts to the Source of your being!

> *Know God, and teach your souls to know*
> *The joys that from religion flow.*

Give your hearts to him who, together with ten thousand blessings, has 'given you his Son, his only Son'![44] Let your continual 'fellowship be with the Father, and with his Son, Jesus Christ'![45] Let God be in all your thoughts, and ye will be men indeed. Let him be your God and your all! The desire of your eyes, the joy of your heart, and your portion for ever!

---

[44] Jn. 3:16.
[45] 1 Jn 1:3.

The New Creation
1785

This sermon is a further elaboration of the core ideas first expressed in The General Deliverance. *Combined, these two sermons present Wesley's most mature thoughts on the eternal state. Guided by his Chain of Being philosophy, Wesley envisions the new heavens and new earth in very material terms, guided in his speculations by the four essential elements: fire, air, water, and earth. This sermon should be read in conjunction with* God's Approbation of His Works *(Works 2:387-99), which discusses the original creation using the same four elements as a blueprint. Therefore, both of these sermons serve a bookends to his mature eschatology. Following standard Christian tradition, Wesley envisions three levels of heavens with only the lower two transformed by the regenerating work of the new creation. This is in keeping with his* Notes *on* 2 Corinthians 12:2 *and* 2 Peter 3:11. *By contrast, Thomas Hartley, whom Wesley read in 1764, proposed that only the lowest atmospheric heaven will be transformed* (Paradise Restored, 78). *The speculations Wesley presents here on the eternal state should be compared to what he expressed in earlier periods: "On the Resurrection of the Dead" (1732, Works (Jackson) 4:474-85),* Upon our Lord's Sermon on Mount VI *III.8 (1748, Works 1:582), and in his* Notes *on* 1 Corinthians 15:22-58 *and* Revelation 21-22. *Concerning the conflagration, compare with* The Great Assize *III.2-4. For Albert Outler's introduction and note on 'inhabitable planets', see Works 2:500, 503.*

Behold, I make all things new.

Revelation 21:5

1. What a strange scene is here opened to our view! How remote from all our natural apprehensions! Not a glimpse of what is here revealed was ever seen in the heathen world. Not only the modern, barbarous, uncivilized heathens have not the least conception of it; but it was equally unknown to the refined, polished heathens of ancient Greece and Rome. And it is almost as little thought of or understood by the generality of Christians: I mean, not barely

those that are nominally such, that have the form of godliness without the power;[1] but even those that in a measure fear God and study to work righteousness.

2. It must be allowed that after all the researches we can make, still our knowledge of the great truth which is delivered to us in these words is exceedingly short and imperfect. As this is a point of mere revelation, beyond the reach of all our natural faculties, we cannot penetrate far into it, nor form any adequate conception of it. But it may be an encouragement to those who have in any degree tasted of the powers of the world to come[2] to go as far as we can go, interpreting Scripture by Scripture, according to the analogy of faith.

3. The Apostle, caught up in the visions of God, tells us in the first verse of the chapter, 'I saw a new heaven and a new earth';[3] and adds, 'He that sat upon the throne said (I believe the only words which he is said to utter throughout the whole book), Behold, I make all things new.'[4]

4. Very many commentators entertain a strange opinion that this relates only to the present state of things, and gravely tell us that the words are to be referred to the flourishing state of the church, which commenced after the heathen persecutions. Nay, some of them have discovered that all which the Apostle speaks concerning the 'new heaven and the new earth' was fulfilled when Constantine the Great poured in riches and honours upon the Christians. What a miserable way is this of making void the whole counsel of God[5] with regard to all that grand chain of events, in reference to his church, yea, and to all mankind, from the time that John was in Patmos unto the end of the world! Nay, the line of this prophecy reaches farther still. It does not end with the present world, but shows us the things that will come to pass when this world is no more.

5. Thus saith the Creator and Governor of the universe, 'Behold, I make all things new': all which are included in that expression of the Apostle, 'a new heaven and a new earth'. 'A new heaven': the original word in Genesis (chapter one) is in the plural number. And indeed this is the constant language of Scripture—not heaven, but heavens. Accordingly the ancient

---

[1] 2 Tim. 3:5.
[2] Heb. 6:5.
[3] Rev. 21:1.
[4] Rev. 21:5.
[5] Lk. 7:30.

Jewish writers are accustomed to reckon three heavens. In conformity to which the apostle Paul speaks of his being 'caught up into the third heaven'.[6] It is this, the third heaven, which is usually supposed to be the more immediate residence of God—so far as any residence can be ascribed to his omnipresent Spirit, who pervades and fills the whole universe. It is here (if we speak after the manner of men) that the Lord sitteth upon his throne, surrounded by angels and archangels, and by all his flaming ministers.

6. We cannot think that this heaven will undergo any change, any more than its great inhabitant. Surely this palace of the Most High was the same from eternity, and will be world without end.[7] Only the inferior heavens are liable to change; the highest of which we usually call the starry heaven. This, St. Peter informs us, is 'reserved unto fire, against the day of judgment and destruction of ungodly men'. In that day, 'being on fire', it shall first shrivel as a parchment scroll; then it shall 'be dissolved', and 'shall pass away with a great noise;[8] lastly it shall 'flee from the face of him that sitteth on the throne',[9] 'and there shall be found no place for it.'[10]

7. At the same time 'the stars shall fall from heaven,'[11] the secret chain being broken which had retained them in their several orbits from the foundation of the world. In the meanwhile the lower or sublunary 'heaven',[12] with 'the elements' (or principles that compose it), 'shall melt with fervent heat,' while 'the earth with the works that are therein shall be burnt up.[13] This is the introduction to a far nobler state of things, such as it has not yet entered into the heart of men to conceive—the universal restoration which is to succeed the universal destruction. For 'we look for', says the Apostle, 'new heavens and a new earth, wherein dwelleth righteousness.'[14]

8. One considerable difference there will undoubtedly be in the starry heaven when it is created anew; there will be no blazing stars, no comets there. Whether those horrid, eccentric orbs are half-formed planets, in a chaotic state (I speak on the supposition of a plurality of worlds) or such as have undergone their general conflagration, they will certainly have no place in the

---

[6] 2 Cor. 12:22.
[7] Eph. 3:21.
[8] 2 Pet. 3:10-12.
[9] Rev. 6:16.
[10] Rev. 20:11.
[11] Matt. 24:29.
[12] That is, this earth and its atmosphere as in Aristotelian and Ptolemaic astronomy.
[13] 2 Pet. 3:10.
[14] 2 Pet. 3:7, 13.

new heaven, where all will be exact order and harmony. There may be many other differences between the heaven that now is and that which will be after the renovation. But they are above our apprehension: we must leave eternity to explain them.

9. We may more easily conceive the changes which will be wrought in the lower heaven, in the region of the air. It will be no more torn by hurricanes, or agitated by furious storms or destructive tempests. Pernicious or terrifying meteors will have no more place therein. We shall have no more occasion to say,

> *There like a trumpet, loud and strong,*
> *Thy thunder shakes our coast;*
> *While the red lightnings wave along,*
> *The banners of thy host!*

No; all will be then light, fair, serene—a lively picture of the eternal day.

10. All the elements (taking that word in the common sense for the principles of which all natural beings are compounded)[15] will be new indeed; entirely changed as to their qualities, although not as to their nature. *Fire* is at present the general destroyer of all things under the sun; dissolving all things that come within the sphere of its action, and reducing them to their primitive atoms. But no sooner will it have performed its last great office of destroying the heavens and the earth (whether you mean thereby one system only, or the whole fabric of the universe—the difference between one and millions of worlds being nothing before the great Creator); when, I say, it has done this, the destruction wrought by fire will come to a perpetual end. It will destroy no more; it will consume no more; it will forget its power to burn, which it possesses only during the present state of things, and be as harmless in the new heavens and earth as it is now in the bodies of men and other animals, and the substance of trees and flowers; in all which (as late experiments show) large quantities of ethereal fire are lodged—if it be not rather an essential component part of every material being under the sun. But it will probably retain its vivifying power, though divested of its power to destroy.

11. It has been already observed that the calm, placid air will be no more disturbed by storms and tempests. There will be no more meteors with their horrid glare, affrighting the poor children of men. May we not add (though at

---

[15] That is, earth, air, fire, and water.

first it may sound like a paradox) that there will be no more rain. It is observable that there was none in paradise; a circumstance which Moses particularly mentions: 'The Lord God had not caused it to rain upon the earth. But there went up a mist from the earth,' which then covered up the abyss of waters, 'and watered the whole face of the ground'[16] with moisture sufficient for all the purposes of vegetation. We have all reason to believe that the case will be the same when paradise is restored. Consequently there will be no more clouds or fogs; but one bright, refulgent day. Much less will there be any poisonous damps or pestilential blasts. There will be no sirocco in Italy; no parching or suffocating winds in Arabia; no keen north-east winds in our own country,

Shattering the graceful locks of yon fair trees;

but only pleasing, healthful breezes,

Fanning the earth with odoriferous wings.

12. But what change will the element of water undergo when all things are made new? It will be in every part of the world clear and limpid, pure from all unpleasing or unhealthful mixtures; rising here and there in crystal fountains to refresh and adorn the earth 'with liquid lapse of murmuring stream'. For undoubtedly, as there were in paradise, there will be various rivers gently gliding along, for the use and pleasure of both man and beast. But the inspired writer has expressly declared, 'there will be no more sea.'[17] We have reason to believe that at the beginning of the world, when God said, 'Let the waters under the heaven be gathered together unto one place, and let the dry land appear,'[18] the dry land spread over the face of the water, and covered it on every side. And so it seems to have done till, in order to the general deluge which he had determined to bring upon the earth at once, 'the windows of heaven were opened, and the fountains of the great deep broken up.'[19] But the sea will then retire within its primitive bounds, and appear on the surface of the earth no more. Neither indeed will there be any more need of the sea. For either as the ancient poet supposes,

Omnis feret omnia tellus—[20]

---

[16] Gen. 2:5-6.
[17] Rev. 21:1.
[18] Gen 1:9.
[19] Gen 7:11.
[20] Virgil, *Eclogues*, iv. 39.

every part of the earth will naturally produce whatever its inhabitants want—or all mankind will procure what the whole earth affords by a much easier and readier conveyance. For all the inhabitants of the earth, our Lord informs us, will then be *isaggeloi*,[21] 'equal to angels'; on a level with them in swiftness as well as strength; so that they can quick as thought transport themselves or whatever they want from one side of the globe to the other.

13. But it seems a greater change will be wrought in the earth than even in the air and water. Not that I can believe that wonderful discovery of Jacob Behmen,[22] which many so eagerly contend for, that the earth itself with all its furniture and inhabitants will then be transparent as glass. There does not seem to be the least foundation for this, either in Scripture or reason. Surely not in Scripture: I know not one text in the Old or New Testament which affirms any such thing. Certainly it cannot be inferred from that text in the Revelation, chapter the fourth, verse the sixth: 'And before the throne there was a sea of glass, like unto crystal.' And yet, if I mistake not, this is the chief, if not the only Scripture which has been urged in favour of this opinion! Neither can I conceive that it has any foundation in reason. It has indeed been warmly alleged that all things would be far more beautiful if they were quite transparent. But I cannot apprehend this; yea, I apprehend quite the contrary. Suppose every part of a human body were made transparent as crystal, would it appear more beautiful than it does now? Nay, rather it would shock us above measure. The surface of the body, and in particular 'the human face divine', is undoubtedly one of the most beautiful objects that can be found under heaven. But could you look through the rosy cheek, the smooth, fair forehead, or the rising bosom, and distinctly see all that lies within, you would turn away from it with loathing and horror.

14. Let us next take a view of those changes which we may reasonably suppose will then take place in the earth. It will no more be bound up with intense cold, nor parched up with extreme heat; but will have such a temperature as will be most conducive to its fruitfulness. If in order to punish its inhabitants God did of old

Bid his angels turn askance
This oblique globe,

---

[21] Lk. 20:36.
[22] An English spelling of Jakob Boehme (1575-1624).

thereby occasioning violent cold on one part, and violent heat on the other; he will undoubtedly then order them to restore it to its original position; so that there will be a final end, on the one hand of the burning heat which makes some parts of it scarce habitable; and on the other of

> *The rage of Arctos, and eternal frost.*

15. And it will then contain no jarring or destructive principles within its own bosom. It will no more have any of those violent convulsions in its own bowels. It will no more be shaken or torn asunder by the impetuous force of earthquakes; and will therefore need neither Vesuvius nor Etna, nor any burning mountains to prevent them. There will be no more horrid rocks or frightful precipices; no wild deserts or barren sands; no impassable morasses or unfaithful bogs to swallow up the unwary traveller. There will doubtless be inequalities on the surface of the earth, which are not blemishes, but beauties. For though I will not affirm that

> *earth hath this variety from heaven*
> *Of pleasure situate in hill and dale*;

yet I cannot think gently rising hills will be any defect, but an ornament of the new-made earth. And doubtless we shall then likewise have occasion to say:

> *Lo there his wondrous skill arrays*
> *The fields in cheerful green!*
> *A thousand herbs his hand displays,*
> *A thousand flowers between!*

16. And what will the general produce of the earth be? Not thorns, briars, or thistles. Not any useless or fetid weed; not any poisonous, hurtful, or unpleasant plant; but every one that can be conducive in any wise either to our use or pleasure. How far beyond all that the most lively imagination is now able to conceive! We shall no more regret the loss of the terrestrial paradise, or sigh at that well-devised description of our great poet;

> *Then shall this mount*
> *Of paradise by might of waves be moved*
> *Out of his place, pushed by the horned flood,*
> *With all its verdure spoiled, and trees adrift,*
> *Down the great river to the opening gulf,*

And there take root, an island salt and bare!

For all the earth shall then be a more beautiful paradise than Adam ever saw.

17. Such will be the state of the new earth with regard to the meaner, the inanimate parts of it. But great as this change will be, it is little, it is nothing, in comparison of that which will then take place throughout all animated nature. In the living part of the creation were seen the most deplorable effects of Adam's apostasy. The whole animated creation, whatever has life, from leviathan to the smallest mite, was thereby 'made subject' to such 'vanity'[23] as the inanimate creatures could not be. They were subject to that fell monster, death, the conqueror of all that breathe. They were made subject to its forerunner, pain, in its ten thousand forms; although 'God made not death, neither hath he pleasure in the death of any living.'[24] How many millions of creatures in the sea, in the air, and on every part of the earth, can now no otherwise preserve their own lives than by taking away the lives of others; by tearing in pieces and devouring their poor, innocent, unresisting fellow-creatures! Miserable lot of such innumerable multitudes, who, insignificant as they seem, are the offspring of one common Father, the creatures of the same God of love! It is probable not only two-thirds of the animal creation, but ninety-nine parts out of a hundred, are under a necessity of destroying others in order to preserve their own life! But it shall not always be so. He that sitteth upon the throne[25] will soon change the face of all things, and give a demonstrative proof to all his creatures that 'his mercy is over all his works.'[26] The horrid state of things which at present obtains will soon be at an end. On the new earth no creature will kill or hurt or give pain to any other. The scorpion will have no poisonous sting, the adder no venomous teeth. The lion will have no claws to tear the lamb; no teeth to grind his flesh and bones. Nay, no creature, no beast, bird, or fish, will have any inclination to hurt any other. For cruelty will be far away, and savageness and fierceness be forgotten. So that violence shall be heard no more, neither wasting or destruction seen on the face of the earth. 'The wolf shall dwell with the lamb' (the words may be literally as well as figuratively understood) 'and the leopard shall lie down with the kid.'[27] 'They shall not hurt or destroy,'[28] from the rising up of the sun to the going down of the same.

---

[23] Rom. 8:20.
[24] Wisdom 1:13.
[25] Cf. Rev. 5:13; 6:16; 7:15.
[26] Ps. 145:9 (BCP).
[27] Is. 11:6.
[28] Is. 11:9.

18. But the most glorious of all will be the change which then will take place on the poor, sinful, miserable children of men. These had fallen in many respects, as from a greater height, so into a lower depth than any other part of the creation. But they shall 'hear a great voice out of heaven, saying, Behold, the tabernacle of God is with men, and he will dwell with them, and they shall be his people, and God himself shall be their God.' Hence will arise an unmixed state of holiness and happiness far superior to that which Adam enjoyed in paradise. In how beautiful and affecting a manner is this described by the Apostle! 'God shall wipe away all tears from their eyes; and there shall be no more death, neither sorrow nor crying, neither shall there be any more pain: for the former things are done away.'[29] As there will be no more death, and no more pain or sickness preparatory thereto; as there will be no more grieving for or parting with friends; so there will be no more sorrow or crying. Nay, but there will be a greater deliverance than all this; for there will be no more sin. And to crown all, there will be a deep, an intimate, an uninterrupted union with God; a constant communion with the Father and his Son Jesus Christ, through the Spirit; a continual enjoyment of the Three-One God, and of all the creatures in him!

---

[29] Rev. 21:3-4.

Of Hell
1788

This is the final sermon of a triad on the eternal state. Wesley draws on traditional sources to develop his doctrine of eternal punishment as loss and torment. To be noted, once again, is Wesley's conception of the eternal state in very material terms. Hell is both a state and a place. The unredeemed have resurrected material bodies capable of suffering the infliction of a material fire that is never quenched. With the new creation, the constitution of material things will be so changed that nothing can be dissolved or consumed (II.5). Therefore, the unredeemed will physically suffer, and will do so eternally. Added to this is Wesley's description of the mental anguish of the poor unhappy souls in hell. Wesley's description of what the unredeemed know should be compared to what he describes in the next sermon on the intermediate state. Other places in this Reader that address final punishment are The Great Assize III.1 *and his* Notes *on* Revelation 14:11 *and* 20:11-15. *For more of Wesley's views on final punishment, see* The Way to the Kingdom II.4 *(Works 1:227),* Upon our Lord's Sermon on the Mount XI I.1-6 *(Works 1:665-68),* On Dives and Lazarus *(Works 4:4-18), and* Walking by Sight and Walking by Faith §21 *(Works 4:58). For Albert Outler's introduction, see Works 3:30.*

Where their worm dieth not, and the fire is not quenched.

Mark 9:48

1. Every truth which is revealed in the oracles of God is undoubtedly of great importance. Yet it may be allowed that some of those which are revealed therein are of greater importance than others, as being more immediately conducive to the grand end of all, the eternal salvation of men. And we may judge of their importance even from this circumstance, that they are not mentioned once only in the sacred writings, but are repeated over and over. A remarkable instance of this we have with regard to the awful truth which is now before us. Our blessed Lord, who uses no superfluous words, who makes no 'vain repetitions',[1] repeats it over and over in the same chapter, and as it

---
[1] Matt. 6:7.

were in the same breath. So verse 43, 44: 'If thy hand offend thee', if a thing or person as useful as a hand be an occasion of sin, and there is no other way to shun that sin, 'cut it off. It is better for thee to enter into life maimed, than having two hands to go into hell; into unquenchable fire, where their worm dieth not, and the fire is not quenched.' So again, verse 45, 46: 'If thy foot offend thee, cut it off. It is better for thee to enter halt into life, than having two feet to be cast into hell; into unquenchable fire, where their worm dieth not, and the fire is not quenched.' And yet again, verse 47, 48: 'If thine eye', a person or thing as dear as thine eye, 'offend thee', hinder thy running the race which is set before thee,[2] 'pluck it out: it is better for thee to enter into the kingdom of God with one eye, than having two eyes to be cast into hell-fire; where their worm dieth not, and the fire is not quenched.'

2. And let it not be thought that the consideration of these terrible truths is proper only for enormous sinners. How is this supposition consistent with what our Lord speaks to those who were then doubtless the holiest men upon earth? 'When innumerable multitudes were gathered together, he said to his disciples' (the apostles) 'first of all, I say unto you, my friends, Fear not them that can kill the body, and after that have no more that they can do. But I say unto you, Fear him who after he hath killed hath power to cast into hell; yea, I say unto you, Fear him!'[3] Yea, fear him under this very notion, of having power to cast into hell; that is, in effect, fear lest he should cast you into the place of torment.[4] And this very fear, even in the children of God, is one excellent means of preserving them from it.

3. It behoves therefore not only the outcasts of men but even 'you, his friends', you that fear and love God, deeply to consider what is revealed in the oracles of God concerning the future state of punishment. How widely distant is this from the most elaborate accounts which are given by the heathen authors! Their accounts are (in many particulars at least) childish, fanciful, and self-inconsistent. So that it is no wonder they did not believe themselves, but only related the tales of the vulgar. So Virgil strongly intimates, when, after the laboured account he had given of the shades beneath, he sends him that had related it out at the ivory gate, through which (as he tells us) only *dreams* pass; thereby giving us to know that all the preceding account is no more than a dream. This he only insinuates; but his brother poet, Juvenal, speaks out flat and plain:

---

[2] Cf. Heb. 12:2.
[3] Lk. 12:1, 4-5.
[4] Lk. 16:28.

Of Hell

Esse aliquos manes, et subterranea regna, . . .
Nec pueri credunt, nisi qui nondum aere lavantur[5]—

'Even our children do not believe a word of the tales concerning another world.'

4. Here, on the contrary, all is worthy of God the Creator, the Governor of mankind. All is awful and solemn, suitable to his wisdom and justice by whom 'Tophet was ordained of old';[6] although originally 'prepared', not for the children of men, but 'for the devil and his angels'.[7]

The punishment of those who in spite of all the warnings of God resolve to have their portion with the devil and his angels will, according to the ancient and not improper division, be either *poena damni,* what they lose, or *poena sensus*, what they feel.[8] After considering these separately I shall touch on a few additional circumstances, and conclude with two or three inferences.

I.1. And, first, let us consider the *poena damni*, the punishment of loss. This commences in that very moment wherein the soul is separated from the body; in that instant the soul loses all those pleasures, the enjoyment of which depends on the outward senses. The smell, the taste, the touch delight no more; the organs that ministered to them are spoiled, and the objects that used to gratify them are removed far away. In the dreary regions of the dead all these things are forgotten; or, if remembered, are only remembered with pain, seeing they are gone for ever. All the pleasures of the imagination are at an end. There is no grandeur in the infernal region; there is nothing beautiful in those dark abodes, no light but that of livid flames. And nothing new, but one unvaried scene of horror upon horror. There is no music but that of groans and shrieks, of weeping, wailing, and gnashing of teeth;[9] of curses and blasphemies against God, or cutting reproaches of one another. Nor is there anything to gratify the sense of honour: no, they are the heirs of shame and everlasting contempt.[10]

2. Thus are they totally separated from all the *things* they were fond of in the present world. At the same instant will commence another loss—that of all

---

[5] Juvenal, *Satires*, ii. 149.
[6] Cf. Is. 30:33.
[7] Matt. 25:41.
[8] "The idea, however, comes from a familiar scholastic distinction between punishment of bereavement and deprivation (*poena damni*), i.e., of what had been valued in this life, and the active punishment of the bodily senses" Outler, *Works* 3:33-34 n 9.
[9] Matt. 8:12; 13:42.
[10] Dan. 12:2.

the *persons* whom they loved. They are torn away from their nearest and dearest relations, their wives, husbands, parents, children, and (what to some will be worse than all this) the friend which was as their own soul.[11] All the pleasure they ever enjoyed in these is lost, gone, vanished away. For there is no friendship in hell. Even the poet who affirms (though I know not on what authority),

> Devil with devil damned
> Firm concord holds;[12]

does not affirm that there is any concord among the human fiends that inhabit the great abyss.

3. But they will then be sensible of a greater loss than that of all they enjoyed on earth. They have lost their place in Abraham's bosom,[13] in the paradise of God.[14] Hitherto indeed it hath not entered into their hearts to conceive what holy souls enjoy in the garden of God,[15] in the society of angels, and of the wisest and best men that have lived from the beginning of the world (not to mention the immense increase of knowledge which they will then undoubtedly receive). But they will then fully understand the value of what they have vilely cast away.

4. But as happy as the souls in paradise are, they are preparing for far greater happiness. For paradise is only the porch of heaven; and it is there the spirits of just men are made perfect.[16] It is in heaven only that there is the fullness of joy, the pleasures that are at God's right hand for evermore.[17] The loss of this by those unhappy spirits will be the completion of their misery. They will then know and feel that God alone is the centre of all created spirits; and consequently that a spirit made for God can have no rest out of him. It seems that the Apostle had this in his view when he spoke of those 'who shall be punished with everlasting destruction from the presence of the Lord'.[18] Banishment from the presence of the Lord is the very essence of destruction to a spirit that was made for God. And if that banishment lasts for ever, it is 'everlasting destruction'.

---

[11] Cf. 1 Sam. 18:1, 3; 20:17.
[12] Milton, *Paradise Lost,* ii.496-97.
[13] Lk. 16:22.
[14] Rev. 2:7.
[15] Eze. 28:13; 31:8, 9.
[16] Heb. 12:23.
[17] Ps. 16:11.
[18] 2 Th. 1:9.

Such is the loss sustained by those miserable creatures on whom that awful sentence will be pronounced, 'Depart from me, ye cursed!'[19] What an unspeakable curse, if there were no other! But alas! This is far from being the whole; for to the punishment of *loss* will be added the punishment of *sense*. What they lose implies unspeakable misery, which yet is inferior to what they feel. This it is which our Lord expresses in those emphatical words, 'where their worm dieth not, and the fire is not quenched'.

II.1. From the time that sentence was pronounced upon man, 'Dust thou art, and unto dust thou shalt return,'[20] it was the custom of all nations, so far as we can learn, to commit dust to dust: it seemed natural to restore the bodies of the dead to the general mother earth. But in process of time another method obtained, chiefly among the rich and great, of burning the bodies of their relations, and frequently in a grand magnificent manner. For which purpose they erected huge funeral piles, with immense labour and expense. By either of these methods the body of man was soon restored to its parent dust. Either the worm or the fire soon consumed the well-wrought frame; after which the worm itself quickly died, and the fire was entirely quenched. But there is likewise a worm that belongs to the future state; and that is a worm that never dieth. And there is a fire hotter than that of the funeral pile; and it is a fire that will never be quenched.

2. The first thing intended by the worm that never dieth seems to be a guilty conscience, including self-condemnation, sorrow, shame, remorse, and a sense of the wrath of God. May not we have some conception of this by what is sometimes felt even in the present world? Is it not of this chiefly that Solomon speaks when he says, 'The spirit of a man may bear his infirmities', his infirmities or griefs of any other kind, 'but a wounded spirit who can bear?'[21] Who can bear the anguish of an awakened conscience, penetrated with a sense of guilt, and the arrows of the Almighty sticking in the soul, and drinking up the spirit![22] How many of the stout-hearted have sunk under it, and chose strangling rather than life![23] And yet what are these wounds, what is all this anguish of a soul while in this present world, in comparison of those they must suffer when their souls are wholly awakened to feel the wrath of an offended God! Add to these all unholy passions, fear, horror, rage; evil desires, desires that can never be satisfied. Add all unholy tempers, envy,

---

[19] Matt. 25:41.
[20] Gen. 3:19.
[21] Pr. 18:14.
[22] Job 6:4.
[23] Job 7:15.

jealousy, malice, and revenge; all of which will incessantly gnaw the soul, as the vulture was supposed to do the liver of Tityus.[24] To these if we add hatred of God and all his creatures—all these united together may serve to give us some little, imperfect idea of the worm that never dieth.

3. We may observe a remarkable difference in the manner wherein our Lord speaks concerning the two parts of the future punishment. He says, 'Where *their* worm dieth not' of the one; 'where *the* fire is not quenched' of the other. This cannot be by chance. What then is the reason for this variation of the expression?

Does it not seem to be this? 'The fire' will be the same, essentially the same, to all that are tormented therein—only perhaps more intense to some than others, according to their degree of guilt. But 'their worm' will not, cannot be the same. It will be infinitely varied according to the various kinds as well as degrees of wickedness. This variety will arise partly from the just judgment of God, 'rewarding every man according to his works'.[25] For we cannot doubt but this rule will take place no less in hell than in heaven. As in heaven 'every man will receive his own reward', incommunicably his own, according to 'his own labours',[26] incommunicably his, that is, the whole tenor of his tempers, thoughts, words, and actions; so undoubtedly every man in fact will receive his own bad reward, according to his own bad labour. And this likewise will be incommunicably *his own*, even as his labour was. Variety of punishment will likewise arise from the very nature of the thing. As they that bring most holiness to heaven will find most happiness there, so on the other hand it is not only true that the more wickedness a man brings to hell the more misery he will find there; but that this misery will be infinitely varied according to the various kinds of his wickedness. It was therefore proper to say 'the fire' in general, but 'their worm' in particular.

4. But it has been questioned by some whether there be any fire in hell—that is, any material fire. Nay, if there be any fire it is unquestionably material. For what is immaterial fire? The same as immaterial water or earth! Both the one and the other is absolute nonsense, a contradiction in terms. Either therefore we must affirm it to be material, or we deny its existence. But if we granted them there is no fire at all there, what would they gain thereby? Seeing this is allowed on all hands, that it is either fire or something worse. And consider this: does not our Lord speak *as if* it were real fire? No one can deny or doubt of this. Is it possible then to suppose that the God of truth

---

[24] Cf. Homer, *odyssey,* xi.576-81.
[25] Matt. 16:27.
[26] 1 Cor. 3:8.

would speak in this manner if it were not so? Does he design to fright his poor creatures? What, with scarecrows? With vain shadows of things that have no being? O let not anyone think so! Impute not such folly to the Most High!

5. But others aver: 'It is not possible that fire should burn always. For by the immutable law of nature it consumes whatever is thrown into it. And by the same law, as soon as it has consumed its fuel, it is itself consumed; it goes out.'

It is most true that in the present constitution of things, during the present laws of nature, the element of fire does dissolve and consume whatever is thrown into it. But here is the mistake: the present laws of nature are not immutable. When the heavens and the earth shall flee away,[27] the present scene will be totally changed; and with the present constitution of things, the present laws of nature will cease. After this great change nothing will be dissolved, nothing will be consumed any more. Therefore if it were true that fire consumes all things now, it would not follow that it would do the same after the whole frame of nature has undergone that vast, universal change.

6. I say, 'If it were true that fire consumes *all things* now.' But indeed it is not true. Has it not pleased God to give us already some proof of what will be hereafter? Is not the *linum asbestum*, the incombustible flax, known in most parts of Europe? If you take a towel or handkerchief made of this (one of which may now be seen in the British Museum) you may throw it into the hottest fire, and when it is taken out again it will be observed, upon the nicest experiment, not to have lost one grain of its weight. Here therefore is a substance before our eyes, which even in the present constitution of things (as if it were an emblem of things to come) may remain in fire without being consumed.

7. Many writers have spoken of other bodily torments added to the being cast into the lake of fire. One of these, even pious Kempis, supposes that misers, for instance, have melted gold poured down their throats; and he supposes many other particular torments to be suited to men's particular sins. Nay, our great poet himself supposes the inhabitants of hell to undergo variety of tortures; not to continue always in the lake of fire, but to be frequently 'by harpy-footed furies haled'[28] into regions of ice, and then back again through 'extremes by change more fierce'. But I find no word, no tittle of this, not the least hint of it, in all the Bible. And surely this is too awful a subject to admit

---

[27] Matt. 24:35, etc.
[28] Milton, *Paradise Lost,* ii.596.

of such play of imagination. Let us keep to the written Word. It is torment enough to dwell with everlasting burnings.[29]

8. This is strongly illustrated by a fabulous story, taken from one of the eastern writers, concerning a Turkish king who, after he had been guilty of all manner of wickedness, once did a good thing; for seeing a poor man falling into a pit, wherein he must have inevitably perished, and kicking him from it, he saved his life. The story adds that when for his enormous wickedness he was cast into hell, that foot wherewith he had saved the man's life was permitted to lie out of the flames. But allowing this to be a real case, what a poor comfort would it be! What if both feet were permitted to lie out of the flames, yea, and both hands, how little would it avail! Nay, if all the body were taken out, and placed where no fire touched it, and only one hand or one foot kept in a burning fiery furnace, would the man meantime be much at ease? Nay, quite the contrary. Is it not common to say to a child, 'Put your finger into that candle: can you bear it even for one minute? How then will you bear hell-fire!' Surely it would be torment enough to have the flesh burnt off from only one finger. What then will it be to have the whole body plunged into a lake of fire burning with brimstone![30]

III. It remains now only to consider two or three circumstances attending the never-dying worm and the unquenchable fire.

1. And first consider the company wherewith everyone is surrounded in that place of torment. It is not uncommon to hear even condemned criminals in our public prisons say, 'O! I wish I was hanged out of the way, rather than to be plagued with these wretches that are round about me.' But what are the most abandoned wretches upon earth, compared to the inhabitants of hell? None of these are as yet perfectly wicked, emptied of every spark of good; certainly not till this life is at an end; probably not till the day of judgment. Nor can any of these exert without control their whole wickedness on their fellow-creatures. Sometimes they are restrained by good men; sometimes even by bad. So even the torturers in the Roman Inquisition are restrained by those that employ them when they suppose the sufferer cannot endure any more. They then order the executioners to forbear; because it is contrary to the rules of the house that a man should die upon the rack. And very frequently, when there is no human help, they are restrained by God, who hath set them their bounds which they cannot pass, and saith, 'Hitherto shall

---

[29] Is. 33:14.
[30] Rev. 19:20.

ye come, and no farther.'[31] Yea, so mercifully hath God ordained that the very extremity of pain causes a suspension of it. The sufferer faints away, and so (for a time at least) sinks into insensibility. But the inhabitants of hell are perfectly wicked, having no spark of goodness remaining. And they are restrained by none from exerting to the uttermost their total wickedness. Not by men; none will be restrained from evil by his companions in damnation. And not by God; for he hath forgotten them, hath delivered them over to the tormentors.[32] And the devils need not fear, like their instruments upon earth, lest they should expire under the torture. They can die no more: they are strong to sustain whatever the united malice, skill, and strength of angels can inflict upon them. And their angelic tormentors have time sufficient to vary their torments a thousand ways. How infinitely may they vary one single torment—horrible appearances! Whereby, there is no doubt, an evil spirit, if permitted, could terrify the stoutest man upon earth to death.

2. Consider, secondly, that all these torments of body and soul are without intermission. They have no respite from pain; but 'the smoke of their torment ascendeth up day and night.'[33] Day and night! That is speaking according to the constitution of the present world, wherein God has wisely and graciously ordained that day and night should succeed each other, so that in every four and twenty hours there comes a

> Daily sabbath, made to rest
> Toiling man and weary beast.[34]

Hence we seldom undergo much labour, or suffer much pain, before

> Tired nature's kind restorer, balmy sleep,[35]

steals upon us by insensible degrees, and brings an interval of ease. But although the damned have uninterrupted night, it brings no interruption of their pain. No sleep accompanies that darkness: whatever either ancient or modern poets, either Homer or Milton, dream, there is no sleep either in hell or heaven. And be their suffering ever so extreme, be their pain ever so intense, there is no possibility of their fainting away—no, not for a moment.

---

[31] Job 38:11.
[32] Matt. 18:34.
[33] Rev. 14:11.
[34] Mark Le Pla, *A Paraphrase on the Song of the Three Children*, st. 21, ll. 7-8.
[35] Edward Young, *Night Thoughts*, i.1.

Again. The inhabitants of earth are frequently diverted from attending to what is afflictive by the cheerful light of the sun, the vicissitudes of the seasons, 'the busy hum of men',[36] and a thousand objects that roll around them with endless variety. But the inhabitants of hell have nothing to divert them from their torments even for a moment:

> Total eclipse: no sun, no moon![37]—

no change of seasons or of companions. There is no business, but one uninterrupted scene of horror, to which they must be all attention. They have no interval of inattention or stupidity: they are all eye, all ear, all sense. Every instant of their duration it may be said of their whole frame that they are

> . . . tremblingly alive all o'er,
> And smart and agonize at every pore.[38]

3. And of this duration *there is no end*! What a thought is this! Nothing but eternity is the term of their torment! And who can count the drops of rain, or the sands of the sea, or the days of eternity? Every suffering is softened if there is any hope, though distant, of deliverance from it. But here,

> Hope never comes, that comes to all[39]

the inhabitants of the upper world! What, sufferings never do end!

> Never! Where sinks the soul at that dread sound!
> Into a gulf how dark, and how profound![40]

Suppose millions of days, of years, of ages elapsed; still we are only on the threshold of eternity! Neither the pain of body nor of soul is any nearer at an end than it was millions of ages ago. When they are once cast into *to pur to asbeston*[41] (how emphatical!), 'the fire, the unquenchable', all is concluded: 'their worm dieth not, and the fire is not quenched!'[42]

---

[36] Milton, *L'Allegro,* l.118.
[37] George Frederick Handel, *Samson, An Oratorio.*
[38] Pope, *Essay on Man,* i.197-98.
[39] Milton, *Paradise Lost,* i.66-67.
[40] Cf. *The Last Day,* iii.156-57.
[41] Mk. 9:43.
[42] Mk. 9:44, 46, 48.

Such is the account which the Judge of all gives of the punishment which he has ordained for impenitent sinners. And what a counterbalance may the consideration of this be to the violence of any temptation! In particular to the fear of man, the very use to which it is applied by our Lord himself. 'Be not afraid of them that kill the body, and after that have no more that they can do: but fear him who after he hath killed hath power to cast into hell.'[43]

What a guard may these considerations be against any temptation from pleasure! Will you lose, for any of these poor, earthly pleasures which perish in the using (to say nothing of the present substantial pleasures of religion), the pleasures of paradise, such 'as eye hath not seen, nor ear heard, neither hath it entered into our hearts to conceive'?[44] Yea, the pleasures of heaven, the society of angels, and of the spirits of just men made perfect,[45] the conversing face to face with God your Father, your Saviour, your Sanctifier, and the drinking of those rivers of pleasure that are at God's right hand for evermore?[46]

Are you tempted by pain either of body or mind? O compare present things with future. What is the pain of body which you do or may endure, to that of lying in a lake of fire burning with brimstone?[47] What is any pain of mind, any fear, anguish, sorrow, compared to 'the worm that never dieth'? That never dieth! This is the sting of all! As for our pains on earth, blessed be God, they are not eternal. There are some intervals to relieve, and there is some period to finish them. When we ask a friend that is sick how he does, 'I am in pain now,' says he, 'but I hope to be easy soon.' This is a sweet mitigation of the present uneasiness. But how dreadful would his case be if he should answer: 'I am all over pain, and I shall never be eased of it. I lie under exquisite torment of body and horror of soul; and I shall feel it for ever.' Such is the case of the damned sinners in hell. Suffer any pain, then, rather than come into that place of torment.[48]

I conclude with one more reflection, taken from Dr. Watts:

> It demands our highest gratitude that we who have long ago deserved this misery are not yet plunged into it, while there are thousands who have been adjudged to this place of punishment before they had continued so long in sin as many of us have done. What an instance is

---

[43] Lk. 12:4-5.
[44] 1 Cor. 2:9.
[45] Heb. 12:23.
[46] Cf. Ps. 36:8; Rev. 16:11.
[47] Rev. 19:20.
[48] Lk. 16:28.

it of divine goodness that we are not under this fiery vengeance! Have we not seen many sinners, on our right and left, cut off in their sins? And what but the tender mercy of God hath spared us week after week, month after month, and given us space for repentance? What shall we render unto the Lord for all his patience and long-suffering, even to this day? How often have we incurred the sentence of condemnation by our repeated rebellion against God? And yet we are still alive in his presence, and are hearing the words of hope and salvation. O let us look back and shudder at the thoughts of that dreadful precipice, on the edge of which we have so long wandered! Let us fly for refuge to the hope that is set before us, and give a thousand thanks to the divine mercy that we are not plunged into this perdition.[49]

---

[49] An abridgment and paraphrase of 'Reflection V' in the discourse "The Nature of the Punishments in Hell" (*Works* I.724).

On Faith
1791

This is Wesley's last written sermon and deals with the intermediate state. The contrast between this sermon and the prior three immediately stands out. Whereas Wesley conceived the eternal state in very material terms, he here moves directly into the immaterial. The departed are disembodied spirits who serve alongside angels or demons, depending on one's state of character and destiny. The righteous serve the heirs of salvation in this present life, while the unrighteous are the cause of all kinds of evils, including storms, earthquakes, meteor showers, diseases, mental illness, and various temptations to sin. In other words, the departed remain very engaged in the affairs of this world and in the eschatological battle between good and evil. Wesley envisions his soon departure as a release from the limitations of the human body, and expects a great increase in knowledge, holiness, and other natural capacities, like the ability to travel at the speed of thought. His opening definition of faith, based on Hebrews 11:1, reaches back to the early 1740s (see An Earnest Appeal to Men of Reason and Religion §6, Works 11:46*). Other sermons to be read in conjunction with this one are* Of Good Angels *(Works 3:4-15),* Of Evil Angels *(Works 3:16-29),* On Dives and Lazarus *(Works 4:4-18),* On the Discoveries of Faith §§8-9 *(Works 4:32-33), and* Human Life a Dream *(Works 4:109-19). Wesley's early views on angels are found in* On Guardian Angels *(Works 4:224-35). Also compare his* Notes on 2 *Corinthians 5:1-8 and* Philippians 1:21-24, *and his* Letter to Mary Bishop *on April 17, 1776 (Telford 6:214). Wesley's rejection of purgatory and his views on the intermediate state of OT saints can found in his* Reply to A Roman Catechism *(Works, Jackson, 10:98-101). For Albert Outler's introduction, see Works 4:187.*

Now faith is the evidence of things not seen.

Hebrews 11:1

1. Many times have I thought, many times have I spoke, many times have I wrote upon these words; and yet there appears to be a depth in them which I

am in no wise able to fathom. Faith is, in one sense of the word, a divine conviction of God and of the things of God; in another (nearly related to, yet not altogether the same) it is a divine conviction of the invisible and eternal world. In this sense I would now consider—

2. I am now an immortal spirit, strangely connected with a little portion of earth; but this is only for a while. In a short time I am to quit this tenement of clay, and to remove into another state,

> *which the living know not,*
> *And the dead cannot, or they may not tell!*[1]

What kind of existence shall I then enter upon? When my spirit has launched out of the body, how shall I feel myself? Perceive my own being? How shall I discern the things that are round about me, either material or spiritual objects? When my eyes no longer transmit the rays of light, how will the naked spirit *see*? When the organs of hearing are mouldered into dust, in what manner shall I *hear*? When the brain is of no farther use, what means of *thinking* shall I have? When my whole body is resolved into senseless earth, what means shall I have of gaining *knowledge*?

3. How strange, how incomprehensible, are the means whereby I shall then take knowledge even of the material world! Will things appear then as they do now? Of the same size, shape, and colour? Or will they be altered in any or all these respects? How will the sun, moon, and stars appear? The sublunary heavens? The planetary heavens? The region of the fixed stars? How the fields of ether,[2] which we may conceive to be millions of miles beyond them? Of all this we know nothing yet—and indeed we need to know nothing.

4. What then can we know of those innumerable objects which properly belong to the invisible world? Which mortal eye hath not seen, nor ear heard, neither hath it entered into our heart to conceive? What a scene will then be opened, when the regions of Hades are displayed without a covering! Our English translators seem to have been much at a loss for a word to render this. Indeed two hundred years ago it was tolerably expressed by the word 'hell', which then signified much the same with the word 'Hades', namely, the invisible world. Accordingly by Christ descending into hell they meant

---

[1] Cf. John Hughes, *The Siege of Damascus,* III.i.203-04.
[2] Cf. Richard Blackmore, 'Creation; A Philosophical Poem', in Chalmers, *British Poets,* X.380.

his body remained in the grave, his soul remained in Hades, which is the receptacle of separate spirits, from death to the resurrection. Here we cannot doubt but the spirits of the righteous are inexpressibly happy. They are, as St. Paul expresses it, 'with the Lord', favoured with so intimate a communion with him as 'is far better'[3] than whatever the chief of the apostles experienced while in this world. On the other hand, we learn from our Lord's own account of Dives and Lazarus that the rich man, from the moment he left the world, entered into a state of torment. And 'there is a great gulf fixed'[4] in Hades between the place of the holy and that of unholy spirits, which it is impossible for either the one or the other to pass over. Indeed a gentleman of great learning, the honourable Mr. Campbell, in his account of the middle state published not many years ago, seems to suppose that wicked souls may amend in Hades, and then remove to a happier mansion. He has great hopes that 'the rich man' mentioned by our Lord, in particular, might be purified by that penal fire, till, in process of time, he might be qualified for a better abode. But who can reconcile this with Abraham's assertion that none can pass over the 'great gulf'?[5]

5. I cannot therefore but think that all those who are with the rich man in the unhappy division of Hades will remain there, howling and blaspheming, cursing God and looking upwards, till they are cast into 'the everlasting fire, prepared for the devil and his angels'.[6] And on the other hand, can we reasonably doubt but that those who are now in paradise, in Abraham's bosom, all those holy souls who have been discharged from the body from the beginning of the world unto this day, will be continually ripening for heaven, will be perpetually holier and happier, till they are received into 'the kingdom prepared for them from the foundation of the world'?[7]

6. But who can inform us in what part of the universe Hades is situated? This abode of both happy and unhappy spirits till they are reunited to their bodies? It has not pleased God to reveal anything concerning it in the Holy Scripture; and consequently it is not possible for us to form any judgment or even conjecture about it. Neither are we informed how either one or the other are employed during the time of their abode there. Yet may we not improbably suppose that the Governor of the world may sometimes permit wicked souls

---

[3] Phil. 1:23.
[4] Lk. 16:26.
[5] For background information on this paragraph see Outler's comments in *Works* 4:190, n. 10, 11.
[6] Matt. 25:41.
[7] Matt. 25:34.

> To do his gloomy errands in the deep?[8]

Or perhaps, in conjunction with evil angels, to inflict vengeance on wicked men. Or will many of them be shut up in the chains of darkness unto the great judgment of the great day? In the meantime, may we not probably suppose that the spirits of the just, though generally lodged in paradise, yet may sometimes, in conjunction with the holy angels, minister to the heirs of salvation? May they not

> Sometimes on errands of love,
> Revisit their brethren below?[9]

It is a pleasing thought that some of these human spirits attending us with, or in the room of, angels, are of the number of those that were dear to us while they were in the body. So that there is no absurdity in the question:

> Have ye your own flesh forgot,
> By a common ransom bought?
> Can death's interposing tide,
> Spirits one in Christ divide?[10]

But be this as it may, it is certain human spirits swiftly increase in knowledge, in holiness, and in happiness, conversing with all the wise and holy souls that lived in all ages and nations from the beginning of the world; with angels and archangels, to whom the children of men are no more than infants; and above all with the eternal Son of God, in whom are hid all the treasures of wisdom and knowledge.[11] And let it be especially considered, whatever they learn they will retain for ever. For they forget nothing. To forget is only incident to spirits that are clothed with flesh and blood.

7. But how will this material universe appear to a disembodied spirit? Who can tell whether any of these objects that surround us will appear the same as they do now? And if we know so little of these, what can we now know concerning objects of a quite different nature? Concerning the spiritual world? It seems it will not be possible for us to discern them at all till we are

---

[8] Milton, *Paradise Lost*, i.152.
[9] Cf. Charles Wesley *Hymns for. . .Redemption* (1747), Hymn XXII, st. 2 (*Poet. Wks.*, IV.240).
[10] John and Charles Wesley, *Hymns and Sacred Poems* (1740), p. 199 (*Poet. Wks.*, I.365).
[11] Cf. Col. 2:3.

furnished with senses of a different nature, which are not yet opened in our souls. These may enable us both to penetrate the inmost substance of things, whereof we now discern only the surface, and to discern innumerable things of the very existence whereof we have not now the least perception. What astonishing scenes will then discover themselves to our newly opening senses! Probably fields of ether, not only tenfold, but ten thousandfold 'the length of this terrene'.[12] And with what variety of furniture, animate and inanimate! How many orders of beings, not discovered by organs of flesh and blood. Perhaps

> Thrones, dominions, princedoms, virtues, powers?[13]—

whether of those that retain their first habitations and primeval strength, or of those that, rebelling against their Creator, have been cast out of heaven? And shall we not then, as far as angel's ken,[14] survey the bounds of creation, and see every place where the Almighty

> Stopped his rapid wheels, and said,
> This be thy just circumference, O world.[15]

Yea, shall we not be able to move, quick as thought, through the wide realms of uncreated night? Above all, the moment we step into eternity, shall we not feel ourselves swallowed up of him who is in this and every place, who filleth heaven and earth? It is only the veil of flesh and blood which now hinders us from perceiving that the great Creator cannot but fill the whole immensity of space. He is every moment above us, beneath us, and on every side. Indeed in this dark abode, this land of shadows, this region of sin and death, the thick cloud which is interposed between conceals him from our sight. But the veil will disappear, and he will appear in unclouded majesty, God over all, blessed for ever![16]

8. How variously are the children of men employed in this world! In treading o'er

> The paths they trod six thousand years before?[17]

---

[12] Milton, *Paradise Lost*, vi.78.
[13] Ibid. v.772, 840; x.460.
[14] Ibid. i.59.
[15] Ibid., vii.224, 230-31.
[16] Rom. 9:5.
[17] Young, *The Last Day,* I.78.

But who knows how we shall be employed after we enter that invisible world? A little of it we may conceive, and that without any doubt, provided we keep to what God himself has revealed in his Word, and what he works in the hearts of his children. Let us consider, first, what may be the employment of unholy spirits from death to the resurrection. We cannot doubt but the moment they leave the body they find themselves surrounded by spirits of their own kind, probably human as well as diabolical. What power God may permit these to exercise over them we do not distinctly know. But it is not improbable he may suffer Satan to employ them, as he does his own angels, in inflicting death or evils of various kinds on the men that know not God. For this end they may raise storms by sea or by land, they may shoot meteors through the air. They may occasion earthquakes, and in numberless ways afflict those whom they are not suffered to destroy. Where they are not permitted to take away life, they may inflict various diseases—and many of these which we judge to be natural are undoubtedly diabolical. I believe this is frequently the case with lunatics. It is observable that many of those mentioned in Scripture who are called lunatics by one of the evangelists are termed demoniacs by another. One of the most eminent physicians I ever knew, particularly in cases of insanity, the late Dr. Deacon, was clearly of opinion that this was the case with many, if not most lunatics. And it is no valid objection to this that these diseases are so often cured by natural means. For a wound inflicted by an evil spirit might be cured as any other; unless that spirit was permitted to repeat the blow.

9. May not some of these evil spirits be likewise employed in conjunction with evil angels in tempting wicked men to sin, and in procuring occasion for them? Yea, and in tempting good men to sin, even after they had escaped the corruption that is in the world? Herein doubtless they put forth all their strength, and greatly glory if they conquer. A passage in an ancient author may greatly illustrate this (although I apprehend he did not intend, though, we should take it literally): 'Satan summoned his powers, and examined what mischief each of them had done. One said, "I have set a house on fire, and destroyed all its inhabitants." Another said, "I have raised a storm at sea, and sunk a ship, and all on board perished in the waters." Satan answered, "Perhaps those that were burnt or drowned were saved." A third said, "I have been forty years tempting a holy man to commit adultery. And I have left him asleep in his sin." Hearing this, Satan rose to do him honour, and all hell resounded with his praise.' Hear this, all ye that imagine you cannot fall from grace!

10. Ought not we then to be perpetually on our guard against those subtle enemies? Though we see them not,

> A constant watch they keep:
> They eye us night and day;
> And never slumber, never sleep,
> Lest they should lose their prey.[18]

Herein they join with 'the rulers of the darkness' (the intellectual darkness) 'of this world';[19] the ignorance, wickedness, and misery diffused through it to hinder all good, and promote all evil! To this end they are continually 'working', with energy, 'in the children of disobedience'.[20] Yea, sometimes they work by them those 'lying wonders'[21] that might almost deceive even the children of God.

11. But meantime, how may we conceive the inhabitants of the other part of Hades, the souls of the righteous, to be employed? It has been positively affirmed by some philosophical men that spirits have no place! But they do not observe that if it were so they must be omnipresent—an attribute which cannot be allowed to any but the Almighty Spirit. The abode of these blessed spirits the ancient Jews were used to term 'paradise'—the same name which our Lord gave it, telling the penitent thief, 'This day shalt thou be with me in paradise.'[22] Yet in what part of the universe this is situated who can tell, or even conjecture, since it has not pleased God to reveal anything concerning it? But we have no reason to think they are confined to this place; or, indeed, to any other. May we not rather say that, 'servants of his', as well as the holy angels, they 'do his pleasure',[23] whether among the inhabitants of earth or in any other part of his dominions? And as we easily believe that they are swifter than the light, even as swift as thought, they are well able to traverse the whole universe in the twinkling of an eye, either to execute the divine commands or to contemplate the works of God. What a field is here opened before them! And how immensely may they increase in knowledge, while they survey his works of creation or providence, or his manifold wisdom in the church! What depth of wisdom, of power, and of goodness do they discover in his methods of bringing many sons to glory! Especially while

---

[18] Charles Wesley, *Hymns and Sacred Poems* (1749), II.119 (*Poet. Wks.*, V.261).
[19] Eph. 6:12.
[20] Eph. 2:2.
[21] 2 Th. 2:9.
[22] Lk. 23:43.
[23] Ps. 103:21 (BCP).

they conversed on any of these subjects with the illustrious dead of ancient days! With Adam, first of men, with Noah, who saw both the primeval and the ruined world. With Abraham, the friend of God, with Moses, who was favoured to speak with God, as it were, 'face to face';[24] with Job, perfected by sufferings, with Samuel, David, Solomon, Isaiah, Daniel, and all the prophets. With the apostles, the noble army of martyrs, and all the saints who have lived and died to the present day; with our elder brethren the holy angels, cherubim, seraphim, and all the companies of heaven! Above all [with the Lord of creation himself,] with Jesus, the Mediator of the new covenant. Meantime how will they advance in holiness, in the whole image of God wherein they were created! In the love of God and man, gratitude to their Creator, and benevolence to all their fellow-creatures. Yet it does not follow (what some earnestly maintain) that this general benevolence will at all interfere with that peculiar affection which God himself implants for our relations, friends, and benefactors. O no! Had you stood by his bedside when that dying saint was crying out, 'I have a father and a mother gone to heaven' (to paradise, the receptacle of happy spirits); 'I have ten brothers and sisters gone to heaven; and now I am going to them, that am the eleventh! Blessed be God that I was born!'[25] would you have replied: 'What if you are going to them? They will be no more to you than any other persons; for you will not know them.' Not know them! Nay, does not all that is in you recoil at that thought? Indeed sceptics may ask, 'How do disembodied spirits know each other?' I answer plainly, I cannot tell. But I am certain that they do. This is as plainly proved from one passage of Scripture as it could be from a thousand. Did not Abraham and Lazarus know each other in Hades, even afar off? Even though they were fixed on different sides of the 'great gulf'?[25] Can we doubt then whether the souls that are together in paradise shall know one another? The Scripture therefore clearly decides this question. And so does the very reason of the thing. For we know every holy temper which we carry with us into paradise will remain in us for ever. But such is gratitude to our benefactors. This therefore will remain for ever. And this implies that the knowledge of our benefactors will remain, without which it cannot exist.

12. And how much will that add to the happiness of those spirits which are already discharged from the body, that they are permitted to minister to those whom they have left behind! An indisputable proof of this we have in the twenty-second chapter of the Revelation. When the Apostle fell down to worship the glorious spirit which he seems to have mistaken for Christ, he

---

[24] Ex. 33:11.
[25] Thomas Halyburton's deathbed scene.
[25] Lk. 16:26.

told him plainly, 'I am of thy fellow-servants, the prophets';[26] not God, not an angel, not a human spirit. And in how many ways may they minister to the heirs of salvation! Sometimes by counteracting wicked spirits whom we cannot resist because we cannot see them; sometimes by preventing our being hurt by men, or beasts, or inanimate creatures. How often may it please God to answer the prayer of good

Bishop Ken:

> O may thine angels while I sleep
> Around my bed their vigils keep!
> Their love angelical instil,
> Stop all the consequence of ill:
> May they celestial joys rehearse,
> And thought to thought with me converse;
> Or in my stead the whole night long
> Sing to my God a grateful song.[27]

And may not the Father of spirits allot this office jointly to angels and human spirits waiting to be made perfect?

13. It may indeed be objected that God has no need of any subordinate agents, of either angelical or human spirits, to guard his children in their waking or sleeping hours; seeing he that keepeth Israel doth neither slumber nor sleep. And certainly he is able to preserve them by his own immediate power, yea, and he is able by his own immediate power, without any instruments at all, to supply the wants of all his creatures, both in heaven and earth. But it is and ever was his pleasure not to work by his own immediate power only, but chiefly by subordinate means, from the beginning of the world. And how wonderfully is his wisdom displayed in adjusting all these to each other! So that we may well cry out: 'O Lord, how manifold are thy works! In wisdom hast thou made them all!'[28]

14. This we know concerning the whole frame and arrangement of the visible world. But how exceeding little do we now know concerning the invisible? And we should have known still less of it had it not pleased the Author of both worlds to give us more than natural light, to give us 'his word to be a

---

[26] Rev. 22:9.
[27] Thomas Ken, 'An Evening Hymn', sts. 10-11, adapted.
[28] Ps. 104:24.

lantern to our feet, and a light in all our paths'.[29] And holy men of old, being assisted by his Spirit, have discovered many particulars of which otherwise we should have had no conception.

15. And without revelation how little certainty of invisible things did the wisest of men obtain! The small glimmerings of light which they had were merely conjectural. At best they were only a faint, dim twilight, delivered from uncertain tradition; and so obscured by heathen fables that it was but one degree better than utter darkness.

16. How uncertain the best of these conjectures was may easily be gathered from their own accounts. The most finished of all these accounts is that of the great Roman poet. Where observe how warily he begins, with that apologetic preface:

Sit mihi fas audita loqui?[30]—
May I be allowed to tell what I have heard?

And in the conclusion, lest anyone should imagine he believed any of these accounts, he sends the relator of them out of Hades by the 'ivory gate', through which he had just informed us that only dreams and shadows pass![31] A very plain intimation that all which has gone before is to be looked upon as a dream!

17. How little regard they had for all these conjectures with regard to the invisible world clearly appears from the words of his brother poet, who affirms without any scruple:

Esse aliquos manes et subterranea regna
Nec pueri credunt[32]—

'That there are ghosts or realms below, not even a man of them now believes.'
So little could even the most improved reason discover concerning the invisible and eternal world. The greater cause have we to praise the Father of lights, who hath opened the eyes of our understanding[33] to discern those

---

[29] Ps. 119:105 (BCP).
[30] Virgil, *Aeneid,* vi.266.
[31] Ibid., vi.893-96.
[32] Juvenal, *Satires,* ii.149, 152.
[33] Eph. 1:18.

things which could not be seen by eyes of flesh and blood; that he who of old time shined out of darkness, hath shined in our hearts, and enlightened us with the light of the glory of God in the face of Jesus Christ,[34] the author and finisher of our faith,[35] by whom he made the worlds;[36] by whom he now sustains whatever he hath made; for

> Till nature shall her Judge survey,
> The King Messiah reigns.[37]

These things we have believed upon the testimony of God, the Creator of all things visible and invisible. By this testimony we already know the things that now exist, though not yet seen, as well as those that will exist in their season, until this visible world will pass away and the Son of man shall come in his glory.

18. Upon the whole, what thanks ought we to render to God, who has vouchsafed this 'evidence of things unseen' to the poor inhabitants of earth, who otherwise must have remained in utter darkness concerning them! How invaluable a gift is even this imperfect light to the benighted sons of men! What a relief is it to the defects of our senses, and consequently of our understanding, which can give us no information of anything but what is first presented by the senses. But hereby a new set of senses (so to speak) is opened in our souls, and by this means,

> The things unknown to feeble sense,
> Unseen by reason's glimmering ray,
> With strong, commanding evidence
>   Their heav'nly origin display.
> Faith lends its realizing light:
> The clouds disperse, the shadows fly;
> Th' Invisible appears in sight,
>   And God is seen by mortal eye![38]

---

[34] 2 Cor. 4:6.
[35] Heb. 12:2.
[36] Heb. 1:2.
[37] Samuel Wesley, Jun., 'An Hymn to God the Son', *Poems* (1736) p. 4.
[38] Charles Wesley, 'The Life of Faith', sts.5-6, in *Hymns and Sacred Poems* (1740), p.7 (*Poet. Wks.*, I.210).

Part Three

John Wesley's Explanatory Notes

on Eschatology

The Teachings of Jesus Christ

The Kingdom of God

John Wesley's views of the kingdom evolved over time. His first attempt to define the kingdom placed it squarely in the ethereal realm, in keeping with his amillennialism (Seek First the Kingdom §6, Works 4:219). His views changed when he embraced the Moravian gospel with its emphasis on present salvation. Wesley now saw the kingdom in two dimensions or phases. The kingdom of grace is Christ's present reign in the heart of the believer through the gospel. The kingdom of glory is Christ's future reign over the world at his second coming. This distinction was commonly held by supporters of the Revival (e.g. Thomas Hartley, Paradise Restored, *81, 93). In the commentary below, Wesley explains each phase of the kingdom and God's redemptive purpose to be fulfilled. What Wesley writes here should be compared to his* Notes *on Daniel 2, Matthew 25,* and *1 Corinthians 15:24, where he distinguishes between the present 'mediatorial' reign of the Son and the future 'immediate' rule of the Father. To explore further Wesley's views on the kingdom, see* An Extract of the Life and Death of Mr. Thomas Haliburton §1 *(Works, Jackson, 14:211),* The Way to the Kingdom *(Works 1:218-32),* Upon our Lord's Sermon on the Mount VI III.8 *(Works 1:581-82),* Christian Perfection II.8 *(Works 2:107-08),* The Scripture Way of Salvation I.1 *(Works 2:156), and* On the Wedding Garment §9 *(Works 4:143).*

Matthew 3:1-2

¹ In those days cometh John the Baptist, preaching in the wilderness of Judea, ² And saying, Repent ye; for the kingdom of heaven is at hand.

---

2. The kingdom of heaven and the kingdom of God are but two phrases for the same thing. They mean, not barely a future happy state in heaven, but a state to be enjoyed on earth, the proper disposition for the glory of heaven, rather than the possession of it. *Is at hand* — As if he had said, God is about to erect that kingdom, spoken of by Daniel, Daniel 2:44; 7:13, 14; the kingdom of the God of heaven. It properly signifies here, the Gospel dispensation, in which subjects were to be gathered to God by his Son, and a

The Kingdom of God

Matthew 13:1-52

¹ The same day went Jesus out of the house, and sat by the sea-side. ² And great multitudes were gathered together to him, so that he went into the <u>vessel</u>, and sat; and all the multitude stood on the shore. ³ And he spake many things to them in parables, saying, Behold, the sower went forth to sow. ⁴ And while he sowed, some *seeds* fell by the <u>highway</u> side, and the <u>birds</u> came and devoured them. ⁵ <u>Others</u> fell upon stony *places*, where they

---

society to be formed, which was to subsist first on earth, and afterward with God in glory. In some places of Scripture, the phrase more particularly denotes the state of it on earth. In others, it signifies only the state of glory; but it generally includes both. The Jews understood it of a temporal kingdom, the seat of which they supposed would be Jerusalem; and the expected sovereign of this kingdom they learned from Daniel to call the Son of man. Both John the Baptist and Christ took up that phrase, the kingdom of heaven, as they found it and gradually taught the Jews (though greatly unwilling to learn) to understand it right. The very demand of repentance, as previous to it, showed it was a spiritual kingdom, and that no wicked man, how politic, brave, or learned soever, could possibly be a subject of it.

Matthew 13 Notes
 1. Mark 4:1; Luke 8:4.
 2. AV ship. *He went into the vessel* — Which constantly waited upon him, while he was on the sea coast.
 3. *In parables* — The word is here taken in its proper sense, for apt similes or comparisons. This way of speaking, extremely common in the eastern countries, drew and fixed the attention of many, and occasioned the truths delivered to sink the deeper into humble and serious hearers. At the same time, by an awful mixture of justice and mercy, it hid them from the proud and careless. In this chapter our Lord delivers seven parables; directing the four former (as being of general concern) to all the people; the three latter to his disciples. *Behold the sower* — How exquisitely proper is this parable to be an introduction to all the rest! In this our Lord answers a very obvious and a very important question. The same sower, Christ, and the same preachers sent by him, always sow the same seed; why has it not always the same effect? He that hath ears to hear, let him hear!
 4. AV way; fowls. *And while he sowed, some seeds fell by the highway side, and the birds came and devoured them* — It is observable, that our Lord points out the grand hindrances of our bearing fruit, in the same order as they occur. The first danger is, that the birds will devour the seed. If it escape this,

had not much earth and they <u>sprung up immediately</u>, because they had not depth of earth. ⁶ And when the sun was up, they were scorched; and because they had not root, they withered away. ⁷ And some fell among thorns; and the thorns sprung up, and choked them. ⁸ And others fell into good ground, and brought forth fruit, some an hundred *fold*, some sixty, some thirty. ⁹ He that hath ears to hear, let him hear. ¹⁰ And the disciples came, and said to him, Why speakest thou to them in parables? ¹¹ He answered and said unto them, Because to you it is given to know the mysteries of the kingdom of heaven, but to them it is not given. ¹² For whosoever hath, to him shall be given, and he shall have abundance; but whosoever hath not, from him shall be taken away even what he hath. ¹³ Therefore I speak to them in parables, because seeing they see not; and hearing they hear not, neither do they understand. ¹⁴

---

there is then another danger, namely, lest it be scorched, and wither away. It is long after this that the thorns spring up and choke the good seed. A vast majority of those who hear the word of God receive the seed as by the highway side. Of those who do not lose it by the birds, yet many receive it as on stony places. Many of them who receive it in a better soil, yet suffer the thorns to grow up, and choke it: so that few even of these endure to the end, and bear fruit unto perfection: yet in all these cases, it is not the will of God that hinders, but their own voluntary perverseness.

5. AV Some; sprung up.

8. *Good ground* — Soft, not like that by the highway side; deep, not like the stony ground; purged, not full of thorns.

11. *To you, who have, it is given to know the mysteries of the kingdom of heaven* — The deep things which flesh and blood cannot reveal, pertaining to the inward, present kingdom of heaven. But to them who have not, *it is not given* — Therefore speak I in parables, that ye may understand, while they do not understand.

12. *Whosoever hath* — That is, improves what he hath, uses the grace given according to the design of the giver; *to him shall be given* — More and more, in proportion to that improvement. *But whosoever hath not* — Improves it not, *from him shall be taken even what he hath* — Here is the grand rule of God's dealing with the children of men: a rule fixed as the pillars of heaven. This is the key to all his providential dispensations; as will appear to men and angels in that day. Matthew 25:29; Mark 4:25; Luke 8:18; 19:26.

13. *Therefore I speak to them in parables, because seeing, they see not* — In pursuance of this general rule, I do not give more knowledge to this people, because they use not that which they have already: having all the

The Kingdom of God

And in them is fulfilled the prophecy of Isaiah, who saith, Hearing, ye will hear, but <u>in nowise</u> understand; and seeing ye shall see, but <u>in nowise</u> perceive. ¹⁵ For the heart of this people is waxed <u>fat</u>, and *their* ears are dull of hearing, and their eyes have they closed; lest at any time they should see with *their* eyes, and hear with *their* ears, and should understand with *their* hearts, and should be converted, and I should heal them. ¹⁶ But blessed are your eyes, for they see; and your ears, for they hear. ¹⁷ For verily I say unto you, That many prophets and righteous men have desired to see the things which ye see, and have not seen *them;* and to hear the things which ye hear, and have not heard *them.*

¹⁸ Hear ye therefore the parable of the sower. ¹⁹ When any one heareth the word of the kingdom, and <u>considereth</u> *it* not, the wicked *one* cometh, and catcheth away what was sown in his heart. This is he who received seed by the <u>highway</u> side. ²⁰ But he who received the seed into stony *places,* is he that heareth the word, and <u>immediately</u> receiveth it with joy; ²¹ Yet hath he not root in himself, and so endureth but for a while; for when tribulation or persecution ariseth because of the word, <u>straightway</u> he is offended. ²² He

---

means of seeing, hearing, and understanding, they use none of them: they do not effectually see, or hear, or understand any thing.

14. AV shall not. *Hearing ye will hear, but in nowise understand* — That is, Ye will surely hear. All possible means will be given you: yet they will profit you nothing; because your heart is sensual, stupid, and insensible; your spiritual senses are shut up; yea, you have closed your eyes against the light; as being unwilling to understand the things of God, and afraid, not desirous that he should heal you. Isaiah 6:9; John 12:40; Acts 28:26.

15. AV gross.

16. *But blessed are your eyes* — For you both see and understand. You know how to prize the light which is given you. Luke 10:23.

19. AV understandeth; way. *When any one heareth the word, and considereth it not* — The first and most general cause of unfruitfulness. *The wicked one cometh* — Either inwardly; filling the mind with thoughts of other things; or by his agent. Such are all they that introduce other subjects, when men should be considering what they have heard.

20. AV anon. *The seed sown on stony places, therefore sprang up soon, because it did not sink deep,* Matthew 13:5. *He receiveth it with joy* — Perhaps with transport, with ecstasy: struck with the beauty of truth, and drawn by the preventing grace of God.

21. AV by and by. *Yet hath he not root in himself* — No deep work of grace: no change in the ground of his heart. Nay, he has no deep conviction;

also that received seed among the thorns is he that heareth the word; and the care of this world, and the deceitfulness of riches, choke the word, and it becometh unfruitful. ²³ But he that received seed on the good ground is he that heareth the word, and <u>considereth</u> *it;* who also beareth fruit, and bringeth forth, some an hundred *fold,* some sixty, some thirty.

²⁴ He proposed to them another parable, saying, The kingdom of heaven is like a man sowing good seed in his field. ²⁵ But while men slept, his enemy came and sowed <u>darnel</u> amidst the wheat, and went away. ²⁶ And

---

and without this, good desires soon wither away. *He is offended* — He finds a thousand plausible pretenses for leaving so narrow and rugged a way.

22. *He that received the seed among the thorns, is he that heareth the word and considereth it* — In spite of Satan and his agents: yea, hath root in himself is deeply convinced, and in a great measure inwardly changed; so that he will not draw back, even when tribulation or persecution ariseth. And yet even in him, together with the good seed, the thorns spring up, Matthew 13:7. (perhaps unperceived at first) till they gradually choke it, destroy all its life and power, and it becometh unfruitful. Cares are thorns to the poor: wealth to the rich; the desire of other things to all. *The deceitfulness of riches* — Deceitful indeed! For they smile, and betray; kiss, and smite into hell. They put out the eyes, harden the heart, steal away all the life of God; fill the soul with pride, anger, love of the world; make men enemies to the whole cross of Christ! And all the while are eagerly desired, and vehemently pursued, even by those who believe there is a God!

23. AV understandeth. *Some a hundred fold, some sixty, some thirty* — That is, in various proportions; some abundantly more than others.

24. *He proposed another parable* — in which he farther explains the case of unfruitful hearers. The kingdom of heaven (as has been observed before) sometimes signifies eternal glory; sometimes the way to it, inward religion; sometimes, as here, the Gospel dispensation. The phrase is likewise used for a person or thing relating to any one of those; so in this place it means, Christ preaching the Gospel, *who is like a man sowing good seed* — The expression, is like, both here and in several other places, only means, that the thing spoken of may be illustrated by the following similitude. *Who sowed good seed in his field* — God sowed nothing but good in his whole creation. Christ sowed only the good seed of truth in his Church.

25. AV tares. *But while men slept* — They ought to have watched; the Lord of the field sleepeth not. *His enemy came and sowed darnel* — This is very like wheat, and commonly grows among wheat rather than among other grain; but tares or vetches are of the pulse kind, and bear no resemblance to wheat.

The Kingdom of God

when the blade was sprung up, and brought forth fruit, then appeared the <u>darnel</u> also. ²⁷ So the servants of the householder came to him, and said, Sir, didst not thou sow good seed in thy field? Whence then hath it <u>darnel</u>? ²⁸ He said to them, An enemy hath done this. The servants said to him, Wilt thou then that we go and gather them up? ²⁹ But he said, No; lest, gather up the <u>darnel</u>, ye root up the wheat with them. ³⁰ Suffer both grow together till the harvest; and at the time of the harvest I will say to the reapers, Gather ye together first the darnel, and bind it in bundles to burn it; but gather the wheat into my barn.

³¹ He proposed to them another parable, saying, The kingdom of heaven is like a grain of mustard seed, which a man took and sowed in his field. ³² Which indeed is the least of all seeds; but when it is grown up, it is the greatest of herbs, and becometh a tree, so that the birds of the air come and lodge in the branches of it.

---

26. *When the blade was sprung up, then appeared the darnel* — It was not discerned before; it seldom appears, as soon as the good seed is sown: all at first appears to be peace, and love, and joy.

27. *Didst not thou sow good seed in thy field? Whence then hath it darnel?* — Not from the parent of good. Even the heathen could say, "No evil can from thee proceed, 'Tis only suffer'd, not decreed; as darkness is not from the sun, nor mount the shades, till he is gone."

28. *He said, An enemy hath done this* — A plain answer to the great question concerning the origin of evil. God made men (as he did angels) intelligent creatures, and consequently free either to choose good or evil; but he implanted no evil in the human soul. An enemy (with man's concurrence) hath done this. Darnel, in the Church, is properly outside Christians, such as have the form of godliness, without the power. Open sinners, such as have neither the form nor the power, are not so properly darnel, as thistles and brambles; these ought to be rooted up without delay, and not suffered in the Christian community. Whereas should fallible men attempt to gather up the darnel they would often root up the wheat with them.

31. *He proposed to them another parable* — The former parables relate chiefly to unfruitful hearers; these that follow, to those who bear good fruit. *The kingdom of heaven* — Both the Gospel dispensation, and the inward kingdom. Mark 4:30; Luke 13:18.

32. *The least* — That is, one of the least: a way of speaking extremely common among the Jews. *It becometh a tree* — In those countries it grows exceeding large and high. So will the Christian doctrine spread in the world, and the life of Christ in the soul.

^{33} He spake another parable to them. The kingdom of heaven is like leaven, which a woman taking covered up in three measures of meal, till the whole was leavened. ^{34} All these things spake Jesus to the multitude in parables; and without a parable spake he not unto them. ^{35} Whereby was fulfilled what was spoken by the prophet, saying, I will open my mouth in parables; I will utter things <u>hid</u> from the foundation of the world.

^{36} Then Jesus, having sent the multitude away, went into the house; and his disciples came to him, saying, Declare to us the parable of the <u>darnel</u> of the field. ^{37} He answering said to them, He that soweth the good seed is the Son of Man. ^{38} The field is the world; the good seed are the children of the kingdom; but the <u>darnel</u> are the children of the wicked one; ^{39} The enemy that sowed them is the devil; the harvest is the end of the world; the reapers are the angels. ^{40} As therefore the <u>darnel</u> is gathered and burned <u>with</u> fire; so shall it be at the end of this world. ^{41} The Son of Man shall send forth his angels, and they shall gather out of his kingdom all things that offend, and them that do iniquity. ^{42} And shall cast them into a furnace of fire; there shall be wailing and the gnashing of teeth. ^{43} Then shall the righteous shine forth as the sun in the kingdom of their Father. He that hath ears to hear, let him hear.

^{44} Again, the kingdom of heaven is like treasure hid in a field; which a man having found hideth, and for joy thereof goeth and selleth all that he hath, and buyeth that field.

---

33. *Three measures* — This was the quantity which they usually baked at once: *till the whole was leavened* — Thus will the Gospel leaven the world and grace the Christian. Luke 13:20.

34. *Without a parable spake he not unto them* — That is, not at that time; at other times he did.

35. AV which have been kept secret. Psalm 78:2.

38. *The good seed are the children of the kingdom* — That is, the children of God, the righteous.

40. AV tares; in the.

41. *They shall gather all things that offend* — Whatever had hindered or grieved the children of God; whatever things or persons had hindered the good seed which Christ had sown from taking root or bearing fruit. The Greek word is, All scandals.

44. The three following parables are proposed, not to the multitude, but peculiarly to the apostles: the two former of them relate to those who receive the Gospel; the third, both to those who receive, and those who preach it. *The kingdom of heaven is like treasure hid in a field* — The kingdom of God

⁴⁵ Again, the kingdom of heaven is like a merchant man, seeking goodly pearls. ⁴⁶ Who, having found one pearl of great value, went and sold all that he had, and bought it.

⁴⁷ Again, the kingdom of heaven is like a net cast into the sea, and gathering of every kind. ⁴⁸ Which, when it was full, they drew to the shore, and sitting down gathered the good into vessels, but cast the bad away. ⁴⁹ So shall it be at the end of the world. The angels shall come forth, and sever the wicked from among the just. ⁵⁰ And shall cast them into the furnace of fire; there shall be the wailing and the gnashing of teeth. ⁵¹ Jesus saith to them, Have ye understood all these things? They say to him, Yea, Lord. ⁵² Then said he to them, Therefore every scribe instructed unto the kingdom of heaven is like an householder, who <u>bringeth out</u> of his treasure things new and old.

Mark 4:21-29

²¹ And he said to them, Is a candle brought to be put under a bushel, or under a bed, and not to be set on a candlestick? ²² For there is nothing hid,

---

within us is a treasure indeed, but a treasure hid from the world, and from the most wise and prudent in it. He that finds this treasure, (perhaps when he thought it far from him) hides it deep in his heart, and gives up all other happiness for it.

45. *The kingdom of heaven* — That is, one who earnestly seeks for it; in verse Matthew 13:47 it means, the Gospel preached, which is like a net gathering of every kind. Just so the Gospel, wherever it is preached, gathers at first both good and bad, who are for a season full of approbation and warm with good desires. But Christian discipline and strong, close exhortation begin that separation in this world, which shall be accomplished by the angels of God in the world to come.

52. AV bringeth forth out. *Every scribe instructed unto the kingdom of heaven* — That is, every duly prepared preacher of the Gospel has a treasure of Divine knowledge, out of which he is able to bring forth all sorts of instructions. The word treasure signifies any collection of things whatsoever, and the places where such collections are kept.

Mark 4 Notes

21. *And he said, Is a candle* — As if he had said, I explain these things to you, I give you this light, not to conceal, but to impart it to others. And if I

which shall not be made manifest, neither was any thing kept secret, but that it might come abroad. ²³ If any man hath ears to hear, let him hear. ²⁴ And he said to them, Take heed what ye hear. With what measure ye mete, it shall be measured to you; and to you that hear, shall more be given. ²⁵ For he that hath, to him shall be given; and he that hath not, from him shall be taken even that which he hath.

²⁶ And he said, So is the kingdom of God, as if a man should cast seed into the ground. ²⁷ And should sleep, and rise night and day, and the seed should spring and grow up he knoweth not how. ²⁸ For the earth bringeth forth fruit of itself; first the blade, then the ear, after that the corn in the ear. ²⁹ But when the fruit is brought forth, immediately he putteth in the sickle, because the harvest is come.

---

conceal any thing from you now, it is only that it may be more effectually manifested hereafter. Matthew 5:15; Luke 8:16; 11:33.

22. Matthew 10:26; Luke 8:17.

24. *Take heed what ye hear* — That is, attend to what you hear, that it may have its due influence upon you. *With what measure you mete* — That is, according to the improvement you make of what you have heard, still farther assistance shall be given. *And to you that hear* — That is, with improvement.

25. *He that hath* — That improves whatever he has received, to the good of others, as well as of his own soul. Matthew 13:12; Luke 8:18.

26. *So is the kingdom of God* — The inward kingdom is like seed which a man casts into the ground. This a preacher of the Gospel casts into the heart. And he *sleeps and rises night and day* — That is, he has it continually in his thoughts. Meantime it *springs and grows up he knows not how* — Even he that sowed it cannot explain how it grows. For as the earth by a curious kind of mechanism, which the greatest philosophers cannot comprehend, does as it were spontaneously bring forth *first the blade, then the ear, then the full corn in the ear*. So the soul, in an inexplicable manner, brings forth, first weak graces, then stronger, then full holiness; and all this of itself, as a machine, whose spring of motion is within itself. Yet observe the amazing exactness of the comparison. The earth brings forth no corn (as the soul no holiness) without both the care and toil of man, and the benign influence of heaven.

29. *He putteth in the sickle* — God cutteth down and gathereth the corn into his garner.

The Kingdom of God

Luke 17:20-37

²⁰ And <u>being asked by</u> the Pharisees, When cometh the kingdom of God? He answered them and said, The kingdom of God cometh not with observation. ²¹ Neither shall they say, Lo here! Or, lo there! For, behold, the kingdom of God is within you. ²² And he said to the disciples, The days will come, when ye shall desire to see one of the days of the Son of Man, and ye shall not see *it*. ²³ And when they shall say to you, See here; see there; <u>go not</u>, nor follow *them*. ²⁴ For as the lightning, that lighteneth out of the one *part* under heaven, shineth to the other *part* under heaven; so shall the Son of Man be in his day. ²⁵ But first must he suffer many things, and be rejected by this generation. ²⁶ And as it was in the days of Noah, so shall it be also in the days of the Son of Man. ²⁷ They ate, they drank, they <u>married</u>, they were given in marriage, till the day that Noah entered into the ark, and the flood came, and destroyed them all. ²⁸ Likewise also as it was in the days of Lot; they ate, they drank, they bought, they sold, they planted, they builded. ²⁹ But the <u>day</u> that Lot went out of Sodom it rained fire and brimstone from heaven, and destroyed them all. ³⁰ Even thus shall it be in the day that the Son of Man is revealed. ³¹ In that day, he that shall be on the house-top, and his <u>goods</u> in the house, let him not go down to take them away; and he that is in the field,

---

20. AV he was demanded of. *The kingdom of God cometh not with observation* — With such outward pomp as draws the observation of every one.

21. *Neither shall they say, Lo here, or lo there* — This shall not be the language of those who are, or shall be sent by me, to declare the coming of my kingdom. *For behold the kingdom of God is within or among you* — Look not for it in distant times or remote places: it is now in the midst of you: it is come: it is present in the soul of every true believer: it is a spiritual kingdom, an internal principle. Wherever it exists, it exists in the heart.

22. *Ye shall desire to see one of the days of the Son of man* — One day of mercy or one day wherein you might converse with me, as you do now.

23. AV go not after them. *They shall say, See, Christ is here, or there* — Limiting his presence to this or that place. Matthew 24:23.

24. *So shall also the Son of man be* — So swift, so wide, shall his appearing be: *In his day* — The last day.

26. *The days of the Son of man* — Those which immediately follow that which is eminently styled his day. Matthew 24:37.

27. AV married wives.

29. AV same day.

let him likewise not return back. ³² Remember Lot's wife. ³³ Whosoever shall seek to save his life shall lose it; and whosoever shall lose *his life* shall preserve it. ³⁴ I tell you, in <u>this</u> night, there shall be two men in one bed; one shall be taken, and the other left. ³⁵ Two women shall be grinding together; one shall be taken, and the other left. ³⁶ Two men shall be in the field; one shall be taken, and the other left. ³⁷ And they answering said to him, Where, Lord? And he said to them, Wheresoever the body *is,* there will the eagles be gathered together.

---

31. AV stuff. *In that day* — (Which will be the grand type of the last day) when ye shall see Jerusalem encompassed with armies.

32. *Remember Lot's wife* — And escape with all speed, without ever looking behind you. Luke 9:24; John 12:25.

33. *The sense of this and the following verses is, Yet as great as the danger will be, do not seek to save your life by violating your conscience: if you do, you will surely lose it: whereas if you should lose it for my sake, you shall be paid with life everlasting. But the most probable way of preserving it now, is to be always ready to give it up: a peculiar Providence shall then watch over you, and put a difference between you and other men.*

34. AV that.

37. Matthew 24:28.

Hymn 72
2 Corinthians 5:1-9

We know, by faith we know,
If this vile house of clay,
This tabernacle, sink below
In ruinous decay,
We have a house above,
Not made with mortal hands;
And firm as our Redeemer's love
That heavenly fabric stands.

It stands securely high,
Indissolubly sure;
Our glorious mansion in the sky
Shall evermore endure;
O were we entered there,
To perfect heaven restored!
O were we all caught up to share
The triumph of our Lord!

Absent, alas! From God,
We in the body mourn;
And pine to quit this mean abode,
And languish to return.
Jesus, regard our vows,
And change our faith to sight,
And clothe us with our nobler house
Of empyrean light!

O let us put on thee
In perfect holiness;
And rise prepared thy face to see,
Thy bright, unclouded face;
Thy grace with glory crown,
Who hast the earnest given,
And now triumphantly come down
And take our souls to heaven.

1746, *Works* 7:171-72

The Fall of Jerusalem and the Parousia of Christ
Matthew 24:1-51; Mark 13:1-37; Luke 21:5-36

Wesley understood salvation history to be the sacred narrative of God restoring his kingdom reign over the entire created order. Regarding the prophetic scriptures, this narrative runs as 'one complete chain of prophecy' from Daniel through the Gospels with the final chapters foretold in the Revelation (Rev. 1:3). In the prophecy below, Jesus foretells the events leading up to the destruction of the Temple in AD 70 (Matt. 24:1-28) followed by his glorious return (Matt. 24:29-31). The gap between these two eschatological events is filled in by the Book of Revelation to form a seamless narrative of God's kingdom rule, from the first coming to the second coming of Christ. As for sources, Wesley acknowledged his debt to Jewish historian Flavius Josephus (Matt. 24:14; Lk. 21:11). A comparison of his Notes *with other commentators demonstrates his views were influenced the most by Johann Bengel.*

Matthew 24:1-51

¹ And Jesus, going out of the temple, departed, and his disciples came to *him*, to show him the buildings of the temple. ² And Jesus said to them, Do ye see all these things? Verily I say to you. There shall not be left here one stone upon another, which shall not be thrown down.

³ And as he sat on the Mount of Olives, his disciples came to him privately, saying, Tell us, when shall these things be? And what *shall be* the sign of thy coming, and of the end of the world? ⁴ And Jesus answering said,

---

1. Mark 13:1; Luke 21:5.

2. *There shall not be left one stone upon another* — This was most punctually fulfilled; for after the temple was burnt, Titus, the Roman general, ordered the very foundations of it to be dug up; after which the ground on which it stood was ploughed up by Turnus Rufus.

3. *As he sat on the mount of Olives* — Whence they had a full view of the temple. When shall these things be? And what shall be the sign of thy coming, *and of the end of the world?* — The disciples inquire confusedly:

1. Concerning the time of the destruction of the temple;

Take heed that no man deceive you. ⁵ For many will come in my name, saying, I am Christ; and will deceive many. ⁶ And ye shall hear of wars and rumours of wars; see that ye be not troubled; for all *these* things must come to pass, but the end is not yet. ⁷ For nation shall rise against nation, and kingdom against kingdom; and there shall be famines, and pestilences, and earthquakes, in divers places. ⁸ All these *are* the beginning of sorrows. ⁹ Then shall they deliver you up to affliction, and will kill you; and ye shall be hated of all nations for my name's sake. ¹⁰ And then will many be offended, and will betray one another, and hate one another. ¹¹ And many false prophets

---

2. Concerning the signs of Christ's coming, and of the end of the world, as if they imagined these two were the same thing.

Our Lord answers distinctly concerning:

1. The destruction of the temple and city, with the signs preceding, ver. 4, etc., 15, etc. Matthew 24:4, 15.
2. His own coming and the end of the world, with the signs thereof, ver. 29-31. Matthew 24:29-31.
3. The time of the destruction of the temple, ver. 32, etc. Matthew 24:32.
4. The time of the end of the world, ver. 36. Matthew 24:36.

4. *Take heed that no man deceive you* — The caution is more particularly designed for the succeeding Christians, whom the apostles then represented. The first sign of my coming is the rise of false prophets. But it is highly probable many of these things refer to more important events which are yet to come.

5. *Many shall come in my name* — First, false Christs; next, false prophets, Matthew 24:11. At length, both together, Matthew 24:24. And indeed never did so many impostors appear in the world as a few years before the destruction of Jerusalem; undoubtedly because that was the time wherein the Jews in general expected the Messiah.

6. *Wars* — Near: *Rumors of wars* — At a distance. *All these things must come to pass* — As a foundation for lasting tranquility. *But the end* — Concerning which ye inquire, *is not yet* — So far from it, that this is but the beginning sorrows.

9. *Then shall they deliver you up to affliction* — As if ye were the cause of all these evils. *And ye shall be hated* of *all nations* — Even of those who tolerate all other sects and parties; but in no nation will the children of the devil tolerate the children of God. Matthew 10:17.

10. *Then shall many be offended* — So as utterly to make shipwreck of faith and a pure conscience. But hold ye fast faith, Matthew 24:11. in spite of

will rise, and will deceive many. ¹² And because iniquity shall abound, the love of many will wax cold. ¹³ But he that shall endure to the end, the same shall be saved. ¹⁴ And this gospel of the kingdom shall be preached in all the world for a testimony to all nations; and then shall the end come. ¹⁵ When therefore ye see the abomination of desolation, spoken of by Daniel the prophet, standing in the holy place (he that readeth, let him understand); ¹⁶ then let them who are in Judea flee to the mountains. ¹⁷ Let not him that is on

---

false prophets: love, even when iniquity and offenses abound, Matthew 24:12. And hope, unto the end, Matthew 24:13. He that does so shall be snatched out of the burning. *The love of many will wax cold* — The generality of those who love God will (like the Church at Ephesus, Revelation 2:4) leave their first love.

13. Matthew 10:22; Mark 13:13; Luke 21:17.

14. AV witness. *This Gospel shall be preached in all the world* — Not universally: this is not done yet: but in general through the several parts of the world, and not only in Judea. And this was done by St. Paul and the other apostles, before Jerusalem was destroyed. *And then shall the end come* — Of the city and temple. Josephus's "History of the Jewish War" is the best commentary on this chapter. it is a wonderful instance of God's providence, that he, an eye witness, and one who lived and died a Jew, should, especially in so extraordinary a manner, be preserved, to transmit to us a collection of important facts, which so exactly illustrate this glorious prophecy, in almost every circumstance. Mark 13:10.

15. *When ye see the abomination of desolation* — Daniel's term is, The abomination that maketh desolate, Daniel 11:31; that is, the standards of the desolating legions, on which they bear the abominable images of their idols: *Standing in the holy place* — Not only the temple and the mountain on which it stood, but the whole city of Jerusalem, and several furlongs of land round about it, were accounted holy; particularly the mount on which our Lord now sat, and on which the Romans afterward planted their ensigns. *He that readeth let him understand* — Whoever reads that prophecy of Daniel, let him deeply consider it. Mark 13:14; Luke 21:20; Daniel 9:27.

16. *Then let them who are in Judea flee to the mountains* — So the Christians did, and were preserved. It is remarkable that after the Romans under Cestus Gallus made their first advances toward Jerusalem, they suddenly withdrew again, in a most unexpected and indeed impolitic manner. This the Christians took as a signal to retire, which they did, some to Pella, and others to Mount Libanus.

The Fall of Jerusalem and the Parousia of Christ

the housetop come down to take any thing out of his house. [18] Neither let him who is in the field return back to take his clothes. [19] But woe to them that are with child, and to them that give suck in those days! [20] And pray ye that your flight be not in the winter, neither on the Sabbath. [21] For then shall be great tribulation, such as was not from the beginning of the world to this time, nor ever shall be. [22] And unless those days were shortened, no flesh would be saved; but for the elect's sake those days shall be shortened. [23] Then if any man shall say to you, Lo, here *is* Christ, or there; believe *it* not. [24] For false Christs and false prophets will arise, and shall show great signs and wonders; so that they would deceive, if possible, even the elect. [25] Behold, I have told you before. [26] Therefore if they say to you, Behold, he is in the desert; go not forth. Behold, *he is* in the secret chambers; believe *it* not. [27] For as the lightning goeth forth from the east, and shineth even to the west, so shall also

---

17. *Let not him that is on the house top come down to take any thing out of his house* — It may be remembered that their stairs used to be on the outside of their houses.

19. *Woe to them that are with child, and to them that give suck* — Because they cannot so readily make their escape.

20. AV Sabbath day. *Pray ye that your flight be not in the winter* — They did so; and their flight was in the spring. *Neither on the Sabbath* — Being on many accounts inconvenient; beside that many would have scrupled to travel far on that day. For the Jews thought it unlawful to walk above two thousand paces (two miles) on the Sabbath day.

21. *Then shall be great tribulation* — Have not many things spoken in the chapter, as well as in Mark 13:14 etc., Luke 21:2 etc. a farther and much more extensive meaning than has been yet fulfilled?

22. *And unless those days were shortened* — By the taking of Jerusalem sooner than could be expected: *No flesh would be saved* — The whole nation would be destroyed. *But for the elect's sake* — That is, for the sake of the Christians.

23. Mark 13:21; Luke 17:23.

24. AV the very. *They would deceive, if possible, the very elect* — But it is not possible that God should suffer the body of Christians to be thus deceived.

the coming of the Son of Man be. ²⁸ For wheresoever the carcase is, there will the eagles be gathered together.

²⁹ Immediately after the tribulation of those days the sun shall be darkened, and the moon shall not give her light, and the stars shall fall from heaven, and the powers of the heavens shall be shaken. ³⁰ And then shall appear the sign of the Son of Man in heaven; and then shall all the tribes of the earth mourn, and shall see the Son of Man coming in the clouds of heaven with power and great glory. ³¹ And he will send forth his angels with a loud-sounding trumpet, and they shall gather together his elect from the four winds, from one end of heaven to the other.

³² Learn a parable from the fig tree; when its branch is now tender, and shooteth forth leaves, ye know that summer *is* nigh. ³³ So likewise when ye

---

27. AV cometh out. *For as the lightning goeth forth* — For the next coming of Christ will be as quick as lightning; so that there will not be time for any such previous warning.

28. *For wheresoever the carcass is, there will the eagles he gathered together* — Our Lord gives this, as a farther reason, why they should not hearken to any pretended deliverer. As if he had said, "Expect not any deliverer of the Jewish nation; for it is devoted to destruction. It is already before God a dead carcass, which the Roman eagles will soon devour." Luke 17:37.

29. *Immediately after the tribulation of those days* — Here our Lord begins to speak of his last coming. But he speaks not so much in the language of man as of God, with whom a thousand years are as one day, one moment. Many of the primitive Christians not observing this, thought he would come immediately, in the common sense of the word: a mistake which St. Paul labors to remove, in his Second Epistle to the Thessalonians. *The powers of the heavens* — Probably the influences of the heavenly bodies. Mark 13:24; Luke 21:25.

30. *Then shall appear the sign of the Son of man in heaven* — It seems a little before he himself descends. The sun, moon, and stars being extinguished (probably not those of our system only), the sign of the Son of man (perhaps the cross) will appear in the glory of the Lord.

31. *They shall gather together his elect* — That is, all that have endured to the end in the faith which worketh by love.

32. *Learn a parable* — Our Lord having spoke of the signs preceding the two grand events, concerning which the apostles had inquired, begins here to speak of the time of them. And to the question proposed, Matthew 24:3, concerning the time of the destruction of Jerusalem, he answers Matthew

see all these things, know that it is nigh, *even* at the doors. ³⁴ Verily I say to you, This generation shall not pass away till all these things be done. ³⁵ Heaven and earth shall pass away, but my words shall not pass away. ³⁶ But of that day and hour knoweth no *man,* neither the angels of heaven, but my Father only. ³⁷ But as the days of Noah, so shall also the coming of the Son of Man be. ³⁸ For as in the days that were before the flood they were eating and drinking, marrying and giving in marriage, til the day that Noah entered into the ark. ³⁹ And knew not till the flood came, and took them all away; so shall also the coming of the Son of Man be.

⁴⁰ Then shall two men be in the field; one is taken, and one is left. ⁴¹ Two women *shall* be grinding in the mill; one is taken, and one is left.

⁴² Watch therefore, for ye know not what hour your Lord cometh. ⁴³ But ye know this, that if the householder had known in what watch the thief would have come, he would have watched, and not have suffered his house to be broken open. ⁴⁴ Therefore be ye also ready; for at an hour ye think not the Son of Man cometh. ⁴⁵ Who then is the faithful and wise servant, whom his lord hath appointed ruler over his household, to give them food in due season? ⁴⁶ Happy *is* that servant, whom his lord coming shall find so doing.

24:34. Concerning the time of the end of the world, he answers Matthew 24:36. Mark 13:28; Luke 21:29.

34. AV fulfilled. *This generation of men now living shall not pass till all these things be done* — The expression implies, that great part of that generation would be passed away, but not the whole. Just so it was. For the city and temple were destroyed thirty-nine or forty years after.

36. *But of that day* — The day of judgment; *Knoweth no man* — Not while our Lord was on earth. Yet it might be afterward revealed to St. John consistently with this.

37. Luke 17:26.

40. *One is taken* — Into God's immediate protection: *and one is left* — To share the common calamities. Our Lord speaks as having the whole transaction present before his eyes.

41. *Two women shall be grinding* — Which was then a common employment of women.

42. *Ye know not what hour your Lord cometh* — Either to require your soul of you, or to avenge himself of this nation. Mark 13:33; Luke 12:35; 21:34.

43. AV goodman of the house; up.

45. AV made; meat. *Who then is the faithful and wise servant* — Which of you aspires after this character? *Wise* — Every moment retaining the

⁴⁷ Verily I say to you, He will appoint him ruler over all his goods. ⁴⁸ But if that evil servant say in his heart, My lord delayeth his coming. ⁴⁹ And shall begin to smite his fellow-servants, and shall eat and drink with the drunken. ⁵⁰ The lord of that servant shall come in a day that he <u>expecteth</u> *him* <u>not</u>, and in an hour that he is not aware of. ⁵¹ And shall cut him asunder, and <u>allot</u> him his portion with the hypocrites; there shall be the weeping and the gnashing of teeth.

Mark 13:1-37

¹ And as he was going out of the temple, one of his disciples saith to him, Master, see what manner of stones and what manner of buildings! ² And Jesus answering said to him, Seest thou these great buildings? There shall not be left one stone upon another, that shall not be thrown down. ³ And as he sat on the Mount of Olives over against the temple, Peter and James and John and Andrew asked him privately, ⁴ Tell us when shall these things be? And what *shall be* the sign when all these things shall be fulfilled? ⁵ And Jesus answering them said, Take heed lest any deceive you. ⁶ For many will come

---

clearest conviction, that all he now has is only entrusted to him as a steward: *Faithful* — Thinking, speaking, and acting continually, in a manner suitable to that conviction.

46. AV Blessed.

48. *But if that evil servant* — Now evil, having put away faith and a good conscience.

50. AV looketh not for *him*.

51. AV appoint. *And allot him his portion with the hypocrites* — The worst of sinners, as upright and sincere as he was once. If ministers are the persons here primarily intended, there is a peculiar propriety in the expression. For no hypocrisy can be baser than to call ourselves ministers of Christ while we are the slaves of avarice, ambition, or sensuality. Wherever such are found, may God reform them by his grace, or disarm them of that power and influence, which they continually abuse to his dishonor, and to their own aggravated damnation!

Mark 13 Notes

1. Matthew 24:1; Luke 21:5.

4. *Two questions are here asked; the one concerning the destruction of Jerusalem: the other concerning the end of the world.*

in my name, saying, I am _he;_ and will deceive many. ⁷ But when ye shall hear of wars and rumours of wars, be not troubled; for *it* must be, but the end *is* not yet. ⁸ For nation shall rise against nation, and kingdom against kingdom; and there shall be earthquakes in divers places, and there shall be famines and troubles; these *are* the beginnings of sorrows.

⁹ But take heed to yourselves; for they will deliver you to councils; and ye shall be beaten in synagogues; and shall stand before rulers and kings for my sake, for a testimony to them. ¹⁰ And the gospel must first be published among all nations. ¹¹ But when they shall hale you, and deliver *you* up, take no thought beforehand what ye shall speak, neither do ye premeditate; but whatsoever shall be given you in that hour, that speak; for it is not ye that speak, but the Holy Ghost. ¹² Now the brother shall betray the brother to death, and the father the son; and children shall rise up against their parents, and cause them to be put to death. ¹³ And ye shall be hated of all men for my name's sake; but he that endureth to the end, he shall be saved.

¹⁴ But when ye shall see the abomination of desolation, spoken of by Daniel the prophet, standing where it ought not (let him that readeth understand), then let them that be in Judea flee to the mountains. ¹⁵ And let not him that is on the housetop go down into the house, neither enter in, to take any thing out of his house. ¹⁶ And let not him that is in the field turn back to take up his garment. ¹⁷ But woe to them that are with child, and to them that give suck in those days! ¹⁸ And pray ye that your flight be not in the winter. ¹⁹ For in those days shall be affliction, such as was not from the beginning of the creation which God created until now, neither shall be. ²⁰ And unless the Lord had shortened those days, no flesh should be saved; but for the elect's sake, whom he hath chosen, he hath shortened those days. ²¹

---

6. AV *Christ.*

9. AV against. Luke 21:12.

10. Matthew 24:14.

11. AV lead. *The Holy Ghost will help you. But do not depend upon any other help; for all the nearest ties will be broken.*

14. *Where it ought not* — That place being set apart for sacred use. Matthew 24:15; Luke 21:20; Daniel 9:27.

19. AV this time. *In those days shall be affliction, such as was not from the beginning of the creation* — May it not be doubted, whether this be yet fully accomplished? Is not much of this affliction still to come?

20. AV the. *The elect* — The Christians: *whom he hath chosen* — That is, hath taken out of, or separated from, the world, through sanctification of the

Then if any man say to you, Lo, here *is* Christ; or, lo, *he is* there; believe *it* not. ²² For false Christs and false prophets shall rise, and shall show signs and wonders, to seduce, if possible, even the elect. ²³ But take ye heed; behold, I have foretold you all things.

²⁴ But in those days, after that tribulation, the sun shall be darkened, and the moon shall not give her light. ²⁵ And the stars of heaven shall <u>be falling</u>, and the powers that are in <u>the heavens</u> shall be shaken. ²⁶ And then shall they see the Son of Man coming in the clouds with great power and glory. ²⁷ And then shall he send his angels, and shall gather together his elect from the four winds, from the uttermost part of the earth to the uttermost part of heaven.

²⁸ Now learn a parable from the fig tree. When its branch is now tender, and putteth forth leaves, ye know that summer is <u>nigh</u>. ²⁹ So likewise when ye see these things come to pass, know that he is nigh, *even* at the door. ³⁰ Verily I say to you, This generation shall in nowise pass, till all these things be done. ³¹ Heaven and earth shall pass away; but my words shall in nowise pass away.

³² But of that day or that hour knoweth no one; no, not the angels that are in heaven, neither the Son, but the Father. ³³ Take heed, watch and pray; for ye know not when the time is. ³⁴ *For the Son of Man is* as a man taking a far journey, who left his house, and gave authority to his servants, and to each his work, and commanded the porter to watch. ³⁵ Watch ye therefore; for ye

---

Spirit and belief of the truth. *He hath shortened* — That is, will surely shorten.

21. AV *him.* Matthew 24:23.

24. *But in those days* — Which immediately precede the end of the world: *after that tribulation* — Above described.

25. AV fall; heaven.

28. AV near. Matthew 24:32; Luke 21:28.

29. *He is nigh* — The Son of man.

30. *All these things* — Relating to the temple and the city.

32. *Of that day* — The day of judgment is often in the Scriptures emphatically called that day. *Neither the Son* — Not as man: as man he was no more omniscient than omnipresent. But as God he knows all the circumstances of it.

33. Matthew 24:42; Luke 21:34.

34. *The Son of man is as a man taking a far journey* — Being about to leave this world and go to the Father, he appoints the services that are to be performed by all his servants, in their several stations. This seems chiefly to

know not when the master of the house cometh, at evening, or at midnight, or at the cockcrowing, or in the morning. ³⁶ Lest coming suddenly he find you sleeping. ³⁷ And what I say to you I say unto all, Watch.

Luke 21:5-36

⁵ And as some spake of the temple, that it was adorned with goodly stones and gifts, he said, ⁶ *As for* these things which ye behold, the days will come, in the which there shall not be left one stone upon another, that shall not be thrown down. ⁷ And they asked him, saying, Master, when shall these things be? And what *is* the sign when these things shall come to pass? ⁸ And he said, Take heed that ye be not deceived; for many shall come in my name, saying, I am *the Christ;* and the time is near; go ye not after them. ⁹ And when ye shall hear of wars and commotions, be not terrified; for these things must be first; but the end *is* not <u>immediately</u>. ¹⁰ Then said he to them, Nation shall rise against nation, and kingdom against kingdom. ¹¹ And great earthquakes shall be in divers places, and famines, and pestilences; and there shall be fearful sights, and great signs from heaven. ¹² But before all these things they shall lay their hands on you, and persecute *you,* delivering *you* up to the synagogues, and into prisons, being brought before kings and rulers for my

---

respect ministers at the day of judgment: but it may be applied to all men, and to the time of death. Matthew 25:14; Luke 19:12.

Luke 21 Notes

5. *Goodly stones* — Such as no engines now in use could have brought, or even set upon each other. *Some of them (as an eye witness who lately measured them writes) were forty* — five cubits long, five high, and six broad; yet brought thither from another country. *And gifts* — Which persons delivered from imminent dangers had, in accomplishment of their vows, hung on the walls and pillars. The marble of the temple was so white, that it appeared like a mountain of snow at a distance. And the gilding of many parts made it, especially when the sun shone, a most splendid and beautiful spectacle. Matthew 24:1; Mark 13:1.

8. AV draweth. *I am the Christ; and the time is near* — When I will deliver you from all your enemies. They are the words of the seducers.

9. AV by and by. *Commotions* — Intestine broils; civil wars.

11. *Fearful sights and signs from heaven* — Of which Josephus gives a circumstantial account.

name's sake. ¹³ And it shall turn to you for a testimony. ¹⁴ Settle it therefore in your hearts, not to <u>premeditate</u> what to answer. ¹⁵ For I will give you a mouth and wisdom, which all your adversaries shall not be able to gainsay nor resist. ¹⁶ But ye shall be betrayed by parents, and brethren, and kinsfolk, and friends; and *some* of you they will cause to be put to death. ¹⁷ And ye shall be hated of all men for my name's sake. ¹⁸ But there shall not an hair of your head perish. ¹⁹ In your patience possess ye your souls. ²⁰ And when ye see Jerusalem compassed with armies, then know that the desolation thereof is nigh. ²¹ Then let them which are in Judea flee to the mountains; and let them that are in the midst of it depart out; and let not them that are in the countries enter into it. ²² For these are the days of vengeance, that all things which are written may be fulfilled. ²³ But woe to them that are with child, and to them that give suck, in those days! For there shall be great distress in the land, and wrath on this people. ²⁴ And they shall fall by the edge of the sword, and shall be led away captive into all nations; and Jerusalem shall be trodden by the Gentiles, until the times of the Gentiles are fulfilled.

---

12. Mark 13:9.

13. *It shall turn to you for a testimony* — Of your having delivered your own souls, and of their being without excuse.

14. AV meditate.

16. Matthew 10:21.

17. Matthew 24:13; Mark 13:13.

18. *Not a hair of your head* — A proverbial expression, *shall perish* — Without the special providence of God. And then, not before the time, nor without A full reward.

19. *In your patience possess ye your souls* — Be calm and serene, masters of yourselves, and superior to all irrational and disquieting passions. By keeping the government of your spirits, you will both avoid much misery, and guard the better against all dangers.

21. *Let them that are in the midst of it* — Where Jerusalem stands (that is, they that are in Jerusalem) depart out of it, before their retreat is cut off by the uniting of the forces near the city, and let not them that are in the adjacent countries by any means enter into it.

22. And things which are written — Particularly in Daniel.

24. *They shall fall by the edge of the sword, and shall be led away captive* — Eleven hundred thousand perished in the siege of Jerusalem, and above ninety thousand were sold for slaves. *So terribly was this prophecy fulfilled! And Jerusalem shall be trodden by the Gentiles* — That is, inhabited. So it was indeed. The land was sold, and no Jew suffered even to come within

^{25} And there shall be signs in the sun and moon, and stars; and upon the earth distress of nations, with perplexity; the sea roaring and tossing; ^{26} Men fainting away for fear, and expectation of the things coming upon the world; for the powers of the heavens shall be shaken. ^{27} And then shall they see the Son of Man coming in a cloud, with power and great glory.

^{28} Now when these things begin to come to pass, look up, and lift up your heads; for your redemption draweth nigh.

^{29} And he spake a parable to them, Behold the fig tree, and all the trees. ^{30} When they now shoot forth, ye see and know of yourselves that summer is now nigh. ^{31} So likewise when ye see these things come to pass, know that the kingdom of God is nigh. ^{32} Verily I say unto you, This generation shall not pass away, till all things be effected. ^{33} Heaven and earth shall pass away; but my words shall in nowise pass away. ^{34} But take heed to yourselves, lest at any time your hearts be overloaded with gluttony, and drunkenness, and

---

sight of Jerusalem. The very foundations of the city were ploughed up, and a heathen temple built where the temple of God had stood. *The times of the Gentiles* — That is, the times limited for their treading the city; which shall terminate in the full conversion of the Gentiles.

25. AV sea and waves roaring. JW added "and tossing." *And there shall be* — Before the great day, which was typified by the destruction of Jerusalem: *signs* — Different from those mentioned Luke 21:11, etc. Matthew 24:29; Mark 13:24.

26. AV Men's hearts failing them; for looking after those; earth; heaven.

28. *Now when these things* — Mentioned Luke 21:8, 10, etc., begin to come to pass, look up with firm faith, and lift up your heads with joy: for your redemption out of many troubles draweth nigh, by God's destroying your implacable enemies.

29. *Behold the fig tree and all the trees* — Christ spake this in the spring, just before the passover; when all the trees were budding on the mount of Olives, where they then were.

30. AV nigh at hand. *Ye know of yourselves* — Though none teach you.

31. AV nigh at hand. *The kingdom of God is nigh* — The destruction of the Jewish city, temple, and religion, to make way for the advancement of my kingdom.

32. AV be fulfilled. *Till all things be effected* — All that has been spoken of the destruction of Jerusalem, to which the question, Luke 21:7, relates: and which is treated of from Luke 21:8-24.

33. AV not.

the cares of this life, and so that day come upon you unawares. ³⁵ For as a snare shall it come on all them that <u>sit</u> on the face of the whole earth. ³⁶ Watch ye therefore, and pray always, that ye may be accounted worthy to escape all these things which will come to pass, and to stand before the Son of Man.

---

34. AV overcharged, surfeiting. *Take heed, lest at any time your hearts be overloaded with gluttony and drunkenness* — And was there need to warn the apostles themselves against such sins as these? Then surely there is reason to warn even strong Christians against the very grossest sins. Neither are we wise, if we think ourselves out of the reach of any sin: *and so that day* — Of judgment or of death, come upon you, even you that are not of this world-Unawares. Matthew 24:42; Mark 13:33; Luke 12:35.

35. AV dwell. *That sit* — Careless and at ease.

36. *Watch ye therefore* — This is the general conclusion of all that precedes. *That ye may be counted worthy* — This word sometimes signifies an honor conferred on a person, as when the apostles are said to be counted worthy to suffer shame for Christ, Acts 5:41. Sometimes meet or becoming: as when John the Baptist exhorts, to bring fruits worthy of repentance, Luke 3:8. And so to be counted worthy to escape, is to have the honor of it, and to be fitted or prepared for it. *To stand* — With joy and triumph: not to fall before him as his enemies.

Hymn 61

How happy are the little flock,
Who safe beneath their guardian rock
    In all commotions rest!
When wars and tumult's waves run high,
Unmoved above the storm they lie,
    They lodge in Jesu's breast.

Such happiness, O Lord, have we,
By mercy gathered into thee
    Before the floods descend:
And while the bursting cloud comes down,
We mark the vengeful day begun,
    And calmly wait the end.

The plague, and dearth, and din of war,
Our Saviour's swift approach declare,
    And bid our hearts arise:
Earth's basis shook confirms our hope,
Its cities' fall but lifts us up
    To meet thee in the skies…

Whatever ills the world befall
A pledge of endless good we call,
    A sign of Jesus near.
His chariot will not long delay;
We hear the rumbling wheels, and pray,
    Triumphant Lord, appear!

1756, *Works* 7:156-57

The Epistles of Paul

The selections below address several eschatological themes in an unsystematic manner, yet reveal important insights in the development of Wesley's end-times 'system' (if it is even possible to speak of such a thing). A good example is Romans 8:18-27, which foreshadows Wesley's new creation eschatology found in The General Deliverance *and* The New Creation. *Others passages, like Romans 11:7-32, 2 Thessalonians 2:1-13, and 2 Timothy 3:1-5 deal with 'signs' that were expected to precede the end of this age. These should be compared to what Wesley wrote later in* The Mystery of Iniquity, The General Spread of the Gospel, *and* The Signs of the Times. *Regarding the papal Antichrist, Wesley's notes below should be read in conjunction with Revelation 13-19 and 1 John 2:18-29. The last passage illustrates how Wesley could at times broaden the identity of the Antichrist to include teachers he sharply disagreed with, like the mystics, latitudinarians, and Count Zinzendorf (Works 18:246; 2:92-93; 26:16, 558). Wesley's views on the Papacy are also found in his reply to* A Roman Catechism *(Works, Jackson, 10:87-89) and the tract* The Advantage of the Members of the Church of England over Those of the Church of Rome *(Works, Jackson, 10:138-39). Concerning the gathering of living believers at Christ's coming, compare what Wesley says at 1 Corinthians 15 and 1 Thessalonians 4:17 with* The Great Assize II.3 *and the 1744 Minutes Q. 16 (Works, Jackson, 8:277-78).*

Groaning for the New Creation
Romans 8:18-27

[18] For I reckon that the sufferings of the present time *are* not worthy *to be compared* with the glory which shall be revealed in us. [19] For the earnest expectation of the <u>creation</u> waiteth for the <u>revelation</u> of the sons of God. [20]

---

18. *For I reckon* — This verse gives the reason why he but now mentioned sufferings and glory. When that glory "shall be revealed in us," then the sons of God will be revealed also.

19. AV creature; manifestation. *For the earnest expectation* — The word denotes a lively hope of something drawing near, and a vehement longing

For the <u>creation</u> was made subject to vanity, not willingly, but <u>by him</u> who subjected *it, in hope* ²¹ that the <u>creation</u> itself shall be delivered from the bondage of corruption into the glorious liberty of the children of God. ²² For we know that the whole creation <u>groaneth together</u> and <u>travaileth together</u> until now. ²³ And not only *they,* but even we ourselves, who have the firstfruits of the Spirit, even we ourselves groan within ourselves, waiting for the adoption, the redemption of our body. ²⁴ For we are saved by hope; but hope that is seen is not hope; for what a man seeth, why doth he yet hope

---

after it. *Of the creation* — Of all visible creatures, believers excepted, who are spoken of apart; each kind, according as it is capable. All these have been sufferers through sin; and to all these (the finally impenitent excepted) shall refreshment redound from the glory of the children of God. Upright heathens are by no means to be excluded from this earnest expectation: nay, perhaps something of it may at some times be found even in the vainest of men; who (although in the hurry of life they mistake vanity for liberty, and partly.

20. AV creature; by reason of him; *the same* in hope (in AV v 21 ends with comma). *The creation was made subject to vanity* — Abuse, misery, and corruption. *By him who subjected it* — Namely, God, Genesis 3:17, 5:29. Adam only made it liable to the sentence which God pronounced; yet not without hope.

21. AV creature. *The creation itself shall be delivered* — Destruction is not deliverance: therefore whatsoever is destroyed, or ceases to be, is not delivered at all. Will, then, *any part of the creation be destroyed? Into the glorious liberty* — The excellent state wherein they were created.

22. AV groaneth; tavaileth in pain together. *For the whole creation groaneth together* — With joint groans, as it were with one voice. *And travaileth* — Literally, is in the pains of childbirth, to be delivered of the burden of the curse. *Until now* — To this very hour; and so on till the time of deliverance.

23. *And even we, who have the first-fruits of the Spirit* — That is, the Spirit, who is the first-fruits of our inheritance. *The adoption* — Persons who had been privately adopted among the Romans were often brought forth into the forum, and there publicly owned as their sons by those who adopted them. So at the general resurrection, when the body itself is redeemed from death, the sons of God shall be publicly owned by him in the great assembly of men and angels. *The redemption of our body* — From corruption to glory and immortality.

for? ²⁵ But if we hope for what we see not, we patiently wait for it. ²⁶ Likewise the Spirit also helpeth our infirmities; for we know not what we should pray for as we ought; but the Spirit itself maketh intercession for us with groanings which cannot be uttered. ²⁷ But he who searcheth the hearts knoweth what *is* the mind of the Spirit, for he maketh intercession for the saints according to God.

The Conversion of the Jews
Romans 11:7-32

⁷ What then? Israel hath not obtained that which he seeketh; but the election hath obtained, and the rest were blinded. ⁸ According as it is written, God hath given them a spirit of slumber, eyes that they should not see, and ears that they should not hear, unto this day. ⁹ And David saith, Let their table become a snare, and a trap, and a stumblingblock, and a recompence to

---

24. *For we are saved by hope* — Our salvation is now only in hope. We do not yet possess this full salvation.

26. *Likewise the Spirit* — Nay, not only the universe, not only the children of God, but the Spirit of God also himself, as it were, groaneth, while he helpeth our infirmities, or weaknesses. Our understandings are weak, particularly in the things of God our desires are weak; our prayers are weak. *We know not* — Many times. *What we should pray for* — Much less are we able to pray for it as we ought: *but the Spirit maketh intercession for us* — In our hearts, even as Christ does in heaven. *With groanings* — The matter of which is from ourselves, but the Spirit forms them; and they are frequently inexpressible, even by the faithful themselves

27. AV to *the will of* God. *But he who searcheth the hearts* — Wherein the Spirit dwells and intercedes. *Knoweth* — Though man cannot utter it. What is the mind of the Spirit, *for he maketh intercession for the saints* — Who are near to God. *According to God* — According to his will, as is worthy of God. and acceptable to him.

Romans 11 Notes

7. *What then* — What is the conclusion from the whole? It is this: that Israel in general hath not obtained justification; but those of them only who believe. *And the rest were blinded* — By their own wilful prejudice.

8. God hath at length withdrawn his Spirit, and so given them up to a spirit of slumber; which is fulfilled unto this day. Isaiah 29:10.

them. ¹⁰ Let their eyes be darkened, that they may not see, and bow down their back always.

¹¹ I say then, Have they stumbled so as to fall? God forbid. But <u>by</u> their fall salvation *is come* to the <u>gentiles</u>, to provoke them to jealousy. ¹² But if their fall *be* the riches of the world, and <u>their loss</u> the riches of the <u>gentiles</u>; how much more their fulness? ¹³ For I speak to you <u>gentiles</u>, as I am the apostle of the <u>gentiles</u>, I magnify my office. ¹⁴ If by any means I may provoke to jealousy *those who are* my flesh, and save some of them. ¹⁵ For if the casting away of them *be* the reconciling of the world, what *will* the receiving *of them be,* but life from the dead? ¹⁶ For if the <u>first-fruits</u> *be* holy, so *is* the lump; and if the root *be* holy, so *are* the branches. ¹⁷ And if some of

---

9. *And David saith* — In that prophetic imprecation, which is applicable to them, as well as to Judas. *A recompence* — Of their preceding wickedness. So sin is punished by sin; and thus the gospel, which should have fed and strengthened their souls, is become a means of destroying them. Psalm 69:22, 23.

11. AV through; Gentiles. Have they stumbled so as to fall — Totally and finally? No But by their fall — Or slip: it is a very soft word in the original. Salvation is come to the gentiles — See an instance of this, Acts 13:46. To provoke them — The Jews themselves, to jealousy.

12. AV the diminishing of them. The first part of this verse is treated of, Romans 11:13, etc.; the latter, *How much more their fullness,* (that is, their full conversion,) Romans 11:23, etc. So many prophecies refer to this grand event, that it is surprising any Christian can doubt of it. And these are greatly confirmed by the wonderful preservation of the Jews as a distinct people to this day. When it is accomplished, it will be so strong a demonstration, both of the Old and New Testament revelation, as will doubtless convince many thousand Deists, in countries nominally Christian; of whom there will, of course, be increasing multitudes among merely nominal Christians. And this will be a means of swiftly propagating the gospel among Mahometans and Pagans; who would probably have received it long ago, had they conversed only with real Christians.

13. *I magnify my office* — Far from being ashamed of ministering to the gentiles, I glory therein; the rather, as it may be a means of provoking my brethren to jealousy.

14. *My flesh* — My kinsmen.

15. *Life from the dead* — Overflowing life to the world, which was dead.

16. AV firstfruit. *And this will surely come to pass. For if the first fruits be holy, so is the lump* — The consecration of them was esteemed the

the branches were broken off, and thou, being a wild olive tree, wert grafted in among them, and with them partakest of the root and fatness of the olive tree; [18] boast not against the branches. But if thou boast, thou bearest not the root, but the root thee. [19] Wilt thou say then, The branches were broken off, that I might be <u>grafted in</u>? [20] Well; they were broken off for unbelief, and thou standest by faith. Be not highminded, but fear. [21] For if God spared not the natural branches, *take heed* lest he also spare not thee.

[22] Behold therefore the goodness and severity of God. Toward them that fell, severity; but toward thee, goodness, if thou continue in *his* goodness; else shalt thou also be cut off. [23] And they, if they do not continue in unbelief, shall be grafted in; for God is able to graft them in again. [24] For if thou wert <u>cut off</u> from the natural wild olive tree, and grafted contrary to nature into a good olive tree; how much more shall these, who are the natural *branches,* be grafted into their own olive tree?

[25] Brethren, I would not that ye should be ignorant of this mystery, lest ye should be wise in your own conceits; that <u>hardness</u> is in part happened to

---

consecration of all and so the conversion of a few Jews is an earnest of the conversion of all the rest. *And if the root be holy* — The patriarchs from whom they spring, surely God will at length make their descendants also holy.

17. *Thou* — O gentile. *Being a wild olive tree* — Had the graft been nobler than the stock, yet its dependance on it for life and nourishment would leave it no room to boast against it. How much less, when, contrary to what is practiced among men, the wild olive tree is engrafted on the good!

18. *Boast not against the branches* — Do not they do this who despise the Jews? or deny their future conversion?

19. AV grafted in.(JW turned the sentence into a question).

20. *They were broken off for unbelief, and thou standest by faith* — Both conditionally, not absolutely: if absolutely, there might have been room to boast. *By faith* — The free gift of God, which therefore ought to humble thee.

21. *Be not highminded, but fear* — We may observe, this fear is not opposed to trust, but to pride and security.

22. *Else shalt thou* — Also, who now "standest by faith," be both totally and finally cut off.

24. AV cut out. *Contrary to nature* — For according to nature, we graft the fruitful branch into the wild stock; but here the wild branch is grafted into the fruitful stock.

The Epistles of Paul

Israel, till the fulness of the <u>gentiles</u> be come in; ²⁶ and so all Israel shall be saved. As it is written, The deliverer shall come out of Sion, and shall turn away <u>iniquity</u> from Jacob. ²⁷ And this *is* my covenant with them, when I shall take away their sins. ²⁸ With regard to the gospel, *they are* enemies for your sake; but as for the election, *they are* beloved, for the sake of their fathers. ²⁹ For the gifts and the calling of God *are* without repentance. ³⁰ <u>As then ye were once disobedient to God</u>, but have now obtained mercy through their <u>disobedience</u>. ³¹ So these also have now been <u>disobedient</u>, that through your mercy they may likewise find mercy. ³² For God hath <u>shut up all together in disobedience</u>, that he might have mercy upon all.

---

25. AV blindness; gentiles. St. Paul calls any truth known but to a few, a mystery. Such had been the calling of the gentiles: such was now the conversion of the Jews. *Lest ye should be wise in your own conceits* — Puffed up with your present advantages; dreaming that ye are the only church; or that the church of Romans cannot fail. *Hardness in part is happened to Israel, till* — Israel therefore is neither totally nor finally rejected. *The fulness of the gentiles be come in* — Till there be a vast harvest amongst the heathens.

26. AV ungodliness. *And so all Israel shall be saved* — Being convinced by the coming of the gentiles. But there will be a still larger harvest among the gentiles, when all Israel is come in. *The deliverer shall come* — Yea, the deliverer is come; but not the full fruit of his coming. Isaiah 59:20

28. *They are now enemies* — To the gospel, to God, and to themselves, which God permits. For your sake: *but as for the election* — That part of them who believe, they are beloved.

29. *For the gifts and the calling of God are without repentance* — God does not repent of his gifts to the Jews, or his calling of the gentiles.

30. AV For as ye in times past have not believed God; unbelief.

31. AV unbelief.

32. AV concluded them all in unbelief. *For God hath shut up all together in disobedience* — Suffering each in their turn to revolt from him. First, God suffered the gentiles in the early age to revolt, and took the family of Abraham as a peculiar seed to himself. Afterwards he permitted them to fall through unbelief, and took in the believing gentiles. And he did even this to provoke the Jews to jealousy, and so bring them also in the end to faith. This was truly a mystery in the divine conduct, which the apostle adores with such holy astonishment.

The Resurrection Body
1 Corinthians 15:22-58

[20] But now is Christ risen from the dead, the first fruit of them that slept. [21] For since by man *came* death, by man *came* also the resurrection of the dead. [22] For as through Adam all die, even so through Christ shall all be made alive. [23] But every one in his own order: Christ the first fruit; afterward they who are Christ's, at his coming. [24] Then *cometh* the end, when he shall have delivered up the kingdom to God, even the Father; when he shall have abolished all rule and all authority and power. [25] For he must reign, till he hath put all enemies under his feet. [26] The last enemy *that* is destroyed *is*

---

22. AV in. *As through Adam all, even the righteous, die, so through Christ all these shall be made alive* — He does not say, "shall revive," (as naturally as they die,) but shall be made alive, by a power not their own.

23. *Afterward* — The whole harvest. At the same time the wicked shall rise also. But they are not here taken into the account.

24. AV put down. *Then* — After the resurrection and the general judgment. *Cometh the end* — Of the world; the grand period of all those wonderful scenes that have appeared for so many succeeding generations. When he shall have delivered up the kingdom to the Father, and he (the Father) shall have abolished all adverse rule, authority, *and power* — Not that the Father will then begin to reign without the Son, nor will the Son then cease to reign. For the divine reign both of the Father and Son is from everlasting to everlasting. But this is spoken of the Son's mediatorial kingdom, which will then be delivered up, and of the immediate kingdom or reign of the Father, which will then commence. Till then the Son transacts the business which the Father hath given him, for those who are his, and by them as well as by the angels, with the Father, and against their enemies. So far as the Father gave the kingdom to the Son, the Son shall deliver it up to the Father, John 13:3. Nor does the Father cease to reign, when he gives it to the Son; neither the Son, when he delivers it to the Father: but the glory which he had before the world began, John 17:5; Hebrews 1:8, will remain even after this is delivered up. Nor will he cease to be a king even in his human nature, Luke 1:33. If the citizens of the new Jerusalem" shall reign for ever," Revelation 22:5, how much more shall he?

25. *He must reign* — Because so it is written. *Till he* — the Father hath put all his enemies under his feet. Psalm 110:1.

death. ²⁷ For he hath put all things under his feet. But when he saith, All things are put under *him, it is* manifest that who did put all things under him is escepted. ²⁸ But when all things shall be put under him, then shall the Son also be subject to him that put all things under him, that God may be all in all. ²⁹ Else what shall they do who are baptized for the dead, if the dead rise not at all? Why are they then baptized for them? ³⁰ Why are we also in danger every hour? ³¹ I protest by your rejoicing, brethren, which I have in Christ Jesus our Lord, I die daily. ³² If after the manner of men, I have fought with wild beasts at Ephesus, what advantageth it me, if the dead rise not? Let us eat and drink; for tomorrow we die. ³³ Be not deceived. Evil

---

26. AV shall be. *The last enemy that is destroyed is death* — Namely, after Satan, Hebrews 2:14, and sin, 1 Corinthians 15:56, are destroyed. In the same order they prevailed. Satan brought in sin, and sin brought forth death. And Christ, when he of old engaged with these enemies, first conquered Satan, then sin, in his death; and, lastly, death, in his resurrection. In the same order he delivers all the faithful from them, yea, and destroys these enemies themselves. Death he so destroys that it shall be no more; sin and Satan, so that they shall no more hurt his people.

27. *Under him* — Under the Son. Psalm 8:6, 7.

28. AV subdued unto. *The Son also shall be subject* — Shall deliver up the mediatorial kingdom. *That the three-one God may be all in all* — All things, (consequently all persons,) without any interruption, without the intervention of any creature, without the opposition of any enemy, shall be subordinate to God. All shall say, "My God, and my all." This is the end. Even an inspired apostle can see nothing beyond this.

29. *Who are baptized for the dead* — Perhaps baptized in hope of blessings to be received after they are numbered with the dead. Or, *"baptized in the room of the dead"* — Of them that are just fallen in the cause of Christ: like soldiers who advance in the room of their companions that fell just before their face.

30. *Why are we* — The apostles. *Also in danger every hour* — It is plain we can expect no amends in this life.

31. *I protest by your rejoicing, which I have* — Which love makes my own. *I die daily* — I am daily in the very jaws of death. Beside that I live, as it were, in a daily martyrdom.

32. AV beasts. *If to speak after the manner of men* — That is, to use a proverbial phrase, *expressive of the most imminent danger I have fought with wild beasts at Ephesus* — With the savage fury of a lawless multitude, Acts 19:29, etc. This seems to have been but just before. Let as eat, etc. — We

communications corrupt good manners. [34] Awake to righteousness, and sin not; for some have not the knowledge of God. I speak *this* to your shame. [35] But some one will say, How are the dead raised up? And with what kind of body do they come? [36] Thou fool, that which thou sowest is not quickened except it die. [37] And that which thou sowest, thou sowest not the body that shall be, but a bare grain, perhaps of wheat, or of some other <u>corn</u>. [38] But God giveth it a body as it hath pleased him, and to each of the seeds its own body. [39] All flesh *is* not the same flesh; but *there is* one *kind of* flesh of men,

---

might, on that supposition, as well say, with the Epicureans, Let us make the best of this short life, seeing we have no other portion.

33. *Be not deceived* — By such pernicious counsels as this. *Evil communications corrupt good manners* — He opposes to the Epicurean saying, *a well* — known verse of the poet Menander. *Evil communications* — Discourse contrary to faith, hope, or love, naturally tends to destroy all holiness.

34. *Awake* — An exclamation full of apostolical majesty. *Shake off your lethargy! To righteousness* — Which flows from the true knowledge of God, and implies that your whole soul be broad awake. *And sin not* — That is, and ye will not sin Sin supposes drowsiness of soul. There is need to press this. *For some among you have not the knowledge of God* — With all their boasted knowledge, they are totally ignorant of what it most concerns them to know. *I speak this to your shame* — For nothing is more shameful, than sleepy ignorance of God, and of the word and works of God; in these especially, considering the advantages they had enjoyed.

35. *But some one possibly will say, How are the dead raised up, after their whole frame is dissolved? And with what kind of bodies do they come again, after these are mouldered into dust?*

36. To the inquiry concerning the manner of rising, and the quality of the bodies that rise, the Apostle answers first by a similitude, 1 Corinthians 15:36-42, and then plainly and directly, 1 Corinthians 15:42, 43. *That which thou sowest, is not quickened into new life and verdure, except it die* — Undergo a dissolution of its parts, a change analogous to death. Thus St. Paul inverts the objection; as if he had said, Death is so far from hindering life, that it necessarily goes before it.

37. AV grain. *Thou sowest not the body that shall be* — Produced from the seed committed to the ground, but a bare, naked grain, widely different from that which will afterward rise out of the earth.

38. *But God* — Not thou, O man, not the grain itself, giveth it a body as it hath pleased him, from the time he distinguished the various Species of

another of beasts, another of birds, another of fishes. ⁴⁰ *There are* also heavenly bodies, and *there are* earthly bodies; but the glory of the heavenly *is* one, and that of the earthly another. ⁴¹ *There is* one glory of the sun, and another glory of the moon, and another glory of the stars; for *one* star differeth from *another* star in glory. ⁴² So also *is* the resurrection of the dead. It is sown in corruption; it is raised in incorruption: ⁴³ It is sown in dishonour; it is raised in glory. It is sown in weakness; it is raised in power. ⁴⁴ It is sown an animal body; it is raised a spiritual body. There is an animal body, and there is a spiritual body. ⁴⁵ And so it is written, The first man

---

beings; and to each of the seeds, not only of the fruits, but animals also, (to which the Apostle rises in the following verse,) its own body; not only peculiar to that species, but proper to that individual, and arising out of the substance of that very grain.

39. *All flesh* — As if he had said, Even earthy bodies differ from earthy, and heavenly bodies from heavenly. What wonder then, if heavenly bodies differ from earthy? or the bodies which rise from those that lay in the grave?

40. AV celestial; terrestrial. *There are also heavenly bodies* — As the sun, moon, and stars; *and there are earthy* — as vegetables and animals. But the brightest luster which the latter can have is widely different from that of the former.

41. *Yea, and the heavenly bodies themselves differ from each other.*

42. *So also is the resurrection of the dead* — So great is the difference between the body which fell, and that which rises. *It is sown* — A beautiful word; committed, as seed, to the ground. *In corruption* — Just ready to putrefy, and, by various degrees of corruption and decay, to return to the dust from whence it came. *It is raised in incorruption* — Utterly incapable of either dissolution or decay.

43. *It is sown in dishonor* — Shocking to those who loved it best, *human nature in disgrace! It is raised in glory* — Clothed with robes of light, fit for those whom the King of heaven delights to honor. *It is sown in weakness* — Deprived even of that feeble strength which it once enjoyed. *It is raised in power* — Endued with vigor, strength, and activity, such as we cannot now conceive.

44. AV natural. *It is sown in this world a merely animal body* — Maintained by food, sleep, and air, like the bodies of brutes: but it is raised of a more refined contexture, needing none of these animal refreshments, and endued with qualities of a spiritual nature, like the angels of God.

Adam was made a living soul; the last Adam *is* a quickening spirit. ⁴⁶ Yet the spiritual *body was* not first; but the animal; afterward the spiritual. ⁴⁷ The first man *was* from the earth, earthy; the second man *is* the Lord from heaven. ⁴⁸ As <u>was</u> the earthy, such *are* they also *that are* earthy; and *as* <u>was</u> the heavenly, such *are* they also that are heavenly. ⁴⁹ And as we have borne the image of the earthy, we shall also bear the image of the heavenly.

⁵⁰ But this I say, brethren, that flesh and blood cannot inherit the kingdom of God; neither doth corruption inherit incorruption. ⁵¹ Behold, I show you a mystery. We shall not all sleep, but we shall all be changed. ⁵² In a moment, in the twinkling of an eye, at the last trumpet; for the trumpet shall sound, and

---

45. *The first Adam was made a living soul* — God gave him such life as other animals enjoy: but the last Adam, Christ, *is a quickening spirit* — As he hath life in himself, so he quickeneth whom he will; giving a more refined life to their very bodies at the resurrection. Genesis 2:7.

47. *The first man was from the earth, earthy; the second man is the Lord from heaven-The first man, being from the earth, is subject to corruption and dissolution, like the earth from which he came. The second man* — St. Paul could not so well say, "Is from heaven, heavenly:" because, though man owes it to the earth that he is earthy, yet the Lord does not owe his glory to heaven. He himself made the heavens, and by descending from thence showed himself to us as the Lord. Christ was not the second man in order of time; but in this respect, that as Adam was a public person, who acted in the stead of all mankind, so was Christ. As Adam was the first general representative of men, Christ was the second and the last. And what they severally did, terminated not in themselves, but affected all whom they represented.

48. AV is. *They that are earthy* — Who continue without any higher principle. *They that are heavenly* — Who receive a divine principle from heaven.

49. *The image of the heavenly* — Holiness and glory.

50. *But first we must be entirely changed; for such flesh and blood as we are clothed with now, cannot enter into that kingdom which is wholly spiritual: neither doth this corruptible body inherit that incorruptible kingdom.*

51. *A mystery* — A truth hitherto unknown; and not yet fully known to any of the sons of men. *We* — Christians. The Apostle considers them all as one, in their succeeding generations. *Shall not all die* — Suffer a separation of soul and body. *But we shall all* — Who do not die, *be changed* — So that this animal body shall become spiritual.

The Epistles of Paul

the dead shall be raised incorruptible, and we shall be changed. ⁵³ For this corruptible must put on incorruption, and this mortal put on immortality. ⁵⁴ So when this corruptible shall have put on incorruption, and this mortal shall have put on immortality, then shall be brought to pass the saying that is written, Death is swallowed up in victory. ⁵⁵ O death, where *is* thy sting? O Hades, where *is* thy victory? ⁵⁶ The sting of death *is* sin; and the strength of sin *is* the law. ⁵⁷ But thanks *be* to God, who hath given us the victory through our Lord Jesus Christ. ⁵⁸ Therefore, my beloved brethren, be ye stedfast, unmovable, always abounding in the work of the Lord, knowing that your labour is not in vain in the Lord.

---

52. *In a moment* — Amazing work of omnipotence! And cannot the same power now change us into saints in a moment? *The trumpet shall sound* — To awaken all that sleep in the dust of the earth.

54. *Death is swallowed up in victory* — That is, totally conquered, abolished for ever.

55. AV grave. *O death, where is thy sting?* — Which once was full of hellish poison. O Hades, the receptacle of separate souls, *where is thy victory* — Thou art now robbed of all thy spoils; all thy captives are set at liberty. Hades literally means the invisible world, and relates to the soul; death, to the body. The Greek words are found in the Septuagint translation of Hosea 13:14. Isaiah 25:8.

56. *The sting of death is sin* — Without which it could have no power. But this sting none can resist by his own strength. *And the strength of sin is the law* — As is largely declared, Romans 7:7, etc.

57. *But thanks be to God, who hath given us the victory* — Over sin, death, and Hades.

58. *Be ye steadfast* — In yourselves. *Unmovable* — By others; continually increasing in the work of faith and labor of love. *Knowing your labor is not in vain in the Lord* — Whatever ye do for his sake shall have its full reward in that day. Let us also endeavor, by cultivating holiness in all its branches, to maintain this hope in its full energy; longing for that glorious day, when, in the utmost extent of the expression, death shall be swallowed up forever, and millions of voices, after the long silence of the grave, shall burst out at once into that triumphant song, O death, where is thy sting? O Hades, where is thy victory?

Hymn 57
1 Thessalonians 4:13-17

Jesus, faithful to his word,
Shall with a shout descend;
All heaven's host their glorious Lord
Shall pompously attend.
Christ shall come with dreadful noise,
Lightnings swift, and thunders loud,
With the great archangel's voice,
And with the trump of God.

First the dead in Christ shall rise;
Then we that yet remain
Shall be caught up to the skies,
And see our Lord again.
We shall meet him in the air,
All rapt up to heaven shall be,
Find, and love, and praise him there,
To all eternity.

Who can tell the happiness,
This glorious hope affords?
Joy unuttered we possess
In these reviving words.
Happy, while on earth we breathe,
Mightier bliss ordained to know,
Trampling down sin, hell, and death,
To the third heaven we go!

1742 *Works* 7:150-51

The Gathering of Believers
1 Thessalonians 4:13-5:11

¹³ Now <u>we</u> would not have you ignorant, brethren, concerning them that are asleep, that ye sorrow not, even as others who have no hope. ¹⁴ For if we believe that Jesus died and rose again, so will God bring with him those also that sleep in Jesus. ¹⁵ For this we say unto you by the word of the Lord, that we who are alive who are left to the <u>appearing</u> of the Lord shall not prevent them that are asleep. ¹⁶ For the Lord himself shall descend from heaven with a shout, with the voice of an archangel, and with the trumpet of God; and the dead in Christ shall rise first. ¹⁷ Then we who are alive <u>who are left</u> shall be caught up together with them in clouds, to meet the Lord in the air; and so shall we be ever with the Lord. ¹⁸ Wherefore comfort one another with these words.

¹ But of the times and seasons, brethren, ye have no need that I write unto you. ² For ye yourselves know perfectly that the day of the Lord so cometh as a thief in the night. ³ When they cry, Peace and safety; then sudden destruction cometh upon them, as travail upon a woman with child; and they

---

13. AV Now I. *Now* — Herein the efficacy of Christianity greatly appears, — that it neither takes away nor embitters, but sweetly tempers, that most refined of all affections, our desire of or love to the dead.

14. *So* — As God raised him. *With him* — With their living head.

15. AV coming. *By the word of the Lord* — By a particular revelation. *We who are left* — This intimates the fewness of those who will be then alive, compared to the multitude of the dead. Believers of all ages and nations make up, as it were, one body; in consideration of which, the believers of that age might put themselves in the place, and speak in the person, of them who were to live till the coming of the Lord. Not that St. Paul hereby asserted (though some seem to have imagined so) that the day of the Lord was at hand.

16. *With a shout* — Properly, a proclamation made to a great multitude. Above this is, the voice of the archangel; above both, the trumpet of God; the voice of God, somewhat analogous to the sound of a trumpet.

17. AV and remain. *Together* — In the same moment. *In the air* — The wicked will remain beneath, while the righteous, being absolved, shall be assessors with their Lord in the judgment. *With the Lord* — In heaven.

1. *But of the precise times when this shall be.*

2. *For this in* general *ye do know; and ye can and need know no more.*

shall not escape. ⁴ But ye, brethren, are not in darkness, that that day should overtake you as a thief. ⁵ Ye are all the children of the light, and children of the day; we are not *children* of the night, nor of darkness. ⁶ Therefore let us not sleep, as the others; but let us awake, and keep awake. ⁷ For they that sleep, sleep in the night; and they that are drunken are drunken in the night. ⁸ But let us, who are of the day, keep awake, having put on the breastplate of faith and love; and for an helmet, the hope of salvation. ⁹ For God hath not appointed us to wrath, but to obtain salvation by our Lord Jesus Christ. ¹⁰ Who died for us, that, whether we wake or sleep, we may live together with him. ¹¹ Wherefore comfort one another, and edify one another, as also ye do.

Apostasy and the Man of Sin
2 Thessalonians 2:1-12

¹ Now I beseech you, brethren, concerning the appearing of our Lord Jesus Christ, and our gathering together unto him, ² that ye be not soon shaken in mind, or terrified, neither by spirit, nor by word, nor by letter as from us, as if the day of the Lord were at hand. ³ Let no man deceive you by any means, for *that day shall not come,* unless the falling away come first,

---

3. *When they* — The men of the world say.

4. *Ye are not in darkness* — Sleeping secure in sin.

6. AV watch; be sober. *Awake, and keep awake* — Being awakened, let us have all our spiritual senses about us.

7. *They usually sleep and are drunken in the night* — These things do not love the light.

8. AV be sober; putting on.

9. *God hath not appointed us to wrath* — As he hath the obstinately impenitent.

10. AV should. *Whether we wake or sleep* — Be alive or dead at his coming.

2 Thessalonians Notes

1. AV coming. Our gathering together to him — In the clouds.

2. AV troubled. *Be not shaken in mind* — In judgment. *Or terrified* — As those easily are who are immoderately fond of knowing future things. Neither by any pretended revelation from the Spirit, nor by pretense of any word spoken by me.

The Epistles of Paul

and the man of sin be revealed, the son of perdition. ⁴ Who opposeth and exalteth himself above all that is called God, or that is worshipped; so that he sitteth in the temple of God as God, <u>declaring</u> himself that he is God. ⁵ Remember ye not, that I told you these things, when I was yet with you? ⁶ And now ye know <u>that which restraineth</u> that he may be revealed in his time. ⁷ For the mystery of iniquity already worketh; only he who now <u>restraineth</u> <u>will restrain</u>, till he be taken out of the way. ⁸ And then will that <u>wicked one</u>

---

3. *Unless the falling away* — From the pure faith of the gospel, come first. This began even in the apostolic age. But the man of sin, *the son of perdition* — Eminently so called, is not come yet. However, in many respects, the Pope has an indisputable claim to those titles. He is, in an emphatic sense, the man of sin, as he increases all manner of sin above measure. And he is, too, properly styled, the son of perdition, as he has caused the death of numberless multitudes, both of his opposers and followers, destroyed innumerable souls, and will himself perish everlastingly. He it is that opposeth himself to the emperor, once his rightful sovereign; and that exalteth himself above all that is called God, *or that is worshipped* — Commanding angels, and putting kings under his feet, both of whom are called gods in scripture; claiming the highest power, the highest honor; suffering himself, not once only, to be styled God or vice-God. Indeed no less is implied in his ordinary title, "Most Holy Lord," or, *"Most Holy Father." So that he sitteth* — Enthroned. *In the temple of God* — Mentioned Revelation 11:1. *Declaring himself that he is God* — Claiming the prerogatives which belong to God alone.

4. AV shewing.

6. AV what withholdeth. *And now ye know* — By what I told you when I was with you. *That which restraineth* — The power of the Roman emperors. When this is taken away, the wicked one will be revealed. *In his time* — His appointed season, and not before.

7. AV letteth; let. *He will surely be revealed; for the mystery* — The deep, secret power of iniquity, just opposite to the power of godliness, already worketh. It began with the love of honor, and the desire of power; and is completed in the entire subversion of the gospel of Christ. This mystery of iniquity is not wholly confined to the Romansish church, but extends itself to others also. It seems to consist of,

  1. Human inventions added to the written word.
  2. Mere outside performances put in the room of faith and love.

be revealed, whom the Lord will consume with the <u>Spirit</u> of his mouth, and destroy with the brightness of his <u>appearing</u>. ⁹ Whose <u>appearing</u> is after the <u>mighty working</u> of Satan with all power and signs and lying wonders; ¹⁰ and with all deceivableness of unrighteousness in them that perish; because they received not the love of the truth, that they might be saved. ¹¹ And therefore God shall send them strong delusion, so that they shall believe <u>the lie</u>. ¹² That they all <u>may be condemned</u> who believed not the truth, but had pleasure in unrighteousness. ¹³ But we <u>ought</u> to give thanks always to God for you, brethren beloved of the Lord, because God hath from the beginning chosen you to salvation through sanctification of the Spirit and belief of the truth. ¹⁴ To which he hath called you by our gospel, to the obtaining of the glory of our Lord Jesus Christ. ¹⁵ Therefore, brethren, stand fast, and hold the traditions which ye have been taught, whether by word, or by our epistle. ¹⁶

---

3. Other mediators besides the man Christ Jesus. The two last branches, together with idolatry and bloodshed, are the direct consequences of the former; namely, the adding to the word of God.

Already worketh — In the church. *Only he that restraineth* — That is, the potentate who successively has Romans in his power. The emperors, heathen or Christian; the kings, Goths or Lombards; the Carolingian or German emperors.

8. AV Wicked; spirit. *And then* — When every prince and power that restrains is taken away. *Will that wicked one* — Emphatically so called, be revealed. *Whom the Lord will soon consume with the spirit of his mouth* — His immediate power. *And destroy* — With the very first appearance of his glory.

9. AV coming; working, JW added 'mighty'.

10. *Because they received not the love of the truth* — Therefore God suffered them to fall into that "strong delusion."

11. AV a lie. *Therefore God shall send them* — That is, judicially permit to come upon them, strong delusion.

12. AV might be damned. *That they all may be condemned* — That is, the consequence of which will be, that they all will be condemned who believed not the truth, *but had pleasure in unrighteousness* — That is, who believed not the truth, because they loved sin.

13. AV are bound. *God hath from the beginning* — Of your hearing the gospel. *Chosen you to salvation* — Taken you out of the world, and placed you in the way to glory.

14. *To which* — Faith and holiness. *He hath called you by our gospel* — That which we preached, accompanied with the power of his Spirit.

Now our Lord Jesus Christ himself, and God, even our Father, who hath loved us, and hath given us everlasting consolation and good hope through grace, ^{17} comfort your hearts, and stablish you in every good word and work.

Marks of the Apostasy
2 Timothy 3:1-5

^{1} But know this, that in the last days <u>grievous</u> times will come. ^{2} For men will be lovers of their themselves, <u>lovers of money</u>, <u>arrogant</u>, proud, <u>evilspeakers</u>, disobedient to parents, ungrateful, unholy, ^{3} without natural affection, <u>implacable</u>, <u>slanderers</u>, <u>intemperate</u>, fierce, despisers of <u>good men</u>, ^{4} traitors, <u>rash</u>, <u>puffed up</u>, lovers of pleasures more than lovers of God; ^{5} having a form of godliness, but denying the power of it; from <u>these also</u> turn away.

---

15. *Hold* — Without adding to, or diminishing from, *the traditions which ye have been taught* — The truths which I have delivered to you. *Whether by word or by our epistle* — He preached before he wrote. And he had written concerning this in his former epistle.

2 Timothy Notes
1. AV perilous. *In the last days* — The time of the gospel dispensation, commencing at the time of our Lord's death, is peculiarly styled the last days. *Grievous* — Troublesome and dangerous.

2. AV covetous; boasters; blasphemers. *For men* — Even in the church. *Will be* — In great numbers, and to an higher degree than ever. *Lovers of themselves* — Only, not their neighbors, the first root of evil. *Lovers of money* — The second.

3. AV trucebreakers; false accusers; incontinent; those that are good. *Without natural affection* — To their own children. Intemperate, *fierce* — Both too soft, and too hard.

4. AV heady; highminded. *Lovers of sensual pleasure* — Which naturally extinguishes all love and sense of God.

5. AV such. *Having the form*—An appearance of godliness, but not regarding, nay, even *denying* and blaspheming, the inward power and reality of it. Is not this eminently fulfilled at this day?

Hymn 54
2 Corinthians 5:10

Thou Judge of quick and dead,
Before whose bar severe,
With holy joy, or guilty dread,
We all shall soon appear;
Our cautioned souls prepare
For that tremendous day,
And fill us now with watchful care,
And stir us up to pray.

To pray, and wait the hour,
That awful hour unknown,
When robed in majesty and power
Thou shalt from heaven come down,
Th'immortal Son of Man,
To judge the human race,
With all they Father's dazzling train,
With all thy glorious grace.

To damp our earthly joys,
T'increase our gracious fears,
Forever let th'archangel's voice
Be sounding in our ears
The solemn midnight cry,
'Ye dead, the Judge is come;
Arise and meet him in the sky,
And meet your instant doom!

O may we thus be found
Obedient to his word,
Attentive to the trumpet's sound,
And looking for our Lord!
O may we thus ensure
A lot among the blest,
And watch a moment, to secure
An everlasting rest!

1749, *Works* 7:147-48

The General Epistles

The next two selections focus on the conflagration of the present cosmos and the spirit of Antichrist working in the present age. We have already seen that Wesley's views on this world's destruction were heavily influenced by the Chain of Being. His commentary below should be compared to what he says in his Notes *on Revelation 20:11 and the sermons* The Great Assize *III.2-4 and* On Eternity *§7 (Works 2:361-62). For his comments elsewhere on the spirit of antichrist and false teachers, see the introductory comment to the Epistles of Paul and the sermon* The Mystery of Iniquity. *This heretical spirit shook Methodism when the enthusiast George Bell began to proclaim (1) the millennium had arrived, (2) angelic perfection was available, and (3) the means of grace were no longer of any use. Soon, Bell claimed the world would be destroyed and this led to open schism in the societies. Wesley's response can be found in the* Plain Account 20-22, 25:108-68 *(see* Annotated Edition*). Wesley also claimed that Protestants had succumbed to the same spirit as Rome when it came to their willingness to persecute and make war on other Christians. This led him to long for Christ's millennial reign when universal peace will rule the world* (Upon our Lord's Sermon on the Mount II III.18, *Works 1:508-09).*

The Conflagration of the Present Cosmos
2 Peter 3:1-14

¹ This second epistle, beloved, I now write to you; in *both* which I stir up your pure minds by way of remembrance. ² That ye may be mindful of the words which were spoken before by the holy prophets, and of the commandment of us the apostles of the Lord and Saviour. ³ Knowing this first, that there will come scoffers in the last days, walking after their own desires. ⁴ And saying, Where is the promise of his coming? For ever since the fathers fell asleep, all things continue as *they were* from the beginning of

---

2, 3. *Be the more mindful thereof, because ye know scoffers will come first* — Before the Lord comes. *Walking after their own evil desires* — Here is the origin of the error, the root of libertinism. Do we not see this eminently fulfilled?

3. AV lusts. See note. "2 Peter 3:2."

the creation. ⁵ For this they willingly are ignorant of, that by the word of God the heavens were of old, and the earth standing out of the water and in the water; ⁶ through which the world that then was, being overflowed with water, perished. ⁷ But the heavens and the earth, that are now, are by his word <u>treasured</u> up, reserved unto fire at the day of judgment and <u>destruction</u> of ungodly men. ⁸ But, beloved, be not ignorant of this one thing, that one day *is* with the Lord as a thousand years, and a thousand years as one day. ⁹ The

---

4. AV For since. *Saying, Where is the promise of his coming* — To judgment (They do not even deign to name him.) We see no sign of any such thing. *For ever since the fathers* — Our first ancestors. Fell asleep, *all things* — Heaven. water, earth. *Continue as they were from the beginning of the creation* — Without any such material change as might make us believe they will ever end.

5. *For this they are willingly ignorant of* — They do not care to know or consider. *That by the almighty word of God* — Which bounds the duration of all things, so that it cannot be either longer or shorter. *Of old* — Before the flood. The aerial heavens were, *and the earth* — Not as it is now, *but standing out of the water and in the water* — Perhaps the interior globe of earth was fixed in the midst of the great deep, the abyss of water; the shell or exterior globe standing out of the water, covering the great deep. This, or some other great and manifest difference between the original and present constitution of the terraqueous globe, seems then to have been so generally known, that St. Peter charges their ignorance of it totally upon their willfulness.

6. *Through which* — Heaven and earth, the windows of heaven being opened, and the fountains of the great deep broken up. *The world that then was* — The whole antediluvian race. Being overflowed with water, *perished* — And the heavens and earth themselves, though they did not perish, yet underwent a great change. So little ground have these scoffers for saying that all things continue as they were from the creation.

7. AV kept in store; perdition. *But the heavens and the earth, that are now* — Since the flood. Are reserved unto fire at the day wherein God will judge the world, and punish the ungodly with everlasting destruction.

8. *But be not ye ignorant* — Whatever they are. *Of this one thing* — Which casts much light on the point in hand. That one day is with the Lord as a thousand years, *and a thousand years as one day* — Moses had said, Psalm 90:4, "A thousand years in thy sight are as one day;" which St. Peter applies with regard to the last day, so as to denote both his eternity, whereby he exceeds all measure of time in his essence and in his operation; his

Lord is not <u>slow</u> concerning his promise (some men count it <u>slowness</u>); but is longsuffering <u>for your sake</u>, not willing that any should perish, but that all should come to repentance. ¹⁰ But the day of the Lord will come as a <u>thief</u>; in which the heavens shall pass away with a great noise, the elements shall melt with fervent heat, and the earth and the works that are therein shall be burned up. ¹¹ Seeing then all these things <u>are</u> dissolved, what manner of persons

---

knowledge, to which all things past or to come are present every moment; his power, which needs no long delay, in order to bring its work to perfection; and his longsuffering, which excludes all impatience of expectation, and desire of making haste. *One day is with the Lord as a thousand years* — That is, in one day, in one moment he can do the work of a thousand years. Therefore he "is not slow:" he is always equally ready to fulfill his promise. *And a thousand years are as one day* — That is, no delay is long to God. A thousand years are as one day to the eternal God. Therefore "he is longsuffering:" he gives us space for repentance, without any inconvenience to himself. In a word, with God time passes neither slower nor swifter than is suitable to him and his economy; nor can there be any reason why it should be necessary for him either to delay or hasten the end of all things. How can we comprehend this? If we could comprehend it, St. Peter needed not to have added, with the Lord.

9. AV slack; slackness; to us-ward. *The Lord is not slow* — As if the time fixed for it were past. *Concerning his promise* — Which shall surely be fulfilled in its season. *But is longsuffering towards us* — Children of men. Not willing that any soul, which he hath made should perish.

10. AV thief in the night. *But the day of the Lord will come as a thief* — Suddenly, unexpectedly. *In which the heavens shall pass away with a great noise* — Surprisingly expressed by the very sound of the original word. *The elements shall melt with fervent heat* — The elements seem to mean, the sun, moon, and stars; not the four, commonly so called; for air and water cannot melt, and the earth is mentioned immediately after. *The earth and all the works* — Whether of nature or art. *That are therein shall be burned up* — And has not God already abundantly provided for this?

1. By the stores of subterranean fire which are so frequently bursting out at Aetna, Vesuvius, Hecla, and many other burning mountains.
2. By the ethereal (vulgarly called electrical) fire, diffused through the whole globe; which, if the secret chain that now binds it up were loosed, would immediately dissolve the whole frame of nature.
3. By comets, one of which, if it touch the earth in its course toward the sun, must needs strike it into that abyss of fire; if in its return from the

ought ye to be in all holy conversation and godliness, ^{12} looking for and hasting on *the* coming of the day of God, wherein the heavens being on fire shall be dissolved, and the elements shall melt with fervent heat? ^{13} Nevertheless we look for new heavens and a new earth, according to his promise, wherein dwelleth righteousness. ^{14} Wherefore, beloved, seeing ye look for these things, labour to be found of him in peace, without spot, and blameless.

---

sun, when it is heated, as a great man computes, two thousand times hotter than a red-hot cannonball, it must destroy all vegetables and animals long before their contact, and soon after burn it up.

11. AV shall be. *Seeing then that all these things are dissolved* — To the eye of faith it appears as done already. *All these things* — Mentioned before; all that are included in that scriptural expression, "the heavens and the earth;" that is, the universe. On the fourth day God made the stars, Genesis 1:16, which will be dissolved together with the earth. They are deceived, therefore, who restrain either the history of the creation, or this description of the destruction, of the world to the earth and lower heavens; imagining the stars to be more ancient than the earth, and to survive it. Both the dissolution and renovation are ascribed, not to the one heaven which surrounds the earth, but to the heavens in general, 2 Peter 3:10, 13, without any restriction or limitation. *What persons ought ye to be in all holy conversation* — With men. *And godliness* — Toward your Creator.

12. *Hastening on* — As it were by your earnest desires and fervent prayers. *The coming of the day of God* — Many myriads of days he grants to men: one, the last, is the day of God himself.

13. *We look for new heavens and a new earth* — Raised as it were out of the ashes of the old; we look for an entire new state of things. *Wherein dwelleth righteousness* — Only righteous spirits. How great a mystery!

14. *Labor that whenever he cometh ye may be found in peace* — May meet him without terror, being sprinkled with his blood, and sanctified by his Spirit, so as to be without spot and blameless. Isaiah 65:17; Isaiah 66:22.

Hymn 522

O happy, happy day
That calls thy exiles home!
The heavens shall pass away,
The earth receives its doom;
Earth we shall view and heaven destroyed,
And shout above the fiery void!

These eyes shall see them fall,
Mountains, and stars, and skies!
These eyes shall see them all
Out of their ashes rise!
These lips his praises shall rehearse
Whose nod restores the universe!

According to his word,
His oath to sinners given,
We look to see restored
The ruined earth and heaven,
In a new world his truth to prove,
A world of righteousness and love.

Then let us wait the sound
That shall our souls release,
And labour to be found
Of him in spotless peace;
In perfect holiness renewed,
Adorned with Christ, and meet for God!

1747, *Works* 7:716-17

The Spirit of Antichrist
1 John 2:18-29

¹⁸ Little children, it is the last time; and as ye have heard that antichrist cometh, *so* even now are there many antichrists; whereby we know that it is the last time. ¹⁹ They went out from us, but they were not of us; for if they had been of us, they would have continued with us; but *they went out,* that they might be made manifest that they were not all of us. ²⁰ But ye have an <u>anointing</u> from the Holy One, and know all things. ²¹ I have not written to you because ye know not the truth, but because ye know it, and that no lie is of the truth. ²² Who is that liar but he that denieth that Jesus is the Christ? He is antichrist who denieth the Father and the Son. ²³ Whosoever denieth the

---

18. *My little children, it is the last time* — The last dispensation of grace, that which is to continue to the end of time, is begun. *Ye have heard that antichrist cometh* — Under the term antichrist, or the spirit of antichrist, he includes all false teachers and enemies to the truth; yea, whatever doctrines or men are contrary to Christ. It seems to have been long after this that the name of antichrist was appropriated to that grand adversary of Christ, "the man of sin," 2 Thessalonians 2:3 Antichrist, in St. John's sense, that is, antichristianism, has been spreading from his time till now; and will do so, till that great adversary arises, and is destroyed by Christ's coming.

19. *They were not of us* — When they went; their hearts were before departed from God, otherwise, they would have continued with us: but they went out, *that they might be made manifest* — That is, this was made manifest by their going out.

20. AV unction. *But ye have an anointing* — A chrism; perhaps so termed in opposition to the name of antichrist; an inward teaching from the Holy Ghost, *whereby ye know all things* — Necessary for your preservation from these seducers, and for your eternal salvation. St. John here but just touches upon the Holy Ghost, of whom he speaks more largely, 1 John 3:24; 4:13; 5:6.

21. *I have written* — Namely, 1 John 2:13. *To you because ye know the truth* — That is, to confirm you in the knowledge ye have already. *Ye know that no lie is of the truth* — That all the doctrines of these antichrists are irreconcilable to it.

22. *Who is that liar* — Who is guilty of that lying, but he who denies that truth which is the sum of all Christianity? That Jesus is the Christ; that he is the Son of God; that he came in the flesh, is one undivided truth, and he that

Son, he hath not the Father; he that acknowledgeth the Son hath the Father also. ²⁴ Therefore let that abide in you which ye have heard from the beginning. If that which ye heard from the beginning <u>abide</u> in you, ye also shall <u>abide</u> in the Son, and in the Father. ²⁵ And this is the promise which he hath promised us, eternal life. ²⁶ These things have I written to you concerning them that seduce you. ²⁷ But the anointing which ye have received of him abideth in you, and ye need not that any should teach you; save as the same anointing teacheth you of all things, and is true, and is no lie, and as it hath taught you, ye shall abide in him.

²⁸ And now, beloved children, abide in him; that, when he shall appear, we may have confidence, and not be ashamed before him at his coming. ²⁹

---

denies any part of this, in effect denies the whole. *He is antichrist* —And the spirit of antichrist, who in denying the Son denies the Father also.

23. *Whosoever denieth the eternal Son of God, he hath not communion with the Father; but he that truly and believingly acknowledgeth the Son, hath communion with the Father also.*

24. AV remain; continue. *If that truth concerning the Father and the Son, which ye have heard from the beginning, abide fixed and rooted in you, ye also shall abide in that happy communion with the Son and the Father.*

25. *He* — The Son. *Hath promised us* — If we abide in him.

26. *These things* — From 1 John 2:21. *I have written to you* — St. John, according to his custom, begins and ends with the same form, and having finished a kind of parenthesis, 1 John 2:20-26, continues, 2:27, what he said in the twentieth verse, concerning them that would seduce you.

27. *Ye need not that any should teach you, save as that anointing teacheth you* — Which is always the same, always consistent with itself. But this does not exclude our need of being taught by them who partake of the same anointing. *Of all things* — Which it is necessary for you to know. *And is no lie* — Like that which antichrist teaches. *Ye shall abide in him* — This is added both by way of comfort and of exhortation. The whole discourse, from verse 18 to this, 1 John 2:18-27 is peculiarly adapted to little children.

28. *And now, beloved children* — Having finished his address to each, he now returns to all in general. Abide in him, *that we* — A modest expression. *May not be ashamed before him at his coming* — O how will ye, Jews, Socinians, nominal Christians, be ashamed in that day!

Since ye know that he is righteous, ye know that every one who <u>practiceth</u> righteousness is born of him.

---

29. AV doeth. *Every one* — And none else. *Who practiceth righteousness* — From a believing, loving heart. *Is born of him* — For all his children are like himself.

The Revelation Of Jesus Christ

Revelation is a study of salvation history, the unfolding of God's redemptive plan to establish Christ's kingdom over the kingdoms of this world (11:15). Wesley understood chapters four and five to be the heart of the prophecy: God is the source and end of all things. Everything flows from him and returns to him (ch. 4). At his ascension Christ was invested with authority to defeat God's enemies, preserve his people, and to return this world's kingdoms back to their rightful master (ch. 5). The rest of the book simply tells the story through apocalyptic symbolism how these ends are accomplished. Therefore, Revelation begins where Jesus' Olivet discourse ends (destruction of Jerusalem in AD 70) and continues the story through the church age to the eternal kingdom (1:3).

While this is the main plot, there is a subplot that weaves through the entire commentary and reflects the core value of the Revival: real versus nominal religion. Beginning with his comments on the seven churches, Wesley is continually drawn to this core value in his commentary. In eighteenth-century England, the Church of Rome was widely viewed as the poster-child of formal religion. Wesley's notes confirms this attitude (9:20-21; 13:7-10, 15; 17:6; 18:24). The reader should pay close attention to this motif and how Wesley develops it from beginning to end (e.g. compare verbal links between chs. 2-3 and 21-22, not found elsewhere in the notes). Wesley's writing of this commentary strengthened his belief that Methodism was destined to be an eschatological movement, called to usher in the millennial reign of Christ. There is no doubt he identified Methodism with the faithful in Revelation. In this light, Wesley's commentary breathes the same themes found in The Mystery of Iniquity, The General Spread of the Gospel, *and* The Signs of the Times.

Wesley's discussion of background information and outline is found in the commentary on 1:1-10 and at the opening of chapter four. Regarding his later views on Bengel, see chapter three in the introduction. The reader is advised to study closely the notes at 6:11, 9:12, 10:6-7, 11:13, 12:14, 13:1, 17:10 and the outlines in chapter five of the introduction to grasp how Wesley (who is abridging Bengel) aligns Revelation to secular history. How Wesley and Bengel interpret the various numbers is quite complex and will take much effort to sort out the details (reader beware!). Wesley and Bengel follow standard Protestant hermeneutics when they identify the wild beast with the Papacy, but part paths somewhat by aligning Babylon with the city or civic powers of Rome, not the Catholic church (17:3). This distinction shapes their interpretation of the future eschatological wild beast, who will rule for 3 1/2 years over the city of Rome (17:8-11). There is a strong sense of imminence in the notes, revealing Wesley's own perspective (1:3; 12:12; 13:1; 17:10; 19:7; 20:3). The reader will find many interesting details, like the evil prophetess Jezebel representing the pastor's wife! Or, a literal interpretation that the two witnesses are two future Jewish evangelists in Jerusalem, and their lying dead for 3 1/2 days is due to the Islamic, Jewish, and Christian Sabbaths (Friday – Sunday). Or, a literal reading that the eschatological wild beast and false prophet will be thrown into the lake of fire without experiencing physical death. Regarding sources, Wesley acknowledges his debt to Bengel, but he also relied heavily on Bartolomeo Plantina for his history of the Papacy (13:1 Prop. 7 #16; 13:3). Wesley's Journal records him preaching from Revelation several times during the 1780s, mostly on chapters 14 and 20.

John Wesley's Introduction

IT is scarce possible for any that either love or fear God not to feel their hearts extremely affected in seriously reading either the beginning or the latter part of the Revelation. These, it is evident, we cannot consider too much; but the intermediate parts I did not study at all for many years; as utterly despairing of understanding them, after the fruitless attempts of so many wise and good men; and perhaps I should have lived and died in this sentiment, had I not seen the works of the great Bengelius. But these revived my hopes of understanding even the prophecies of this book; at least many of them in some good degree; for perhaps some will not be opened but in eternity. Let us, however, bless God for the measure of light we may enjoy, and improve it to his glory.

The following notes are mostly those of that excellent man; a few of which are taken from his *Gnomon Novi Testamenti*, but far more from his *Ekklarte Offenbarung*, which is a full and regular comment on the Revelation. Every part of this I do not undertake to defend. But none should condemn him without reading his proofs at large. It did not suit my design to insert these: they are above the capacity of ordinary readers. Nor had I room to insert the entire translation of a book which contains near twelve hundred pages.

All I can do is, partly to translate, partly abridge, the most necessary of his observations; allowing myself the liberty to alter some of them, and to add a few notes where he is not full. His text, it may be observed, I have taken almost throughout, which I apprehend he has abundantly defended both in the *Gnomon* itself, and in his *Apparatus* and *Crisis in Apocalypsin*.

Yet I by no means pretend to understand or explain all that is contained in this mysterious book. I only offer what help I can to the serious inquirer, and shall rejoice if any be moved thereby more carefully to read and more deeply to consider the words of this prophecy. Blessed is he that does this with a single eye. His labor shall not be in vain.

Chapter 1

¹ The revelation of Jesus Christ, which God gave unto him, to show his servants the things which must shortly come to pass; and he sent and signified *them* by his angel to his servant John. ² Who hath testified the word

---

Ch 1. 1. AV *it. The Revelation* — Properly so called; for things covered before are here revealed, or unveiled. No prophecy in the Old Testament has this title; it was reserved for this alone in the New. It is, as it were, a manifesto, wherein the Heir of all things declares that all power is given him in heaven and earth, and that he will in the end gloriously exercise that power, maugre all the opposition of all his enemies.

Of Jesus Christ — Not of "John the Divine," a title added in latter ages. Certain it is, that appellation, the Divine, was not brought into the church, much less was it affixed to John the apostle, till long after the apostolic age. It was St. John, indeed, who wrote this book, but the author of it is Jesus Christ.

Which God gave unto him — According to his holy, glorified humanity, as the great Prophet of the church. God gave the Revelation to Jesus Christ; Jesus Christ made it known to his servants.

To show — This word recurs, Revelation 22:6; and in many places the parts of this book refer to each other. Indeed the whole structure of it breathes the art of God, comprising, in the most finished compendium, things to come, many, various; near, intermediate, remote; the greatest, the least; terrible, comfortable; old, new; long, short; and these interwoven together, opposite, composite; relative to each other at a small, at a great, distance; and therefore sometimes, as it were, disappearing, broken off, suspended, and afterwards unexpectedly and most seasonably appearing again. In all its parts it has an admirable variety, with the most exact harmony, beautifully illustrated by those very digressions which seem to interrupt it. In this manner does it display the manifold wisdom of God shining in the economy of the church through so many ages.

of God, and the testimony of Jesus Christ, whatsoever things he saw. ³ Happy is he that readeth, and they that hear the words of *this* prophecy, and keep the things which are written therein: for the time *is* near.

His servants — Much is comprehended in this appellation. It is a great thing to be a servant of Jesus Christ. This book is dedicated particularly to the servants of Christ in the seven churches in Asia; but not exclusive of all his other servants, in all nations and ages. It is one single revelation, and yet sufficient for them all, from the time it was written to the end of the world. Serve thou the Lord Jesus Christ in truth: so shalt thou learn his secret in this book; yea, and thou shalt feel in thy heart whether this book be divine, or not.

The things which must shortly come to pass — The things contained in this prophecy did begin to be accomplished shortly after it was given; and the whole might be said to come to pass shortly, in the same sense as St. Peter says, "The end of all things is at hand;" and our Lord himself, "Behold, I come quickly." There is in this book a rich treasure of all the doctrines pertaining to faith and holiness. But these are also delivered in other parts of holy writ; so that the Revelation need not to have been given for the sake of these. The peculiar design of this is, to show the things which must come to pass. And this we are especially to have before our eyes whenever we read or hear it. It is said afterward, "Write what thou seest;" and again, "Write what thou hast seen, and what is, and what shall be hereafter;" but here, where the scope of the hook is shown, it is only said, the things which must come to pass. Accordingly, the showing things to come, is the great point in view throughout the whole. And St. John writes what he has seen, and what is, only as it has an influence on, or gives light to, what shall be.

And he — Jesus Christ. *Sent and signified them* — Showed them by signs or emblems; so the Greek word properly means. *By his angel* — Peculiarly called, in the sequel, "the angel of God," and particularly mentioned, Revelation 17:1; 21:9; 22:6, 16. *To his servant John* — A title given to no other single person throughout the book.

2. AV bare record of. *Who hath testified* — In the following book. *The word of God* — Given directly by God. *And the testimony of Jesus* — Which he hath left us, as the faithful and true witness. *Whatsoever things he saw* — In such a manner as was a full confirmation of the divine original of this book.

3. AV Blessed; at hand. *Happy is he that readeth, and they that hear, the words of this prophecy* — Some have miserably handled this book. Hence others are afraid to touch it; and, while they desire to know all things else, reject only the knowledge of those which God hath shown. They inquire after anything rather than this; as if it were written, "Happy is he that doth not read this prophecy." Nay, but happy is he that readeth, and they that hear, *and keep the words thereof* — Especially at this time, when so considerable a part of them is on the point of being fulfilled. Nor are helps wanting whereby any sincere and diligent inquirer may understand what he reads therein. The book itself is written in the most accurate manner possible. It distinguishes the several things whereof it treats by seven epistles, seven seals, seven trumpets, seven phials; each of which sevens is divided into four and three.

Many things the book itself explains; as the seven stars; the seven candlesticks; the lamb, his seven horns and seven eyes; the incense; the dragon; the heads and horns of the beasts; the fine linen; the testimony of Jesus: and much light arises from comparing it with the ancient prophecies, and the predictions in the other books of the New Testament. In this book our Lord has comprised what was wanting in those prophecies touching the time which followed his ascension and the end of the Jewish polity.

Accordingly, it reaches from the old Jerusalem to the new, reducing all things into one sum, in the exactest order, and with a near resemblance to the ancient prophets. The introduction and conclusion agree with Daniel; the description of the man child, and the promises to Zion, with Isaiah; the judgment of Babylon, with Jeremiah; again, the determination of times, with Daniel; the architecture of the holy city, with Ezekiel; the emblems of the horses, candlesticks, etc., with Zechariah. Many things largely described by the prophets are here summarily repeated; and frequently in the same words. To them we may then usefully have recourse. Yet the Revelation suffices for the explaining itself, even if we do not yet understand those prophecies; yea, it casts much light upon them.

Frequently, likewise, where there is a resemblance between them, there is a difference also; the Revelation, as it were, taking a stock from one of the old prophets, and inserting a new graft into it. Thus Zechariah speaks of two olive trees; and so does St. John; but with a different meaning. Daniel has a beast with ten horns; so has St. John; but not with quite the same signification. And here the difference of words, emblems, things, times, ought studiously to be observed. Our Lord foretold many things before his passion; but not all things; for it was not yet seasonable. Many things, likewise, his Spirit foretold in the writings of the apostles, so far as the necessities of those times required: now he comprises them all in one short book; therein presupposing all the other prophecies, and at the same time explaining, continuing, and perfecting them in one thread. It is right therefore to compare them; but not to measure the fullness of these by the scantiness of those preceding. Christ, when on earth, foretold what would come to pass in a short time; adding a brief description of the last things.

⁴ John to the seven churches which are in Asia: Grace *be* unto you, and peace, from him who is, and who was, and who is cometh; and from the seven spirits that are before his throne; ⁵ and from Jesus Christ, the faithful

---

Here he foretells the intermediate things; so that both put together constitute one complete chain of prophecy. This book is therefore not only the sum and the key of all the prophecies which preceded, but likewise a supplement to all; the seals being closed before. Of consequence, it contains many particulars not revealed in any other part of scripture. They have therefore little gratitude to God for such a revelation, reserved for the exaltation of Christ, who boldly reject whatever they find here which was not revealed, or not so clearly, in other parts of scripture. *He that readeth and they that hear* — St. John probably sent this book by a single person into Asia, who read it in the churches, while many heard. But this, likewise, in a secondary sense, refers to all that shall duly read or hear it in all ages. *The words of this prophecy* — It is a revelation with regard to Christ who gives it; a prophecy, with regard to John who delivers it to the churches. *And keep the things which are written therein* — In such a manner as the nature of them requires; namely, with repentance, faith, patience, prayer, obedience, watchfulness, constancy. It behoves every Christian, at all opportunities, to read what is written in the oracles of God; and to read this precious book in particular, frequently, reverently, and attentively. *For the time* — Of its beginning to be accomplished. *Is near* — Even when St. John wrote. How much nearer to us is even the full accomplishment of this weighty prophecy!

4. *John* — The dedication of this book is contained in the fourth, fifth, and sixth verses; but the whole Revelation is a kind of letter. *To the seven churches which are in Asia* — That part of the Lesser Asia which was then a Roman province. There had been several other churches planted here; but it seems these were now the most eminent; and it was among these that St. John had labored most during his abode in Asia. In these cities there were many Jews. Such of them as believed in each were joined with the gentile believers in one church. Grace be unto you, *and peace* — The favor of God, with all temporal and eternal blessings. From him who is, and who was, and who cometh, or, *who is to come* — A wonderful translation of the great name JEHOVAH: he was of old, he is now, he cometh; that is, will be for ever. *And from the seven spirits which are before his throne* — Christ is he who "hath the seven spirits of God." "The seven lamps which burn before the throne are the seven spirits of God." " The lamb hath seven horns and seven eyes, which are the seven spirits of God." Seven was a sacred number in the Jewish church: but it did not always imply a precise number. It sometimes is to be taken figuratively, to denote completeness or perfection. By these seven

witness, the first begotten of the dead, and the prince of the kings of the earth. To him that loveth us, and hath washed us from our sins with his own blood, ⁶ and hath made us kings and priests unto God and Father; to him be glory and <u>might</u> for ever.

⁷ Behold, he cometh with clouds; and every eye shall see him, and they who have pierced him; and all the <u>tribes</u> of the earth shall wail because of him. Yea, Amen. ⁸ I am the Alpha and the <u>Omega, saith</u> the <u>Lord God</u>, who is, and who was, and who <u>cometh</u>, the Almighty.

---

spirits, not seven created angels, but the Holy Ghost is to be understood. The angels are never termed spirits in this book; and when all the angels stand up, while the four living creatures and the four and twenty elders worship him that sitteth on the throne, and the Lamb, the seven spirits neither stand up nor worship. To these "seven spirits of God," the seven churches, to whom the Spirit speaks so many things, are subordinate; as are also their angels, yea, and "the seven angels which stand before God." He is called the seven spirits, not with regard to his essence, which is one, but with regard to his manifold operations.

5. *And from Jesus Christ, the faithful witness, the first begotten from the dead, and the prince of the kings of the earth* — Three glorious appellations are here given him, and in their proper order. He was the faithful witness of the whole will of God before his death, and in death, and remains such in glory. He rose from the dead, as "the first fruits of them that slept;" and now hath all power both in heaven and earth. He is here styled a prince: but by and by he hears his title of king; yea, King of kings, and Lord of lords." This phrase, the kings of the earth, signifies their power and multitude, and also the nature of their kingdom. It became the Divine Majesty to call them kings with a limitation; especially in this manifesto from his heavenly kingdom; for no creature, much less a sinful man, can bear the title of king in an absolute sense before the eyes of God.

6. AV dominion. *To him that loveth us, and, out of that free, abundant love, hath washed us from the guilt and power of our sins with his own blood, and hath made us kings* — Partakers of his present, and heirs of his eternal, kingdom. *And priests unto his God and Father* — To whom we continually offer ourselves, an holy, living sacrifice. *To him be the glory* — For his love and redemption. *And the might* — Whereby he governs all things.

7. AV kindreds. *Behold* — In this and the next verse is the proposition, and the summary of the whole book. *He cometh* — Jesus Christ. Throughout this book, whenever it is said, He cometh, it means his glorious coming. The preparation for this began at the destruction of Jerusalem, and more particularly at the time of writing this book; and goes on, without any

⁹ I John, your brother, and companion in the <u>affliction</u>, and in the kingdom and patience of Jesus, was in the island Patmos, for the word of God, and for the testimony of Jesus. ¹⁰ I was in the Spirit on the Lord's day,

---

interruption, till that grand event is accomplished. Therefore it is never said in this book, He will come; but, He cometh. And yet it is not said, He cometh again: for when he came before, it was not like himself, but in "the form of a servant." But his appearing in glory is properly his coming; namely, in a manner worthy of the Son of God. *And every eye* — Of the Jews in particular. *Shall see him* — But with what different emotions, according as they had received or rejected him. *And they who have pierced him* — They, above all, who pierced his hands, or feet, or side. Thomas saw the print of these wounds even after his resurrection; and the same, undoubtedly, will be seen by all, when he cometh in the clouds of heaven. *And all the tribes of the earth* — The word tribes, in the Revelation, always means the Israelites: but where another word, such as nations or people, is joined with it, it implies likewise (as here) all the rest of mankind. *Shall wail because of him* — For terror and pain, if they did not wail before by true repentance. Yea, *Amen* — This refers to, every eye shall see him. He that cometh saith, Yea; he that testifies it, Amen. The word translated yea is Greek; Amen is Hebrews: for what is here spoken respects both Jew and gentile.

8. AV Omega, the beginning and the ending, saith; Lord, JW added 'God'; is to come. *I am the Alpha and the Omega, saith the Lord God* — Alpha is the first, Omega, the last, letter in the Greek alphabet. Let his enemies boast and rage ever so much in the intermediate time, yet the Lord God is both the Alpha, or beginning, and the Omega, or end, of all things. God is the beginning, as he is the Author and Creator of all things, and as he proposes, declares, and promises so great things: he is the end, as he brings all the things which are here revealed to a complete and glorious conclusion. Again, the beginning and end of a thing is in scripture styled the whole thing. Therefore God is the Alpha and the Omega, the beginning and the end; that is, one who is all things, and always the same.

9. AV tribulation. *I John* — The instruction and preparation of the apostle for the work are described from the ninth to the twentieth verse. Revelation 1:9-20, *Your brother* — In the common faith. *And companion in the affliction* — For the same persecution which carried him to Patmos drove them into Asia.

This book peculiarly belongs to those who are under the cross. It was given to a banished man; and men in affliction understand and relish it most. Accordingly, it was little esteemed by the Asiatic church, after the time of Constantine; but highly valued by all the African churches, as it has been

and heard behind me a great voice, as of a trumpet, ¹¹ saying, What thou seest, write in a book, and send to the seven churches; to Ephesus, and to Smyrna, and to Pergamos, and to Thyatira, and to Sardis, and to Philadelphia,

---

since by all the persecuted children of God. In the affliction, *and kingdom and patience of Jesus* — The kingdom stands in the midst. It is chiefly under various afflictions that faith obtains its part in the kingdom; and whosoever is a partaker of this kingdom is not afraid to suffer for Jesus, 2 Timothy 2:12. *I was in the island Patmos* — In the reign of Domitian and of Nerva. And there he saw and wrote all that follows. It was a place peculiarly proper for these visions. He had over against him, at a small distance, Asia and the seven churches; going on eastward, Jerusalem and the land of Canaan; and beyond this, Antioch, yea, the whole continent of Asia. To the west, he had Romans, Italy, and all Europe, swimming, as it were, in the sea; to the south, Alexandria and the Nile with its outlets, Egypt, and all Africa; and to the north, what was afterwards called Constantinople, on the straits between Europe and Asia. So he had all the three parts of the world which were then known, with all Christendom, as it were, before his eyes; a large theatre for all the various scenes which were to pass before him: as if this island had been made principally for this end, to serve as an observatory for the apostle. For preaching the word of God he was banished thither, *and for the testimony of Jesus* — For testifying that he is the Christ.

10. *I was in the Spirit* — That is, in a trance, a prophetic vision; so overwhelmed with the power, and filled with the light, of the Holy Spirit, as to be insensible of outward things, and wholly taken up with spiritual and divine. What follows is one single, connected vision, which St. John saw in one day; and therefore he that would understand it should carry his thought straight on through the whole, without interruption. The other prophetic books are collections of distinct prophecies, given upon various occasions: but here is one single treatise, whereof all the parts exactly depend on each other. Revelation 4:1 is connected with Revelation 1:19 and what is delivered in the fourth chapter goes on directly to the twenty-second. *On the Lord's day* — On this our Lord rose from the dead: on this the ancients believed he will come to judgment. It was, therefore, with the utmost propriety that St. John on this day both saw and described his coming. *And I heard behind me* — St. John had his face to the east: our Lord, likewise, in this appearance looked eastward toward Asia, whither the apostle was to write. A great voice, *as of a trumpet* — Which was peculiarly proper to proclaim the coming of the great King, and his victory over all his enemies.

and to Laodicea. ¹² And I turned to see the voice that spake with me. And being turned, I saw seven golden candlesticks. ¹³ And in the midst of the candlesticks *one,* like a <u>son</u> of man, clothed with a garment down to the foot, and girt about at the breat with a golden girdle. ¹⁴ His head and hairs *were*

---

11. AV Saying, I am Alpha and Omega, the first and the last: and, What. *Saying, What thou seest* — And hearest. He both saw and heard. This command extends to the whole book. All the books of the New Testament were written by the will of God; but none were so expressly commanded to be written. *In a book* — So all the Revelation is but one book: nor did the letter to the angel of each church belong to him or his church only; but the whole book was sent to them all. *To the churches* — Hereafter named; and through them to all churches, in all ages and nations. *To Ephesiansesus* — Mark. Thomas Smith, who in the year 1671 traveled through all these cities, observes, that from Ephesus to Smyrna is forty-six English miles; from Smyrna to Pergamos, sixty-four; from Pergamos to Thyatira, forty-eight; from Thyatira to Sardis, thirty-three; from Sardis to Philadelphia, twenty-seven; from Philadelphia to Laodicea, about forty-two miles.

12, 13. AV Son. *And I turned to see the voice* — That is, to see him whose voice it was. And being turned, *I saw* — It seems, the vision presented itself gradually. First he heard a voice; and, upon looking behind, he saw the golden candlesticks, and then, in the midst of the candlesticks, which were placed in a circle, *he saw one like a son of man* — That is, in an human form. As a man likewise our Lord doubtless appears in heaven: though not exactly in this symbolical manner, wherein he presents himself as the head of his church. He next observed that our Lord was clothed with a garment down to the foot, *and girt with a golden girdle* — Such the Jewish high priests wore. But both of them are here marks of royal dignity likewise. *Girt about at the breast* — he that is on a journey girds his loins. Girding the breast was an emblem of solemn rest. It seems that the apostle having seen all this, looked up to behold the face of our Lord: but was beat back by the appearance of his flaming eyes, which occasioned his more particularly observing his feet. Receiving strength to raise his eyes again, he saw the stars in his right hand, and the sword coming out of his mouth: but upon beholding the brightness of his glorious countenance, which probably was much increased since the first glance the apostle had of it, he "fell at his feet as dead." During the time that St. John was discovering these several particulars, our Lord seems to have been speaking. And doubtless even his voice, at the very first, bespoke the God: though not so insupportably as his glorious appearance.

white as white wool, as snow, and his eyes as a flame of fire. ¹⁵ And his feet like fine brass, as if they burned in a furnace; and his voice as the voice of many waters. ¹⁶ And he had in his right hand seven stars; and out of his mouth went a sharp two-edged sword; and his countenance was as the sun shineth in his strength. ¹⁷ And when I saw him, I fell at his feet as dead. And he laid his right hand upon me, saying, Fear not; I am the first and the last. ¹⁸

---

14. *His head and his hair* — That is, the hair of his head, not his whole head. *Were white as white wool* — Like the Ancient of Days, represented in Daniel's vision, Daniel 7:9. Wool is commonly supposed to be an emblem of eternity. *As snow* — Betokening his spotless purity. *And his eyes as a flame of fire* — Piercing through all things; a token of his omniscience.

15. *And his feet like fine brass* — Denoting his stability and strength. *As if they burned in a furnace* — As if having been melted and refined, they were still red hot. *And his voice* — To the comfort of his friends, and the terror of his enemies. *As the voice of many waters* — Roaring aloud, and bearing down all before them.

16. *And he had in his right hand seven stars* — In token of his favor and powerful protection. *And out of his mouth went a sharp two-edged sword* — Signifying his justice and righteous anger, continually pointed against his enemies as a sword; sharp, to stab; two-edged, to hew. *And his countenance was as the sun shineth in his strength* — Without any mist or cloud.

17. *And I fell at his feet as dead* — Human nature not being able to sustain so glorious an appearance. Thus was he prepared (like Daniel of old, whom he peculiarly resembles) for receiving so weighty a prophecy. A great sinking of nature usually precedes a large communication of heavenly things. St. John, before our Lord suffered, was so intimate with him, as to lean on his breast, to lie in his bosom. Yet now, near seventy years after, the aged apostle is by one glance struck to the ground. What a glory must this be! Ye sinners, be afraid cleanse your hands: purify your hearts. Ye saints, be humble, prepare: rejoice. But rejoice unto him with reverence: an increase of reverence towards this awful majesty can be no prejudice to your faith. Let all petulancy, with all vain curiosity, be far away, while you are thinking or reading of these things. *And he laid his right hand upon me* — The same wherein he held the seven stars. What did St. John then feel in himself? Saying, *Fear not* — His look terrifies, his speech strengthens. He does not call John by his name, (as the angels did Zechariah and others,) but speaks as his well known master. What follows is also spoken to strengthen and encourage him. *I am* — When in his state of humiliation he spoke of his glory, he frequently spoke in the third person, as Matthew 26:64. But he now

And he that liveth and was dead; and, behold, I am alive for evermore; and have the keys of death and of <u>Hades</u>. ¹⁹ Write the things which thou hast seen, and which are, and which shall be hereafter. ²⁰ The mystery of the seven stars which thou sawest in my right hand, and *of* the seven golden candlesticks. The seven stars are angels of the seven churches; and the seven candlesticks are seven churches.

---

speaks of his own glory, without any veil, in plain and direct terms. *The first and the last* — That is, the one, eternal God, who is from everlasting to everlasting, Isaiah 41:4.

18. AV hell. *And he that liveth* — Another peculiar title of God. *And I have the keys of death and of Hades* — That is, the invisible world. In the intermediate state, the body abides in death, the soul in Hades. Christ hath the keys of, that is, the power over, both; killing or quickening of the body, and disposing of the soul, as it pleaseth him. He gave St. Peter the keys of the kingdom of heaven; but not the keys of death or of Hades. How comes then his supposed successor at Romans by the keys of purgatory? From the preceding description, mostly, are taken the titles given to Christ in the following letters, particularly the four first.

19. *Write the things which thou hast seen* — This day: which accordingly are written, Revelation 1:11-18. *And which are* — The instructions relating to the present state of the seven churches. These are written, Revelation 1:20 - Revelation 3:22. *And which shall be hereafter* — To the end of the world; written, Revelation 4:1, etc.

20. *Write first the mystery* — *The mysterious meaning of the seven stars* — St. John knew better than we do, in how many respects these stars were a proper emblem of those angels: how nearly they resembled each other, and how far they differed in magnitude, brightness, & other circumstances. *The seven stars are angels of the seven churches* — Mentioned in the eleventh verse. Revelation 1:11 In each church there was one pastor or ruling minister, to whom all the rest were subordinate. This pastor, bishop, or overseer, had the peculiar care over that flock: on him the prosperity of that congregation in a great measure depended, and he was to answer for all those souls at the judgment seat of Christ. *And the seven candlesticks are seven churches* — How significant an emblem is this! For a candlestick, though of gold, has no light of itself; neither has any church, or child of man. But they receive from Christ the light of truth, holiness, comfort, that it may shine to all around them. As soon as this was spoken St. John wrote it down, even all that is contained in this first chapter. Afterwards what was contained in the second and third chapters was dictated to him in like manner.

Chapter 2

¹ To the angel of the church at Ephesus write, These things saith he that holdeth the seven stars in his right hand, that walketh in the midst of the seven golden candlesticks. ² I know thy works, and thy labour, and thy

---

Ch 2. Of the following letters to the angels of the seven churches it may be necessary to speak first in general, and then particularly. In general we may observe, when the Israelites were to receive the law at Mount Sinai, they were first to be purified; and when the kingdom of God was at hand, John the Baptist prepared men for it by repentance. In like manner we are prepared by these letters for the worthy reception of this glorious revelation. By following the directions given herein, by expelling incorrigibly wicked men, and putting away all wickedness, those churches were prepared to receive this precious depositum. And whoever in any age would profitably read or hear it, must observe the same admonitions. These letters are a kind of sevenfold preface to the book. Christ now appears in the form of a man, (not yet under the emblem of a lamb,) and speaks mostly in proper, not in figurative, words. It is not till Revelation 4:1, that St. John enters upon that grand vision which takes up the residue of the book. There is in each of these letters:

1. A command to write to the angel of the church.
2. A glorious title of Christ.
3. An address to the angel of that church, containing A testimony of his mixed, or good, or bad state; An exhortation to repentance or steadfastness; A declaration of what will be; generally, of the Lord's coming.
4. A promise to him that overcometh, together with the exhortation, "He that hath an ear to hear, let him hear."

The address in each letter is expressed in plain words, the promise, in figurative. In the address our Lord speaks to the angel of each church which then was, and to the members thereof directly; whereas in the promise he speaks of all that should overcome, in whatever church or age, and deals out to them one of the precious promises, (by way of anticipation,) from the last chapters of the book.

1. *Write* — So Christ dictated to him every word. *These things saith he who holdeth the seven stars in his right hand* — Such is his mighty power! Such his favor to them and care over them, that they may indeed shine as stars, *both by purity of doctrine and holiness of life! Who walketh* — According to his promise, "I am with you always, *even to the end of the world." In the midst of the golden candlesticks* — Beholding all their works

patience, that thou canst not bear evil men; and thou hast tried those who say they are apostles, and are not, and hast found them liars. ³ And hast patience, and hast borne for my name's sake, and hast not fainted. ⁴ But I have against thee, that thou hast left thy first love. ⁵ Remember therefore from whence thou art fallen, and repent and do the first works; if not, I come to thee, and

---

and thoughts, and ready to "remove the candlestick out of its place," if any, being warned, will not repent. Perhaps here is likewise an allusion to the office of the priests in dressing the lamps, which was to keep them always burning before the Lord.

2. *I know* — Jesus knows all the good and all the evil, which his servants and his enemies suffer and do. Weighty word, "I know," how dreadful will it one day sound to the wicked, how sweet to the righteous! The churches and their angels must have been astonished, to find their several states so exactly described, even in the absence of the apostle, and could not but acknowledge the all-seeing eye of Christ and of his Spirit. With regard to us, to every one of us also he saith, "I know thy works." Happy is he that conceives less good of himself, than Christ knows concerning him. *And thy labor* — After the general, three particulars are named, and then more largely described in an inverted order:

1. Thy labor (v 2)	6. Thou hast born…for my name's sake…and hast not fainted (v 3)
2. Thy patience (v2)	5. Thou hast patience (v 3)
3. Thou canst not (v2)	4. Thou hast tried those who say they are (bear evil men) apostles, and are not, and hast found them liars.

And thy patience — Notwithstanding which thou canst not bear that incorrigibly wicked men should remain in the flock of Christ. And thou hast tried those who say they are apostles, *and are not* — For the Lord hath not sent them.

4. *But I have against thee, that thou hast left thy first love* — That love for which all that church was so eminent when St. Paul wrote his epistle to them. He need not have left this. He might have retained it entire to the end. And he did retain it in part, or there could not have remained so much of what was commendable in him. But he had not kept, as he might have done, the first tender love in its vigor and warmth. Reader, hast thou?

will remove thy candlestick out of its place, unless thou repent. ⁶ But thou hast this, that thou hatest the <u>works</u> of the Nicolaitans, which I also hate. ⁷ He

---

5. *It is not possible for any to recover the first love, but by taking these three steps*: 1. Remember; 2. Repent; 3. Do the first works.

Remember from whence thou art fallen — From what degree of faith, love, holiness, though perhaps insensibly. *And repent* — Which in the very lowest sense implies a deep and lively conviction of thy fall. Of the seven angels, two, at Ephesus and at Pergamos, were in a mixed state; two, at Sardis and at Laodicea, were greatly corrupted: all these are exhorted to repent; as are the followers of Jezebel at Thyatira: two, at Smyrna and Philadelphia, were in a flourishing state, and are therefore only exhorted to steadfastness.

There can be no state, either of any pastor, church, or single person, which has not here suitable instructions. All, whether ministers or hearers, together with their secret or open enemies, in all places and all ages, may draw hence necessary self-knowledge, reproof, commendation, warning, or confirmation. Whether any be as dead as the angel at Sardis, or as much alive as the angel at Philadelphia, this book is sent to him, and the Lord Jesus hath something to say to him therein. For the seven churches with their angels represent the whole Christian church, dispersed throughout the whole world, as it subsists, not, as some have imagined, in one age after another, but in every age. This is a point of deep importance, and always necessary to be remembered: that these seven churches are, as it were, a sample of the whole church of Christ, as it was then, as it is now, and as it will be in all ages.

Do the first works — Outwardly and inwardly, or thou canst never regain the first love. *But if not* — By this word is the warning sharpened to those five churches which are called to repent; for if Ephesus was threatened, how much more shall Sardis and Laodicea be afraid! And according as they obey the call or not, there is a promise or a threatening, Revelation 2:5, 16, 22; Revelation 3:3, 20. But even in the threatening the promise is implied, in case of true repentance. I come to thee, *and will remove thy candlestick out of its place* — I will remove, unless thou repent, the flock now under thy care to another place, where they shall be better taken care of. But from the flourishing state of the church of Ephesus after this, there is reason to believe he did repent.

6. AV deeds. *But thou hast this* — Divine grace seeks whatever may help him that is fallen to recover his standing. *That thou hatest the works of the Nicolaitans* — Probably so called from Nicolas, one of the seven deacons, Acts 6:5. Their doctrines and lives were equally corrupt. They allowed the most abominable lewdness and adulteries, as well as sacrificing to idols; all

that hath an ear, let him hear what the Spirit saith to the churches. To him that overcometh will I give to eat of the tree of life, which is in the paradise of my God.

⁸ And to the angel of the church at Smyrna write, These things saith the first and the last, who was dead and is alive. ⁹ I know <u>thy affliction</u>, and poverty (but thou art rich), and the <u>reviling</u> of those who say they are Jews,

---

which they placed among things indifferent, and pleaded for as branches of Christian liberty.

7. *He that hath an ear, let him hear* — Every man, whoever can hear at all, ought carefully to hear this. *What the Spirit saith* — In these great and precious promises. *To the churches* — And in them to every one that overcometh; that goeth on from faith and by faith to full victory over the world, and the flesh, and the devil.

In these seven letters twelve promises are contained, which are an extract of all the promises of God. Some of them are not expressly mentioned again in this book, as "the hidden manna," the inscription of "the name of the new Jerusalem," the "sitting upon the throne." Some resemble what is afterwards mentioned, as "the hidden name," Revelation 19:12; "the ruling the nations," Revelation 19:15; "the morning star," Revelation 22:16. And some are expressly mentioned, as "the tree of life," Revelation 22:2; freedom from "the second death," Revelation 20:6; the name in "the book of life," Revelation 20:12; 21:27; the remaining "in the temple of God," Revelation 7:15; the inscription of "the name of God and of the Lamb," Revelation 14:1; 22:4.

In these promises sometimes the enjoyment of the highest goods, sometimes deliverance from the greatest evils, is mentioned. And each implies the other, so that where either part is expressed, the whole is to be understood. That part is expressed which has most resemblance to the virtues or works of him that was spoken to in the letter preceding. *To eat of the tree of life* — The first thing promised in these letters is the last and highest in the accomplishment, Revelation 22:2, 14, 19. The tree of life and the water of life go together, Revelation 22:1, 2; both implying the living with God eternally. *In the paradise of my God* — The word paradise means a garden of pleasure. In the earthly paradise there was one tree of life: there are no other trees in the paradise of God.

8. *These things saith the first and the last, who was dead and is alive* — How directly does this description tend to confirm him against the fear of death! verses 10, 11. Revelation 2:10, 11 Even with the comfort wherewith St. John himself was comforted, Revelation 1:17, 18, shall the angel of this church be comforted.

and are not, but a synagogue of Satan. ¹⁰ Fear none of those things which thou art about to suffer; behold, the devil is about to cast some of you into prison, that ye may be tried; and ye shall have <u>affliction</u> ten days; be thou faithful unto death, and I will give thee the crown of life. ¹¹ He that hath an ear, let him hear what the Spirit saith to the churches. He that overcometh shall not be hurt by the second death.

¹² And to the angel of the church at Pergamos write, These things saith he who hath the sharp two-edged sword. ¹³ I know where thou dwellest, where the throne of Satan *is*; and thou holdest fast my name, and hast not denied my

---

9. AV thy works, and tribulation; blasphemy. *I know thy affliction and poverty* — A poor prerogative in the eyes of the world! The angel at Philadelphia likewise had in their sight but "a little strength." And yet these two were the most honorable of all in the eyes of the Lord. *But thou art rich* — In faith and love, of more value than all the kingdoms of the earth. *Who say they are Jews* — God's own people. *And are not* — They are not Jews inwardly, not circumcised in heart. *But a synagogue of Satan* — Who, like them, was a liar and a murderer from the beginning.

10. AV tribulation. The first and last words of this verse are particularly directed to the minister; whence we may gather, that his suffering and the affliction of the church were at the same time, and of the same continuance. Fear none of those things which thou art about to suffer — Probably by means of the false Jews. Behold — This intimates the nearness of the affliction. Perhaps the ten days began on the very day that the Revelation was read at Smyrna, or at least very soon after. The devil — Who sets all persecutors to work; and these more particularly. Is about to cast some of you — Christians at Smyrna; where, in the first ages, the blood of many martyrs was shed. Into prison, that ye may be tried — To your unspeakable advantage, 1 Peter 4:12, 14. And ye shall have affliction — Either in your own persons, or by sympathizing with your brethren. Ten days — (Literally taken) in the end of Domitian's persecution, which was stopped by the edict of the emperor Nerva. Be thou faithful — Our Lord does not say, "till I come," as in the other letters, but unto death — Signifying that the angel of this church should quickly after seal his testimony with his blood; fifty years before the martyrdom of Polycarp, for whom some have mistaken him. And I will give thee the crown of life — The peculiar reward of them who are faithful unto death.

11. *The second death* — The lake of fire, the portion of the fearful, who do not overcome, Revelation 21:8.

12. *The sword* — With which I will cut off the impenitent, verse 16. Revelation 2:16.

faith, even in the days wherein Antipas *was* my faithful witness, who was slain among you, where Satan dwelleth. ¹⁴ But I have a few things against thee, that thou hast there them that hold the doctrine of Balaam, who taught Balak to cast a stumbling-block before the sons of Israel, to eat things sacrificed to idols, and to commit fornication. ¹⁵ In like manner thou also hast them that hold the doctrine of the Nicolaitans, which I hate. ¹⁶ Repent therefore; if not, I come to thee, and will fight against them with the sword of my mouth. ¹⁷ He that hath an ear let him hear what the Spirit saith to the churches. To him that overcometh will I give of the hidden manna, and will give him a white stone, and on the stone a new name written, which none knoweth but he that receiveth it.

---

13. *Where the throne of Satan is* — Pergamos was above measure given to idolatry: so Satan had his throne and full residence there. *Thou holdest fast my name* — Openly and resolutely confessing me before men. *Even in the days wherein Antipas* — Martyred under Domitian. *Was my faithful witness* — Happy is he to whom Jesus, the faithful and true witness, giveth such a testimony!

14. AV children. *But thou hast there* — Whom thou oughtest to have immediately cast out from the flock. *Them that hold the doctrine of Balaam* — Doctrine nearly resembling his. *Who taught Balak* — And the rest of the Moabites. *To cast a stumblingblock before the sons of Israel* — They are generally termed, the children, but here, the sons, of Israel, in opposition to the daughters of Moab, by whom Balaam enticed them to fornication and idolatry. *To eat things sacrificed to idols* — Which, in so idolatrous a city as Pergamos, was in the highest degree hurtful to Christianity. *And to commit fornication* — Which was constantly joined with the idol-worship of the heathens.

15. *In like manner thou also* — As well as the angel at Ephesus. *Hast them that hold the doctrine of the Nicolaitans* — And thou sufferest them to remain in the flock.

16. *If not, I come to thee* — who wilt not wholly escape when I punish them. *And will fight with them* — Not with the Nicolaitans, who are mentioned only by the by, but the followers of Balaam. *With the sword of my mouth* — With my just and fierce displeasure. Balaam himself was first withstood by the angel of the Lord with "his sword drawn," Numbers 22:23, and afterwards "slain with the sword," Numbers 31:8.

17. *To him that overcometh* — And eateth not of those sacrifices. *Will I give of the hidden manna* — Described, John vi. The new name answers to this: it is now "hid with Christ in God." The Jewish manna was kept in the

^{18} And to the angel of the church at Thyatira write, These things saith the Son of God, who hath eyes as a flame of fire, and feet like fine brass. ^{19} I know <u>thy love</u> and faith, and thy service and patience; and thy last works more than the first. ^{20} But I have against thee, that thou sufferest that woman Jezebel, who calleth herself a prophetess, and teacheth and to seduceth my servants to commit fornication, and to eat things sacrificed to idols. ^{21} And I

---

ancient ark of the covenant. The heavenly ark of the covenant appears under the trumpet of the seventh angel, Revelation 11:19, where also the hidden manna is mentioned again. It seems properly to mean, the full, glorious, everlasting fruition of God. *And I will give him a white stone* — The ancients, on many occasions, gave their votes in judgment by small stones; by black, they condemned; by white ones they acquitted. Sometimes also they wrote on small smooth stones. Here may be an allusion to both. *And a new name* — So Jacob, after his victory, gained the new name of Israel. Wouldest thou know what thy new name will be? The way to this is plain, — overcome. Till then all thy inquiries are vain. Thou wilt then read it on the white stone.

18. *And to the angel of the church at Thyatira* — Where the faithful were but a little flock. *These things saith the Son of God* — See how great he is, who appeared "like a son of man!" Revelation 1:13. *Who hath eyes as a flame of fire* — "Searching the reins and the heart," verse 23. Revelation 2:23 *And feet like fine brass* — Denoting his immense strength. Job comprises both these, his wisdom to discern whatever is amiss, and his power to avenge it, in one sentence, Job 42:2, "No thought is hidden from him, and he can do all things."

19. AV thy works, and charity. *I know thy love* — How different a character is this from that of the angel of the church at Ephesus! The latter could not bear the wicked, and hated the works of the Nicolaitans; but had left his first love and first works. The former retained his first love, and had more and more works, but did bear the wicked, did not withstand them with becoming vehemence. Mixed characters both; yet the latter, not the former, is reproved for his fall, and commanded to repent. And faith, and thy service, *and patience* — Love is shown, exercised, and improved by serving God and our neighbor; so is faith by patience and good works.

20. *But thou sufferest that woman Jezebel* — who ought not to teach at all, 1 Timothy 2:12. *To teach and seduce my servants* — At Pergamos were many followers of Balaam; at Thyatira, one grand deceiver. Many of the ancients have delivered, that this was the wife of the pastor himself. Jezebel of old led the people of God to open idolatry. This Jezebel, fitly called by her name, from the resemblance between their works, led them to partake in the idolatry of the heathens. This she seems to have done by first enticing them to

gave her time to repent of her fornication; but she will not repent. ²² Behold, I will cast her into a bed, and them that commit adultery with her into great <u>affliction</u>, unless they repent of her works. ²³ And I will kill her children with death; and all the churches shall know that I am he who searcheth the reins and hearts; and I will give you every one according to your works. ²⁴ But I say to you, the rest that are at Thyatira, as many as do not hold this doctrine, who have not known the depths of Satan, as they speak. I will lay upon you no other burden. ²⁵ But what ye have hold fast till I come. ²⁶ And he that overcometh, and keepeth my works unto the end, to him will I give power over the nations. ²⁷ And he shall rule them with a rod of iron; they shall be

---

fornication, just as Balaam did: whereas at Pergamos they were first enticed to idolatry, and afterwards to fornication.

21. *And I gave her time to repent* — So great is the power of Christ! *But she will not repent* — So, though repentance is the gift of God, man may refuse it; God will not compel.

22. AV tribulation. I will cast her into a bed-into great affliction-and them that commit either carnal or spiritual adultery with her, *unless they repent* — She had her time before. *Of her works* — Those to which she had enticed their and which she had committed with them. It is observable, the angel of the church at Thyatira was only blamed for suffering her. This fault ceased when God took vengeance on her. Therefore he is not expressly exhorted to repent, though it is implied.

23. *And I will kill her children* — Those which she hath born in adultery, and them whom she hath seduced. *With death* — This expression denotes death by the plague, or by some manifest stroke of God's hand. Probably the remarkable vengeance taken on her children was the token of the certainty of all the rest. *And all the churches* — To which thou now writest. *Shall know that I search the reins* — The desires. *And hearts* — Thoughts.

24. *But I say to you who do not hold this doctrine* — Of Jezebel. *Who have not known the depths of Satan* — O happy ignorance! *As they speak* — That were continually boasting of the deep things which they taught. Our Lord owns they were deep, even deep as hell: for they were the very depths of Satan. *Were these the same of which Martin Luther speaks? It is well if there are not some of his countrymen now in England who know them too well! I will lay upon you no other burden* — Than that you have already suffered from Jezebel and her adherents.

25. *What ye* — Both the angel and the church have.

26. *By works* — Those which I have commanded. *To him will I give power over the nations* — That is, I will give him to share with me in that

<u>dashed in pieces</u> like a potter's vessels; as I also have received of my Father. ²⁸ And I will give him the morning star. ²⁹ He that hath an ear, let him hear what the Spirit saith to the churches.

Chapter 3

¹ And to the angel of the church at Sardis write, These things saith he that hath the seven <u>spirits</u> of God, and the seven stars. I know thy works, that thou hast a name that thou livest, but art dead. ² Be watchful, and strengthen the things which remain, which were ready to die: for I have not found thy works <u>complete</u> before my God. ³ Remember therefore how thou hast received and heard, and hold fast, and repent. If thou watch not, I will come as a thief, and thou shalt not know at what hour I will come upon thee. ⁴ Yet thou hast a few names in Sardis who have not defiled their garments; and they shall walk

---

glorious victory which the Father hath promised me over all the nations who as yet resist me, Psalm 2:8, 9.

27. AV broken to shivers. *And he shall rule them* — That is, shall share with me when I do this. *With a rod of iron* — With irresistible power, employed on those only who will not otherwise submit; *who will hereby be dashed in pieces* — Totally conquered.

28. *I will give him the morning star* — Thou, O Jesus, art the morning star! O give thyself to me! Then will I desire no sun, only thee, who art the sun also. He whom this star enlightens has always morning and no evening. The duties and promises here answer each other; the valiant conqueror has power over the stubborn nations. And he that, after having conquered his enemies, keeps the works of Christ to the end, shall have the morning star, an unspeakable brightness and peaceable dominion in him.

Ch 3. 1. AV Spirits. *The seven spirits of God* — The Holy Spirit, from whom alone all spiritual life and strength proceed. *And the seven stars* — which are subordinate to him. *Thou hast a name that thou livest* — A fair reputation, a goodly outside appearance. But that Spirit seeth through all things, and every empty appearance vanishes before him.

2. AV perfect. *The things which remain* — In thy soul; knowledge of the truth, good desires, and convictions. *Which were ready to die* — Wherever pride, indolence, or levity revives, all the fruits of the Spirit are ready to die.

3. *Remember how* — Humbly, zealously, seriously. Thou didst receive the grace of God once, *and hear* — His word. *And hold fast* — The grace thou hast received. *And repent* — According to the word thou hast heard.

with me in white; they are worthy. ⁵ He that overcometh, he shall be clothed in white raiment; and I will not blot his name out of the book of life, and I will confess his name before my Father, and before his angels. ⁶ He that hath an ear, let him hear what the Spirit saith to the churches.

⁷ And to the angel of the church at Philadelphia write, These things saith the holy one, the true one, he that hath the key of David, he that openeth, and none shutteth; and shutteth, and none openeth. ⁸ I know thy works (behold, I have given before thee an open door, none can shut it), that thou hast a little strength, and hast kept my word, and hast not denied my name. ⁹ Behold, I bring them of the synagogue of Satan, who say they are Jews, and are not, but lie; behold, I will make them come and <u>bow down</u> before thy feet, and know

---

4. *Yet thou hast a few names* — That is, persons. But though few, they had not separated themselves from the rest; otherwise, the angel of Sardis would not have had them. Yet it was no virtue of his, that they were unspotted; whereas it was his fault that they were but few. *Who have not defiled their garments* — Either by spotting themselves, or by partaking of other men's sins. *They shall walk with me in white* — in joy; in perfect holiness; in glory. *They are worthy* — A few good among many bad are doubly acceptable to God. O how much happier is this worthiness than that mentioned, Revelation 16:6.

5. *He shall be clothed in white raiment* — The color of victory, joy, and triumph. *And I will not blot his name out of the book of life* — Like that of the angel of the church at Sardis: but he shall live for ever. *I will confess his name* — As one of my faithful servants and soldiers.

7. *The holy one, the true one* — Two great and glorious names *He that hath the key of David* — A master of a family, or a prince, has one or more keys, wherewith he can open and shut all the doors of his house or palace. So had David a key, a token of right and sovereignty, which was afterward adjudged to Eliakim, Isaiah 22:22. Much more has Christ, the Son of David, the key of the spiritual city of David, the New Jerusalem; the supreme right, power, and authority, as in his own house. He openeth this to all that overcome, and none shutteth: he shutteth it against all the fearful, and none openeth. Likewise when he openeth a door on earth for his works or his servants, none can shut; and when he shutteth against whatever would hurt or defile, none can open.

8. *I have given before thee an opened door* — To enter into the joy of thy Lord; and, meantime, to go on unhindered in every good work. *Thou hast a little strength* — But little outward human strength; a little, poor, mean, despicable company. *Yet thou hast kept my word* — Both in judgment and practice.

that I have loved thee. ¹⁰ Because thou hast kept the word of my patience, I also will keep thee from the hour of temptation, which shall come upon the whole world, to try them that dwell upon the earth. ¹¹ <u>I come</u> quickly; hold fast what thou hast, that none take thy crown. ¹² He that overcometh, I will make him a pillar in the temple of my God, and he shall go out no more; and I will write upon him the name of my God, and the name of the city of my God, the new Jerusalem, which cometh down out of heaven from my God: and my new name. ¹³ He that hath an ear, let him hear what the Spirit saith to the churches.

---

9. AV worship. *Behold, I* — who have all power; and they must then comply. *I will make them come and bow down before thy feet* — Pay thee the lowest homage. *And know* — At length, that all depends on my love, and that thou hast a place therein. O how often does the judgment of the people turn quite round, when the Lord looketh upon them! Job 42:7, etc.

10. Because thou hast kept the word of my patience — The word of Christ is indeed a word of patience. I also will keep thee — O happy exemption from that spreading calamity! From the hour of temptation — So that thou shalt not enter into temptation; but it shall pass over thee. The hour denotes the short time of its continuance; that is, at any one place. At every one it was very sharp, though short; wherein the great tempter was not idle, Revelation 2:10. Which hour shall come upon the whole earth — The whole Roman empire. It went over the Christians, and over the Jews and heathens; though in a very different manner. This was the time of the persecution under the seemingly virtuous emperor Trajan. The two preceding persecutions were under those monsters, Nero and Domitian; but Trajan was so admired for his goodness, and his persecution was of such a nature, that it was a temptation indeed, and did throughly try them that dwelt upon the earth.

11. AV Behold, I come. *Thy crown* — Which is ready for thee, if thou endure to the end.

12. *I will make him a pillar in the temple of my God* — I will fix him as beautiful, as useful, and as immovable as a pillar in the church of God. *And he shall go out no more* — But shall be holy and happy for ever. *And I will write upon him the name of my God* — So that the nature and image of God shall appear visibly upon him. *And the name of the city of my God* — Giving him a title to dwell in the New Jerusalem. *And my new name* — A share in that joy which I entered into, after overcoming all my enemies.

¹⁴ And to the angel of the church at Laodicea write, These things saith the Amen, the faithful and true witness, the beginning of the creation of God. ¹⁵ I know thy works, that thou art neither cold nor hot. O that thou wert cold or hot! ¹⁶ So because thou art lukewarm, and neither cold nor hot, I am about to spue thee out of my mouth. ¹⁷ Because thou sayest, I am rich, and <u>have enriched myself</u>, and have need of nothing; and knowest not that thou art wretched, and <u>pitiable</u>, and poor, and blind, and naked. ¹⁸ I counsel thee to buy of me gold purified in the fire, that thou mayest be rich; and white raiment, that thou mayest be clothed, and the shame of thy nakedness may not appear; and eyesalve to anoint thine eyes, that thou mayest see. ¹⁹ Whomsoever I love, I rebuke and chasten; be zealous, and repent. ²⁰ Behold,

---

14. *To the angel of the church at Laodicea* — For these St. Paul had had a great concern, Colossians 2:1. *These things saith the Amen* — That is, the True One, the God of truth. *The beginning* — The Author, Prince, and Ruler. *Of the creation of God* — Of all creatures; the beginning, or Author, by whom God made them all.

15. *I know thy works* — Thy disposition and behavior, though thou knowest it not thyself. *That thou art neither cold* — An utter stranger to the things of God, having no care or thought about them. *Nor hot* — As boiling water: so ought we to be penetrated and heated by the fire of love. *O that thou wert* — This wish of our Lord plainly implies that he does not work on us irresistibly, as the fire does on the water which it heats. *Cold or hot* — Even if thou wert cold, without any thought or profession of religion, there would be more hope of thy recovery.

16. *So because thou art lukewarm* — The effect of lukewarm water is well known. *I am about to spue thee out of my mouth* — I will utterly cast thee from me; that is, unless thou repent.

17. AV increased with goods; miserable. *Because thou sayest* — Therefore "I counsel thee," etc. *I am rich* — In gifts and grace, as well as worldly goods. *And knowest not that thou art* — In God's account, wretched and pitiable.

18. *I counsel thee* — who art poor, and blind, and naked. *To buy of me* — Without money or price. *Gold purified in the fire* — True, living faith, which is purified in the furnace of affliction. *And white raiment* — True holiness. *And eyesalve* — Spiritual illumination; the "unction of the Holy One," which teacheth all things.

19. Whomsoever I love — Even thee, thou poor Laodicean! O how much has his unwearied love to do! I rebuke — For what is past. And chasten — That they may amend for the time to come.

I stand at the door, and knock; if any man hear my voice, and open the door, I will come in to him, and sup with him, and he with me. [21] He that overcometh, I will give him to sit with me on my throne, as I also have overcame, and sat down with my Father on his throne. [22] He that hath an ear, let him hear what the Spirit saith to the churches.

Chapter 4

---

20. *I stand at the door, and knock* — Even at this instant; while he is speaking this word. *If any man open* — Willingly receive me. *I will sup with him* — Refreshing him with my graces and gifts, and delighting myself in what I have given. *And he with me* — In life everlasting.

21. *I will give him to sit with me on my throne* — In unspeakable happiness and glory. Elsewhere, heaven itself is termed the throne of God: but this throne is in heaven.

22. *He that hath an ear, let him hear, etc.* — This stands in the three former letters before the promise; in the four latter, after it; clearly dividing the seven into two parts; the first containing three, the last, four letters. The titles given our Lord in the three former letters peculiarly respect his power after his resurrection and ascension, particularly over his church; those in the four latter, his divine glory, and unity with the Father and the Holy Spirit. Again, this word being placed before the promises in the three former letters, excludes the false apostles at Ephesus, the false Jews at Smyrna, and the partakers with the heathens at Pergamos, from having any share therein. In the four latter, being placed after them, it leaves the promises immediately joined with Christ's address to the angel of the church, to show that the fulfilling of these was near; whereas the others reach beyond the end of the world. It should be observed, that the overcoming, or victory, (to which alone these peculiar promises are annexed,) is not the ordinary victory obtained by every believer; but a special victory over great and peculiar temptations, by those that are strong in faith.

Ch 4. We are now entering upon the main prophecy. The whole Revelation may be divided thus:

> The first, second, and third chapters contain the introduction;
> The fourth and fifth, the proposition;
> The sixth, seventh, eighth, and ninth describe things which are already fulfilled;
> The tenth to the fourteenth, things which are now fulfilling;
> The fifteenth to the nineteenth, things which will be fulfilled shortly;

¹ After these things I saw, and, behold, a door opened in heaven; and the first voice which I had heard, as of a trumpet talking with me, said, Come up hither, and I will show thee things which must be hereafter. ² And immediately I was in the spirit; and, behold, a throne was set in heaven, and one sitting on the throne. ³ And he that sat was in appearance like a jasper

---

The twentieth, twenty-first, and twenty-second, things at a greater distance.

1. AV looked. *After these things* — As if he had said, After I had written these letters from the mouth of the Lord. By the particle and, the several parts of this prophecy are usually connected: by the expression, after these things, they are distinguished from each other, Revelation 7:9; 19:1. By that expression, and after these things, they are distinguished, and yet connected, Revelation 7:1; 15:5; 18:1. St. John always saw and heard, and then immediately wrote down one part after another: and one part is constantly divided from another by some one of these expressions. *I saw* — Here begins the relation of the main vision, which is connected throughout; as it appears from "the throne, and him that sitteth thereon;" "the Lamb;" (who hitherto has appeared in the form of a man;) " the four living creatures;" and " the four and twenty elders," represented from this place to the end. From this place, it is absolutely necessary to keep in mind the genuine order of the texts, as it stands in the preceding table. *A door opened in heaven* — Several of these openings are successively mentioned. Here a door is opened; afterward, "the temple of God in heaven," Revelation 11:19; 15:5; and, at last, "heaven" itself, 19:11. By each of these St. John gains a new and more extended prospect. *And the first voice which I had heard* — Namely, that of Christ: afterward, he heard the voices of many others. Said, *Come up hither* — Not in body, but in spirit; which was immediately done.

2. AV sat. *And immediately I was in the spirit* — Even in an higher degree than before, Revelation 1:10. And, behold, *a throne was set in heaven* — St. John is to write "things which shall be;" and, in order thereto, he is here shown, after an heavenly manner, how whatever "shall be," whether good or bad, flows out of invisible fountains; and how, after it is done on the visible theatre of the world and the church, it flows back again into the invisible world, as its proper and final scope. Here commentators divide: some proceed theologically; others, historically; whereas the right way is, to join both together. The court of heaven is here laid open; and the throne of God is, as it were, the center from which everything in the visible world goes forth, and to which everything returns. Here, also, the kingdom of Satan is disclosed; and hence we may extract the most important things out of the most

and a sardine stone; and a rainbow *was* round about the throne, in appearance like an emerald. ⁴ And round about the throne *are* four and twenty <u>thrones</u> and on the <u>thrones</u> four and twenty elders sitting, clothed in white raiment; and upon their heads crowns of gold. ⁵ And out of the throne go forth lightnings and voices and thunders; and seven lamps of fire burn before the

---

comprehensive and, at the same time, most secret history of the kingdom of hell and heaven. But herein we must be content to know only what is expressly revealed in this book. This describes, not barely what good or evil is successively transacted on earth, but how each springs from the kingdom of light or darkness, and continually tends to the source whence it sprung: So that no man can explain all that is contained therein, from the history of the church militant only. And yet the histories of past ages have their use, as this book is properly prophetical. The more, therefore, we observe the accomplishment of it, so much the more may we praise God, in his truth, wisdom, justice, and almighty power, and learn to suit ourselves to the time, according to the remarkable directions contained in the prophecy. *And one sat on the throne* — As a king, governor, and judge. Here is described God, the Almighty, the Father of heaven, in his majesty, glory, and dominion.

3. *And he that sat was in appearance* — Shone with a visible lustre, like that of sparkling precious stones, such as those which were of old on the high priest's breastplate, and those placed as the foundations of the new Jerusalem, Revelation 21:19, 20. If there is anything emblematical in the colors of these stones, possibly the jasper, which is transparent and of a glittering white, with an intermixture of beautiful colors, may be a symbol of God's purity, with various other perfections, which shine in all his dispensations. The sardine stone, of a blood-red color, may be an emblem of his justice, and the vengeance he was about to execute on his enemies. An emerald, being green, may betoken favor to the good; a rainbow, the everlasting covenant. See Genesis 9:9. And this being round about the whole breadth of the throne, fixed the distance of those who stood or sat round it.

4. AV seats. *And round about the throne* — In a circle, are four and twenty thrones, *and on the thrones four and twenty elders* — The most holy of all the former ages, Isaiah 24:23; Hebrews 12:1; representing the whole body of the saints. *Sitting* — In general; but falling down when they worship. *Clothed in white raiment* — This and their golden crowns show, that they had already finished their course and taken their place among the citizens of heaven. They are never termed souls, and hence it is probable that they had glorified bodies already. Compare Matthew 27:52.

throne, which are the seven spirits of God. ⁶ And before the throne *is* a <u>sea as of glass</u>, like crystal; and in the midst of the throne, and round about the throne, four <u>living creatures</u>, full of eyes before and behind. ⁷ And the first <u>living creature</u> *is* like a lion, and the second <u>living creature</u> *is* like a calf, and

---

5. *And out of the throne go forth lightnings* — Which affect the sight. *Voices* — Which affect the hearing. *Thunderings* — Which cause the whole body to tremble. Weak men account all this terrible; but to the inhabitants of heaven it is a mere source of joy and pleasure, mixed with reverence to the Divine Majesty. Even to the saints on earth these convey light and protection; but to their enemies, terror and destruction.

6. AV sea of glass; beasts. *And before the throne is a sea as of glass, like crystal* — Wide and deep, pure and clear, transparent and still. Both the "seven lamps of fire" and this sea are before the throne; and both may mean "the seven spirits of God," the Holy Ghost; whose powers and operations are frequently represented both under the emblem of fire and of water. We read again, Revelation 15:2, of "a sea as of glass," where there is no mention of "the seven lamps of fire;" but, on the contrary, the sea itself is "mingled with fire." We read also, Revelation 22:1, of "a stream of water of life, clear as crystal." Now, the sea which is before the throne, and the stream which goes out of the throne, may both mean the same; namely, the Spirit of God. *And in the midst of the throne* — With respect to its height. *Round about the throne* — That is, toward the four quarters, east, west, north, and south. *Were four living creatures* — Not beasts, no more than birds. These seem to be taken from the cherubim in the visions of Isaiah and Ezekiel, and in the holy of holies. They are doubtless some of the principal powers of heaven; but of what order, it is not easy to determine. It is very probable that the twenty-four elders may represent the Jewish church: their harps seem to intimate their having belonged to the ancient tabernacle service, where they were wont to be used. If so, the living creatures may represent the Christian church. Their number, also, is symbolical of universality, and agrees with the dispensation of the gospel, which extended to all nations under heaven. And the "new song" which they all sing, saying, "Thou hast redeemed us out of every kindred, and tongue, and people, and nation," Revelation 5:9, could not possibly suit the Jewish without the Christian church. *The first living creature was like a lion* — To signify undaunted courage. The second, *like a calf* — Or ox, Ezekiel 1:10, to signify unwearied patience. The third, *with the face of a man* — To signify prudence and compassion. The fourth, *like an eagle* — To signify activity and vigor. *Full of eyes* — To betoken wisdom and knowledge. *Before* — To see the face of him that sitteth on the throne. *And behind* — To see what is done among the creatures.

the third <u>living creature</u> hath a face as a man, and the fourth *is* like a flying eagle. ⁸ And the four <u>living creatures</u> had each of them six wings; round about and within they are full of eyes; and they rest not day and night, saying, Holy, holy, holy, <u>Lord God, the Almighty</u>, who was, and who is, and <u>who cometh</u>. ⁹ And when the living creatures give glory and honour and thanks to

---

7. AV beast; *was. And the first* — Just such were the four cherubim in Ezekiel, who supported the moving throne of God; whereas each of those that overshadowed the mercy-seat in the holy of holies had all these four faces: whence a late great man supposes them to have been emblematic of the Trinity, and the incarnation of the second Person. *A flying eagle* — That is, with wings expanded.

8. AV Lord God Almighty; is to come. *Each of them hath six wings* — As had each of the seraphim in Isaiah's vision. "Two covered his face," in token of humility and reverence: "two his feet," perhaps in token of readiness and diligence for executing divine commissions. Round about and within they are full of eyes. *Round about* — To see everything which is farther off from the throne than they are themselves. *And within* — On the inner part of the circle which they make with one another. First, they look from the center to the circumference, then from the circumference to the center. *And they rest not* — O happy unrest! *Day and night* — As we speak on earth. But there is no night in heaven. And say, Holy, holy, *holy* — Is the Three-One God. There are two words in the original, very different from each other; both which we translate holy. The one means properly merciful; but the other, which occurs here, implies much more. This holiness is the sum of all praise, which is given to the almighty Creator, for all that he does and reveals concerning himself, till the new song brings with it new matter of glory. This word properly signifies separated, both in Hebrews and other languages. And when God is termed holy, it denotes that excellence which is altogether peculiar to himself; and the glory flowing from all his attributes conjoined, shining forth from all his works, and darkening all things besides itself, whereby he is, and eternally remains, in an incomprehensible manner separate and at a distance, not only from all that is impure, but likewise from all that is created. God is separate from all things. He is, and works from himself, out of himself, in himself, through himself, for himself. Therefore, he is the first and the last, the only one and the Eternal, living and happy, endless and unchangeable, almighty, omniscient, wise and true, just and faithful, gracious and merciful. Hence it is, that holy and holiness mean the same as God and Godhead: and as we say of a king, "His Majesty;" so the scripture says of God, "His Holiness," Hebrews 12:10. The Holy Spirit is the Spirit of God. When God is spoken of, he is often named "the Holy One:" and as God swears by his

him that sitteth upon the throne, that liveth for ever and ever, ¹⁰ the four and twenty elders fall down before him that sitteth upon the throne, and worship him that liveth for ever and ever, and cast their crowns before the throne, saying, ¹¹ Worthy art thou, O Lord our God, to receive glory, and the honour, and the power; for thou hast created all things, and through thy will they were and are created.

---

name, so he does also by his holiness; that is, by himself. This holiness is often styled glory: often his holiness and glory are celebrated together, Leviticus 10:3; Isaiah 6:3. For holiness is covered glory, and glory is uncovered holiness. The scripture speaks abundantly of the holiness and glory of the Father, the Son, and the Holy Ghost. And hereby is the mystery of the Holy Trinity eminently confirmed. That is also termed holy which is consecrated to him, and for that end separated from other things: and so is that wherein we may be like God, or united to him. In the hymn resembling this, recorded by Isaiah, Isaiah 6:3, is added, "The whole earth is full of his glory." But this is deferred in the Revelation, till the glory of the Lord (his enemies being destroyed) fills the earth.

9, 10. *And when the living creatures give glory-the elders fall down* — That is, as often as the living creatures give glory, immediately the elders fall down. The expression implies, that they did so at the same instant, and that they both did this frequently. The living creatures do not say directly, "Holy, holy, holy art thou;" but only bend a little, out of deep reverence, and say, "Holy, holy, holy is the Lord." But the elders, when they are fallen down, may say, "Worthy art thou, O Lord our God."

11. AV O Lord (JW added 'our God'). *Worthy art thou to receive* — This he receives not only when he is thus praised, but also when he destroys his enemies and glorifies himself anew. *The glory and the honor and the power* — Answering the thrice-holy of the living creatures, verse 9. Revelation 4:9, *For thou hast created all things* — Creation is the ground of all the works of God: therefore, for this, as well as for his other works, will he be praised to all eternity. *And through thy will they were* — They began to be. It is to the free, gracious and powerfully-working will of Him who cannot possibly need anything that all things owe their first existence. *And are created* — That is, continue in being ever since they were created.

Chapter 5

¹ And I saw in the right hand of him that sat on the throne a book written within and without, sealed with seven seals. ² And I saw a strong angel proclaiming with a loud voice, Who *is* worthy to open the book, and to loose

---

Ch 5. 1. *And I saw* — This is a continuation of the same narrative. *In the right hand* — The emblem of his all-ruling power. He held it openly, in order to give it to him that was worthy. It is scarce needful to observe, that there is not in heaven any real book of parchment or paper or that Christ does not really stand there, in the shape of a lion or of a lamb. Neither is there on earth any monstrous beast with seven heads and ten horns. But as there is upon earth something which, in its kind, answers such a representation; so there are in heaven divine counsels and transactions answerable to these figurative expressions. All this was represented to St. John at Patmos, in one day, by way of vision. But the accomplishment of it extends from that time throughout all ages. Writings serve to inform us of distant and of future things. And hence things which are yet to come are figuratively said to be "written in God's book;" so were at that time the contents of this weighty prophecy. But the book was sealed. Now comes the opening and accomplishing also of the great things that are, as it were, the letters of it. *A book written within and without* — That is, no part of it blank, full of matter. *Sealed with seven seals* — According to the seven principal parts contained in it, one on the outside of each. The usual books of the ancients were not like ours, but were volumes or long pieces of parchment, rolled upon a long stick, as we frequently roll silks. Such was this represented, which was sealed with seven seals. Not as if the apostle saw all the seals at once; for there were seven volumes wrapped up one within another, each of which was sealed: so that upon opening and unrolling the first, the second appeared to be sealed up till that was opened, and so on to the seventh. The book and its seals represent all power in heaven and earth given to Christ. A copy of this book is contained in the following chapters. By "the trumpets," contained under the seventh seal, the kingdom of the world is shaken, that it may at length become the kingdom of Christ. By "the vials," under the seventh trumpet, the power of the beast, and whatsoever is connected with it, is broken. This sum of all we should have continually before our eyes: so the whole Revelation flows in its natural order.

the seals thereof? ³ And none in heaven, or on earth, neither under the earth, was able to open the book, neither to look thereon. ⁴ And I wept much, that none was found worthy to open the book, neither to look thereon. ⁵ And one of the elders saith to me, Weep not; behold, the Lion of the tribe of Judah, the root of David, hath prevailed to open the book, and the seven seals thereof. ⁶ And I beheld in the midst of the throne and of the four <u>living creatures</u>, and in the midst of the elders, a Lamb standing as if he had been slain, having seven horns and seven eyes, which are the seven <u>spirits</u> of God sent forth into all the earth. ⁷ And he came and took the book out of the right hand of him that

---

2. *And I saw a strong angel* — This proclamation to every creature was too great for a man to make, and yet not becoming the Lamb himself. It was therefore made by an angel, and one of uncommon eminence.

3. *And none* — No creature; no, not Mary herself. In heaven, or in earth, *neither under the earth* — That is, none in the universe. For these are the three great regions into which the whole creation is divided. *Was able to open the book* — To declare the counsels of God. *Nor to look thereon* — So as to understand any part of it.

4. *And I wept much* — A weeping which sprung from greatness of mind. The tenderness of heart which he always had appeared more clearly now he was out of his own power. The Revelation was not written without tears; neither without tears will it be understood. How far are they from the temper of St. John who inquire after anything rather than the contents of this book! yea, who applaud their own clemency if they excuse those that do inquire into them!

5. *And one of the elders* — Probably one of those who rose with Christ, and afterwards ascended into heaven. Perhaps one of the patriarchs. Some think it was Jacob, from whose prophecy the name of Lion is given him, Genesis 49:9. *The Lion of the tribe of Judah* — The victorious prince who is, like a lion, able to tear all his enemies in pieces. *The root of David* — As God, the root and source of David's family, Isaiah 11:1, 10. *Hath prevailed to open the book* — Hath overcome all obstructions, and obtained the honor to disclose the divine counsels.

6. AV beasts; Spirits. *And I saw* — First, Christ in or on the midst of the throne; secondly, the four living creatures making the inner circle round him; and, thirdly, the four and twenty elders making a larger circle round him and them. *Standing* — He lieth no more; he no more falls on his face; the days of his weakness and mourning are ended. He is now in a posture of readiness to execute all his offices of prophet, priest, and king. *As if he had been slain* — Doubtless with the prints of the wounds which he once received. And

sat upon the throne. ⁸ And when he took the book, the four living creatures and four and twenty elders fell down before the Lamb, having every an harp, and golden phials full of incense, which are the prayers of saints. ⁹ And they sing a new song, saying, Worthy art thou to take the book, and to open the seals thereof; for thou wast slain, and hast redeemed us to God by thy blood

---

because he was slain, he is worthy to open the book, verse 9, Revelation 5:9 to the joy of his own people, and the terror of his enemies. *Having seven horns* — As a king, the emblem of perfect strength. *And seven eyes* — The emblem of perfect knowledge and wisdom. By these he accomplishes what is contained in the book, namely, by his almighty and all-wise Spirit. To these seven horns and seven eyes answer the seven seals and the sevenfold song of praise, verse 12. Revelation 5:12 In Zechariah, likewise, 3:9; 4:10. Zechariah 3:9, Zechariah 4:10 mention is made of "the seven eyes of the Lord, *which go forth over all the earth.*" *Which* — Both the horns and the eyes. *Are the seven spirits of God sent forth into all the earth* — For the effectual working of the Spirit of God goes through the whole creation; and that in the natural, as well as spiritual, world. For could mere matter act or move? Could it gravitate or attract? Just as much as it can think or speak.

7. *And he came* — Here was "Ask of me," Psalm 2:8, fulfilled in the most glorious manner. *And took* — it is one state of exaltation that reaches from our Lord's ascension to his coming in glory. Yet this state admits of various degrees. At his ascension, "angels, and principalities, and powers were subjected to him." Ten days after, he received from the Father and sent the Holy Ghost. *And now he took the book out of the right hand of him that sat upon the throne* — who gave it him as a signal of his delivering to him all power in heaven and earth. He received it, in token of his being both able and willing to fulfill all that was written therein.

8. AV vials; odours. *And when he took the book, the four living creatures fell down* — Now is homage done to the Lamb by every creature. These, together with the elders, make the beginning; and afterward, Revelation 5:14, the conclusion. They are together surrounded with a multitude of angels, Revelation 5:11, and together sing the new song, as they had before praised God together, Revelation 4:8, etc. *Having every one* — The elders, not the living creatures. *An harp* — Which was one of the chief instruments used for thanksgiving in the temple service: a fit emblem of the melody of their hearts. *And golden phials* — Cups or censers. Full of incense, *which are the prayers of the saints* — Not of the elders themselves, but of the other saints still upon earth, whose prayers were thus emblematically represented in heaven.

out of every <u>tribe</u>, and tongue, and people, and nation. ¹⁰ And hast made <u>them</u> unto our God kings and priests; and <u>they</u> shall reign over the earth. ¹¹ And I saw and heard a voice of many angels, round about the throne and the <u>living creatures</u> and the elders; and the number of them was ten thousand times ten thousand, and thousands of thousands. ¹² Saying with a loud voice, Worthy is the Lamb that was slain to receive power, and riches, and wisdom, and strength, and honour, and glory, and blessing. ¹³ And every creature which is in heaven, and on the earth, and under the earth, and <u>on the sea</u>, and all that are in them, I heard them all saying, To him that sitteth on the throne, and to the Lamb, *is* the blessing, and the honour, and the glory, and the strength, for ever and ever. ¹⁴ And the four <u>living creatures</u> said, Amen. And <u>the elders</u> fell down and <u>worshipped</u>.

---

9. AV sung; kindred. *And they sing a new song* — One which neither they nor any other had sung before. *Thou hast redeemed us* — So the living creatures also were of the number of the redeemed. This does not so much refer to the act of redemption, which was long before, as to the fruit of it; and so more directly to those who had finished their course, "who were redeemed from the earth," Revelation 14:1, out of every tribe, and tongue, and people, *and nation* — That is, out of all mankind.

10. AV us; we. *And hast made them* — The redeemed. So they speak of themselves also in the third person, out of deep self-abasement. *They shall reign over the earth* — The new earth: herewith agree the golden crowns of the elders. The reign of the saints in general follows, under the trumpet of the seventh angel; particularly after the first resurrection, as also in eternity, Revelation 11:18;15:7;20:4;22:5; Daniel 7:27; Psalm 49:14.

11. *And I saw* — The many angels. *And heard* — The voice and the number of them. *Round about the elders* — So forming the third circle. It is remarkable, that men are represented through this whole vision as nearer to God than any of the angels. *And the number of them was* — At least two hundred millions, and two millions over. And yet these were but a part of the holy angels. Afterward, Revelation 7:11, St. John heard them all.

12. *Worthy is the Lamb* — The elders said, Revelation 5:9, "Worthy art thou." They were more nearly allied to him than the angels. To receive the power, etc. — This sevenfold applause answers the seven seals, of which the four former describe all visible, the latter all invisible, things, made subject to the Lamb. And every one of these seven words bears a resemblance to the seal which it answers.

13. AV such as are in the sea. *And every creature* — In the whole universe, good or bad. In the heaven, on the earth, under the earth, *on the sea*

Chapter 6

— With these four regions of the world, agrees the fourfold word of praise. What is in heaven, says blessing; what is on earth, honor; what is under the earth, glory: what is on the sea, strength; is unto him. This praise from all creatures begins before the opening of the first seal; but it continues from that time to eternity, according to the capacity of each. His enemies must acknowledge his glory; but those in heaven say, Blessed be God and the Lamb. This royal manifesto is, as it were, a proclamation, showing how Christ fulfils all things, and "every knee bows to him," not only on earth, but also in heaven, and under the earth. This book exhausts all things, 1 Corinthians 15:27, 28, and is suitable to an heart enlarged as the sand of the sea. It inspires the attentive and intelligent reader with such a magnanimity, that he accounts nothing in this world great; no, not the whole frame of visible nature, compared to the immense greatness of what he is here called to behold, yea, and in part, to inherit. St. John has in view, through the whole following vision, what he has been now describing, namely, the four living creatures, the elders, the angels, and all creatures, looking together at the opening of the seven seals.

14. AV beasts; four *and* twenty elders; worshipped him that liveth for ever and ever.

Ch 6. The seven seals are not distinguished from each other by specifying the time of them. They swiftly follow the letters to the seven churches, and all begin almost at the same time. By the four former is shown, that all the public occurrences of all ages and nations, as empire, war, provision, calamities, are made subject to Christ. And instances are intimated of the first in the east, the second in the west, the third in the south, the fourth in the north and the whole world. The contents, as of the phials and trumpets, so of the seals, are shown by the songs of praise and thanksgiving annexed to them. They contain therefore "the power, and riches, and wisdom, and strength, and honor, and glory, and blessing," which the Lamb received.

The four former have a peculiar connection with each other; and so have the three latter seals. The former relate to visible things, toward the four quarters to which the four living creatures look. Before we proceed, it may be observed,
1. No man should constrain either himself or another to explain everything in this book. It is sufficient for every one to speak just so far as he understands.
2. We should remember that, although the ancient prophets wrote the occurrences of those kingdoms only with which Israel had to do, yet the

¹ And I saw when the Lamb opened one of the seven seals, and I heard one of the four living creatures saying, as the voice of thunder, Come *and* see. ² And I saw, and behold a white horse; and he that sat on him had a bow; and a crown was given him; and he went forth conquering and to conquer.

Revelation contains what relates to the whole world, through which the Christian church is extended. Yet,
3. We should not prescribe to this prophecy, as if it must needs admit or exclude this or that history, according as we judge one or the other to be of great or small importance. "God seeth not as a man seeth;" therefore what we think great is often omitted, what we think little inserted, in scripture history or prophecy.
4. We must take care not to overlook what is already fulfilled; and not to describe as fulfilled what is still to come. We are to look in history for the fulfilling of the four first seals, quickly after the date of the prophecy. In each of these appears a different horseman. In each we are to consider, first, the horseman himself; secondly, what he does. The horseman himself, by an emblematical *prosopopoeia*, represents a swift power, bringing with it either,

1. A flourishing state; or,
2. Bloodshed; or,
3. Scarcity of provisions; or,
4. Public calamities.

With the quality of each of these riders the color of his horse agrees. The fourth horseman is expressly termed "death;" the first, with his bow and crown, "a conqueror;" the second, with his great sword, is a warrior, or, as the Roman termed him, Mars; the third, with the scales, has power over the produce of the land. Particular incidents under this or that Roman emperor are not extensive enough to answer any of these horsemen. The action of every horseman intimates farther,

1. Toward the east, wide spread empire, and victory upon victory:
2. Toward the west, much bloodshed:
3. Toward the south, scarcity of provisions:
4. Toward the north, the plague and various calamities.

1. AV beasts; noise. I heard one-That is, the first. Of the living creatures — Who looks forward toward the east.
2. *And I saw, and behold a white horse, and he that sat on him had a bow* — This color, and the bow shooting arrows afar off, betoken victory, triumph, prosperity, enlargement of empire, and dominion over many people. Another

³ And when he opened the second seal, I heard the second <u>living creature</u> say, <u>Come</u>. ⁴ And there went out another horse *that was* red; and to him that sat thereon <u>it was given</u> to take peace from the earth, that they should kill one another; and there was given him a great sword.

---

horseman, indeed, and of quite another kind, appears on a white horse, Revelation 19:11. But he that is spoken of under the first seal must be so understood as to bear a proportion to the horsemen in the second, third, and fourth seal. Nerva succeeded the emperor Domitian at the very time when the Revelation was written, in the year of our Lord 96. He reigned scarce a year alone; and three months before his death he named Trajan for his colleague and successor, and died in the year 98. Trajan's accession to the empire seems to be the dawning of the seven seals. *And a crown was given him* — This, considering his descent, Trajan could have no hope of attaining. But God gave it him by the hand of Nerva; and then the east soon felt his power. *And he went forth conquering and to conquer* — That is, from one victory to another. In the year 108 the already victorious Trajan went forth toward the east, to conquer not only Armenia, Assyria, and Mesopotamia, but also the countries beyond the Tigris, carrying the bounds of the Roman empire to a far greater extent than ever. We find no emperor like him for making conquests. He aimed at nothing else; he lived only to conquer. Meantime, in him was eminently fulfilled what had been prophesied of the fourth empire, Daniel 2:40, 7:23, that he should "devour, tread down, and break in pieces the whole earth."

3. AV beast; Come and see. *And when he had opened the second seal, I heard the second living creature* — Who looked toward the west. Saying, *Come* — At each seal it was necessary to turn toward that quarter of the world which it more immediately concerned.

4. AV power was given. *There went forth another horse that was red* — A color suitable to bloodshed. *And to him that sat thereon it was given to take peace from the earth* — Vespasian, in the year 75, had dedicated a temple to Peace; but after a time we hear little more of peace. All is full of war and bloodshed, chiefly in the western world, where the main business of men seemed to be, to kill one another. To this horseman there was given a great sword; and he had much to do with it; for as soon as Trajan ascended the throne, peace was taken from the earth. Decebalus, king of Dacia, which lies westward from Patmos, put the Romans to no small trouble. The war lasted five years, and consumed abundance of men on both sides; yet was only a prelude to much other bloodshed, which followed for a long season. All this was signified by the great sword, which strikes those who are near, as the bow does those who are at a distance.

⁵ And when he opened the third seal, I heard the third living creature say, Come. And I saw, and behold a black horse; and he that sat on him had a pair of scales in his hand. ⁶ And I heard a voice in the midst of the four living creatures say, A measure of wheat for a penny, and three measures of barley for a penny; and hurt not the oil and the wine.

---

5. AV Come and see; balances. *And when he had opened the third seal, I heard the third living creature* — Toward the south. Saying, Come. *And behold a black horse* — A fit emblem of mourning and distress; particularly of black famine, as the ancient poets term it. *And he that sat on him had a pair of scales in his hand* — When there is great plenty, men scarce think it worth their while to weigh and measure everything, Genesis 41:49. But when there is scarcity, they are obliged to deliver them out by measure and weight, Ezekiel 4:16. Accordingly, these scales signify scarcity. They serve also for a token, that all the fruits of the earth, and consequently the whole heavens, with their courses and influences; that all the seasons of the year, with whatsoever they produce, in nature or states, are subject to Christ. Accordingly his hand is wonderful, not only in wars and victories, but likewise in the whole course of nature.

6. *And I heard a voice* — It seems, from God himself. *Saying* — To the horseman, "Hitherto shalt thou come, *and no farther." Let there be a measure of wheat for a penny* — The word translated measure, was a Grecian measure, nearly equal to our quart. This was the daily allowance of a slave. The Roman penny, as much as a laborer then earned in a day, was about sevenpence halfpenny English. According to this, wheat would be near twenty shillings per bushel. This must have been fulfilled while the Grecian measure and the Roman money were still in use; as also where that measure was the common measure, and this money the current coin. It was so in Egypt under Trajan. *And three measures of barley for a penny* — Either barley was, in common, far cheaper among the ancients than wheat, or the prophecy mentions this as something peculiar. *And hurt not the oil and the wine* — Let there not be a scarcity of everything. Let there he some provision left to supply the want of the rest This was also fulfilled in the reign of Trajan, especially in Egypt, which lay southward from Patmos. In this country, which used to be the granary of the empire, there was an uncommon dearth at the very beginning of his reign; so that he was obliged to supply Egypt itself with corn from other countries. The same scarcity there was in the thirteenth year of his reign, the harvest failing for want of the rising of the Nile: and that not only in Egypt, but in all those other parts of Africa, where the Nile uses to overflow.

⁷ And when he opened the fourth seal, I heard the voice of the fourth living creature say, Come. ⁸ And I saw, and behold a pale horse; and he that sat on him, his name is Death (and Hades followed even with him); and power was given him over the fourth part of the earth, to kill with the scimitar, and with famine, and with death, and by the wild beasts of the earth.

---

7. AV Come and see. I heard the voice of the fourth living creature — Toward the north.

8. AV Hell; them; sword; hunger; beasts (JW added wild). *And I saw, and behold a pale horse* — Suitable to pale death, his rider. *And Hades* — The representative of the state of separate souls. *Followeth even with him* — The four first seals concern living men. Death therefore is properly introduced. Hades is only occasionally mentioned as a companion of death. So the fourth seal reaches to the borders of things invisible, which are comprised in the three last seals. *And power was given to him over the fourth part of the earth* — What came single and in a lower degree before, comes now together, and much more severely. The first seal brought victory with it: in the second was "a great sword;" but here a scimitar. In the third was moderate dearth; here famine, and plague, and wild beasts beside. And it may well be, that from the time of Trajan downwards, the fourth part of men upon the earth, that is, within the Roman empire, died by sword, famine, pestilence, and wild beasts. "At that time," says Aurelius Victor, "the Tyber overflowed much more fatally than under Nerva, with a great destruction of houses and there was a dreadful earthquake through many provinces, and a terrible plague and famine, *and many places consumed by fire.*" *By death* — That is, by pestilence wild beasts have, at several times, destroyed abundance of men; and undoubtedly there was given them, at this time, an uncommon fierceness and strength. It is observable that war brings on scarcity, and scarcity pestilence, through want of wholesome sustenance; and pestilence, by depopulating the country, leaves the few survivors an easier prey to the wild beasts. And thus these judgments make way for one another in the order wherein they are here represented. What has been already observed may be a fourfold proof that the four horsemen, as with their first entrance in the reign of Trajan, (which does by no means exhaust the contents of the four first seals,) so with all their entrances in succeeding ages, and with the whole course of the world and of visible nature, are in all ages subject to Christ, subsisting by his power, and serving his will, against the wicked, and in defense of the righteous. Herewith, likewise, a way is paved for the trumpets which regularly succeed each other; and the whole prophecy, as to what is future, is confirmed by the clear accomplishment of this part of it.

⁹ And when he opened the fifth seal, I saw under the altar the souls of them that had been slain for the word of God, and for the testimony which they held. ¹⁰ And they cried with a loud voice, saying, How long, O Lord, thou Holy One and true, dost thou not judge and avenge our blood on them that dwell upon the earth? ¹¹ And there was given to them, to every one, a white robe; and it was said to them, that they should rest yet for a time, till

---

9. *And when he opened the fifth seal* — As the four former seals, so the three latter, have a close connection with each other. These all refer to the invisible world; the fifth, to the happy dead, particularly the martyrs; the sixth, to the unhappy; the seventh, to the angels, especially those to whom the trumpets are given. *And I saw* — Not only the church warring under Christ, and the world warring under Satan; but also the invisible hosts, both of heaven and hell, are described in this book. And it not only describes the actions of both these armies upon earth; but their respective removals from earth, into a more happy or more miserable state, succeeding each other at several times, distinguished by various degrees, celebrated by various thanksgivings; and also the gradual increase of expectation and triumph in heaven, and of terror and misery in hell. *Under the altar* — That is, at the foot of it. Two altars are mentioned in the Revelation, "the golden altar" of incense, Revelation 9:13; and the altar of burnt-offerings, mentioned here, and Revelation 8:5, 14:18, 16:7. At this the souls of the martyrs now prostrate themselves. By and by their blood shall be avenged upon Babylon; but not yet, whence it appears that the plagues in the fourth seal do not concern Romans in particular.

10. AV holy and true. *And they cried* — This cry did not begin now, but under the first Roman persecution. The Romans themselves had already avenged the martyrs slain by the Jews on that whole nation. *How long* — They knew their blood would be avenged; but not immediately, as is now shown them. *O Lord* — The Greek word properly signifies the master of a family: it is therefore beautifully used by these, who are peculiarly of the household of God. *Thou Holy One and true* — Both the holiness and truth of God require him to execute judgment and vengeance. *Dost thou not judge and avenge our blood?* — There is no impure affection in heaven: therefore, this desire of theirs is pure and suitable to the will of God. The martyrs are concerned for the praise of their Master, of his holiness and truth: and the praise is given him, Revelation 19:2, where the prayer of the martyrs is changed into a thanksgiving:- Thou holy One and true: "True and right are thy judgments." How long dost thou not judge "He hath judged the great whore, and avenge our blood? and hath avenged the blood of his servants."

their fellowservants also and their brethren should be fulfilled, who should be killed even as they *were*.

¹² And I saw when he opened the sixth seal, and there was a great earthquake, and the sun became black as sackcloth of hair, and the moon became as blood. ¹³ And the stars of heaven fell to the earth, as a fig tree casteth its untimely figs, when it is shaken by a mighty wind. ¹⁴ And the heaven departed as a <u>book</u> that is rolled together; and every mountain and island were moved out of their places. ¹⁵ And the kings of the earth, and the

---

11. *And there was given to every one a white robe* — An emblem of innocence, joy, and victory, in token of honor and favorable acceptance. *And it was said to them* — They were told how long. They were not left in that uncertainty. *That they should rest* — Should cease from crying. They rested from pain before. *A time* — This word has a peculiar meaning in this book, to denote which, we may retain the original word chronos. Here are two classes of martyrs specified, the former killed under heathen Romans, the latter, under papal Romans. The former are commanded to rest till the latter are added to them. There were many of the former in the days of John: the first fruits of the latter died in the thirteenth century. Now, a time, or chronos, is 1111 years. This chronos began A. C. 98, and continued to the year 1209; or from Trajan's persecution, to the first crusade against the Waldenses. *Till* — It is not said, Immediately after this time is expired, vengeance shall be executed; but only, that immediately after this time their brethren and fellow servants will come to them. This event will precede the other; and there will be some space between.

12. *And I saw* — This sixth seal seems particularly to point out God's judgment on the wicked departed. St. John saw how the end of the world was even then set before those unhappy spirits. This representation might be made to them, without anything of it being perceived upon earth. The like representation is made in heaven, Revelation 11:18. *And there was a great earthquake* — Or shaking, not of the earth only, but the heavens. This is a farther description of the representation made to those unhappy souls.

13. *And the stars fell to, or towards, the earth* — Yea, and so they surely will, let astronomers fix their magnitude as they please. As a fig tree casteth its untimely figs, *when it is shaken by a mighty wind* — How sublimely is the violence of that shaking expressed by this comparison!

14. AV scroll. *And the heavens departed as a book that is rolled together* — When the scripture compares some very great with a little thing, the majesty and omnipotence of God, before whom great things are little, is highly exalted. *Every mountain and island* — What a mountain is to the land, that an island is to the sea.

great men, and the chief captains, and the rich, and the mighty, and every slave, and freeman hid themselves in the caves and in the rocks of the mountains; ⁱ⁶ and said to the mountains and rocks, Fall on us, and hide us from the face of him that sitteth on the throne, and from the wrath of the Lamb. ¹⁷ For the great day of his wrath is come; and who <u>is able</u> to stand?

Chapter 7

¹ And after these things I saw four angels standing on the four corners of the earth, holding the four winds, that the wind should not blow on the earth, nor on the sea, nor on any tree. ² And I saw another angel ascending from the

---

15. *And the kings of the earth* — They who had been so in their day. *And the great men and chief captains* — The generals and nobles. *Hid themselves* — So far as in them lay. *In the rocks of the mountains* — There are also rocks on the plains; but they were rocks on high, which they besought to fall upon them.

16. *To the mountains and the rocks* — Which were tottering already, verse 12. Revelation 6:12 *Hide us from the face of him* — Which "is against the ungodly," Psalm 34:16.

17. AV shall be able.

Ch 7. 1. *And after these things* — What follows is a preparation for the seventh seal, which is the weightiest of all. It is connected with the sixth by the particle and; whereas what is added, verse 9, Revelation 6:9 stands free and unconnected. *I saw four angels* — Probably evil ones. They have their employ with the four first trumpets, as have other evil angels with the three last; namely, the angel of the abyss, the four bound in the Euphrates, and Satan himself. These four angels would willingly have brought on all the calamities that follow without delay. But they were restrained till the servants of God were sealed, and till the seven angels were ready to sound: even as the angel of the abyss was not let loose, nor the angels in the Euphrates unbound, neither Satan cast to the earth, till the fifth, sixth, and seventh angels severally sounded. *Standing on the four corners of the earth* — East, west, south, north. In this order proceed the four first trumpets. *Holding the four winds* — Which else might have softened the fiery heat, under the first, second, and third trumpet. That the wind should not blow upon the earth, nor on the sea, *nor on any tree* — It seems, that these expressions betoken the several quarters of the world; that the earth signifies that to the east of Patmos, Asia, which was nearest to St. John, and where the trumpet of the first angel had its accomplishment. Europe swims in the sea over against this;

rising of the sun, having the seal of the living God; and he cried with a loud voice to the four angels, to whom it was given to hurt the earth and the sea, ³ saying, Hurt ye not the earth, neither the sea, neither the trees, till we have sealed the servants of our God <u>on</u> their foreheads. ⁴ And I heard the number of them that were sealed; an hundred forty four thousand were sealed out of all the tribes of the children of Israel:

⁵ Of the tribe of Judah *were* sealed twelve thousand.
 Of the tribe of Reuben *were* sealed twelve thousand.
 Of the tribe of Gad *were* sealed twelve thousand.
⁶ Of the tribe of Aser *were* sealed twelve thousand.
 Of the tribe of Nepthalim *were* sealed twelve thousand.
 Of the tribe of Manasses *were* sealed twelve thousand.
⁷ Of the tribe of Simeon *were* sealed twelve thousand.
 Of the tribe of Levi *were* sealed twelve thousand.
 Of the tribe of Issachar *were* sealed twelve thousand.

---

and is accordingly termed by the prophets, "the islands." The third part, Africa, seems to be meant, Revelation 8:7, 8, 10, by "the streams of water," or "the trees," which grow plentifully by them.

2. AV east. *And I saw another (a good) angel ascending from the east* — The plagues begin in the east; so does the sealing. Having the seal of the only living and true God: *and he cried with a loud voice to the four angels* — Who were hasting to execute their charge. *To whom it was given to hurt the earth and the sea* — First, and afterwards "the trees."

3. AV in. *Hurt not the earth, till we* — Other angels were joined in commission with him. *Have sealed the servants of our God on their foreheads* — Secured the servants of God of the twelve tribes from the impending calamities; whereby they shall be as clearly distinguished from the rest, as if they were visibly marked on their foreheads.

4. *Of the children of Israel* — To these will afterwards be joined a multitude out of all nations. But it may be observed, this is not the number of all the Israelites who are saved from Abraham or Moses to the end of all things; but only of those who were secured from the plagues which were then ready to fall on the earth. It seems as if this book had, in many places, a special view to the people of Israel.

5. Judah is mentioned first, in respect of the kingdom, and of the Messiah sprung therefrom.

7. After the Levitical ceremonies were abolished, Levi was again on a level with his brethren.

⁸ Of the tribe of Zabulon *were* sealed twelve thousand.
Of the tribe of Joseph *were* sealed twelve thousand.
Of the tribe of Benjamin *were* sealed twelve thousand.

⁹ After these things I saw, and, behold, a great multitude, which no man could number, of all nations, and <u>tribes</u>, and people, and tongues, <u>standing</u> before the throne, and before the Lamb, clothed with white robes, and palms in their hands. ¹⁰ And they <u>cry</u> with a loud voice, saying, Salvation to our God who sitteth on the throne, and to the Lamb. ¹¹ And all the angels stood round about the throne, and the elders, and the four <u>living creatures</u>, and they fell before the throne on their faces, and worshipped God, ¹² saying, Amen. The blessing, and the glory, and the wisdom, and the thanksgiving, and the

---

8. *Of the tribe of Joseph* — Or Ephraim; perhaps not mentioned by name, as having been, with Daniel, the most idolatrous of all the tribes. It is farther observable of Daniel, that it was very early reduced to a single family; which family itself seems to have been cut off in war, before the time of Ezra; for in the Chronicles, where the posterity of the patriarchs is recited, Daniel is wholly omitted.

9. AV kindreds; stood. *A great multitude* — Of those who had happily finished their course. Such multitudes are afterwards described, and still higher degrees of glory which they attain after a sharp fight and magnificent victory, Revelation 14:1; 15:2; 19:1; 20:4. There is an inconceivable variety in the degrees of reward in the other world. Let not any slothful one say, "If I get to heaven at all, I will be content:" such an one may let heaven go altogether. In worldly things, men are ambitious to get as high as they can. Christians have a far more noble ambition. The difference between the very highest and the lowest state in the world is nothing to the smallest difference between the degrees of glory. *But who has time to think of this? Who is at all concerned about it? Standing before the throne* — In the full vision of God. *And palms in their hands* — Tokens of joy and victory.

10. AV cried. *Salvation to our God* — Who hath saved us from all evil into all the happiness of heaven. The salvation for which they praise God is described, verse 15; Revelation 7:15 that for which they praise the Lamb, verse 14; Revelation 7:14 and both, in the sixteenth and seventeenth verses. Revelation 7:16, 17.

11. AV beasts. *And all the angels stood* — In waiting. Round about the throne, *and the elders and the four living creatures* — That is, the living creatures, next the throne; the elders, round these; and the angels, round them both. *And they fell on their faces* — So do the elders, once only, Revelation 11:16. The heavenly ceremonial has its fixed order and measure.

honour, and the power, and the strength, *be* to our God for ever and ever. ¹³ And one of the elders answered, saying to me, Who are these that are clothed in white robes? And whenceare they come? ¹⁴ And I said to him, <u>My lord</u>, thou knowest. And he said to me, These are they who come out of great <u>affliction</u>, and they have washed their robes, and made them white in the blood of the Lamb. ¹⁵ Therefore are they before the throne of God, and serve him day and night in his temple; and he that sitteth upon the throne shall <u>have his tent over</u> them. ¹⁶ They shall hunger no more, neither thirst any more;

---

12. *Amen* — With this word all the angels confirm the words of the "great multitude;" but they likewise carry the praise much higher. The blessing, and the glory, and the wisdom, and the thanksgiving, and the honor, and the power, and the strength, *be unto our God for ever and ever* — Before the Lamb began to open the seven seals, a sevenfold hymn of praise was brought him by many angels, Revelation 5:12. Now he is upon opening the last seal, and the seven angels are going to receive seven trumpets, in order to make the kingdoms of the world subject to God. All the angels give sevenfold praise to God.

13. *And one of the elders* — What stands, verses 13-17, Revelation 7:13-17 might have immediately followed the tenth verse; but that the praise of the angels, which was at the same time with that of the "great multitude," came in between. *Answered* — He answered St. John's desire to know, not any words that he spoke.

14. AV Sir; tribulation. *My Lord* — Or, my master; a common term of respect. So Zechariah, likewise, bespeaks the angel, Zechariah 1:9; 4:4; 6:4. *Thou knowest* — That is, I know not; but thou dost. *These are they* — Not martyrs; for these are not such a multitude as no man can number. But as all the angels appear here, so do all the souls of the righteous who had lived from the beginning of the world. *Who come* — He does not say, who did come; but, who come now also: to whom, likewise, pertain all who will come hereafter. *Out of great affliction* — Of various kinds, wisely and graciously allotted by God to all his children. *And have washed their robes* — From all guilt. *And made them white* — In all holiness. *By the blood of the Lamb* — Which not only cleanses, but adorns us also.

15. AV dwell among. *Therefore* — Because they came out of great affliction, and have washed their robes in his blood. *Are they before the throne* — It seems, even nearer than the angels. *And serve him day and night* — Speaking after the manner of men; that is, continually. *In his temple* — Which is in heaven. *And he shall have his tent over them* — Shall spread his glory over them as a covering.

neither shall the sun light on them, nor any heat. ¹⁷ For the Lamb who is in the midst of the throne will feed them, and will lead them to living fountains of waters; and God will wipe away all tears from their eyes.

Chapter 8

¹ And when he had opened the seventh seal, there was silence in heaven about half an hour. ² And I saw the seven angels who stood before God; and seven trumpets were given them. ³ And another angel came and stood at the

---

16. *Neither shall the sun light on them* — For God is there their sun. Nor any painful heat, or inclemency of seasons.

17. *For the Lamb will feed them* — With eternal peace and joy; so that they shall hunger no more. *And will lead them to living fountains of water* — The comforts of the Holy Ghost; so that they shall thirst no more. Neither shall they suffer or grieve any more; for God "will wipe away all tears from their eyes."

Ch 8. 1. *And when he had opened the seventh seal, there was silence in heaven* – Such a silence is mentioned but in this one place. It was uncommon, and highly observable: for praise is sounding in heaven day and night. In particular, immediately before this silence, all the angels, and before them the innumerable multitude, had been crying with a loud voice; and now all is still at once: there is an universal pause. Hereby the seventh seal is very remarkably distinguished from the six preceding. This silence before God shows that those who were round about him were expecting, with the deepest reverence, the great things which the Divine Majesty would farther open and order. Immediately after, the seven trumpets are heard, and a sound more august than ever. Silence is only a preparation: the grand point is, the sounding the trumpets to the praise of God. *About half an hour* – To St. John, in the vision, it might seem a common half hour.

2. *And I saw* – The seven trumpets belong to the seventh seal, as do the seven phials to the seventh trumpet. This should be carefully remembered, that we may not confound together the times which follow each other. And yet it may be observed, in general, concerning the times of the incidents mentioned in this book, it is not a certain rule, that every part of the text is fully accomplished before the completion of the following part begins. All things mentioned in the epistles are not full accomplished before the seals are opened; neither are all things mentioned under the seals fulfilled before the trumpets begin; nor yet is the seventh trumpet wholly past before the phials are poured out. Only the beginning of each part goes before the beginning of

altar, having a golden censer; and much incense was given him, that he might place *it* with the prayers of all saints upon the golden altar which is before the throne. ⁴ And the smoke of the incense ascended before God out of the

---

the following. Thus the epistles begin before the seals, the seals before the trumpets, the trumpets before the phials. One epistle begins before another, one seal before another, one trumpet especially before another, one phial before another. Yet, sometimes, what begins later than another thing ends sooner; and what begins earlier than another thing ends later: so the seventh trumpet begins earlier than the phials, and yet extends beyond them all.

The seven angels which stood before God – A character of the highest eminence. *And seven trumpets were given them* – When men desire to make known openly a thing of public concern, they give a token that may be seen or heard far and wide; and, among such, none are more ancient than trumpets, Lev 25:9 ; Num 10:2; Amos 3:6.The Israelites, in particular, used them, both in the worship of God and in war; therewith openly praising the power of God before, after, and in, the battle, Josh 6:4 ; 2Ch 13:14, &c. And the angels here made known by these trumpets the wonderful works of God, whereby all opposing powers are successively shaken, till the kingdom of the world becomes the kingdom of God and his Anointed.

These trumpets reach nearly from the time of St. John to the end of the world; and they are distinguished by manifest tokens. The place of the four first is specified; namely, east, west, south, and north successively: in the three last, immediately after the time of each, the place likewise is pointed out. forth of the second woe: but the trumpets were given to him and the other six together; (as were afterward the phials to the seven angels;) and it is accordingly said of all the seven together, that "they prepared themselves to sound." These, therefore, were not men, as some have thought, but angels, properly so called.

3. *And* – In the second verse, Rev 7:2, "trumpets were given" to the seven angels; and in the sixth, Rev 7:6, "prepared to sound." But between these, the incense of this angel and the prayers of the saints are mentioned; the interposing of which shows, that the prayers of the saints and the trumpets of the angels go together: and these prayers, with the effects of them, may well be supposed to extend through all the seven. *Another angel* – Another created angel. Such are all that are here spoken of. In this part of the Revelation, Christ is never termed an angel; but, "the Lamb." *Came and stood at the altar* – Of burnt-offerings. *And there was given him a golden censer* – A censer was a cup on a plate or saucer. This was the token and the business of the office. *And much incense was given* – Incense generally signifies prayer: here it signifies the longing desires of the angels, that the holy counsel of God

angel's hand with the prayers of the saints. ⁵ And the angel took the censer, and filled it with fire of the altar, and threw it upon the earth; and there were thunderings, and lightnings, and voices, and an earthquake.

⁶ And the seven angels who had the seven trumpets prepared themselves to sound. ⁷ The <u>first sounded</u>, and there was hail and fire mingled with blood, and they were cast upon the earth; and <u>the third part of earth was burned up</u>, and the third part of the trees was burned up, and all the green grass was burnt up.

---

might be fulfilled. And there was much incense; for as the prayers of all the saints in heaven and earth are here joined together: so are the desires of all the angels which are brought by this angel. *That he might place it* – It is not said, offer it; for he was discharging the office of an angel, not a priest. *With the prayers of all the saints* – At the same time; but not for the saints. The angels are fellow servants with the saints, not mediators for them.

4. And the smoke of the incense came up before God, with the prayers of the saints — A token that both were accepted.

5. *And there were thunderings, and lightnings, and voices, and an earthquake* — These, especially when attended with fire, are emblems of God's dreadful judgments, which are immediately to follow.

6. *And the seven angels prepared themselves to sound* — That each, when it should come to his turn, might sound without delay. But while they do sound, they still stand before God.

7. AV first angel sounded; omitted in AV (JW added entire phrase). *And the first sounded* – And every angel continued to sound, till all which his trumpet brought was fulfilled and till the next began. There are intervals between the three woes, but not between the four first trumpets. And there was hail and fire mingled with blood, and *there were cast upon the earth* – The earth seems to mean Asia; Palestine, in particular. Quickly after the Revelation was given, the Jewish calamities under Adrian began: yea, before the reign of Trajan was ended. And here the trumpets begin. Even under Trajan, in the year 114, the Jews made an insurrection with a most dreadful fury; and in the parts about Cyrene, in Egypt, and in Cyprus, destroyed four hundred and sixty thousand persons. But they were repressed by the victorious power of Trajan, and afterward slaughtered themselves in vast multitudes. The alarm spread itself also into Mesopotamia, where Lucius Quintius slew a great number of them. They rose in Judea again in the second year of Adrian; but were presently quelled. Yet in 133 they broke out more violently than ever, under their false messiah Barcochab; and the war continued till the year 135, when almost all Judea was desolated. In the Egyptian plague also hail and fire were together. But here hail is to be taken

⁸ And the second angel sounded, and as it were a great mountain burning with fire was cast into the sea; and the third part of the sea became blood; ⁹ And the third part of the creatures that were in the sea which had life, died; and the third part of the ships were destroyed.

---

figuratively, as also blood, for a vehement, sudden, powerful, hurtful invasion; and fire betokens the revenge of an enraged enemy, with the desolation therefrom. *And they were cast upon the earth* – That is, the fire and hail and blood. But they existed before they were cast upon the earth. The storm fell, the blood flowed, and the flames raged round Cyrene, and in Egypt, and Cyprus, before they reached Mesopotamia and Judea. *And the third part of the earth was burnt up* – Fifty well-fortified cities, and nine hundred and eighty-five well-inhabited towns of the Jews, were wholly destroyed in this war. Vast tracts of land were likewise left desolate and without inhabitant. And the third part of the trees was burned up, and *all the green grass was burned up* – Some understand by the trees, men of eminence among the Jews; by the grass, the common people. The Romans spared many of the former: the latter were almost all destroyed.

Thus vengeance began at the Jewish enemies of Christ's kingdom; though even then the Romans did not quite escape. But afterwards it came upon them more and more violently: the second trumpet affects the Roman heathens in particular; the third, the dead, unholy Christians; the fourth, the empire itself.

8. *And the second angel sounded, and as it were a great mountain burning with fire was cast into the sea* – By the sea, particularly as it is here opposed to the earth, we may understand the west, or Europe; and chiefly the middle parts of it, the vast Roman empire. A mountain here seems to signify a great force and multitude of people. Jer 51:25; so this may point at the irruption of the barbarous nations into the Roman empire. The warlike Goths broke in upon it about the year 250: and from that time the irruption of one nation after another never ceased till the very form of the Roman empire, and all but the name, was lost. The fire may mean the fire of war, and the rage of those savage nations. *And the third part of the sea became blood* – This need not imply, that just a third part of the Romans was slain; but it is certain an inconceivable deal of blood was shed in all these invasions.

9. *And the third part of the creatures that were in the sea* – That is, of all sorts of men, of every station and degree. *Died* – By those merciless invaders. *And the third part of the ships were destroyed* – It is a frequent thing to resemble a state or republic to a ship, wherein many people are embarked together, and share in the same dangers. And how many states were utterly destroyed by those inhuman conquerors! Much likewise of this was literally

¹⁰ And the third angel sounded, and there fell from heaven a great star burning <u>as a torch</u>, and it fell on the third part of the rivers, and on the fountains of waters. ¹¹ And the name of the star is called Wormwood; and the third part of the waters became wormwood; and many men died of the waters, because they were made bitter.

---

fulfilled. How often was the sea tinged with blood! How many of those who dwelt mostly upon it were killed! And what number of ships destroyed!

10. AV *as it were a lamp*. *And the third angel sounded, and there fell from heaven a great star, and it fell on the third part of the rivers* – It seems Africa is meant by the rivers; (with which this burning part of the world abounds in an especial manner;) Egypt in particular, which the Nile overflows every year far and wide. In the whole African history, between the irruption of the barbarous nations into the Roman empire, and the ruin of the western empire, after the death of Valentinian the Third, there is nothing more momentous than the Arian calamity, which sprung up in the year 315. It is not possible to tell how many persons, particularly at Alexandria, in all Egypt, and in the neighboring countries, were destroyed by the rage of the Arians. Yet Africa fared better than other parts of the empire, with regard to the barbarous nations, till the governor of it, whose wife was a zealous Arian, and aunt to Genseric, king of the Vandals, was, under that pretence, unjustly accused before the empress Placidia. He was then prevailed upon to invite the Vandals into Africa; who under Genseric, in the year 428, founded there a kingdom of their own, which continued till the year 533. Under these Vandal kings the true believers endured all manner of afflictions and persecutions. And thus Arianism was the inlet to all heresies and calamities, and at length to Mahometanism itself. This great star was not an angel, (angels are not the agents in the two preceding or the following trumpet,) but a teacher of the church, one of the stars in the right hand of Christ. Such was Arius. He fell from on high, as it were from heaven, into the most pernicious doctrines, and made in his fall a gazing on all sides, being great, and now burning as a torch. *He fell on the third part of the rivers* – His doctrine spread far and wide, particularly in Egypt. *And on the fountains of water* – wherewith Africa abounds.

11. *And the name of the star is called Wormwood* — The unparalleled bitterness both of Arius himself and of his followers show the exact propriety of his title. *And the third part of the waters became wormwood* — A very considerable part of Afric was infected with the same bitter doctrine and Spirit. *And many men (though not a third part of them) died* — By the cruelty of the Arians.

¹² And the fourth angel sounded, and the third part of the sun was smitten, and the third part of the moon, and the third part of the stars; so that the third part of them was darkened, and the day shone not for a third part thereof, and the night likewise.

---

12. *And the fourth angel sounded, and the third part of the sun was smitten* – Or struck. After the emperor Theodosius died, and the empire was divided into the eastern and the western, the barbarous nations poured in as a flood. The Goths and Hunns in the years 403 and 405 fell upon Italy itself with an impetuous force; and the former, in the year 410, took Rome by storm, and plundered it without mercy. In the year 452 Attila treated the upper part of Italy in the same manner. In 455 Valentinian the Third was killed, and Genseric invited from Africa. He plundered Rome for fourteen days together. Recimer plundered it again in 472. During all these commotions, one province was lost after another, till, in the year 476, Odoacer seized upon Rome, deposed the emperor, and put an end to the empire itself.

An eclipse of the sun or moon is termed by the Hebrews, *astroke*. Now, as such a darkness does not come all at once, but by degrees, so likewise did the darkness which fell on the Roman, particularly the western empire; for the stroke began long before Odoacer, namely, when the barbarians first conquered the capital city. And the third part of the moon, and the third part of the stars; *so that the third part of them was darkened* – As under the first, second, and third trumpets by "the earth," "sea," and "rivers," are to be understood the men that inhabit them; so hereby the sun, moon, and stars, may be understood the men that live under them, who are so overwhelmed with calamities in those days of darkness, that they can no longer enjoy the light of heaven: unless it may be thought to imply their being killed; so that the sun, moon, and stars shine to them no longer. The very same expression we find in 32:8. "I will darken all the lights of heaven over them." As then the fourth seal transcends the three preceding seals, so does the fourth trumpet the three preceding trumpets. For in this not the third part of the earth, or sea, or rivers only, but of all who are under the sun, are affected. *And the day shone not for a third part thereof* – That is, shone with only a third part of its usual brightness. *And the night likewise* – The moon and stars having lost a third part of their lustre, either with regard to those who, being dead, saw them no longer, or those who saw them with no satisfaction.

The three last trumpets have the time of their continuance fixed, and between each of them there is a remarkable pause: whereas between the four former there is no pause, nor is the time of their continuance mentioned; but all together these four seem to take up a little less than four hundred years.

¹³ And I saw, and heard an angel flying in the midst of heaven, saying with a loud voice, Woe, woe, woe, to the inhabitants of the earth by reason of the other voices of the trumpets of the three angels, which are yet to sound!

Chapter 9

¹ And the fifth angel sounded, and I saw a star falling from heaven to the earth; and to him was given the key of the bottomless pit. ² And he opened the bottomless pit; and there ascended a smoke out of the pit, as the smoke of a great furnace; and the sun and the air were darkened by the smoke of the

---

13. *And I saw, and heard an angel flying* – Between the trumpets of the fourth and fifth angel. *In the midst of heaven* – The three woes, as we shall see, stretch themselves over the earth from Persia eastward, beyond Italy, westward; all which space had been filled with the gospel by the apostles. In the midst of this lies Patmos, where St. John saw this angel, saying, *Woe, woe, woe* – Toward the end of the fifth century, there were many presages of approaching calamities. *To the inhabitants of the earth* – All without exception. Heavy trials were coming on them all. Even while the angel was proclaiming this, the preludes of these three woes were already in motion. These fell more especially on the Jews. As to the prelude of the first woe in Persia, Isdegard II., in 454, was resolved to abolish the Sabbath, till he was, by Rabbi Mar, diverted from his purpose. Likewise in the year 474, Phiruz afflicted the Jews much, and compelled many of them to apostatize. A prelude of the second woe was the rise of the Saracens, who, in 510, fell into Arabia and Palestine. To prepare for the third woe, Innocent I., and his successors, not only endeavored to enlarge their episcopal jurisdiction beyond all bounds, but also their worldly power, by taking every opportunity of encroaching upon the empire, which as yet stood in the way of their unlimited monarchy.

Ch 9. 1. *And the fifth angel sounded, and I saw a star* — Far different from that mentioned, Revelation 8:11. This star belongs to the invisible world. The third woe is occasioned by the dragon cast out of heaven; the second takes place at the loosing of the four angels who were bound in the Euphrates. The first is here brought by the angel of the abyss, which is opened by this star, or holy angel. *Falling to the earth* — Coming swiftly and with great force. *And to him was given* — when he was come. *The key of the bottomless pit* — A deep and hideous prison; but different from "the lake of fire."

pit. ³ And out of the smoke there came forth locusts upon the earth; and power was given them, as the scorpions of the earth have power. ⁴ And it was commanded them not to hurt the grass of the earth, neither any green thing, neither any tree; but only <u>the men</u> who have not the seal of God on their foreheads. ⁵ And it was given them not to kill them, but that they should be tormented five months; and the torment of them *is* as the torment of a

---

2. *And there arose a smoke out of the pit* — The locusts, who afterwards rise out of it, seem to be, as we shall afterwards see, the Persians; agreeable to which, this smoke is their detestable idolatrous doctrine, and false zeal for it, which now broke out in an uncommon paroxysm. *As the smoke of a great furnace* — where the clouds of it rise thicker and thicker, spread far and wide, and press one upon another, so that the darkness increases continually. *And the sun and the air were darkened* — A figurative expression, denoting heavy affliction. This smoke occasioned more and more such darkness over the Jews in Persia.

3. *And out of the smoke* — Not out of the bottomless pit, but from the smoke which issued thence. *There went forth locusts* — A known emblem of a numerous, hostile, hurtful people. Such were the Persians, from whom the Jews, in the sixth century, suffered beyond expression. In the year 540 their academies were stopped, nor were they permitted to have a president for near fifty years. In 589 this affliction ended; but it began long before 540. The prelude of it was about the year 455 and 474: the main storm came on in the reign of Cabades, and lasted from 483 to 532. Toward the beginning of the sixth century, Mar Rab Isaac, president of the academy, was put to death. Hereon followed an insurrection of the Jews, which lasted seven years before they were conquered by the Persians. Some of them were then put to death, but not many; the rest were closely imprisoned. And from this time the nation of the Jews were hated and persecuted by the Persians, till they had well nigh rooted them out. *The scorpions of the earth* — The most hurtful kind. The scorpions of the air have wings.

4. AV those men. *And it was commanded them* — By the secret power of God. Not to hurt the grass, neither any green thing, *nor any tree* — Neither those of low, middling, or high degree, *but only such of them as were not sealed* — Principally the unbelieving Israelites. But many who were called Christians suffered with them.

scorpion when he stingeth a man. ⁶ And in those days the men shall seek death, but not find it; and shall desire to die, but death will flee from them.

⁷ And the <u>appearances</u> of the locusts *are* like horses <u>made ready</u> for battle; and on their heads *are* as it were crowns like gold, and their faces *are* as the faces of men. ⁸ And they had hair as the hair of women, and their teeth were as the *teeth* of lions. ⁹ And they had breastplates, as it were breastplates of iron; and the noise of their wings *was* as the noise of chariots of many horses running to battle. ¹⁰ And they have tails like scorpions, and stings were in their tails; their power *is*, to hurt men five months. ¹¹ And they have over them a king, the angel of the bottomless pit; his name in the Hebrew is Abaddon, but in the Greek he hath the name Apollyon. ¹² One woe is past; behold, there come yet two woes after these things.

---

5. *Not to kill them* — Very few of them were killed: in general, they were imprisoned and variously tormented.

6. *The men* — That is, the men who are so tormented.

7. AV shapes; prepared. *And the appearances* — This description suits a people neither thoroughly civilized, nor entirely savage; and such were the Persians of that age. *Of the locusts are like horses* — With their riders. The Persians excelled in horsemanship. *And on their heads are as it were crowns* — Turbans. *And their faces are as the faces of men* — Friendly and agreeable.

8. *And they had hair as the hair of women* — All the Persians of old gloried in long hair. *And their teeth were as the teeth of lions* — Breaking and tearing all things in pieces.

9. *And the noise of their wings was as the noise of chariots of many horses* — With their war-chariots, drawn by many horses, they, as it were, flew to and fro.

10. *And they have tails like scorpions* — That is, each tail is like a scorpion, not like the tail of a scorpion. *To hurt the unsealed men five months* — Five prophetic months; that is, seventy-nine common years So long did these calamities last.

11. *And they have over them a king* — One by whom they are peculiarly directed and governed. *His name is Abaddon* — Both this and Apollyon signify a destroyer. By this he is distinguished from the dragon, whose proper name is Satan.

12. *One woe is past; behold, there come yet two woes after these things* — The Persian power, under which was the first woe, was now broken by the Saracens: from this time the first pause made a wide way for the two succeeding woes. In 589, when the first woe ended, Mahomet was twenty

¹³ And the sixth angel sounded, and I heard a voice from the four corners of the golden altar which is before God, ¹⁴ saying to the sixth angel who had the trumpet, Loose the four angels who are bound in the great river Euphrates. ¹⁵ And the four angels were loosed, who were prepared for the hour, and day, and month, and year, to kill the third part of men. ¹⁶ And the

---

years old, and the contentions of the Christians with each other were exceeding great. In 591 Chosroes II. reigned in Persia, who, after the death of the emperor, made dreadful disturbances in the east, Hence Mahomet found an open door for his new religion and empire. And when the usurper Phocas had, in the year 606, not only declared the Bishop of Romans, Boniface III., universal bishop, but also the church of Romans the head of all churches, this was a sure step to advance the Papacy to its utmost height. Thus, after the passing away of the first woe, the second, yea, and the third, quickly followed; as indeed they were both on the way together with it before the first effectually began.

13. AV horns. *And the sixth angel sounded* — Under this angel goes forth the second woe. *And I heard a voice from the four corners of the golden altar* — This golden altar is the heavenly pattern of the Levitical altar of incense. This voice signified that the execution of the wrath of God, mentioned verses 20, 21, Revelation 9:20, 21 should, at no intercession, be delayed any longer.

14. *Loose the four angels* — To go every way; to the four quarters. These were evil angels, or they would not have been bound. Why, or how long, they were bound we know not.

15. *And the four angels were loosed, who were prepared* — By loosing them, as well as by their strength and rage. *To kill the third part of men* — That is, an immense number of them. For the hour, and day, and month, *and year* — All this agrees with the slaughter which the Saracens made for a long time after Mahomet's death. And with the number of angels let loose agrees the number of their first and most eminent caliphs. These were Ali, Abubeker, Omar, and Osman. Mahomet named Ali, his cousin and son-in-law, for his successor; but he was soon worked out by the rest, till they severally died, and so made room for him. They succeeded each other, and each destroyed innumerable multitudes of men. There are in a prophetic...

	Com. Years.	Com. Days.
Hour:		8
Day:		196
Month:	15	318
Year:	196	117
In all...	212 years	

number of the army of horsemen *was* two hundred millions. I heard their number. ¹⁷ And thus I saw the horses in the vision, and them that sat on them, having breastplates of fire, and hyacinth, and brimstone; and the heads of the horses *are* as the heads of lions; and out of their mouths goeth fire and smoke and brimstone. ¹⁸ By <u>these three plagues</u> were the third part of men killed, by

---

[Editor: Wesley adds 1 year for the 8 & 196 Com. Days to arrive at 212 years.]

Now, the second woe, as also the beginning of the third, has its place between the ceasing of the locusts and the rising of the beast out of the sea, even at the time that the Saracens, who were chiefly cavalry, were in the height of their carnage; from their, first caliph, Abubeker, till they were repulsed from Romans under Leo IV.

These 212 years may therefore be reckoned from the year 634 to 847. The gradation in reckoning the time, beginning with the hour and ending with a year, corresponds with their small beginning and vast increase. Before and after Mahomet's death, they had enough to do to settle their affairs at home. Afterwards Abubeker went farther, and in the year 634 gained great advantage over the Persians and Romans in Syria. Under Omar was the conquest of Mesopotamia, Palestine, and Egypt made. Under Osman, that of Afric, (with the total suppression of the Roman government in the year 647,) of Cyprus, and of all Persia in 651. After Ali was dead, his son Ali Hasen, a peaceable prince, was driven out by Muavia; under whom, and his successors, the power of the Saracens so increased, that within fourscore years after Mahomet's death they had extended their conquests farther than the warlike Romans did in four hundred years.

16. *And the number of the horsemen was two hundred millions* — Not that so many were ever brought into the field at once, but (if we understand the expression literally) in the course of "the hour, and day, and month, and year." So neither were "the third part of men killed" at once, but during that course of years.

17. *And thus I saw the horses and them that sat on them in the vision* — St. John seems to add these words, in the vision, to intimate that we are not to take this description just according to the letter. *Having breastplates of fire* — Fiery red. *And hyacinth* — Dun blue. *And brimstone* — A faint yellow. Of the same color with the fire and smoke and brimstone, which go out of the mouths of their horses. *And the heads of their horses are as the heads of lions* — That is, fierce and terrible. *And out of their mouth goeth fire and smoke and brimstone* — This figurative expression may denote the consuming, blinding, all-piercing rage, fierceness, and force of these horsemen.

the fire, and the smoke, and the brimstone, which went out of their mouths. [19] For the power of the horses is in their mouths, and in their tails; for their tails *are* like serpents, having heads, and with them they do hurt.

[20] And the rest of the men who were not killed by these plagues yet repented not of the works of their hands, that they should not worship devils, and idols of gold, and silver, and brass, and stone, and of wood; which can neither see, nor hear, nor walk; [21] neither repented of their murders, nor of their sorceries, nor of their fornications, nor of their thefts.

---

18. AV these plagues. *By these three* — Which were inseparably joined. *Were the third part of men* — In the countries they over-ran. *Killed* — Omar alone, in eleven years and a half, took thirty-six thousand cities or forts. How many men must be killed therein!

19. *For the power of these horses is in their mouths, and in their tails* — Their riders fight retreating as well as advancing: so that their rear is as terrible as their front. For their tails are like serpents, *having heads* — Not like the tails of serpents only. They may be fitly compared to the amphisbena, a kind of serpent, which has a short tail, not unlike a head from which it throws out its poison as if it had two heads.

20. *And the rest of the men who were not killed* — Whom the Saracens did not destroy. It is observable, the countries they over-ran were mostly those where the gospel had been planted. *By these plagues* — Here the description of the second woe ends. *Yet repented not* — Though they were called Christians. *Of the works of their hands* — Presently specified. *That they should not worship devils* — The invocation of departed saints, whether true, or false, or doubtful, or forged, crept early into the Christian church, and was carried farther and farther; and who knows how many who are invoked as saints are among evil, not good, angels; or how far devils have mingled with such blind worship, *and with the wonders wrought on those occasions? And idols* — About the year 590, men began to venerate images; and though upright men zealously opposed it, yet, by little and little, images grew into manifest idols. For after much contention, both in the east and west, in the year 787, the worship of images was established by the second Council of Nice. Yet was image worship sharply opposed some time after, by the emperor Theophilus. But when he died, in 842, his widow, Theodora, established it again; as did the Council at Constantinople in the year 863, and again in 871.

21. *Neither repented of their murders, nor of their sorceries* — Whoever reads the histories of the seventh, eighth, and ninth centuries, will find numberless instances of all these in every part of the Christian world. But though God cut off so many of these scandals to the Christian name, yet the

Chapter 10

¹ And I saw another mighty angel coming down from heaven, clothed with a cloud and a rainbow upon his head, and his face as the sun, and his feet as pillars of fire. ² And he had in his hand a little book open; and he set his right foot upon the sea, and his left foot upon the earth. ³ And he cried

---

rest went on in the same course. Some of them, however, might repent under the plagues which follow.

Ch 10. From the first verse of this chapter to chap. xi. 13, preparation is made for the important trumpet of the seventh angel. It consists of two parts, which run parallel to each other: the former reaches from the first to the seventh verse of this chapter; the latter, from the eighth of this to the thirteenth verse of the eleventh chapter: whence, also, the sixth verse of this chapter is parallel to the eleventh verse. The period to which both these refer begins during the second woe, as appears, chap. xi. 14; but, being once begun, it extends in a continued course far into the trumpet of the seventh angel. Hence many things are represented here which are not fulfilled till long after. So the joyful "consummation of the mystery of God" is spoken of in the seventh verse of this chapter, which yet is not till after "the consummation of the wrath of God," Rev. 16:1. So the ascent of the beast "out of the bottomless pit" is mentioned, Rev. 11:7, which nevertheless is still to come, Rev. xvii. 8; and so "the earthquake," by which a tenth part of the great city falls, and the rest are converted, Rev. 11:13, is really later than that by which the same city is "split into three parts," Rev. 16:19. This is a most necessary observation, whereby we may escape many and great mistakes.

1. *And I saw another mighty angel* — Another from that "mighty angel," mentioned, Revelation 5:2; yet he was a created angel; for he did not swear by himself, verse 6. Revelation 5:6 *Clothed with a cloud* — In token of his high dignity. *And a rainbow upon his head* — A lovely token of the divine favor. And yet it is not too glorious for a creature: the woman, Revelation 12:1, is described more glorious still. *And his face as the sun* — Nor is this too much for a creature: for all the righteous "shall shine forth as the sun," Matthew 13:43. *And his feet as pillars of fire* — Bright as flame.

2. *And he had in his hand* — His left hand: he swore with his right. He stood with his right foot on the sea, toward the west; his left, on the land, toward the east: so that he looked southward. And so St. John (as Patmos lies near Asia) could conveniently take the book out of his left hand. This sealed book was first in the right hand of him that sat on the throne: thence the Lamb took it, and opened the seals. And now this little book, containing the

with a loud voice, as a lion roareth; and when he cried, seven thunders uttered their voices. ⁴ And when the seven thunders had uttered their voices, I was about to write; and I heard a voice from heaven, saying, Seal up the things which the seven thunders have uttered, and write them not. ⁵ And the angel whom I saw standing upon the sea and upon the earth lifted up his right hand toward heaven; ⁶ and sware by him that liveth for ever and ever, who created

---

remainder of the other, is given opened, as it was, to St. John. From this place the Revelation speaks more clearly and less figuratively than before. *And he set his right foot upon the sea* — Out of which the first beast was to come. *And his left foot upon the earth* — Out of which was to come the second. The sea may betoken Europe; the earth, Asia; the chief theatres of these great things.

3. *And he cried* — Uttering the words set down, verse 6. Revelation 10:6 And while he cried, *or was crying* — At the same instant. *Seven thunders uttered their voices* — In distinct words, each after the other. Those who spoke these words were glorious, heavenly powers, whose voice was as the loudest thunder.

4. *And I heard a voice from heaven* — Doubtless from him who had at first commanded him to write, and who presently commands him to take the book; namely, Jesus Christ. Seal up those things which the seven thunders have uttered, *and write them not* — These are the only things of all which he heard that he is commanded to keep secret: so something peculiarly secret was revealed to the beloved John, besides all the secrets that are written in this book. At the same time we are prevented from inquiring what it was which these thunders uttered: suffice that we may know all the contents of the opened book, and of the oath of the angel.

5. *And the angel* — This manifestation of things to come under the trumpet of the seventh angel hath a twofold introduction: first, the angel speaks for God, verse 7; Revelation 10:7 then Christ speaks for himself, Revelation 11:3. The angel appeals to the prophets of former times; Christ, to his own two witnesses. Whom I saw standing upon the earth and upon the sea, *lifted up his right hand toward heaven* — As yet the dragon was in heaven. When he is cast thence he brings the third and most dreadful woe on the earth and sea: so that it seems as if there would be no end of calamities. Therefore the angel comprises, in his posture and in his oath, both heaven, sea, and earth, and makes on the part of the eternal God and almighty Creator, a solemn protestation, that he will assert his kingly authority against all his enemies. *He lifted up his right hand toward heaven* — The angel in Daniel, Daniel 12:7, (not improbably the same angel,) lifted up both his hands.

the heaven, and the things that are therein, and the earth, and the things that are therein, and the sea, and the things that are therein, that there should be time no time. ⁷ But in the days of the voice of the seventh angel, while he shall sound, the mystery of God shall be fulfilled, as he hath declared to his servants the prophets.

---

6. *And swear* — The six preceding trumpets pass without any such solemnity. It is the trumpet of the seventh angel alone which is confirmed by so high an oath. *By him that liveth for ever and ever* — Before whom a thousand years are but a day. Who created the heaven, the earth, the sea, *and the things that are therein* — And, consequently, has the sovereign power over all: therefore, all his enemies, though they rage a while in heaven, on the sea, and on the earth, yet must give place to him. *That there shall be no more a time* — "But in the days of the voice of the seventh angel, the mystery of God shall be fulfilled:" that is, a time, a chronos, shall not expire before that mystery is fulfilled. A chronos (1111 years) will nearly pass before then, but not quite. The period, then, which we may term a non-chronos (not a whole time) must be a little, and not much, shorter than this. The non-chronos here mentioned seems to begin in the year 800, (when Charles the Great instituted in the west a new line of emperors, or of "many kings,") to end in the year 1836; and to contain, among other things, the "short time" of the third woe, the "three times and a half" of the woman in the wilderness, and the "duration" of the beast.

7. *But in the days of the voice of the seventh angel* — Who sounded not only at the beginning of those days, but from the beginning to the end. *The mystery of God shall be fulfilled* — It is said, Revelation 17:17, "The word of God shall be fulfilled." The word of God is fulfilled by the destruction of the beast; the mystery, by the removal of the dragon. But these great events are so near together, that they are here mentioned as one. The beginning of them is in heaven, as soon as the seventh trumpet sounds; the end is on the earth and the sea. So long as the third woe remains on the earth and the sea, the mystery of God is not fulfilled. And the angel's swearing is peculiarly for the comfort of holy men, who are afflicted under that woe. Indeed the wrath of God must be first fulfilled, by the pouring out of the phials: and then comes the joyful fulfilling of the mystery of God. *As he hath declared to his servants the prophets* — The accomplishment exactly answering the prediction. The ancient prophecies relate partly to that grand period, from the birth of Christ to the destruction of Jerusalem; partly to the time of the seventh angel, wherein they will be fully accomplished. To the seventh trumpet belongs all that occurs from Revelation 11:15 — Revelation 22:5.

⁸ And the voice which I heard from heaven spake with me again, and said, Go, take <u>the book</u> which is open in the hand of the angel who standeth on the sea and on the earth. ⁹ And I went to the angel, saying to him, Give me <u>the book</u>. And he saith to me, Take and eat it up; and it will make thy belly bitter, but it will be sweet as honey in thy mouth. ¹⁰ And I took <u>the book</u> out of the angel's hand and eat it up; and it was in my mouth sweet as honey; but when I had eaten it, my belly was bitter. ¹¹ And he saith to me, Thou must prophesy again concerning people, and nations, and tongues, and <u>many kings</u>.

And the third woe, which takes place under the same, properly stands, Revelation 12:12, 13:1-18.

8. AV the little book. *And* — what follows from this verse to chap. 11:13, Revelation 11:13 runs parallel with the oath of the angel, and with "the fulfilling of the mystery of God," as it follows under the trumpet of the seventh angel; what is said, verse 11, Revelation 11:11 concerning St. John's "prophesying again," is unfolded immediately after; what is said, verse 7, Revelation 11:7 concerning "the fulfilling the mystery of God," is unfolded, Revelation 11:15-19 and in the following chapters.

9. *Eat it up* — The like was commanded to Ezekiel. This was an emblem of thoroughly considering and digesting it. And it will make thy belly bitter, *but it will be sweet as honey in thy mouth* — The sweetness betokens the many good things which follow, Revelation 11:1, 15, etc.; the bitterness, the evils which succeed under the third woe.

11. AV kings. *Thou must prophesy again* — Of the mystery of God; of which the ancient prophets had prophesied before. And he did prophesy, by "measuring the temple," Revelation 11:1; as a prophecy may be delivered either by words or actions. Concerning people, and nations, and tongues, *and many kings* — The people, nations, and tongues are contemporary; but the kings, being many, succeed one another. These kings are not mentioned for their own sake, but with a view to the "holy city," Revelation 11:2. Here is a reference to the great kingdoms in Spain, England, Italy, etc., which arose from the eighth century; or at least underwent a considerable change, as France and Germany in particular; to the Christian, afterward Turkish, empire in the east; and especially to the various potentates, who have successively reigned at or over Jerusalem, and do now, at least titularly, reign over it.

Chapter 11

¹ And there was given me a reed like a <u>measuring rod</u>; and <u>he said</u>, Arise, and measure the temple of God, and the altar, and them that worship therein. ² But the court which is about the temple <u>cast out</u>, and measure it not; for it is given to the gentiles; and they shall <u>tread</u> the holy city forty-two months. ³ And I will <u>give to</u> my two witnesses, to prophesy a twelve hundred *and* sixty

---

Ch 11. In this chapter is shown how it will fare with "the holy city," till the mystery of God is fulfilled; in the twelfth, what will befall the woman, who is delivered of the man-child; in the thirteenth, how it will be with the kingdom of Christ, while the "two beasts" are in the height of their power. *And there was given me* — By Christ, as appears from the third verse. And he said, *Arise* — Probably he was sitting to write. *And measure the temple of God* — At Jerusalem, where he was placed in the vision. Of this we have a large description by Ezekiel, Ezekiel 40:1-48:35; concerning which we may observe:

1. Ezekiel's prophecy was not fulfilled at the return from the Babylonish captivity.
2. Yet it does not refer to the "New Jerusalem," which is far more gloriously described.
3. It must infallibly be fulfilled even then "when they are ashamed of all that they have done," Ezekiel 43:11.
4. Ezekiel speaks of the same temple which is treated of here.
5. As all things are there so largely described, St. John is shorter and refers thereto.

1. AV rod; and the angel stood, saying.
2. AV leave out; tread underfoot. *But the court which is without the temple* — The old temple had a court in the open air, for the heathens who worshipped the God of Israel. *Cast out* — Of thy account. *And measure it not* — As not being holy In so high a degree. *And they shall tread* — Inhabit. *The holy city* — Jerusalem, Matthew 4:5. So they began to do, before St. John wrote. And it has been trodden almost ever since by the Romans, Persians, Saracens, and Turks. But that severe kind of treading which is here peculiarly spoken of, will not be till under the trumpet of the seventh angel, and toward the end of the troublous times. This will continue but forty-two common months, or twelve hundred and sixty common days; being but a small part of the non-chronos.

days, clothed in sackcloth. ⁴ These are the two olive trees, and the two candlesticks, standing before the Lord of the earth. ⁵ And if any one would hurt them, fire proceedeth out of their mouth, and devoureth their enemies; and if any would kill them, he must thus be killed. ⁶ These have power to shut heaven, that it rain not in the days of their prophesying; and have power over waters to turn them into blood, and to smite the earth with all plagues, as often as they will.

⁷ And when they shall have finished their testimony, the wild beast that ascendeth out of the bottomless pit shall make war with them, and conquer

---

3. AV give power to. *And I* — Christ. *Will give to my two witnesses* — These seem to be two prophets; two select, eminent instruments. Some have supposed (though without foundation) that they are Moses and Elijah, whom they resemble in several respects. *To prophesy twelve hundred and sixty days* — Common days, that is, an hundred and eighty weeks. So long will they prophesy, (even while that last and sharp treading of the holy city continues,) both by word and deed, witnessing that Jesus is the Son of God, the heir of all things, and exhorting all men to repent, and fear, and glorify God. *Clothed in sackcloth* — The habit of the deepest mourners, out of sorrow and concern for the people.

4. AV Lord God. *These are the two olive trees* — That is, as Zerubbabel and Joshua, the two olive trees spoken of by Zechariah, Zechariah 3:9, 4:10, were then the two chosen instruments in God's hand, even so shall these. be in their season. Being themselves full of the unction of the Holy One, they shall continually transmit the same to others also. *And the two candlesticks* — Burning and shining lights. *Standing before the Lord of the earth* — Always waiting on God, without the help of man, and asserting his right over the earth and all things therein.

5. AV hurt. *If any would kill them* — As the Israelites would have done Moses and Aaron, Numbers 16:41. *He must be killed thus* — By that devouring fire.

6. These have power — And they use that power. See verse 10. Revelation 11:10 To shut heaven, that it rain not in the days of their prophesying — During those "twelve hundred and sixty days." And have power over the waters — In and near Jerusalem. To turn them into blood — As Moses did those in Egypt. And to smite the earth with all plagues, as often as they will — This is not said of Moses or Elijah, or any mere man besides. And how is it possible to understand this otherwise than of two individual persons?

them, and kill them. ⁸ And their dead bodies *shall be* in the street of the great city, which is called spiritually Sodom and Egypt, where also their Lord was crucified. ⁹ And *some* of the people and tribes and tongues and nations behold their dead bodies three days and a half, and they shall not suffer their dead bodies to be put in a grave. ¹⁰ And they that dwell upon the earth rejoice over them, and they shall make merry, and send gifts to one another; because these two prophets tormented them that dwelt on the earth. ¹¹ And after the three days and an half the spirit of life from God came into them, and they

---

7. AV beast; conquer. *And when they shall have finished their testimony* — Till then they are invincible. *The wild beast* — Hereafter to be described. *That ascendeth* — First out of the sea, Revelation 13:1, and then out of the bottomless pit, Revelation 17:8. *Shall make war with them* — It is at his last ascent, not out of the sea, but the bottomless pit, that the beast makes war upon the two witnesses. And even hereby is fixed the time of "treading the holy city," and of the "two witnesses." That time ends after the ascent of the beast out of the abyss, and yet before the fulfilling of the mystery. *And shall conquer them* — The fire no longer proceeding out of their mouth when they have finished their work. *And kill them* — These will be among the last martyrs, though not the last of all.

8. AV our. *And their bodies shall be* — Perhaps hanging on a cross. *In the street of the great city* — Of Jerusalem, a far greater city, than any other in those parts. This is described both spiritually and historically: spiritually, as it is called Sodom Isaiah 1:9 etc. and Egypt; on account of the same abominations abounding there, at the time of the witnesses, as did once in Egypt and Sodom. Historically: *Where also their Lord was crucified* — This possibly refers to the very ground where his cross stood. Constantine the Great enclosed this within the walls of the city. Perhaps on that very spot will their bodies be exposed.

9. AV kindreds. *Three days and a half* — So exactly are the times set down in this prophecy. If we suppose this time began in the evening, and ended in the morning, and included (which is no way impossible) Friday, Saturday, and Sunday, the weekly festival of the Turkish people, the Jewish tribes, and the Christian tongues; then all these together, with the heathen nations, would have full leisure to gaze upon and rejoice over them.

10. *And they that dwell upon the earth* — Perhaps this expression may peculiarly denote earthly-minded men. *Shall make merry* — As did the Philistines over Samson. *And send gifts to one another* — Both Turks, and Jews, and heathens, and false Christians.

stood upon their feet; and great fear fell upon them that saw them. ¹² And I heard a great voice saying from heaven to them, Come up hither. And they went up to heaven in a cloud; and their enemies beheld them. ¹³ And in that hour there was a great earthquake, and the tenth part of the city fell, and there were slain in the earthquake seven thousand men, and the rest were terrified, and gave glory to the God of heaven. ¹⁴ The second woe is past; behold, the third woe cometh quickly.

---

11. AV Spirit. *And great fear fell upon them that saw them* — And now knew that God was on their side.

12. *And I heard a great voice* — Designed for all to hear. And they went up to heaven, *and their enemies beheld them* — who had not taken notice of their rising again; by which some had been convinced before.

13. *And there was a great earthquake and the tenth part of the city fell* — We have here an unanswerable proof that this city is not Babylon or Romans, but Jerusalem. For Babylon shall be wholly burned before the fulfilling of the mystery of God. But this city is not burned at all; on the contrary, at the fulfilling of that mystery, a tenth part of it is destroyed by an earthquake, and the other nine parts converted. *And there were slain in the earthquake seven thousand men* — Being a tenth part of the inhabitants, who therefore were seventy thousand in all. *And the rest* — The remaining sixty-three thousand were converted: a grand step toward the fulfilling of the mystery of God. Such a conversion we no where else read of. So there shall be a larger as well as holier church at Jerusalem than ever was yet. *Were terrified — Blessed terror! And gave glory* — The character of true conversion, Jeremiah 13:16. *To the God of heaven* — He is styled, "The Lord of the earth," verse 4, Revelation 11:4 when he declares his right over the earth by the two witnesses; but the God of heaven, when he not only gives rain from heaven after the most afflicting drought, but also declares his majesty from heaven, by taking his witnesses up into it. When the whole multitude gives glory to the God of heaven, then that "treading of the holy city" ceases. This is the point so long aimed at, the desired "fulfilling of the mystery of God," when the divine promises are so richly fulfilled on those who have gone through so great afflictions. All this is here related together, that whereas the first and second woe went forth in the east, the rest of the eastern affairs being added at once, the description of the western might afterwards remain unbroken.

It may be useful here to see how the things here spoken of, and those hereafter described, follow each other in their order.

1. The angel swears; the non-chronos begins; John eats the book; the many kings arise.

¹⁵ And the seventh angel sounded; and there were great voices in heaven, saying, The <u>kingdom</u> of this world is become *the <u>kingdom</u>* of our Lord and of his Christ; and he shall reign for ever and ever. ¹⁶ And the four and twenty

---

2. The non-chronos and the "many kings" being on the decline, that treading" begins, and the "two witnesses" appear.
3. The beast, after he has with the ten kings destroyed Babylon, wars with them and kills them. After three days and an half they revive and ascend to heaven. There is a great earthquake in the holy city: seven thousand perish, and the rest are converted. The "treading" of the city by the gentiles ends.
4. The beast, and the kings of the earth, and their armies are assembled to fight against the Great King.
5. Multitudes of his enemies are killed, and the beast and the false prophet cast alive into the lake of fire.
6. while John measures the temple of God and the altar with the worshippers, the true worship of God is set up. The nations who had trodden the holy city are converted. Hereby the mystery of God is fulfilled.
7. Satan is imprisoned. Being released for a time, he, with Gog and Magog, makes his last assault upon Jerusalem.

14. *The second woe is past* — The butchery made by the Saracens ceased about the year 847, when their power was so broken by Charles the Great that they never recovered it. Behold, *the third woe cometh quickly* — Its prelude came while the Roman see took all opportunities of laying claim to its beloved universality, and enlarging its power and grandeur. And in the year 755 the bishop of Romans became a secular prince, by king Pepin's giving him the exarchate of Lombardy. The beginning of the third woe itself stands, Revelation 12:12.

15. AV kingdoms. *And the seventh angel sounded* — This trumpet contains the most important and joyful events, and renders all the former trumpets matter of joy to all the inhabitants of heaven. The allusion therefore in this and all the trumpets is to those used in festal solemnities. All these seven trumpets were heard in heaven: perhaps the seventh shall once be heard on earth also, 1 Thessalonians 4:16. *And there were great voices* — From the several citizens of heaven. At the opening of the seventh seal "there was silence in heaven;" at the sounding of the seventh trumpet, great voices. This alone is sufficient to show that the seven seals and seven trumpets do not run parallel to each other. As soon as the seventh angel sounds, the kingdom falls to God and his Christ. This immediately appears in heaven, and is there

elders, who sat before God on their thrones, fell on their faces and worshipped God, ¹⁷ saying, We give thee thanks, O <u>Lord God, the Almighty</u>, who is, and who <u>was</u>; because thou hast taken thy great power, and hast reigned. ¹⁸ And the nations were <u>wroth</u>, and thy wrath is come, and the time of the dead, that they be judged, and to give a reward to thy servants the

---

celebrated with joyful praise. But on earth several dreadful occurrences are to appear first. This trumpet comprises all that follows from these voices to Revelation 22:5. *The kingdom of the world* — That is, the royal government over the whole world, and all its kingdoms, Zechariah 14:9. *Is become the kingdom of the Lord* — This province has been in the enemy's hands: it now returns to its rightful Master. In the Old Testament, from Moses to Samuel, God himself was the King of his own people. And the same will be in the New Testament: he will himself reign over the Israel of God. *And of his Christ* — This appellation is now first given him, since the introduction of the book, on the mention of the kingdom devolving upon him, under the seventh trumpet. Prophets and priests were anointed, but more especially kings: whence that term, the anointed, is applied only to a king. Accordingly, whenever the Messiah is mentioned in scripture, his kingdom is implied. *Is become* — In reality, all things (and so the kingdom of the world) are God's in all ages: yet Satan and the present world, with its kings and lords, are risen against the Lord and against his Anointed. God now puts an end to this monstrous rebellion, and maintains his right to all things. And this appears in an entirely new manner, as soon as the seventh angel sounds.

16. *And the four and twenty elders* — These shall reign over the earth, Revelation 5:10. *Who sit before God on their thrones* — which we do not read of any angel.

17. AV Lord God Almighty; wast, and art to come. *The Almighty* — He who hath all things in his power as the only Governor of them. Who is, *and who was* — God is frequently styled, "He who is, and who was, and who is to come." but now he is actually come, the words, "who is to come," are, as it were, swallowed up. When it is said, We thank thee that thou hast taken thy great power, it is all one as, "We thank thee that thou art come." This whole thanksgiving is partly an enlargement on the two great points mentioned in the fifteenth verse; Revelation 11:15 partly a summary of what is hereafter more distinctly related. Here it is mentioned, how the kingdom is the Lord's; afterwards, how it is the kingdom of his Christ. *Thou hast taken thy great power* — This is the beginning of what is done under the trumpet of the seventh angel. God has never ceased to use his power; but he has suffered his enemies to oppose it, which he will now suffer no more.

prophets, and to the saints, and to them that fear thy name, small and great; and to destroy them that destroyed the earth.

^{19} And the temple of God was opened in heaven; and the ark of the covenant was seen in the temple, and there were lightnings, and voices, and thunders, and an earthquake, and great hail.

---

18. AV angry. *And the heathen nations were wroth* — At the breaking out of the power and kingdom of God. This wrath of the heathens now rises to the highest pitch; but it meets the wrath of the Almighty, and melts away. In this verse is described both the going forth and the end of God's wrath, which together take up several ages. *And the time of the dead is come* — Both of the quick and dead, of whom those already dead are far the more numerous part. *That they be judged* — This, being infallibly certain, they speak of as already present. *And to give a reward* — At the coming of Christ, Revelation 22:12; but of free grace, not of debt,

1. To his servants the prophets:
2. To his saints: to them who were eminently holy:
3. To them that fear his name: these are the lowest class.

Those who do not even fear God will have no reward from him. *Small and great* — All universally, young and old, high and low, rich and poor. *And to destroy them that destroyed the earth* — The earth was destroyed by the "great whore" in particular, Revelation 19:2; 17:2, 5; but likewise in general, by the open rage and hate of wicked men against all that is good; by wars, and the various destruction and desolation naturally flowing therefrom; by such laws and constitutions as hinder much good, and occasion many offenses and calamities; by public scandals, whereby a door is opened for all dissoluteness and unrighteousness; by abuse of secular and spiritual powers; by evil doctrines, maxims, and counsels; by open violence and persecution; and by sins crying to God to send plagues upon the earth. This great work of God, destroying the destroyers, under the trumpet of the seventh angel, is not the third woe, but matter of joy, for which the elders solemnly give thanks. All the woes, and particularly the third, go forth over those "who dwell upon the earth;" but this destruction, over those "who destroy the earth," and were also instruments of that woe.

19. AV testament. *And the temple of God*-The inmost part of it. *Was opened in heaven* — And hereby is opened a new scene of the most momentous things, that we may see how the contents of the seventh trumpet are executed; and, notwithstanding the greatest opposition, (particularly by the third woe,) brought to a glorious conclusion. *And the ark of the covenant was seen in his temple* — The ark of the covenant which was made by Moses

Chapter 12

¹ And a great <u>sign</u> was seen in heaven; a woman clothed with the sun, and the moon under her feet, and on her head a crown of twelve stars. ² And

---

was not in the second temple, being probably burnt with the first temple by the Chaldeans. But here is the heavenly ark of the everlasting covenant, the shadow of which was under the Old Testament, Hebrews 9:4. The inhabitants of heaven saw the ark before: St. John also saw it now; for a testimony, that what God had promised, should be fulfilled to the uttermost. And there were lightnings, and voices, and thunders, and an earthquake, *and great hail —* The very same there are, and in the same order, when the seventh angel has poured out his phial; Revelation 16:17-21: one place answers the other. What the trumpet here denounces in heaven, is there executed by the phial upon earth. First it is shown what will be done; and afterwards it is done.

Ch. 12. The great vision of this book goes straight forward, from the fourth to the twenty-second chapter. Only the tenth, with part of the eleventh chapter, was a kind of introduction to the trumpet of the seventh angel; after which it is said, "The second woe is past: behold, the third woe cometh quickly." Immediately the seventh angel sounds, under whom the third woe goes forth. And to this trumpet belongs all that is related to the end of the book.

1. AV wonder. *And a great sign was seen in heaven —* Not only by St. John, but many heavenly spectators represented in the vision. A sign means something that has an uncommon appearance, and from which we infer that some unusual thing will follow. *A woman —* The emblem of the church of Christ, as she is originally of Israel, though built and enlarged on all sides by the addition of heathen converts; and as she will hereafter appear, when all her "natural branches are again "grafted in." She is at present on earth; and yet, with regard to her union with Christ, may be said to be in heaven, Ephesians 2:6. Accordingly, she is described as both assaulted and defended in heaven, verses 4, 7. Revelation 12:4, 7 Clothed with the sun, and the moon under her feet, *and on her head a crown of twelve stars —* These figurative expressions must he so interpreted as to preserve a due proportion between them. So, in Joseph's dream, the sun betokened his father; the moon, his mother; the stars, their children. There may be some such resemblance here; and as the prophecy points out the "power over all nations," perhaps the sun may betoken the Christian world; the moon, the Mahometans, who also carry the moon in their ensigns; and the crown of twelve stars, the twelve tribes of

being with child she crieth, travailing in birth, and pained to be delivered. ³ And another <u>sign</u> was seen in heaven; and behold a great red dragon, having seven heads and ten horns, and seven <u>diadems</u> on his heads. ⁴ And his tail draweth the third part of the stars of heaven, and casteth them to the earth; and the dragon stood before the woman who was ready to be delivered, that when she had brought forth, he might devour her child. ⁵ And she brought forth a man child, who was to rule all the nations with a rod of iron; and her child was caught up to God, and to his throne. ⁶ And the woman fled into the

---

Israel; which are smaller than the sun and moon. The whole of this chapter answers the state of the church from the ninth century to this time.

2. *And being with child she crieth, travailing in birth* — The very pain, without any outward opposition, would constrain a woman in travail to cry out. These cries, throes, and pains to be delivered, were the painful longings, the sighs, and prayers of the saints for the coming of the kingdom of God. The woman groaned and travailed in spirit, that Christ might appear, as the Shepherd and King of all nations.

3. AV wonder; crowns. *And behold a great red dragon* — His fiery-red color denoting his disposition. *Having seven heads* — Implying vast wisdom. *And ten horns* — Perhaps on the seventh head; emblems of mighty power and strength, which he still retained. *And seven diadems on his heads* — Not properly crowns, but costly bindings, such as kings anciently wore; for, though fallen, he was a great potentate still, even "the prince of this world."

4. *And his tail* — His falsehood and subtilty. *Draweth* — As a train. *The third part* — A very large number. *Of the stars of heaven* — The Christians and their teachers, who before sat in heavenly places with Christ Jesus. *And casteth them to the earth* — Utterly deprives them of all those heavenly blessings. This is properly a part of the description of the dragon, who was not yet himself on earth, but in heaven: consequently, this casting them down was between the beginning of the seventh trumpet and the beginning of the third woe; or between the year 847 and the year 947; at which time pestilent doctrines, particularly that of the Manichees in the east, drew abundance of people from the truth. And the dragon stood before the woman, that when she had brought forth, *he might devour the child* — That he might hinder the kingdom of Christ from spreading abroad, as it does under this trumpet.

5. *And she brought forth a man child* — Even Christ, considered not in his person, but in his kingdom. In the ninth age, many nations with their princes were added to the Christian church. *Who was to rule all nations* — When his time is come. *And her child* — Which was already in heaven, as were the woman and the dragon. *Was caught up to God* — Taken utterly out of his reach.

wilderness, where she hath a place prepared by God, that they may feed her there twelve hundred *and* sixty days.

⁷ And there was war in heaven. Michael and his angels <u>warred with</u> the dragon; and the dragon warred and his angels. ⁸ But he prevailed not; neither was his place found any more in heaven. ⁹ And the great dragon was cast out, the <u>ancient</u> serpent, who is called the Devil, and Satan, who deceiveth the whole world; he was cast out unto the earth, and his angels were cast out with

---

6. *And the woman fled into the wilderness* — This wilderness is undoubtedly on earth, where the woman also herself is now supposed to be. It betokens that part of the earth where, after having brought forth, she found a new abode. And this must be in Europe; as Asia and Africa were wholly in the hands of the Turks and Saracens; and in a part of it where the woman had not been before. In this wilderness, God had already prepared a place; that is, made it safe and convenient for her. The wilderness is, those countries of Europe which lie on this side the Danube; for the countries which lie beyond it had received Christianity before. *That they may feed her* — That the people of that place may provide all things needful for her. *Twelve hundred and sixty days* — So many prophetic days, which are not, as some have supposed, twelve hundred and sixty, but seven hundred and seventy-seven, common years. This Bengelius has shown at large in his German Introduction. These we may compute from the year 847 to 1524. So long the woman enjoyed a safe and convenient place in Europe, which was chiefly Bohemia; where she was fed, till God provided for her more plentifully at the Reformation.

7. AV fought against. *And there was war in heaven* — Here Satan makes his grand opposition to the kingdom of God; but an end is now put to his accusing the saints before God. The cause goes against him, verses 10, 11, Revelation 12:10, 11 and Michael executes the sentence. That Michael is a created angel, appears from his not daring, in disputing with Satan, Jude 9, to bring a railing accusation; but only saying, "The Lord rebuke thee." And this modesty is implied in his very name; for Michael signifies, "Who is like God?" which implies also his deep reverence toward God, and distance from all self-exaltation. Satan would be like God: the very name of Michael asks, "Who is like God?" Not Satan; not the highest archangel. It is he likewise that is afterward employed to seize, bind, and imprison that proud spirit.

8. *And he prevailed not* — The dragon himself is principally mentioned; but his angels, likewise, are to be understood. *Neither was this place found any more in heaven* — So till now he had a place in heaven. How deep a mystery is this! One may compare this with Luke 10:18; Ephesians 2:2; 4:8; 6:12.

him. ¹⁰ And I heard a loud voice saying in heaven, Now is come the salvation, and the <u>might</u>, and the kingdom of our God, and the power of his Christ; for the accuser of our brethren is cast <u>out</u>, who accused them before our God day and night. ¹¹ And they have overcome him by the blood of the Lamb, and by the word of their testimony; and they loved not their lives unto the death. ¹² Therefore rejoice, ye heavens, and ye that dwell in them. Woe <u>to</u>

---

9. AV old. *And the great dragon was cast out* — It is not yet said, *unto the earth* — He was cast out of heaven; and at this the inhabitants of heaven rejoice. He is termed the great dragon, as appearing here in that shape, to intimate his poisonous and cruel disposition. *The ancient serpent* — In allusion to his deceiving Eve in that form. Dragons are a kind of large serpent. *Who is called the Devil and Satan* — These are words of exactly the same meaning; only the former is Greek; the latter, Hebrews; denoting the grand adversary of all the saints, whether Jews or gentiles. *He has deceived the whole world* — Not only in their first parents, but through all ages, and in all countries, into unbelief and all wickedness; into the hating and persecuting faith and all goodness. *He was cast out unto the earth* — He was cast out of heaven; and being cast out thence, himself came to the earth. Nor had he been unemployed on the earth before, although his ordinary abode was in heaven.

10. AV strength; down. *Now is come* — Hence it is evident that all this chapter belongs to the trumpet of the seventh angel. In the eleventh chapter, from the fifteenth to the eighteenth verse, are proposed the contents of this extensive trumpet; the execution of which is copiously described in this and the following chapters. *The salvation* — Of the saints. *The might* — Whereby the enemy is cast out. *The kingdom* — Here the majesty of God is shown. *And the power of his Christ* — Which he will exert against the beast; and when he also is taken away, then will the kingdom be ascribed to Christ himself, Revelation 19:16; 20:4. *The accuser of our brethren* — So long as they remained on earth. This great voice, therefore, was the voice of men only. *Who accused them before our God day and night* — Amazing malice of Satan, and patience of God!

11. *And they have overcome him* — Carried the cause against him. *By the blood of the Lamb* — Which cleanses the soul from all sin, and so leaves no room for accusing. *And by the word of their testimony* — The word of God, which they believed and testified, even unto death. So, for instance, died Olam, king of Sweden, in the year 900, whom his own subjects would have compelled to idolatry; and, upon his refusal, slew as a sacrifice to the idol which he would not worship. So did multitudes of Bohemian Christians, in the year 916, when queen Drahomire raised a severe persecution, wherein many "loved not their lives unto the death."

<u>the earth</u> and of the sea! For the devil is come down to you, having great wrath, because he knoweth he hath but a <u>little</u> time.

---

12. AV the inhabitants of the earth; short. *Woe to the earth and the sea* — This is the fourth and last denunciation of the third woe, the most grievous of all. The first was only, the second chiefly, on the earth, Asia; the third, both on the earth and the sea, Europe. The earth is mentioned first, because it began in Asia, before the beast brought it on Europe. *He knoweth he hath but a little time* — Which extends from his casting out of heaven to his being cast into the abyss. We are now come to a most important period of time. The non- chronos hastens to an end. We live in the little time wherein Satan hath great wrath; and this little time is now upon the decline. We are in the "time, times, and half a time," wherein the woman is "fed in the wilderness;" yea, the last part of it, "the half time," is begun. We are, as will be shown, towards the close of the "forty-two months" of the beast; and when his number is fulfilled, grievous things will be. Let him who does not regard the being seized by the wrath of the devil; the falling unawares into the general temptation; the being born away, by the most dreadful violence, into the worship of the beast and his image, and, consequently, drinking the unmixed wine of the wrath of God, and being tormented day and night for ever and ever in the lake of fire and brimstone; let him also who is confident that he can make his way through all these by his own wisdom and strength, without need of any such peculiar preservative as the word of this prophecy affords; let him, I say, go hence. But let him who does not take these warnings for senseless outcries, and blind alarms, beg of God, with all possible earnestness, to give him his heavenly light herein. God has not given this prophecy, in so solemn a manner, only to show his providence over his church, but also that his servants may know at all times in what particular period they are. And the more dangerous any period of time is, the greater is the help which it affords. But where may we fix the beginning and end of the little time? which is probably four-fifths of a chronos, or somewhat above 888 years. This, which is the time of the third woe, may reach from 947, to the year 1836. For,

1. The short interval of the second woe, (which woe ended in the year 840,) and the 777 years of the woman, which began about the year 847, quickly after which followed the war in heaven, fix the beginning not long after 864: and thus the third woe falls in the tenth century, extending from 900 to 1000; called the dark, the iron, the unhappy age.

2. If we compare the length of the third woe with the period of time which succeeds it in the twentieth chapter, it is but a little time to that vast

¹³ And when the dragon saw that he was cast to the earth, he persecuted the woman that had brought forth the male child. ¹⁴ And there were given to the woman the two wings of the great eagle, that she might fly into the wilderness, to her place, where she is <u>fed</u> for a time, and times, and half a time, from the face of the serpent. ¹⁵ And the serpent cast out of his mouth

---

space which reaches from the beginning of the non-chronos to the end of the world.

13. *And when the dragon saw* — That he could no longer accuse the saints in heaven, he turned his wrath to do all possible mischief on earth. *He persecuted the woman* — The ancient persecutions of the church were mentioned, Revelation 1:9, 2:10, 7:14; but this persecution came after her flight, verse 6, Revelation 12:6 just at the beginning of the third woe. Accordingly, in the tenth and eleventh centuries, the church was furiously persecuted by several heathen powers. In Prussia, king Adelbert was killed in the year 997, king Brunus in 1008; and when king Stephen encouraged Christianity in Hungary, he met with violent opposition. After his death, the heathens in Hungary set themselves to root it out, and prevailed for several years. About the same time, the army of the emperor, Henry the Third, was totally overthrown by the Vandals. These, and all the accounts of those times, show with what fury the dragon then persecuted the woman.

14. AV nourished. *And there were given to the woman the two wings of the great eagle, that she might fly into the wilderness to her place* — Eagles are the usual symbols of great potentates. So Ezekiel 17:3, by "a great eagle', means the king of Babylon. Here the great eagle is the Roman empire; the two wings, the eastern and western branches of it. A place in the wilderness was mentioned in the sixth verse also; Revelation 12:6 but it is not the same which is mentioned here. In the text there follow one after the other,

1. The dragon's waiting to devour the child.
2. The birth of the child, which is caught up to God.
3. The fleeing of the woman into the wilderness.
4. The war in heaven, and the casting out of the dragon.
5. The beginning of the third woe.
6. The persecution raised by the dragon against the woman.
7. The woman's flying away upon the eagle's wings.

In like manner there follow one after the other,
1. The beginning of the twelve hundred and sixty days.
2. The beginning of the little time.
3. The beginning of the time, times, and half a time.

This third period partly coincides both with the first and the second. After the beginning of the twelve hundred and sixty days, or rather of the third woe, Christianity was exceedingly propagated, in the midst of various persecutions. About the year 948 it was again settled in Denmark; in 965, in Poland and Silesia; in 980, through all Russia. In 997 it was brought into Hungary; into Sweden and Norway, both before and after. Transylvania received it about 1000; and, soon after, other parts of Dacia. Now, all the countries in which Christianity was settled between the beginning of the twelve hundred and sixty days, and the imprisonment of the dragon, may be understood by the wilderness, and by her place in particular. This place contained many countries; so that Christianity now reached, in an uninterrupted tract, from the eastern to the western empire; and both the emperors now lent their wings to the woman, and provided a safe abode for her. *Where she is fed* — By God rather than man; having little human help. For a time, and times, *and half a time* — The length of the several periods here mentioned seems to be nearly this:

YEARS
   1. The non-chronos contains less than 1111
   2. The little time 888
   3. The time, times, and half a time 777
   4. The time of the beast 666

And comparing the prophecy and history together, they seem to begin and end nearly thus:

   1. The non-chronos extends from about 800 to 1836
   2. The 1260 days of the woman from 847-1524
   3. The little time 947-1836
   4. The time, time, and half 1058-1836
   5. The time of the beast is between the beginning and end of the three times and a half.

In the year 1058 the empires had a good understanding with each other, and both protected the woman. The bishops of Romans, likewise, particularly Victor II., were duly subordinate to the emperor. We may observe, the twelve hundred and sixty days of the woman, from 847 to 1524, and the three times and a half, refer to the same wilderness. But in the former part of the twelve hundred and sixty days, before the three times and an half began, namely, from the year 847 to 1058, she was fed by others, being little able to help herself; whereas, from 1058 to 1524, she is both fed by others, and has food herself. To this the sciences transplanted into the west from the eastern

after the woman water as a <u>river</u>, that he might cause her to be carried away by the <u>stream</u>. ¹⁶ But the earth helped the woman, and opened her mouth, and swallowed up the river which the dragon had cast out of his mouth. ¹⁷ And the dragon was wroth with the woman, and <u>went forth</u> to make war with the <u>rest</u> of her seed, who keep the commandments of God, and <u>retain</u> the testimony of Jesus Christ.

Chapter 13

¹ And I stood on the sand of the sea, and saw a <u>wild beast</u> coming up out of the sea, having seven heads and ten horns, and upon his horns ten <u>diadems</u>, and upon his heads a name of blasphemy. ² And the <u>wild beast</u> which I saw

---

countries much contributed; the scriptures, in the original tongues, brought into the west of Europe by the Jews and Greeks, much more; and most of all, the Reformation, grounded on those scriptures.

15. AV flood; flood. Water is an emblem of a great people; this water, of the Turks in particular. About the year 1060 they overran the Christian part of Asia. Afterward, they poured into Europe, and spread farther and farther, till they had overflowed many nations.

16. *But the earth helped the woman* — The powers of the earth; and indeed she needed help through this whole period. "The time" was from 1058 to 1280; during which the Turkish flood ran higher and higher, though frequently repressed by the emperors, or their generals, helping the woman. "The" two "times" were from 1280 to 1725. During these likewise the Turkish power flowed far and wide; but still from time to time the princes of the earth helped the woman, that she was not carried away by it. "The half time" is from 1725 to 1836. In the beginning of this period the Turks began to meddle with the affairs of Persia: wherein they have so entangled themselves, as to be the less able to prevail against the two remaining Christian empires. Yet this flood still reaches the woman "in her place;" and will, till near the end of the "half time," itself be swallowed up, perhaps by means of Russia, which is risen in the room of the eastern empire.

17. AV went; remnant; have. *And the dragon was wroth* — Anew, because he could not cause her to be carried away by the stream. *And he went forth* — Into other lands. *To make war with the rest of her seed* — Real Christians, living under heathen or Turkish governors.

Ch 13. 1. AV beast; crowns. *And I stood on the sand of the sea* — This also was in the vision. *And I saw* — Soon after the woman flew away. *A wild* *beast coming up* — He comes up twice; first from the sea, then from the abyss. He comes from the sea before the seven phials; "the great whore" comes after them. O reader, this is a subject wherein we also are deeply concerned, and which must be treated, not as a point of curiosity, but as a solemn warning from God! The danger is near. Be armed both against force and fraud, even with the whole armor of God. *Out of the sea* — That is, Europe. So the three woes (the first being in Persia, the second about the Euphrates) move in a line from east to west. This beast is the Romanish Papacy, as it came to a point six hundred years since, stands now, and will for some time longer. To this, and no other power on earth, agrees the whole text, and every part of it in every point; as we may see, with the utmost evidence, from the **propositions** following:

PROP. 1. It is one and the same beast, having seven heads, and ten horns, which is described in this and in the seventeenth chapter. Of consequence, his heads are the same, and his horns also.

PROP. 2. This beast is a spiritually secular power, opposite to the kingdom of Christ. A power not merely spiritual or ecclesiastical, nor merely secular or political but a mixture of both. He is a secular prince; for a crown, yea, and a kingdom are ascribed to him. And yet he is not merely secular; for he is also a false prophet.

PROP. 3. The beast has a strict connection with the city of Romans. This clearly appears from the seventeenth chapter.

PROP. 4. The beast is now existing. He is not past. for Romans is now existing; and it is not till after the destruction of Romans that the beast is thrown into the lake. He is not altogether to come: for the second woe is long since past, after which the third came quickly; and presently after it began, the beast rose out of the sea. Therefore, whatever he is, he is now existing.

PROP. 5. The beast is the Romanish Papacy. This manifestly follows from the third and fourth propositions; the beast has a strict connection with the city of Romans; and the beast is now existing: therefore, either there is some other power more strictly connected with that city, or the Pope is the beast.

PROP. 6. The Papacy, or papal kingdom, began long ago. The most remarkable particulars relating to this are here subjoined; taken so high as abundantly to show the rise of the beast, and brought down as low as our own time, in order to throw a light on the following part of the prophecy:

> A.D. 1033. Benedict the Ninth, a child of eleven years old, is bishop of Romans, and occasions grievous disorders for above twenty years.

A.D. 1048. Damasus II. introduces the use of the triple crown.

A.D. 1058. The church of Milan is, after long opposition, subjected to the Roman.

A.D. 1073. Hildebrand, or Gregory VII., comes to the throne.

A.D. 1076. He deposes and excommunicates the emperor.

A.D. 1077. He uses him shamefully and absolves him.

A.D. 1080. He excommunicates him again, and sends a crown to Rodulph, his competitor.

A.D. 1083. Romans is taken. Gregory flees. Clement is made Pope, and crowns the emperor.

A.D. 1085. Gregory VII. dies at Salerno.

A.D. 1095. Urban II. holds the first Popish council, at Clermont and gives rise to the crusades.

A.D. 1111. Paschal II. quarrels furiously with the emperor.

A.D. 1123. The first western general council in the Lateran. The marriage of priests is forbidden.

A.D. 1132. Innocent II declares the emperor to be the Pope's liege-man, or vassal.

A.D. 1143. The Romans set up a governor of their own, independent on Innocent II. He excommunicates them, and dies. Celestine II. is, by an important innovation, chosen to the Popedom without the suffrage of the people; the right of choosing the Pope is taken from the people, and afterward from the clergy, and lodged in the Cardinals alone.

A.D. 1152. Eugene II. assumes the power of canonizing saints.

A.D. 1155. Adrian IV. puts Arnold of Brixia to death for speaking against the secular power of the Papacy.

A.D. 1159. Victor IV. is elected and crowned. But Alexander III. conquers him and his successor.

A.D. 1168. Alexander III. excommunicates the emperor, and brings him so low, that,

A.D. 1177. he submits to the Pope's setting his foot on his neck.

A.D. 1204. Innocent III. sets up the Inquisition against the Vaudois.

A.D. 1208. He proclaims a crusade against them.

A.D. 1300. Boniface VIII. introduces the year of jubilee.

A.D. 1305. The Pope's residence is removed to Avignon.

A.D. 1377. It is removed back to Romans.

A.D. 1378. The fifty years' schism begins.

A.D. 1449. Felix V., the last Antipope, submits to Nicholas V.

A.D. 1517. The Reformation begins.

A.D. 1527. Romans is taken and plundered.

A.D. 1557. Charles V. resigns the empire; Ferdinand I. thinks the being crowned by the Pope superfluous.
A.D. 1564. Pius IV. confirms the Council of Trent.
A.D. 1682. Doctrines highly derogatory to the Papal authority are openly taught in France.
A.D. 1713. The constitution Unigenitus.
A.D. 1721. Pope Gregory VII. canonized anew.

He who compares this short table with what will be observed, verse 3, Revelation 13:3 and Revelation 17:10, will see that the ascent of the beast out of the sea must needs be fixed toward the beginning of it; and not higher than Gregory VII., nor lower than Alexander III. The secular princes now favored the kingdom of Christ; but the bishops of Romans vehemently opposed it. These at first were plain ministers or pastors of the Christian congregation at Romans, but by degrees they rose to an eminence of honor and power over all their brethren till, about the time of Gregory VII. (and so ever since) they assumed all the ensigns of royal majesty; yea, of a majesty and power far superior to that of all other potentates on earth. We are not here considering their false doctrines, but their unbounded power. When we think of those, we are to look at the false prophet, who is also termed a wild beast at his ascent out of the earth. But the first beast then properly arose, when, after several preludes thereto, the Pope raised himself above the emperor.

PROP. 7. Hildebrand, or Gregory VII., is the proper founder of the papal kingdom. All the patrons of the Papacy allow that he made many considerable additions to it; and this very thing constituted the beast, by completing the spiritual kingdom: the new maxims and the new actions of Gregory all proclaim this. Some of his maxims are,

1. That the bishop of Romans alone is universal bishop.
2. That he alone can depose bishops, or receive them again.
3. That he alone has power to make new laws in the church.
4. That he alone ought to use the ensigns of royalty.
5. That all princes ought to kiss his foot.
6. That the name of Pope is the only name under heaven; and that his name alone should be recited in the churches.
7. That he has a power to depose emperors.
8. That no general synod can be convened but by him.
9. That no book is canonical without his authority.
10. That none upon earth can repeal his sentence, but he alone can repeal any sentence.
11. That he is subject to no human judgment.

12. That no power dare to pass sentence on one who appeals to the Pope.
13. That all weighty causes everywhere ought to be referred to him.
14. That the Roman church never did, nor ever can, err.
15. That the Roman bishop, canonically ordained, is immediately made holy, by the merits of St. Peter.
16. That he can absolve subjects from their allegiance. These the most eminent Romanish writers own to be his genuine sayings. And his actions agree with his words.

Hitherto the Popes had been subject to the emperors, though often unwillingly; but now the Pope began himself, under a spiritual pretext, to act the emperor of the whole Christian world: the immediate dispute was, about the investiture of bishops, the right of which each claimed to himself. And now was the time for the Pope either to give up, or establish his empire forever: to decide which, Gregory excommunicated the emperor Henry IV.; "having first," says Platina, "deprived him of all his dignities." The sentence ran in these terms: "Blessed Peter, prince of the apostles, incline, I beseech thee, thine ears, and hear me thy servant. In the name of the omnipotent God, Father, Son, and Holy Ghost, I cast down the emperor Henry from all imperial and regal authority, and absolve all Christians, that were his subjects, from the oath whereby they used to swear allegiance to true kings. And moreover, because he had despised mine, yea, thy admonitions, I bind him with the bond of an anathema." The same sentence he repeated at Rome in these terms: "Blessed Peter, prince of the apostles, and thou Paul, teacher of the gentiles, incline, I beseech you, your ears to me, and graciously hear me. Henry, whom they call emperor, hath proudly lifted up his horns and his head against the church of God, — who came to me, humbly imploring to be absolved from his excommunication, — I restored him to communion, but not to his kingdom, — neither did I allow his subjects to return to their allegiance. Several bishops and princes of Germany, taking this opportunity, in the room of Henry, justly deposed, chose Rodulph emperor, who immediately sent ambassadors to me, informing me that he would rather obey me than accept of a kingdom, and that he should always remain at the disposal of God and us. Henry then began to be angry, and at first entreated us to hinder Rodulph from seizing his kingdom. I said I would see to whom the right belonged, and give sentence which should be preferred. Henry forbad this. Therefore I bind Henry and all his favorers with the bond of an anathema, and again take from him all regal power. I absolve all Christians from their oath of allegiance, forbid them to obey Henry in anything, and command them to receive Rodulph as their king. Confirm this, therefore, by your authority, ye most holy princes of the apostles, that all may now at length know, as ye have power to bind and loose in heaven, so we have power to give and take away on earth, empires, kingdoms, principalities, and whatsoever men can have."

When Henry submitted, then Gregory began to reign without control. In the same year, 1077, on September 1, he fixed a new era of time, called the Indiction, used at Romans to this day. Thus did the Pope claim to himself the whole authority over all Christian princes. Thus did he take away or confer kingdoms and empires, as a king of kings. Neither did his successors fail to tread in his steps. It is well known, the following Popes have not been wanting to exercise the same power, both over kings and emperors. And this the later Popes have been so far from disclaiming, that three of them have sainted this very Gregory, namely, Clement VIII., Paul V., and Benedict XIII.

Here is then the beast, that is, the king: in fact such, though not in name: according to that remarkable observation of Cardinal Bellarmine, "Antichrist will govern the Roman empire, yet without the name of Roman emperor." His spiritual title prevented his taking the name, while he exerciseth all the power. Now Gregory was at the head of this novelty. So Aventine himself, "Gregory VII was the first founder of the pontifical empire." Thus the time of the ascent of the beast is clear. The apostasy and mystery of iniquity gradually increased till he arose, "who opposeth and exalteth himself above all." 2 Thessalonians 2:4. Before the seventh trumpet the adversary wrought more secretly; but soon after the beginning of this, the beast openly opposes his kingdom to the kingdom of Christ.

PROP 8. The empire of Hildebrand properly began in the year 1077. Then it was, that upon the emperor's leaving Italy, Gregory exercised his power to the full. And on the first of September, in this year, he began his famous epocha. This may be farther established and explained by the following observations:

OBS. 1. The beast is the Romanish Papacy, which has now reigned for some ages.

OBS. 2. The beast has seven heads and ten horns.

OBS. 3. The seven heads are seven hills, and also seven kings. One of the heads could not have been, "as it were, mortally wounded," had it been only a hill.

OBS. 4. The ascent of the beast out of the sea is different from his ascent out of the abyss; the Revelation often mentions both the sea and the abyss but never uses the terms promiscuously.

OBS. 5. The heads of the beast do not begin before his rise out of the sea, but with it.

OBS. 6. These heads, as kings, succeed each other.

OBS. 7. The time which they take up in this succession is divided into three parts. "Five" of the kings signified thereby "are fallen: one is, the other is not yet come."

OBS. 8. "One is:" namely, while the angel was speaking this. He places himself and St. John in the middlemost time, that he might the more commodiously point out the first time as past, the second as present, the third as future.

OBS. 9. The continuance of the beast is divided in the same manner. The beast "was, is not, will ascend out of the abyss," Revelation 17:8, 11. Between these two verses, that is interposed as parallel with them, "Five are fallen, one is, the other is not yet come."

OBS. 10. Babylon is Romans. All things which the Revelation says of Babylon, agree to Romans, and Romans only. It commenced "Babylon," when it commenced "the great." When Babylon sunk in the east, it arose in the west; and it existed in the time of the apostles, whose judgment is said to be "avenged on her."

OBS. 11. The beast reigns both before and after the reign of Babylon. First, the beast reigns, Revelation 13:1, etc.; then Babylon, Revelation 17:1, etc.; and then the beast again, Revelation 17:8, etc.

OBS. 12. The heads are of the substance of the beast; the horns are not. The wound of one of the heads is called "the wound of the beast" itself, verse 3; Revelation 13:3 but the horns, or kings, receive the kingdom "with the beast," Revelation 17:12. That word alone, "the horns and the beast," Revelation 17:16, sufficiently shows them to be something added to him.

OBS. 13. The forty-two months of the beast fall within the first of the three periods. The beast rose out of the sea in the year 1077. A little after, power was given him for forty-two months. This power is still in being.

OBS. 14. The time when the beast "is not," and the reign of "Babylon," are together. The beast, when risen out of the sea, raged violently, till "his kingdom was darkened" by the fifth phial. But it was a kingdom still; and the beast having a kingdom, though darkened, was the beast still. But it was afterwards said, "the beast was," (was the beast, that is, reigned,) "and is not;" is not the beast; does not reign, having lost his kingdom. Why? because "the woman sits upon the beast," who "sits a queen," reigning over the kings of the earth: till the beast, rising out of the abyss, and taking with him the ten kings, suddenly destroys her.

OBS. 15. The difference there is between Romans and the Pope, which has always subsisted, will then be most apparent. Romans, distinct from the Pope, bears three meanings; the city itself, the Roman church, and the people of Romans. In the last sense of the word, Romans with its dutchy, which contained part of Tuscany and Campania, revolted from the Greek emperor in 726, and became a free state, governed by its senate. From this time the senate, and not the Pope, enjoyed the supreme civil power. But in 796, Leo III., being chosen Pope, sent to Charles the Great, desiring him to come and subdue the senate and people of Romans, and constrain them to swear allegiance to him. Hence arose a sharp contention between the Pope and the Roman people, who seized and thrust him into a monastery. He escaped and fled to the emperor, who quickly sent him back in great state. In the year 800 the emperor came to Romans, and shortly after, the Roman people, who had hitherto chosen their own bishops, and looked upon themselves and their senate as having the same rights with the ancient senate and people of Romans, chose Charles for their emperor, and subjected themselves to him, in the same manner as the ancient Romans did to their emperors. The Pope crowned him, and paid him homage on his knees, as was formerly done to the Roman emperors: and the emperor took an oath "to defend the holy Roman church in all its emoluments." He was also created consul, and styled himself thenceforward Augustus, Emperor of the Romans. Afterwards he gave the government of the city and dutchy of Romans to the Pope, yet still subject to himself. What the Roman church is, as distinct from the Pope, appears,

    1. When a council is held before the Pope's confirmation;
    2. When upon a competition, judgment is given which is the true Pope;
    3. When the See is vacant;
    4. When the Pope himself is suspected by the Inquisition

How Romans, as it is a city, differs from the Pope, there is no need to show.

OBS. 16. In the first and second period of his duration, the beast is a body of men; in the third, an individual. The beast with seven heads is the Papacy of many ages: the seventh head is the man of sin, antichrist. He is a body of men from Revelation 13:1 — Revelation 17:7; he is a body of men and an individual, Revelation 17:8 — Revelation 17:11; he is an individual, Revelation 17:12 — Revelation 19:20.

OBS. 17. That individual is the seventh head of the beast, or, the other king after the five and one, himself being the eighth, though one of the seven. As he is a Pope, he is one of the seven heads. But he is the eighth, or not a head, but the beast himself, not, as he is a Pope, but as he bears a new and singular character at his coming from the abyss. To illustrate this by a comparison: suppose a tree of seven branches, one of which is much larger than the rest; if those six are cut away, and the seventh remain, that is the tree.

OBS. 18. "He is the wicked one, the man of sin, the son of perdition" usually termed antichrist.

OBS. 19. The ten horns, or kings, "receive power as kings with the wild beast one hour," Revelation 17:12; with the individual beast, "who was not." But he receives his power again, and the kings with it, who quickly give their new power to him.

OBS. 20. The whole power of the Roman monarchy, divided into ten kingdoms, will be conferred on the beast, Revelation 17:13, 16, 17.

OBS. 21. The ten horns and the beast will destroy the whore, Revelation 17:16.

OBS. 22. At length the beast, the ten horns, and the other kings of the earth, will fall in that great slaughter, Revelation 19:19.

OBS. 23. Daniel's fourth beast is the Roman monarchy, from the beginning of it, till the thrones are set.

This, therefore, comprises both the apocalyptic beast, and the woman, and many other things. This monarchy is like a river which runs from its fountain in one channel, but in its course sometimes takes in other rivers, sometimes is itself parted into several streams, yet is still one continued river. The Roman power was at first undivided; but it was afterwards divided into various channels, till the grand division into the eastern and western empires, which likewise underwent various changes. Afterward the kings of the Heruli. Goths, Lombards, the exarchs of Ravenna, the Romans themselves the emperors, French and German, besides other kings, seized several parts of the Roman power. Now whatever power the Romans had before Gregory VII., that Daniel's beast contains; whatever power the Papacy has had from Gregory VII., this the apocalyptic beast represents, but this very beast (and so Romans with its last authority) is comprehended under that of Daniel. *And upon his heads a name of blasphemy* — To ascribe to a man what belongs to God alone is blasphemy. Such a name the beast has, not on his horns, nor on one head, but on all. The beast himself bears that name, and indeed through his whole duration. This is the name of Papa or Pope; not in the innocent sense wherein it was formerly given to all bishops, but in that high and peculiar sense wherein it is now given to the bishop of Romans by himself, and his followers: a name which comprises the whole pre-eminence of the highest and most holy father upon earth. Accordingly among the above cited

was like a leopard, and his feet were as *the feet* of a bear, and his mouth as the mouth of a lion; and the dragon gave him his power, and his throne, and great authority. ³ And *I saw* one of his heads as it were wounded to death; and his deadly wound was healed; and the whole earth wondered after the wild beast, ⁴ and worshipped the dragon, because he gave the authority to the

---

sayings of Gregory, those two stand together, that his "name alone should be recited in the churches;" and that it is "the only name in the world." So both the church and the world were to name no other father on the face of the earth.

2. AV beast; seat. The three first beasts in Daniel are like "a leopard," "a bear," and "a lion." In all parts, except his feet and mouth, this beast was like a leopard or female panther; which is fierce as a lion or bear, but is also swift and subtle. Such is the Papacy, which has partly by subtlety, partly by force, gained power over so many nations. The extremely various usages, manners, and ways of the Pope, may likewise be compared to the spots of the leopard. And his feet were as the feet of a bear — Which are very strong, and armed with sharp claws. And, as clumsy as they seem, he can therewith walk, stand upright, climb, or seize anything. So does this beast seize and take for his prey whatever comes within the reach of his claws. And his mouth was as the mouth of a lion — To roar, and to devour. And the dragon — Whose vassal and vicegerent he is. Gave him his power — His own strength and innumerable forces. And his throne — So that he might command whatever he would, having great, absolute authority. The dragon had his throne in heathen Romans, so long as idolatry and persecution reigned there. And after he was disturbed in his possession, yet would he never wholly resign, till he gave it to the beast in Christian Romans, so called.

3. *And I saw one* — Or the first. *Of his heads as it were wounded* — So it appeared as soon as ever it rose. The beast is first described more generally, then more particularly, both in this and in the seventeenth chapter. The particular description here respects the former parts; there, the latter parts of his duration: only that some circumstances relating to the former are repeated in the seventeenth chapter. Revelation 17:1-18 This deadly wound was given him on his first head by the sword, verse 14; Revelation 13:14 that is, by the bloody resistance of the secular potentates, particularly the German emperors. These had for a long season had the city of Romans, with her bishop, under their jurisdiction. Gregory determined to cast off this yoke from his own, and to lay it on the emperor's shoulders. He broke loose, and excommunicated the emperor, who maintained his right by force, and gave the Pope such a blow, that one would have thought the beast must have been killed thereby, immediately after his coming up. But he recovered, and grew stronger than

wild beast; and worshipped the wild beast, saying, Who *is* like the wild beast? And who can make war with him? ⁵ And there was given him a mouth speaking great things and blasphemy; and authority was given him forty and two months. ⁶ And he opened his mouth in blasphemy against God, to

---

before. The first head of the beast extends from Gregory VII., at least to Innocent III. In that tract of time the beast was much wounded by the emperors. But, notwithstanding, the wound was healed. Two deadly symptoms attended this wound:

1. Schisms and open ruptures in the church. For while the emperors asserted their right, there were from the year 1080 to the year 1176 only, five open divisions, and at least as many antipopes, some of whom were, indeed, the rightful Popes. This was highly dangerous to the papal kingdoms. But a still more dangerous symptom was,

2. The rising of the nobility at Romans, who would not suffer their bishop to be a secular prince, particularly over themselves. Under Innocent II. they carried their point, re-established the ancient commonwealth, took away from the Pope the government of the city, and left him only his episcopal authority. "At this," says the historian, "Innocent II. And Celestine II. fretted themselves to death: Lucius II., as he attacked the capitol, wherein the senate was, sword in hand, was struck with a stone, and died in a few days: Eugene III., Alexander III., and Lucius III., were driven out of the city: Urban III. and Gregory VIII. spent their days in banishment At length they came to an agreement with Clement III., who was himself a Roman." And the whole earth — The whole western world. Wondered after the wild beast — That is, followed him with wonder, in his councils, his crusades, and his jubilees. This refers not only to the first head, but also to the four following.

4. AV **power.** *And they worshipped the dragon* — Even in worshipping the beast, although they knew it not. *And worshipped the wild beast* — Paying him such honor as was not paid to any merely secular potentate. That very title, "Our most holy Lord," was never given to any other monarch on earth. Saying, *Who is like the wild beast* — "Who is like him?" is a peculiar attribute of God; but that this is constantly attributed to the beast, the books of all his adherents show.

5. *And there was given him* — By the dragon, through the permission of God. *A mouth speaking great things and blasphemy* — The same is said of the little horn on the fourth beast in Daniel. Nothing greater, nothing more blasphemous, can be conceived, than what the Popes have said of themselves,

blaspheme his name and his tabernacle, even them that dwell in heaven. ⁷ And it was given him to make war with the saints, and to overcome them; and <u>authority</u> was given him over all <u>tribe, and people</u>, and tongue, and nation. ⁸ And all that dwell upon the earth will worship him, whose name is not written in the book of life of the Lamb who was slain from the foundation of the world. ⁹ If any one have an ear, let him hear. ¹⁰ If any leadeth into

---

especially before the Reformation. *And authority was given him forty-two months* — The beginning of these is not to be dated immediately from his ascent out of the sea, but at some distance from it.

6. *To blaspheme his name* — Which many of the Popes have done explicitly, and in the most dreadful manner. And his tabernacle, *even them that dwell in heaven* — (For God himself dwelleth in the inhabitance of heaven.) Digging up the bones of many of them, and cursing them with the deepest execrations.

7. AV power; kindred; JW added 'and people'. *And it was given him* — That is, God permitted him. *To make war with his saints* — With the Waldenses and Albigenses. It is a vulgar mistake, that the Waldenses were so called from Peter Waldo of Lyons. They were much more ancient than him; and their true name was Vallenses or Vaudois from their inhabiting the valleys of Lucerne and Agrogne. This name, Vallenses, after Waldo appeared about the year 1160, was changed by the Papists into Waldenses, on purpose to represent them as of modern original. The Albigenses were originally people of Albigeois, part of Upper Languedoc, where they considerably prevailed, and possessed several towns in the year 1200. Against these many of the Popes made open war. Till now the blood of Christians had been shed only by the heathens or Arians; from this time by scarce any but the Papacy. In the year 1208 Innocent III. proclaimed a crusade against them. In June, 1209, the army assembled at Toulouse; from which time abundance of blood was shed, and the second army of martyrs began to be added to the first, who had cried "from beneath the altar." And ever since, the beast has been warring against the saints, and shedding their blood like water. *And authority was given him over every tribe and people* — Particularly in Europe. And when a way was found by sea into the East Indies, and the West, these also were brought under his authority.

8. *And all that dwell upon the earth will worship him* — All will be carried away by the torrent, but the little flock of true believers. The name of these only is written in the Lamb's book of life. And if any even of these "make shipwreck of the faith," he will blot them "out of his book;" although they were written therein from (that is, before) the foundation of the world, Revelation 17:8.

captivity, he goeth into captivity; if any man kill with the sword, he must be killed with the sword. Here is the patience and the <u>faithfulness</u> of the saints.

¹¹ And I saw another <u>wild beast</u> coming up out of the earth; and he had two horns like a lamb, but he spake like a dragon. ¹² And he exerciseth all the <u>authority</u> of the first <u>wild beast</u> before him, and causeth the earth and them that dwelt therein to worship the first <u>wild beast</u>, whose deadly wound was healed. ¹³ And he doeth great wonders, so that he even maketh fire to come down out of heaven to the earth in the sight of men. ¹⁴ And he deceiveth them that dwell on the earth by the <u>wonders</u> which it is given him to do before the <u>wild beast</u>; saying to them that dwell on the earth, to make an image to the <u>wild beast</u>, which had the wound by a sword, and yet lived. ¹⁵

---

9. *If any one have an ear, let him hear* — It was said before, "He that hath an ear, let him hear." This expression, if any, seems to imply, that scarce will any that hath an ear be found. *Let him hear* — With all attention the following warning, and the whole description of the beast.

10. AV faith. *If any man leadeth into captivity* — God will in due time repay the followers of the beast in their own kind. Meanwhile, here is the patience and faithfulness of the saints exercised: their patience, by enduring captivity or imprisonment; their faithfulness, by resisting unto blood.

11. *And I saw another wild beast* — So he is once termed to show his fierceness and strength, but in all other places, "the false prophet." He comes to confirm the kingdom of the first beast. *Coming up* — After the other had long exercised his authority. *Out of the earth* — Out of Asia. But he is not yet come, though he cannot be far off for he is to appear at the end of the forty-two months of the first beast. *And he had two horns like a lamb* — A mild, innocent appearance. *But he spake like a dragon* — Venomous, fiery, dreadful. So do those who are zealous for the beast.

12. *And he exerciseth all the authority of the first wild beast* — Described in the second, fourth, fifth, and seventh verses. Revelation 13:2, 3, 5, 7 *Before him* — For they are both together. *Whose deadly wound was healed* — More throughly healed by means of the second beast.

13. *He maketh fire* — Real fire. *To come down* — By the power of the devil.

14. AV miracles. *Before the wild beast* — Whose usurped majesty is confirmed by these wonders. *Saying to them* — As if it were from God. *To make an image to the wild beast* — Like that of Nebuchadnezzar, whether of gold, silver, or stone. The original image will be set up where the beast himself shall appoint. But abundance of copies will be taken, which may be carried into all parts, like those of Diana of Ephesians.

And <u>it was given him</u> to give <u>breath</u> to the image of the <u>wild beast</u>, so that the image of the <u>wild beast</u> should speak; and he will cause, that as many as will not worship the image of the <u>wild beast</u> shall be killed. ¹⁶ And he causeth all, small and great, both rich and poor, both free and slaves, to receive a mark on the right hand, or on the forehead; ¹⁷ that no man might buy or sell, but he that had the mark, the name of the <u>wild beast</u>, or the number of his name. ¹⁸ Here is wisdom. Let him that hath understanding count the number of the wild beast; for it is the number of a man; and his number is six hundred sixty-six.

---

15. AV he had power; life. *So that the image of the wild beast should speak* — Many instances of this kind have been already among the Papists, as well as the heathens. *And as many as will not worship* — When it is required of them; as it will be of all that buy or sell. *Shall be killed* — By this the Pope manifests that he is antichrist, directly contrary to Christ. It is Christ who shed his own blood; it is antichrist who sheds the blood of others. And yet, it seems, his last and most cruel persecution is to come. This persecution, the reverse of all that preceded, will, as we may gather from many scriptures, fall chiefly on the outward court worshippers, the formal Christians. It is probable that few real, inward Christians shall perish by it: on the contrary, those who "watch and pray always" shall be "accounted worthy to escape all these things, and to stand before the Son of man," Luke 21:36.

16. *On their forehead* — The most zealous of his followers will probably choose this. Others may receive it on their hand.

17. *That no man might buy or sell* — Such edicts have been published long since against the poor Vaudois. But he that had the mark, namely, the name of the first beast, *or the number of his name* — The name of the beast is that which he bears through his whole duration; namely, that of Papa or Pope: the number of his name is the whole time during which he bears this name. Whosoever, therefore, receives the mark of the beast does as much as if he said expressly, "I acknowledge the present Papacy, as proceeding from God;" or, "I acknowledge that what St. Gregory VII. has done, according to his legend, (authorized by Benedict XIII.,) and what has been maintained in virtue thereof, by his successors to this day, is from God." By the former, a man hath the name of the beast as a mark; by the latter, the number of his name. In a word, to have the name of the beast is, to acknowledge His papal Holiness; to have the number of his name is, to acknowledge the papal succession. The second beast will enforce the receiving this mark under the severest penalties.

18. *Here is the wisdom* — To be exercised. "The patience of the saints" availed against the power of the first beast: the wisdom God giveth them will

Chapter 14

¹ And I looked, and, behold, the Lamb <u>standing</u> on the mount Zion, and with him an hundred forty-four thousand, having <u>his name and</u> the name of his Father written on their foreheads. ² And I heard a <u>sound</u> out of heaven, as a sound of many waters, and as a sound of a great thunder; and the sound which I heard *was* as of harpers harping on their harps. ³ And they <u>sing</u> a new song before the throne, and before the four <u>living creatures</u>, and the elders; and none could learn the song but the hundred forty-four thousand, who were redeemed from the earth. ⁴ These are they who had not been defiled with

---

avail against the subtilty of the second. *Let him that hath understanding —* Which is a gift of God, subservient to that wisdom. *Count the number of the wild beast —* Surely none can be blamed for attempting to obey this command. *For it is the number of a man —* A number of such years as are common among men. *And his number is six hundred and sixty-six years —* So long shall he endure from his first appearing.

Ch 14. 1. AV stood; JW added 'his name and'. *And I saw on mount Zion —* The heavenly Zion. *An hundred forty-four thousand —* Either those out of all mankind who had been the most eminently holy, or the most holy out of the twelve tribes of Israel the same that were mentioned, Revelation 7:4, and perhaps also, Revelation 16:2. But they were then in the world, and were sealed in their foreheads, to preserve them from the plagues that were to follow. They are now in safety, and have the name of the Lamb and of his Father written on their foreheads, as being the redeemed of God and of the Lamb, his now unalienable property. This prophecy often introduces the inhabitants of heaven as a kind of chorus with great propriety and elegance. The church above, making suitable reflections on the grand events which are foretold in this book, greatly serves to raise the attention of real Christians, and to teach the high concern they have in them. Thus is the church on earth instructed, animated, and encouraged, by the sentiments temper, and devotion of the church in heaven.

2. AV voice. *And I heard a sound out of heaven —* Sounding clearer and clearer: first, at a distance, as the sound of many waters or thunders; and afterwards, being nearer, it was as of harpers harping on their harps. It sounded vocally and instrumentally at once.

3. AV sung; beasts. *And they —* The hundred forty-four thousand-Sing a new song *— and none could learn that song —* To sing and play it in the same manner. But the hundred forty-four thousand who were redeemed from the earth *— From among men; from all sin.*

women; for they are virgins. These are they who follow the Lamb whithersoever he goeth. These were redeemed from among men, firstfruits to God and the Lamb. ⁵ And in their mouth there was found no guile; they are without fault.

⁶ And I saw another angel flying in the midst of heaven, having an everlasting gospel to preach to them that dwell on the earth, and to every nation, and tribe, and tongue, and people, ⁷ saying with a loud voice, Fear God and give glory to him; for the hour of his judgment is come; and worship him that made the heaven, and the earth, and the sea, and fountains of waters.

---

4. *These are they who had not been defiled with women* — It seems that the deepest defilement, and the most alluring temptation, is put for every other. *They are virgins* — Unspotted souls; such as have preserved universal purity. *These are they who follow the Lamb* — Who are nearest to him. This is not their character, *but their reward Firstfruits* — Of the glorified spirits. Who is ambitious to be of this number?

5. AV before the throne of God. *And in their mouth there was found no guile* — Part for the whole. Nothing untrue, unkind, unholy. *They are without fault* — Having preserved inviolate a virgin purity both of soul and body.

6. AV kindred. *And I saw another angel* — A second is mentioned, verse 8; a third, verse 9. Revelation 14:8, 9 These three denote great messengers of God with their assistants; three men who bring messages from God to men. The first exhorts to the fear and worship of God; the second proclaims the fall of Babylon; the third gives warning concerning the beast. *Happy are they who make the right use of these divine messages! Flying* — Going on swiftly. *In the midst of heaven* — Breadthways. *Having an everlasting gospel* — Not the gospel, properly so called; but a gospel, or joyful message, which was to have an influence on all ages. To preach to every nation, and tribe, and tongue, *and people* — Both to Jew and gentile, even as far as the authority of the beast had extended.

7. *Fear God and give glory to him; for the hour of his judgment is come* — The joyful message is properly this, that the hour of God's judgment is come. And hence is that admonition drawn, Fear God and give glory to him. They who do this will not worship the beast, neither any image or idol whatsoever. *And worship him that made* — Whereby he is absolutely distinguished from idols of every kind. The heaven, and the earth, and the sea, *and fountains of water* — And they who worship him shall be delivered when the angels pour out their phials on the earth, sea, fountains of water, on the sun, and in the air.

⁸ And another angel followed, saying, Babylon <u>the great</u> is fallen, is <u>fallen</u>, she that hath made all nations drink of the <u>wine of her</u> fornication.

⁹ And a third angel followed them, saying with a loud voice, If any one worship the <u>wild beast</u> and his image, and receive *his* mark on his forehead, or on his hand, ¹⁰ he shall also drink of the wine of the wrath of God, which

---

8. AV JW added 'the great'; fallen, that great city; wine of the wrath of her. *And another angel followed, saying, Babylon is fallen* — With the overthrow of Babylon, that of all the enemies of Christ, and, consequently, happier times, are connected. *Babylon the great* — So the city of Romans is called upon many accounts. Babylon was magnificent, strong, proud, powerful. So is Romans also. Babylon was first, Romans afterwards, the residence of the emperors of the world. What Babylon was to Israel of old, Romans hath been both to the literal and spiritual "Israel of God." Hence the liberty of the ancient Jews was connected with the overthrow of the Babylonish empire. And when Romans is finally overthrown, then the people of God will be at liberty. Whenever Babylon is mentioned in this book, the great is added, to teach us that Romans then commenced Babylon, when it commenced the great city; when it swallowed up the Grecian monarchy and its fragments, Syria in particular; and, in consequence of this, obtained dominion over Jerusalem about sixty years before the birth of Christ. Then it began, but it will not cease to be Babylon till it is finally destroyed. Its spiritual greatness began in the fifth century, and increased from age to age. It seems it will come to its utmost height just before its final overthrow. Her fornication is her idolatry; invocation of saints and angels; worship of images; human traditions; with all that outward pomp, yea, and that fierce and bloody zeal, wherewith she pretends to serve God. But with spiritual fornication, as elsewhere, so in Romans, fleshly fornication is joined abundantly. Witness the stews there, licensed by the Pope, which are no inconsiderable branch of his revenue. This is fitly compared, to wine, because of its intoxicating nature. Of this wine she hath, indeed, *made all nations drink* — More especially by her later missions. We may observe, this making them drink is not ascribed to the beast, but to Babylon. For Romans itself, the Roman inquisitions, congregations, and Jesuits, continually propagate the idolatrous doctrines and practices, with or without the consent of this or that Pope, who himself is not secure from their censure.

9. *And a third angel followed* — At no great distance of time. Saying, *If any one worship the wild beast* — This worship consists, partly in an inward submission, a persuasion that all who are subject to Christ must be subject to the beast or they cannot receive the influences of divine grace, or, as their

is poured unmixed into the cup of his indignation; and he shall be tormented with fire and brimstone, in the presence of the <u>angels</u>, and in the presence of the Lamb. ¹¹ And the smoke of their torments ascendeth for ever and ever; and they have no rest day or night, who worshipped the <u>wild beast</u> and his image, and whosoever receiveth the mark of his name. ¹² Here is the patience of the saints; who keep the commandments of God, and the faith of Jesus.

¹³ And I heard a voice out of heaven saying, Write, from henceforth <u>happy</u> are the dead who die in the <u>Lord</u>. Yea, saith the Spirit, that they may rest from their labours. Their works follow them.

---

expression is, there is no salvation out of their church; partly in a suitable outward reverence to the beast himself, and consequently to his image.

10. AV holy angels. *He shall drink* — With Babylon, Revelation 16:19. *And shall be tormented* — With the beast, Revelation 20:10. In all the scripture there is not another so terrible threatening as this. And God by this greater fear arms his servants against the fear of the beast. The wrath of God, *which is poured unmixed* — Without any mixture of mercy; without hope. *Into the cup of his indignation* — And is no real anger implied in all this? O what will not even wise men assert, to serve an hypothesis!

11. *And the smoke* — From the fire and brimstone wherein they are tormented. *Ascendeth for ever and ever* — God grant thou and I may never try the strict, literal eternity of this torment!

12. *Here is the patience of the saints* — Seen, in suffering all things rather than receive this mark. *Who keep the commandments of God* — The character of all true saints; and particularly the great command to believe in Jesus.

13. AV blessed; Lord from henceforth. *And I heard a voice* — This is most seasonably heard when the beast is in his highest power and fury. *Out of heaven* — Probably from a departed saint. *Write* — He was at first commanded to write the whole book. Whenever this is repeated it denotes something peculiarly observable. *Happy are the dead* — From henceforth particularly:

1. Because they escape the approaching calamities:
2. Because they already enjoy so near an approach to glory.

Who die in the Lord — In the faith of the Lord Jesus. *For they rest* — No pain, no purgatory follows; but pure, unmixed happiness. *From their labors* — And the more laborious their life was, the sweeter is their rest. How different this state from that of those, verse 11, Revelation 14:11 who "have no rest day or night!" Reader, *which wilt thou choose? Their works* — Each one's peculiar works. *Follow* — or accompany them; that is, the fruit of their

¹⁴ And I looked, and behold a white cloud, and on the cloud one sitting like a <u>son</u> of man, having a golden crown on his head, and a sharp sickle in his hand. ¹⁵ And another angel came out of the temple, crying with a loud voice to him that sat on the cloud, Thrust in thy sickle, and reap; for the time to reap is come; for the harvest of the earth is ripe. ¹⁶ And he that sat on the cloud thrust in his sickle upon the earth; and the earth was reaped.

¹⁷ And another angel came out of the temple which is in heaven, and he also had a sharp sickle. ¹⁸ And another angel came out from the altar, who had power over fire; and cried with a loud cry to him that had the sharp sickle, saying, Thrust in <u>thy sickle</u>, and <u>lop off</u> the clusters of the vine of the earth; for her grapes are fully ripe. ¹⁹ And the angel thrust in his sickle upon the earth, and lopped off the vine of the earth, and cast *it* into the great winepress of the wrath of God. ²⁰ And the winepress was trodden without the

---

works. Their works do not go before to procure them admittance into the mansions of joy; but they follow them when admitted.

14. AV Son. *In the following verses, under the emblem of an harvest and a vintage, are signified two general visitations; first, many good men are taken from the earth by the harvest; then many sinners during the vintage. The latter is altogether a penal visitation; the former seems to be altogether gracious. Here is no reference in either to the day of judgment, but to a season which cannot be far off. And I saw a white cloud* — An emblem of mercy. *And on the cloud sat one like a son of man* — An angel in an human shape, sent by Christ, the Lord both of the vintage and of the harvest. *Having a golden crown on his head* — In token of his high dignity. *And a sharp sickle in his hand* — The sharper the welcome to the righteous.

15. *And another angel came out of the temple* — "Which is in heaven," verse 17. Revelation 14:17 Out of which came the judgments of God in the appointed seasons.

16. *Crying* — By the command of God. Thrust in thy sickle, *for the harvest is ripe* — This implies an high degree of holiness in those good men, and an earnest desire to be with God.

18. AV thy sharp sickle; gather. *And another angel from the altar* — Of burnt offering; from whence the martyrs had cried for vengeance. *Who had power over fire* — As "the angel of the waters," Revelation 16:5, had over water. Cried, saying, *Lop off the clusters of the vine of the earth* — All the wicked are considered as constituting one body.

city, and blood came out of the winepress, even to the horses' bridles, one thousand six hundred furlongs.

Chapter 15

¹ And I saw another sign in heaven, great and <u>wonderful</u>, seven angels having the seven last plagues; for by them the wrath of God is <u>fulfilled</u>. ² And I saw as it were a sea of glass mingled with fire; and them that gained the victory over the <u>wild beast</u>, and over his image, and over the number of his name, standing at the sea of glass, and having the harps of God. ³ And they sing the song of Moses the servant of God, and the song of the Lamb, saying, Great and <u>wonderful</u> *are* thy works, Lord God Almighty; <u>righteous</u>

---

20. *And the winepress was trodden* — By the Son of God, Revelation 19:15. *Without the city* — Jerusalem. They to whom St. John writes, when a man said, "The city," immediately understood this. And blood came out of the winepress, *even to the horses' bridles* — *So deep at its first flowing from the winepress! One thousand six hundred furlongs* — So far! at least two hundred miles, through the whole land of Palestine.

Ch 15. 1. AV marvelous; filled full. *And I saw seven holy angels having the seven last plagues* — Before they had the phials, which were as instruments whereby those plagues were to be conveyed. They are termed the last, *because by them the wrath of God is fulfilled* — Hitherto. God had born his enemies with much longsuffering; but now his wrath goes forth to the uttermost, pouring plagues on the earth from one end to the other, and round its whole circumference. But, even after these plagues, the holy wrath of God against his other enemies does not cease, Revelation 20:15.

2. AV beast. The song was sung while the angels were coming out, with their plagues, who are therefore mentioned both before and after it, verses 1-6. Revelation 15:1-6, *And I saw as it were a sea of glass mingled with fire* — It was before "clear as crystal," Revelation 4:6, but now mingled with fire, which devours the adversaries. And them that gained, or were gaining, *the victory over the wild beast* — More of whom were yet to come. The mark of the beast, the mark of his name, and the number of his name, seem to mean here nearly the same thing. *Standing at the sea of glass* — Which was before the throne. *Having the harps of God* — Given by him, and appropriated to his praise.

and true are thy ways, O King of the nations. ⁴ Who would not fear thee, O Lord, and glorify thy name? For thou only *art* gracious; for all nations shall come and worship before thee; for thy judgments are made manifest.

⁵ And after these things I looked, and the temple of the tabernacle of the testimony was open in heaven. ⁶ And the seven angels that had the seven plagues came out of the temple, clothed in pure white linen, and having their breasts girt with golden girdles. ⁷ And one of the four living creatures gave

---

3. AV marvelous; just; saints. *And they sing the song of Moses* — So called, partly from its near agreement, with the words of that song which he sung after passing the Red Sea, Exodus 15:11, and of that which he taught the children of Israel a little before his death, Deuteronomy 32:3, 4. But chiefly because Moses was the minister and representative of the Jewish church, as Christ is of the church universal. Therefore it is also termed the sons of the Lamb. It consists of six parts, which answer each other: 1.Great and wonderful are thy 2.For thou only art gracious. works, Lord God Almighty. 3.Just and true are thy ways, O 4. For all the nations shall come King of the nations. and worship before thee. 5.Who would not fear thee, O 6.For thy judgments are made Lord, and glorify thy name? manifest. We know and acknowledge that all thy works in and toward all the creatures are great and wonderful; that thy ways with all the children of men, good and evil, are just and true. *For thou only art gracious* — And this grace is the spring of all those wonderful works, even of his destroying the enemies of his people. Accordingly in Psalm 136:1-26., that clause, "For his mercy endureth for ever," is subjoined to the thanksgiving for his works of vengeance as well as for his delivering the righteous. *For all the nations shall come and worship before thee* — They shall serve thee as their king with joyful reverence. This is a glorious testimony of the future conversion of all the heathens. The Christians are now a little flock: they who do not worship God, an immense multitude. But all the nations shall come, from all parts of the earth, to worship him and glorify his name. *For thy judgments are made manifest* — And then the inhabitants of the earth will at length learn to fear him.

4. AV holy.

5. *After these things the temple of the tabernacle of the testimony* — The holiest of all. *Was opened* — Disclosing a new theatre for the coming forth of the judgments of God now made manifest.

6. *And the seven angels came out of the temple* — As having received their instructions from the oracle of God himself. St. John saw them in heaven, verse 1, Revelation 15:1 before they went into the temple. They appeared in habits like those the high priest wore when he went into the most holy place to consult the oracle. In this was the visible testimony of God's

the seven angels seven golden <u>phials</u> full of the wrath of God, who liveth for ever. ⁸ And the temple was filled with smoke from the glory of God, and from his power; and none <u>could go</u> into the temple, till the seven plagues of the seven angels were fulfilled.

Chapter 16

¹ And I heard a <u>loud</u> voice out of the temple saying to the seven angels, <u>Go, pour</u> out the <u>seven phials</u> of the wrath of God upon the earth. ² And the first went, and poured out his <u>phial</u> upon the earth; and there <u>came</u> a <u>grievous ulcer</u> on the men that had the mark of the <u>wild beast</u>, and that worshipped his

---

presence. *Clothed in pure white linen* — Linen is the habit of service and attendance. *Pure* — unspotted, unsullied. *White* — Or bright and shining, which implies much more than bare innocence. *And having their breasts girt with golden girdles* — In token of their high dignity and glorious rest.

7. AV beasts; vials. *And one of the four living creatures gave the seven angels* — After they were come out of the temple. *Seven golden phials* — Or bowls. The Greek word signifies vessels broader at the top than at the bottom. *Full of the wrath of God, who liveth for ever and ever* — A circumstance which adds greatly to the dreadfulness of his wrath.

8. AV was able to enter. *And the temple was filled with smoke* — The cloud of glory was the visible manifestation of God's presence in the tabernacle and temple. It was a sign of protection at erecting the tabernacle and at the dedication of the temple. But in the judgment of Korah the glory of the Lord appeared, when he and his companions were swallowed up by the earth. So proper is the emblem of smoke from the glory of God, or from the cloud of glory, to express the execution of judgment, as well as to be a sign of favor. Both proceed from the power of God, and in both he is glorified. *And none* — Not even of those who ordinarily stood before God. *Could go into the temple* — That is, into the inmost part of it. *Till the seven plagues of the seven angels were fulfilled* — Which did not take up a long time, like the seven trumpets, but swiftly followed each other.

Ch 16. 1. AV great; God your ways, and pour; vials. *Pour out the seven phials* — The epistles to the seven churches are divided into three and four: the seven seals, and so the trumpets and phials, into four and three. The trumpets gradually, and in a long tract of time, overthrow the kingdom of the world: the phials destroy chiefly the beast and his followers, with a swift and impetuous force. The four first affect the earth, the sea, the rivers, the sun; the rest fall elsewhere, and are much more terrible.

image. ³ And the <u>second</u> poured out his <u>phial</u> upon the sea; and it <u>became blood, as</u> *the blood* of a dead man; and every living soul in the sea died. ⁴ And the <u>third</u> poured out his <u>phial</u> on the rivers and on fountains of waters; and they became blood. ⁵ And I heard the angel of the waters saying, Righteous art <u>thou</u>, who art, and who <u>wast</u>, <u>the Gracious one</u>, because thou hast judged thus. ⁶ For they have shed the blood of saints and prophets, and thou hast given them blood to drink; they are worthy. ⁷ And I heard *another* from the altar saying, Yea, Lord God Almighty, true and righteous *are* thy judgments. ⁸ And the <u>fourth</u> poured out his <u>phial</u> upon the sun; and <u>it</u> was

---

2. AV fell; noisome and grievous sore; beast. *And the first went* — So the second, third, etc., without adding angel, to denote the utmost swiftness; of which this also is a token, that there is no period of time mentioned in the pouring out of each phial. They have a great resemblance to the plagues of Egypt, which the Hebrews generally suppose to have been a month distant from each other. Perhaps so may the phials; but they are all yet to come. *And poured out his phial upon the earth* — Literally taken. *And there came a grievous ulcer* — As in Egypt, Exodus 9:10, 11. *On the men who had the mark of the wild beast* — All of them, and them only. All those plagues seem to be described in proper, not figurative, words.

3. AV second angel; became as (JW added 'blood,'). *The second poured out his phial upon the sea* — As opposed to the dry land. And it become blood, *as of a dead man* — Thick, congealed, and putrid. *And every living soul* — Men, beasts, and fishes, whether on or in the sea, died.

4. AV third angel. The third poured out his phial on the rivers and fountains of water — Which were over all the earth. And they became blood — So that none could drink thereof.

5. AV thou, O Lord; wast, and shalt be; JW added 'the Gracious one'. *The Gracious one* — So he is styled when his judgments are abroad, and that with a peculiar propriety. In the beginning of the book he is termed "The Almighty." In the time of his patience, he is praised for his power, which otherwise might then be less regarded. In the time of his taking vengeance, for his mercy. Of his power there could then be no doubt.

6. *Thou hast given then, blood to drink* — Men do not drink out of the sea, but out of fountains and rivers. Therefore this is fitly added here. *They are worthy* — Is subjoined with a beautiful abruptness.

7. *Yea* — Answering the angel of the waters, and affirming of God's judgments in general, what he had said of one particular judgment.

given him to scorch men with fire. ⁹ And the men were scorched <u>exceedingly</u>, and blasphemed the name of God, who had power over these plagues; but they repented not to give him glory. ¹⁰ And the <u>fifth</u> poured out his <u>phial</u> upon the <u>throne</u> of the <u>wild beast</u>; and his kingdom was <u>darkened</u>; and they gnawed their tongues for pain, ¹¹ and blasphemed the God of heaven, because of their pains and because of their <u>ulcers</u>, and repented not of their <u>works</u>. ¹² And the <u>sixth</u> poured out his <u>phial</u> upon the great river Euphrates; and the water of it was dried up, that the way of the kings from the east might be prepared. ¹³ And I saw out of the mouth of the dragon, and out

---

8. AV fourth angel; vial; power. *The fourth poured out his phial upon the sun* — Which was likewise affected by the fourth trumpet. There is also a plain resemblance between the first, second, and third phials, and the first, second, and third trumpet. *And it was given him* — The angel. *To scorch the men* — Who had the mark of the beast. *With fire* — As well as with the beams of the sun. So these four phials affected earth, water, fire, and air.

9. AV with great heat. *And the men blasphemed God, who had power over these plagues* — They could not but acknowledge the hand of God, yet did they harden themselves against him.

10. AV fifth angel; vial; seat; beast; full of darkness. *The four first phials are closely connected together; the fifth concerns the throne of the beast, the sixth the Mahometans, the seventh chiefly the heathens. The four first phials and the four first trumpets go round the whole earth; the three last phials and the three last trumpets go lengthways over the earth in a straight line. The fifth poured out his phial upon the throne of the wild beast* — It is not said, "on the beast and his throne." Perhaps the sea will then be vacant. *And his kingdom was darkened* — With a lasting, not a transient, darkness. However the beast as yet has his kingdom. Afterward the woman sits upon the beast. and then it is said, "The wild beast is not," Revelation 17:3, 7, 8.

11. AV sores; deeds. *And they* — His followers. *Gnawed their tongues* — Out of furious impatience. *Because of their pains and because of their ulcers* — Now mentioned together, and in the plural number, to signify that they were greatly heightened and multiplied.

12. AV sixth angel; vial. *And the sixth poured out his phial upon the great river Euphrates* — Affected also by the sixth trumpet. *And the water of it* — And of all the rivers that flow into it. *Was dried up* — The far greater part of the Turkish empire lies on this side the Euphrates. The Romanish and Mahometan affairs ran nearly parallel to each other for several ages. In the seventh century was Mahomet himself; and, a little before him, Boniface III., with his universal bishopric. In the eleventh, both the Turks and Gregory VII.

of the mouth of the <u>wild beast</u>, and out of the mouth of the false prophet, three unclean spirits like frogs <u>go forth</u>, [14] (they are the spirits of devils, working miracles), to the kings of the whole world, to gather them unto the battle of that great day of <u>God the Almighty</u>. [15] (Behold, I come as a thief. <u>Happy</u> is he that watcheth, and keepeth his garments, lest he walk naked, and they see his shame.) [16] And they gathered them together to the place which is called in the Hebrew Armageddon. [17] And the <u>seventh</u> poured out his <u>phial</u>

---

carried all before them. In the year 1300, Boniface appeared with his two swords at the newly-erected jubilee. In the self-same year arose the Ottoman Porte; yea, and on the same day. And here the phial, poured out on the throne of the beast, is immediately followed by that poured out on the Euphrates; *that the way of the kings from the east might be prepared* — Those who lie east from the Euphrates, in Persia, India, etc., who will rush blindfold upon the plagues which are ready for them, toward the Holy Land, which lies west of the Euphrates.

13. AV beast; JW added 'go forth'.. *Out of the mouth of the dragon, the wild beast, and the false prophet* — It seems, the dragon fights chiefly against God; the beast, against Christ; the false prophet, against the Spirit of truth; and that the three unclean spirits which come from them, and exactly resemble them, endeavor to blacken the works of creation, of redemption, and of sanctification. *The false prophet* — So is the second beast frequently named, after the kingdom of the first is darkened; for he can then no longer prevail by main strength, and so works by lies and deceit. Mahomet was first a false prophet, and afterwards a powerful prince: but this beast was first powerful as a prince; afterwards a false prophet, a teacher of lies. *Like frogs* — Whose abode is in fens, marshes, and other unclean places. *To the kings of the whole world* — Both Mahometan and pagan. *To gather them* — To the assistance of their three principals.

14. AV God Almighty.

15. AV Blessed. *Behold, I come as a thief* — Suddenly, unexpectedly. Observe the beautiful abruptness. *I* — Jesus Christ. Hear him. Happy is he that watcheth. — *Looking continually for him that "cometh quickly." And keepeth on his garments* — Which men use to put off when they sleep. Lest he walk naked, *and they see his shame* — Lest he lose the graces which he takes no care to keep, and others see his sin and punishment.

16. *And they gathered them together to Armageddon* — Mageddon, or Megiddo, is frequently mentioned in the Old Testament. Armageddon signifies the city or the mountain of Megiddo; to which the valley of Megiddo adjoined. This was a place well known in ancient times for many memorable occurrences; in particular, the slaughter of the kings of Canaan,

upon the air; and there went forth a loud voice, out of the temple from the throne, saying, It is done. ¹⁸ And there were lightnings, and voices, and thunders; and a great earthquake, such as had not been since men were upon the earth, such an earthquake, so great. ¹⁹ And the great city was split into three parts, and the cities of the nations fell; and Babylon the great was remembered before God, to give her the cup of the wine of the fierceness of his wrath. ²⁰ And every island fled away, and the mountains were not found. ²¹ And a great hail, every hail-stone about the weight of a talent, falleth out of heaven upon the men; and the men blasphemed God, because of the plague of the hail; for the plague thereof is exceeding great.

Chapter 17

¹ And there came one of the seven angels which had the seven phials, and talked with me, saying, Come hither; I will show thee the judgment of the great whore that sitteth upon many waters. ² With whom the kings of the

---

related, Judges 5:19. Here the narrative breaks off. It is resumed, Revelation 19:19.

17. AV seventh angel; vial into; came; great. *And the seventh poured out his phial upon the air* — Which encompasses the whole earth. This is the most weighty phial of all, and seems to take up more time than any of the preceding. *It is done* — What was commanded, verse 1. Revelation 16:1 The phials are poured out.

18. AV so mighty. A great earthquake, such as had not been since men were upon the earth — It was therefore a literal, not figurative, earthquake.

19. AV divided. *And the great city* — Namely, Jerusalem, here opposed to the heathen cities in general, and in particular to Romans. *And the cities of the nations fell* — Were utterly overthrown. *And Babylon was remembered before God* — He did not forget the vengeance which was due to her, though the execution of it was delayed.

20. Every island and mountain was "*moved out of its place*," Revelation 6:14; but here they all flee away. What a change must this make in the face of the terraqueous globe! And yet the end of the world is not come.

21. *And a great hail falleth out of heaven* — From which there was no defense. From the earthquake men would fly into the fields; but here also they are met by the hail: nor were they secure if they returned into the houses, when each hail-stone weighed sixty pounds.

earth have committed fornication, and the inhabitants of the earth have been made drunk with the wine of her fornication. ³ And he carried me away in the spirit into <u>a wilderness</u>; and I saw a woman sitting upon a scarlet <u>wild beast</u>, full of names of blasphemy, having seven heads and ten horns. ⁴ And the woman was arrayed in purple and <u>scarlet</u>, and <u>adorned</u> with gold and precious stones and pearls, having in her hand a golden cup, full of

---

Ch 17. 1. AV vials. *And there came one of the seven angels, saying, Come hither* — This relation concerning the great whore, and that concerning the wife of the Lamb, Revelation 21:9, 10, have the same introduction, in token of the exact opposition between them. *I will show thee the judgment of the great whore* — Which is now circumstantially described. *That sitteth as a queen* — In pomp, power, ease, and luxury. *Upon many waters* — Many people and nations, verse 15. Revelation 17:15.

2. *With whom the kings of the earth* — Both ancient and modern, for many ages. *Have committed fornication* — By partaking of her idolatry and various wickedness. *And the inhabitants of the earth* — The common people. *Have been made drunk with the wine of her fornication* — No wine can more thoroughly intoxicate those who drink it, than false zeal does the followers of the great whore.

3. AV the wilderness; coloured beast. *And he carried me away* — In the vision. *Into a wilderness* — The campagna di Romansa, the country round about Romans, is now a wilderness, compared to what it was once. *And I saw a woman* — Both the scripture and other writers frequently represent a city under this emblem. *Sitting upon a scarlet wild beast* — The same which is described in the thirteenth chapter. Revelation 13:1-18 But he was there described as he carried on his own designs only: here, as he is connected with the whore. There is, indeed, a very close connection between them; the seven heads of the beast being "seven hills on which the woman sitteth." And yet there is a very remarkable difference between them, — between the papal power and the city of Romans. This woman is the city of Romans, with its buildings and inhabitants; especially the nobles. The beast, which is now scarlet-colored, (bearing the bloody livery, as well as the person, of the woman,) appears very different from before. Therefore St. John says at first sight, I saw a beast, not the beast, *full of names of blasphemy* — He had' before "a name of blasphemy upon his head," Revelation 13:1: now he has many. From the time of Hildebrand, the blasphemous titles of the Pope have been abundantly multiplied. *Having seven heads* — Which reach in a succession from his ascent out of the sea to his being cast into the lake of fire. *And ten horns* — Which are contemporary with each other, and belong to his last period.

abomination and filthiness of her fornication. ⁵ And on her forehead a name written, MYSTERY, BABYLON THE GREAT, THE MOTHER OF HARLOTS AND ABOMINATIONS OF THE EARTH. ⁶ And I saw the woman drunk with the blood of the saints, and with the blood of the witnesses of Jesus. And when I saw, I wondered exceedingly.

⁷ And the angel said to me, Wherefore didst thou wonder? I will tell thee the mystery of the woman, and of the wild beast that carrieth her, which hath the seven heads and the ten horns. ⁸ The wild beast which thou sawest was, and is not, and shall ascend out of the bottomless pit, and go into perdition;

---

4. AV scarlet colour; decked. *And the woman was arrayed* — With the utmost pomp and magnificence. *In purple and scarlet* — These were the colors of the imperial habit: the purple, in times of peace; and the scarlet, in times of war. *Having in her hand a golden cup* — Like the ancient Babylon, Jeremiah 51:7. *Full of abominations* — The most abominable doctrines as well as practices.

5. *And on her forehead a name written* — Whereas the saints have the name of God and the Lamb on their foreheads. *Mystery* — This very word was inscribed on the front of the Pope's mitre, till some of the Reformers took public notice of it. *Babylon the great* — Benedict XIII., in his proclamation of the jubilee, A.D. 1725, explains this sufficiently. His words are, "To this holy city, famous for the memory of so many holy martyrs, run with religious alacrity. Hasten to the place which the Lord hath chose. Ascend to this new Jerusalem, whence the law of the Lord and the light of evangelical truth hath flowed forth into all nations, from the very first beginning of the church: the city most rightfully called 'The Palace,' placed for the pride of all ages, the city of the Lord, the Zion of the Holy One of Israel. This catholic and apostolical Roman church is the head of the world, the mother of all believers, the faithful interpreter of God and mistress of all churches." But God somewhat varies the style. *The mother of harlots* — The parent, ringleader, patroness, and nourisher of many daughters, that losely copy after her. *And abominations* — Of every kind, spiritual and fleshly. *Of the earth* — In all lands. In this respect she is indeed catholic or universal.

6. AV martyrs; with great admiration. *And I saw the woman drunk with the blood of the saints* — So that Romans may well be called, "The slaughter-house of the martyrs." She hath shed much Christian blood in every age; but at length she is even drunk with it, at the time to which this vision refers. *The witnesses of Jesus* — The preachers of his word. *And I wondered exceedingly* — At her cruelty and the patience of God.

7. AV marvel; beast. *I will tell thee the mystery* — The hidden meaning of this.

and they that dwell on the earth (whose names are not written in the book of life from the foundation of the world) shall wonder, when they behold the <u>wild beast</u>, that was, and is not, and <u>yet will be</u>. ⁹ Here *is* the mind that hath wisdom. The seven heads are seven <u>hills,</u> on which the woman sitteth. ¹⁰ And they are seven kings: five are fallen, one is, the other is not yet come; when he cometh, he must continue a short space. ¹¹ And the <u>wild beast</u> that was,

---

8. AV beast; yet is. *The beast which thou sawest* (namely, verse 3) Revelation 17:3 was, etc. This is a very observable and punctual description of the beast, verses 8, 10, 11. Revelation 17:8, 10, 11 His whole duration is here divided into three periods, which are expressed in a fourfold manner:

I. He,
  1. Was; 2 And is not; 3. And will ascend out of the bottomless pit, and go into perdition.
II. He,
  1. Was; 2. And is not; 3. And will be again.
III. The seven heads are seven hills and seven kings:
  1. Five are fallen; 2. One is; 3. The other is not come; and when he cometh, he must continue a short space.
IV. He,
  1. Was; 2. And is not; 3 Even he is the eighth, and is one of the seven, and goeth into perdition.

The first of these three is described in the thirteenth chapter. Revelation 13:1-18 This was past when the angel spoke to St. John. The second was then in its course; the third woe to come. *And is not* — The fifth phial brought darkness upon his kingdom: the woman took this advantage to seat herself upon him. Then it might be said, He is not. *Yet shall he afterwards ascend out of the bottomless pit* — Arise again with diabolical strength and fury. But he will not reign long: soon after his ascent he goeth into perdition for ever.

9. AV mountains. *Here is the mind that hath wisdom* — Only those who are wise will understand this. The seven heads are seven hills.

10. *And they are seven kings* — Anciently there were royal palaces on all the seven Roman bills. These were the Palatine, Capitoline, Coelian, Exquiline, Viminal, Quirinal, Aventine hills. But the prophecy respects the seven hills at the time of the beast, when the Palatine was deserted and the Vatican in use. Not that the seven heads mean hills distinct from kings; but they have a compound meaning, implying both together. Perhaps the first head of the beast is the Coelian hill, and on it the Lateran, with Gregory VII. and his successors; the second, the Vatican with the church of St. Peter, chosen by Boniface VIII. the third, the Quirinal, with the church of St. Mark,

and is not, even he is the eighth, and is of the seven, and goeth into perdition. ¹² And the ten horns which thou sawest are ten kings, who have not received the kingdom; but receive authority as kings one hour with the <u>wild beast</u>. ¹³

---

and the Quirinal palace built by Paul II. and the fourth, the Exquiline hill, with the temple of St. Maria Maggiore, where Paul V. reigned. The fifth will be added hereafter. Accordingly, in the papal register, four periods are observable since Gregory VII. In the first almost all the bulls made in the city are dated in the Lateran; in the second, at St. Peter's; in the third, at St. Mark's, or in the Quirinal; in the fourth, at St. Maria Maggiore. But no fifth, sixth, or seventh hill has yet been the residence of any Pope. Not that the hill was deserted, when another was made the papal residence; but a new one was added to the other sacred palaces. Perhaps the times hitherto mentioned might be fixed thus:- 1058. Wings are given to the woman. 1077. The beast ascends out of the sea. 1143. The forty-two months begin. 1810. The forty-two months end. 1832. The beast ascends out of the bottomless pit. 1836. The beast finally overthrown. The fall of those five kings seems to imply, not only the death of the Popes who reigned on those hills, but also such a disannulling of all they had done there, that it will be said, The beast is not; the royal power, which had so long been lodged in the Pope, being then transferred to the city. One is, *the other is not yet come* — These two are remarkably distinguished from the five preceding, whom they succeed in their turns. The former of them will continue not a short space, as may be gathered from what is said of the latter: the former is under the government of Babylon; the latter is with the beast. In this second period, one is, at the same time that the beast is not. Even then there will be a Pope, though not with the power which his predecessors had. And he will reside on one of the remaining hills, leaving the seventh for his successor.

11. *And the wild beast that was, and is not, even he is the eighth* — When the time of his not being is over. The beast consists, as it were, of eight parts. The seven heads are seven of them; and the eighth is his whole body, or the beast himself. Yet the beast himself, though he is in a sense termed the eighth, is of the seven, yea, contains them all. The whole succession of Popes from Gregory VII. are undoubtedly antichrist. Yet this hinders not, but that the last Pope in this succession will be more eminently the antichrist, the man of sin, adding to that of his predecessors a peculiar degree of wickedness from the bottomless pit. This individual person, as Pope, is the seventh head of the beast; as the man of sin, he is the eighth, or the beast himself.

12. *The ten horns are ten kings* — It is nowhere said that these horns are on the beast, or on his heads. And he is said to have them, not as he is one of the seven, but as he is the eighth. They are ten secular potentates,

These have one mind, and give their power and authority to the wild beast. ¹⁴ These shall make war with the Lamb, and the Lamb shall overcome them; for he is Lord of lords, and King of kings; and they that *are* with him *are* called, and chosen, and faithful.

¹⁵ And he saith to me, The waters which thou sawest, where the whore sitteth, are people, and multitudes, and nations, and tongues. ¹⁶ And the ten horns which thou sawest, and the wild beast, these shall hate the whore, and shall make her desolate and naked, and shall eat her flesh, and burn her with fire. ¹⁷ For God hath put *it* into their hearts to execute his sentence, and to agree, and give their kingdom to the wild beast, till the words of God shall be fulfilled. ¹⁸And the woman whom thou sawest is the great city, which reigneth over the kings of the earth.

---

contemporary with, not succeeding, each other, who receive authority as kings with the beast, probably in some convention, which, after a very short space, they will deliver up to the beast. Because of their short continuance, only authority as kings, not a kingdom, is ascribed to them. While they retain this authority together with the beast, he will be stronger than ever before; but far stronger still, when their power is also transferred to him.

13. AV strength; beast. In the thirteenth and fourteenth verses Revelation 17:13, 14 is summed up what is afterwards mentioned, concerning the horns and the beast, in this and the two following chapters. *These have one mind, and give* — They all, with one consent, give their warlike power and royal authority to the wild beast.

14. *These* — Kings with the beast. *He is Lord of lords* — Rightful sovereign of all, and ruling all things well. *And King of kings* — As a king he fights with and conquers all his enemies. *And they that are with him* — Beholding his victory, are such as were, while in the body, called, by his word and Spirit. *And chosen* — Taken out of the world, when they were enabled to believe in him. *And faithful* — Unto death.

15. *People, and multitudes, and nations, and tongues* — It is not said tribes: for Israel hath nothing to do with Romans in particular.

16. AV sawest upon the beast. *And shall eat her flesh* — Devour her immense riches.

17. AV fulfill his will; beast. *For God hath put it into their heart* — Which indeed no less than almighty power could have effected. *To execute his sentence — till the words of God* — Touching the overthrow of all his enemies, should be fulfilled.

18. *The woman is the great city, which reigneth* — Namely, while the beast "is not," and the woman "sitteth upon him."

Chapter 18

¹ And after these things I saw another angel come down <u>out of</u> heaven, having great power; and the earth was enlightened with his glory. ² And he cried mightily with a <u>loud</u> voice, saying, Babylon the great is fallen, is fallen, and is become an habitation of devils, and an hold of every unclean spirit, and a cage of every <u>unclean</u> and hateful bird. ³ For all nations have drank of the <u>wine of her</u> fornication, and the kings of the earth have committed fornication with her, and the merchants of the earth are waxed rich through the abundance of her delicacies.

⁴ And I heard another voice out of heaven, saying, Come out of her, my people, that ye be not partakers of her sins, and that ye receive not of her plagues. ⁵ For her sins have reached even to heaven, and God hath

---

Ch 18. 1. AV from. *And I saw another angel coming down out of heaven* — Termed another, with respect to him who "came down out of heaven," Revelation 10:1. *And the earth was enlightened with his glory* — To make his coming more conspicuous. If such be the luster of the servant, what images can display the majesty of the Lord, who has "thousand thousands" of those glorious attendants "ministering to him, and ten thousand times ten thousand standing before him?"

2. AV strong; foul. *And he cried, Babylon is fallen* — This fall was mentioned before, Revelation 14:8; but is now declared at large. *And is become an habitation* — A free abode. Of devils, *and an hold* — A prison. *Of every unclean spirit* — Perhaps confined there where they had once practiced all uncleanness, till the judgment of the great day. How many horrid inhabitants hath desolate Babylon! of invisible beings, devils, and unclean spirits; of visible, every unclean beast, every filthy and hateful bird. Suppose, then, Babylon to mean heathen Romans; what have the Romanists gained, seeing from the time of that destruction, which they say is past, these are to be its only inhabitants for ever.

3. AV wine of the wrath of her.

4. *And I heard another voice* — Of Christ, whose people, secretly scattered even there, are warned of her approaching destruction. *That ye be not partakers of her sins* — That is, of the fruits of them. What a remarkable providence it was that the Revelation was printed in the midst of Spain, in the great Polyglot Bible, before the Reformation! Else how much easier had it been for the Papists to reject the whole book, than it is to evade these striking parts of it.

remembered her iniquities. ⁶ Reward her even as she hath rewarded, and give her double according to her works; in the cup which she <u>mingled mingle</u> to her double. ⁷ As much as she hath glorified herself, and lived deliciously, so much torment and sorrow give her; because she saith in her heart, I sit as a queen, and am no widow, and shall see no sorrow. ⁸ Therefore shall her plagues come in one day, death, and <u>sorrow</u>, and famine; and she shall be <u>burned</u> with fire; for strong *is* the Lord God who judgeth her. ⁹ And the kings of the earth, who had committed fornication and lived deliciously with her, shall <u>weep</u> and <u>mourn</u> over her, when they see the smoke of her burning, ¹⁰ standing afar off for fear of her torment, saying, Alas, alas, thou great city Babylon, thou <u>strong</u> city! In one hour is thy judgment come. ¹¹ And the merchants of the earth weep and mourn over her; for none buyeth their merchandise any more: ¹² merchandise of gold, and silver, and precious

---

5. *Even to heaven* — An expression which implies the highest guilt.

6. AV filled; fill. *Reward her* — This God speaks to the executioners of his vengeance. *Even as she hath rewarded* — Others; in particular, the saints of God. *And give her double* — This, according to the Hebrews idiom, implies only a full retaliation.

7. *As much as she hath glorified herself* — By pride, and pomp, and arrogant boasting. *And lived deliciously* — In all kinds of elegance, luxury, and wantonness. *So much torment give her* — Proportioning the punishment to the sin. *Because she saith in her heart* — As did ancient Babylon, Isai 47:8, 9. *I sit* — Her usual style. Hence those expressions, "The chair, the see of Romans: *he sat so many years.*" *As a queen* — Over many kings, "mistress of all churches; the supreme; the infallible; the only spouse of Christ; *out of which there is no salvation.*" *And am no widow* — But the spouse of Christ. *And shall see no sorrow* — From the death of my children, or any other calamity; for God himself will defend "the church."

8. AV mourning; utterly burned. *Therefore* — as both the natural and judicial consequence of this proud security. *Shall her plagues come* — The death of her children, with an incapacity of bearing more. *Sorrow* — of every kind. *And famine* — In the room of luxurious plenty: the very things from which she imagined herself to be most safe. *For strong is the Lord God who judgeth her* — Against whom therefore all her strength, great as it is, will not avail.

9. AV bewail; lament.

10. AV mighty. *Thou strong city* — Romans was anciently termed by its inhabitants, Valentia, that is, strong. And the word Romans itself, in Greek, signifies strength. This name was given it by the Greek strangers.

stone, and pearl, and fine linen, and purple, and silk, and scarlet, and all thyine wood, and all sorts of vessels of ivory, and all sorts of vessels of most precious wood, and of brass, and iron, and marble, ¹³ and cinnamon, and amomum, and odours, and ointment, and frankincense, and wine, and oil, and fine flour, and wheat, and beasts, and sheep, and merchandise of horses and of chariots, and of bodies and souls of men. ¹⁴ And the fruits which thy soul desireth are departed from thee, and all things that were dainty and splendid are perished from thee, and thou shalt find them no more. ¹⁵ The merchants of these things, who became rich by her, shall stand afar off, for the fear of her torment, weeping and mourning, ¹⁶ saying, Alas, alas the great city, that was clothed in fine linen, and purple, and scarlet, and adorned with gold, and precious stones, and pearl! ¹⁷ In one hour so great riches are become desolate. And every ship-master, and all the company belonging to ships, and sailors, and all who trade by sea, stood afar off, ¹⁸ and cried when they saw the smoke of her burning, saying, What *city was* like the great city! ¹⁹ And they cast dust on their heads, and cried, weeping and mourning, saying, Alas,

---

12. *Merchandise of gold, etc.* — Almost all these are still in use at Romans, both in their idolatrous service, and in common life. *Fine linen* — The sort of it mentioned in the original is exceeding costly. *Thyine wood* — A sweet-smelling wood not unlike citron, used in adorning magnificent palaces. *Vessels of most precious wood* — Ebony, in particular, which is often mentioned with ivory: the one excelling in whiteness, the other in blackness; and both in uncommon smoothness.

13. AV omitted (JW added); omitted (JW added); slaves.. *Amomum* — A shrub whose wood is a fine perfume. *And beasts* — Cows and oxen. *And of chariots* — a purely Latin word is here inserted in the Greek. This St. John undoubtedly used on purpose, in describing the luxury of Romans. *And of bodies* — A common term for slaves. *And souls of men* — For these also are continually bought and sold at Romans. And this of all others is the most gainful merchandise to the Roman traffickers.

14. AV goodly. *And the fruits* — From what was imported they proceed to the domestic delicates of Romans; none of which is in greater request there, than the particular sort which is here mentioned. The word properly signifies, pears, peaches, nectarines, and all of the apple and plum kinds. *And all things that are dainty* — To the taste. *And splendid* — To the sight; as clothes, buildings, furniture.

15. AV wailing.

16. AV decked.

17. AV come to naught.

alas the great city, wherein were made rich all that had ships in the sea, by reason of her <u>magnificence</u>! For in one hour she is made desolate. ²⁰ Rejoice over her, thou heaven, and ye <u>saints, and</u> apostles, and prophets; for God hath avenged you on her.

²¹ And a mighty angel took up a stone like a great mill-stone, and <u>threw</u> *it* into the sea, saying, Thus with violence shall Babylon, the great city, be thrown down, and shall be found no more at all. ²² And the voice of harpers, and musicians, and pipers, and trumpeters, shall be heard no more at all in thee; and no <u>artificer</u> of any kind shall be found any more in thee; and the sound of a mill-stone shall be heard no more at all in thee; ²³ And the light of a candle shall shine no more at all in thee; and the voice of the bridegroom and the bride shall be heard no more in thee; for thy merchants were the great

---

19. AV **wailing; costliness.** *And they cast dust on their heads* — As mourners. Most of the expressions here used in describing the downfall of Babylon are taken from Ezekiel's description of the downfall of Tyre, Ezekiel 26:1 — Ezekiel 28:19.

20. AV **omitted (JW added).** *Rejoice over her, thou heaven* — That is, all the inhabitants of it; and more especially, ye saints; and among the saints still more eminently, ye apostles and prophets.

21. AV **cast.** *And a mighty angel took up a stone, and threw it into the sea* — By a like emblem Jeremiah fore-showed the fall of the Chaldean Babylon, Jeremiah 51:63, 64.

22. AV **craftsman.** *And the voice of harpers* — Players on stringed instruments. *And musicians* — Skilful singers in particular. *And pipers* — Who played on flutes, chiefly on mournful, whereas trumpeters played on joyful, occasions. Shall be heard no more in thee; *and no artificer* — Arts of every kind, particularly music, sculpture, painting, and statuary, were there carried to their greatest height. No, *nor even the sound of a mill-stone shall be heard any more in thee* — Not only the arts that adorn life, but even those employments without which it cannot subsist, will cease from thee for ever. All these expressions denote absolute and eternal desolation. *The voice of harpers* — Music was the entertainment of the rich and great; trade, the business of men of middle rank; preparing bread and the necessaries of life, the employment of the lowest people: marriages, in which lamps and songs were known ceremonies, are the means of peopling cities, as new births supply the place of those that die. The desolation of Romans is therefore described in such a manner, as to show that neither rich nor poor, neither persons of middle rank, nor those of the lowest condition, should be able to live there any more. Neither shall it be re-peopled by new marriages, but remain desolate and uninhabited for ever.

men of the earth; for by thy sorceries were all nations deceived. ²⁴ And in her was found the blood of prophets, and saints, and of all that had been slain upon the earth.

Chapter 19

¹ And after these things I heard a <u>loud</u> voice of <u>great multitude</u> in heaven, saying, Hallelujah; the Salvation, and the <u>glory</u>, and the power to our God. ²

---

23. *For thy merchants were the great men of the earth* — A circumstance which was in itself indifferent, and yet led them into pride, luxury, and numberless other sins.

24. *And in her was found the blood of the prophets and saints* — The same angel speaks still, yet he does not say "in thee," but in her, now so sunk as not to hear these last words. *And of all that had been slain* — Even before she was built. See Matthew 23:35. There is no city under the sun which has so clear a title to catholic blood-guiltiness as Romans. The guilt of the blood shed under the heathen emperors has not been removed under the Popes, but hugely multiplied. Nor is Romans accountable only for that which hath been shed in the city, but for that shed in all the earth. For at Romans under the Pope, as well as under the heathen emperors, were the bloody orders and edicts given: and wherever the blood of holy men was shed, there were the grand rejoicings for it. And what immense quantities of blood have been shed by her agents! Charles IX., of France, in his letter to Gregory XIII., boasts, that in and not long after the massacre of Paris, he had destroyed seventy thousand Huguenots. Some have computed, that, from the year 1518, to 1548, fifteen millions of Protestants have perished by the Inquisition. This may be overcharged; but certainly the number of them in those thirty years, as well as since, is almost incredible. To these we may add innumerable martyrs, in ancient, middle, and late ages, in Bohemia, Germany, Holland, France, England, Ireland, and many other parts of Europe, Africa, and Asia.

Ch 19. 1. AV great; much people; glory, and honour. *I heard a loud voice of a great multitude* — Whose blood the great whore had shed. Saying, *Hallelujah* — This Hebrews word signifies, Praise ye Jah, or Him that is. God named himself to Moses, EHEIEH, that is, I will be, Exodus 3:14; and at the same time, "Jehovah," that is, "He that is, and was, and is to come:" during the trumpet of the seventh angel, he is styled, "He that is and was," Revelation 16:5; and not "He that is to come;" because his long-expected coming is under this trumpet actually present. At length he is styled, "Jah," "He that is;" the past together with the future being swallowed up in the

For true and righteous *are* his judgments; for he hath judged the great whore, who corrupted the earth with her fornication, and hath avenged the blood of his servants at her hand. ³ (And again they said, Hallelujah.) And her smoke ascendeth for ever and ever. ⁴ And the four and twenty elders and the four <u>living creatures</u> fell down, and worshipped God that sat on the throne, saying, Amen; Hallelujah. ⁵ And a voice came forth from the throne, saying, Praise our God, all ye his servants, and ye that fear him, small and great. ⁶ And I heard as it were a voice of a great multitude, and as a voice of many waters, and as a voice of mighty thunders, saying, hallelujah; for the <u>Lord God, the Almighty</u> reigneth. ⁷ Let us be glad and rejoice, and give <u>the glory</u> to him; for the marriage of the Lamb is come, and his wife hath made herself ready. ⁸

---

present, the former things being no more mentioned, for the greatness of those that now are. This title is of all others the most peculiar to the everlasting God. *The salvation* — Is opposed to the destruction which the great whore had brought upon the earth. *His power and glory* — Appear from the judgment executed on her, and from the setting up his kingdom to endure through all ages.

2. *For true and righteous are his judgments* — Thus is the cry of the souls under the altar changed into a song of praise.

4. AV beasts. *And the four and twenty elders, and the four living creatures felt down* — The living creatures are nearer the throne than the elders. Accordingly they are mentioned before them, with the praise they render to God, Revelation 4:9, 10; 5:8, 14; inasmuch as there the praise moves from the center to the circumference. But here, when God's judgments are fulfilled, it moves back from the circumference to the center. Here, therefore, the four and twenty elders are named before the living creatures.

5. *And a voice came forth from the throne* — Probably from the four living creatures, saying, *Praise our God* — The occasion and matter of this song of praise follow immediately after, verses 6, Revelation 19:6 etc.; God was praised before, for his judgment of the great whore, verses 1-4. Revelation 19:1-4 Now for that which follows it: for that the Lord God, the Almighty, takes the kingdom to himself, and avenges himself on the rest of his enemies. Were all these inhabitants of heaven mistaken? If not, there is real, yea, and terrible anger in God.

6. AV Lord God omnipotent. *And I heard the voice of a great multitude. So all his servants did praise him. The Almighty reigneth* — More eminently and gloriously than ever before.

7. AV honour. *The marriage of the Lamb is come* — Is near at hand, to be solemnized speedily. What this implies, none of "the spirits of just men,"

And it is <u>given to</u> her to be arrayed in fine linen, white and clean; the fine linen is the righteousness of saints.

⁹ And he saith to me, Write, <u>Happy</u> *are* they who are <u>invited</u> to the marriage supper of the Lamb. And he saith to me, These are the true sayings of God. ¹⁰ And I fell <u>before</u> his feet to worship him. But he saith to me, See *thou do it* not. I am thy fellow servant, and of thy brethren that keep the testimony of Jesus. Worship God; the testimony of Jesus is the spirit of prophecy.

¹¹ And I saw the heaven opened, and behold a white horse, and he that sitteth on him, called Faithful and True, and in righteousness he judgeth and maketh war. ¹² His eyes *are* a flame of fire, and upon his head *are* many

---

even in paradise, yet know. O what things are those which are yet behind! And what purity of heart should there be, *to meditate upon them! And his wife hath made herself ready* — Even upon earth; but in a far higher sense, in that world. After a time allowed for this, the new Jerusalem comes down, both made ready and adorned, Revelation 21:2.

8. AV granted. *And it is given to her* — By God. The bride is all holy men, the whole invisible church. To be arrayed in fine linen, *white and clean — This is an emblem of the righteousness of the saints* — Both of their justification and sanctification.

9. AV Blessed; called. *And he* — The angel, saith to me, *Write* — St. John seems to have been so amazed at these glorious sights, that he needeth to be reminded of this. *Happy are they who are invited to the marriage supper of the Lamb* — Called to glory. *And he saith* — After a little pause.

10. AV at. *And I fell before his feet to worship him* — It seems, mistaking him for the angel of the covenant. But he saith, *See thou do it not* — In the original, it is only, See not, with a beautiful abruptness. To pray to or worship the highest creature is flat idolatry. *I am thy fellow servant and of thy brethren that have the testimony of Jesus* — I am now employed as your fellow servant, to testify of the Lord Jesus, by the same Spirit which inspired the prophets of old.

11. *And I saw the heaven opened* — This is a new and peculiar opening of it, in order to show the magnificent expedition of Christ and his attendants, against his great adversary. *And behold a white horse* — Many little regarded Christ, when he came meek, "riding upon an ass;" but what will they say, when he goes forth upon his white horse, *with the sword of his mouth? White* — Such as generals use in solemn triumph. And he that sitteth on him, *called Faithful* — In performing all his promises. *And True* — In executing all his

diadems, and he hath a name written, which none knoweth but himself. ¹³ And <u>he *is*</u> clothed in a vesture dipped in blood; and his name is called The Word of God. ¹⁴ And the armies which were in heaven followed him on white horses, clothed in <u>clean, fine linen</u>. ¹⁵ And out of his mouth goeth a sharp <u>two-edged</u> sword, that with it he might smite the nations. And he shall rule them with a rod of iron; and he treadeth the winepress of the fierceness of the wrath of God, the Almighty. ¹⁶ And he hath on his vesture and on his thigh a name written, KING OF KINGS, AND LORD OF LORDS. ¹⁷ And I saw an angel standing in the sun; and he cried with a loud voice, saying to all the <u>birds</u> that fly in the midst of heaven, Come, and gather yourselves

---

threatenings. *And in righteousness* — With the utmost justice. *He judgeth and maketh war* — Often the sentence and execution go together.

12. AV *were as*; crowns. *And his eyes are a flame of fire* — They were said to be as or like a flame of fire, before, Revelation 1:14; an emblem of his omniscience. *And upon his head are many diadems* — For he is king of all nations. And he hath a name written, *which none knoweth but himself* — As God he is incomprehensible to every creature.

13. AV he *was*. *And he is clothed in a vesture dipped in blood* — The blood of the enemies he hath already conquered. Isaiah 63:1, etc.

14. AV fine linen, white and clean.

15. AV omitted (JW added). *And he shall rule them* — Who are not slain by his sword. *With a rod of iron* — That is, if they will not submit to his golden scepter. *And he treadeth the wine press of the wrath of God* — That is, he executes his judgments on the ungodly. This ruler of the nations was born (or appeared as such) immediately after the seventh angel began to sound. He now appears, not as a child, but as a victorious warrior. The nations have long ago felt his "iron rod," partly while the heathen Romans, after their savage persecution of the Christians, themselves groaned under numberless plagues and calamities, by his righteous vengeance; partly, while other heathens have been broken in pieces by those who bore the Christian name. For although the cruelty, for example, of the Spaniards in America, was unrighteous and detestable, yet did God therein execute his righteous judgment on the unbelieving nations; but they shall experience his iron rod as they never did yet, and then will they all return to their rightful Lord.

16. *And he hath on his vesture and on his thigh* — That is, on the part of his vesture which is upon his thigh. *A name written* — It was usual of old, for great personages in the eastern countries, to have magnificent titles affixed to their garments.

together to the <u>great supper of God</u>. ¹⁸ That ye may eat the flesh of kings, and the flesh of <u>chief</u> captains, and the flesh of mighty men, and the flesh of horses, and of those that sit on them, and the flesh of all men, both free and slaves, both small and great. ¹⁹ And I saw the <u>wild beast</u>, and the kings of the earth, and their armies, gathered together to make war with him that sat on the horse, and with his army. ²⁰ And the <u>wild beast</u> was taken, and with him the false prophet who had wrought the miracles before him, with which he had deceived them who had the mark of the <u>wild beast</u>, and them who had worshipped his image. These two were cast alive into the lake of fire burning with brimstone. ²¹ And the <u>rest</u> were slain by the sword of him that sat upon the horse, which went forth out of his mouth; and all the <u>birds</u> were <u>satisfied</u> with their flesh.

---

17. AV fowls; supper of great God. *Gather yourselves together to the great supper of God* — As to a great feast, which the vengeance of God will soon provide; a strongly figurative expression, (taken from Ezekiel 39:17,) denoting the vastness of the ensuing slaughter.

18. AV omitted (JW added).

19. AV beast. *And I saw the kings of the earth* — The ten kings mentioned Revelation 17:12; who had now drawn the other kings of the earth to them, whether Popish, Mahometan, or pagan. *Gathered together to make war with him that sat upon the horse* — All beings, good and evil, visible and invisible, will be concerned in this grand contest. See Zechariah 14:1, etc.

20. *The false prophet, who had wrought the miracles before him* — And therefore shared in his punishment; *these two ungodly men were cast alive* — Without undergoing bodily death. *Into the lake of fire* — And that before the devil himself, Revelation 20:10. Here is the last of the beast. After several repeated strokes of omnipotence, he is gone alive into hell. There were two that went alive into heaven; perhaps there are two that go alive into hell. It may be, Enoch and Elijah entered at once into glory, without first waiting in paradise; the beast and the false prophet plunge at once into the extremest degree of torment, without being reserved in chains of darkness till the judgment of the great day. Surely, none but the beast of Romans would have hardened himself thus against the God he pretended to adore, or refused to have repented under such dreadful, repeated visitations! Well is he styled a beast, from his carnal and vile affections; a wild beast, *from his savage and cruel spirit! The rest were slain* — A like difference is afterwards made between the devil, and Gog and Magog, Revelation 20:9, 10.

21. AV remnant; fowls; filled. Here is a most magnificent description of the overthrow of the beast and his adherents. It has, in particular, one exquisite beauty; that, after exhibiting the two opposite armies, and all the

Chapter 20

¹ And I saw an angel <u>descending out of</u> heaven, having the key of the bottomless pit and a great chain in his hand. ² And he laid hold on the dragon, the old serpent, who is the devil, and Satan, and bound him a thousand years. ³ And cast him into the bottomless pit, and shut *him* up, and

---

apparatus for a battle, verses 11-19; Revelation 19:11-19 then follows immediately, verse 20, 19:20 the account of the victory, without one word of an engagement or fighting. Here is the most exact propriety; for what struggle can there be between omnipotence, and the power of all the creation united against it! Every description must have fallen short of this admirable silence.

Ch 20. 1. AV come down from. *And I saw an angel descending out of heaven* — Coming down with a commission from God. Jesus Christ himself overthrew the beast: the proud dragon shall be bound by an angel; even as he and his angels were cast out of heaven by Michael and his angels. *Having the key of the bottomless pit* — Mentioned before, Revelation 9:1. *And a great chain in his hand* — The angel of the bottomless pit was shut up therein before the beginning of the first woe. But it is now first that Satan, after he had occasioned the third woe, is both chained and shut up.

2. *And he laid hold on the dragon* — With whom undoubtedly his angels were now cast into the bottomless pit, as well as finally "into everlasting fire," Matthew 25:41. *And bound him a thousand years* — That these thousand do not precede, or run parallel with, but wholly follow, the times of the beast, may manifestly appear:

1. From the series of the whole book, representing one continued chain of events.
2. From the circumstances which precede. The woman's bringing forth is followed by the casting of the dragon out of heaven to the earth. With this is connected the third woe, whereby the dragon through, and with, the beast, rages horribly. At the conclusion of the third woe the beast is overthrown and cast into "the lake of fire." At the same time the other grand enemy, the dragon, shall be bound and shut up.
3. These thousand years bring a new, full, and lasting immunity from all outward and inward evils, the authors of which are now removed, and an affluence of all blessings. But such time the church has never yet seen. Therefore it is still to come.
4. These thousand years are followed by the last times of the world, the letting loose of Satan, who gathers together Gog and Magog, and is

set a seal upon him, that he <u>might</u> deceive the nations no more, till the thousand years should be fulfilled; after this he must be loosed for a <u>small time</u>.

> thrown to the beast and false prophet "in the lake of fire." Now Satan's accusing the saints in heaven, his rage on earth, his imprisonment in the abyss, his seducing Gog and Magog, and being cast into the lake of fire, evidently succeed each other.
>
> 5. What occurs from Revelation 20:11 — Revelation 22:5, manifestly follows the things related in the nineteenth chapter. The thousand years came between; whereas if they were past, neither the beginning nor the end of them would fall within this period. In a short time those who assert that they are now at hand will appear to have spoken the truth. Meantime let every man consider what kind of happiness he expects therein. The danger does not lie in maintaining that the thousand years are yet to come; but in interpreting them, whether past or to come, in a gross and carnal sense. The doctrine of the Son of God is a mystery. So is his cross; and so is his glory. In all these he is a sign that is spoken against. Happy they who believe and confess him in all!

3. AV should; little season. *And set a seal upon him* — How far these expressions are to be taken literally, how far figuratively only, *who can tell? That he might deceive the nations no more* — One benefit only is here expressed, as resulting from the confinement of Satan. But how many and great blessings are implied! For the grand enemy being removed, the kingdom of God holds on its uninterrupted course among the nations; and the great mystery of God, so long foretold, is at length fulfilled; namely, when the beast is destroyed and Satan bound. This fulfillment approaches nearer and nearer; and contains things of the utmost importance, the knowledge of which becomes every day more distinct and easy. In the mean time it is highly necessary to guard against the present rage and subtlety of the devil. Quickly he will be bound: when he is loosed again, the martyrs will live and reign with Christ. Then follow his coming in glory, the new heaven, new earth, and new Jerusalem. The bottomless pit is properly the devil's prison; afterwards he is cast into the lake of fire. He can deceive the nations no more till the "thousand years," mentioned before, verse 2, Revelation 20:2 are fulfilled. *Then he must be loosed* — So does the mysterious wisdom of God permit. *For a small time* — Small comparatively: though upon the whole it cannot be very short, because the things to be transacted therein, verses 8, 9, Revelation 20:8, 9 must take up a considerable space. We are very shortly to expect, one after another, the calamities occasioned by the second beast, the harvest and the vintage, the pouring out of the phials, the judgment of

⁴ And I saw thrones, and they that sat on them, and judgment was given to them; and *I saw* the souls of them that had been beheaded for the testimony of Jesus, and for the word of God, and those who had not worshipped the wild beast, nor his image, neither had received the mark on their forehead, or on their hand; and they lived and reigned with Christ a thousand years. ⁵ The

---

Babylon, the last raging of the beast and his destruction, the imprisonment of Satan. How great things these! and how short the time! What is needful for us? Wisdom, patience, faithfulness, watchfulness. It is no time to settle upon our lees. This is not, if it be rightly understood, an acceptable message to the wise, the mighty, the honorable, of this world. Yet that which is to be done, shall be done: there is no counsel against the Lord.

4. AV witness; which; beast. *And I saw thrones* — Such as are promised the apostles, Matthew 19:28; Luke 22:30. *And they* — Namely, the saints, whom St. John saw at the same time, Daniel 7:22, sat upon them; and Judgment was given to them. 1 Corinthians 6:2. Who, and how many, these are, is not said. But they are distinguished from the souls, or persons, mentioned immediately after; and from the saints already raised. *And I saw the souls of those who had been beheaded* — With the axe: so the original word signifies. One kind of death, which was particularly inflicted at Romans, is mentioned for all. For the testimony of Jesus, *and for the word of God* — The martyrs were sometimes killed for the word of God in general; sometimes particularly for the testimony of Jesus: the one, while they refused to worship idols; the other, while they confessed the name of Christ. And those who had not worshipped the wild beast, *nor his image* — These seem to be a company distinct from those who appeared, Revelation 15:2. Those overcame, probably, in such contests as these had not. Before the number of the beast was expired, the people were compelled to worship him, by the most dreadful violence. But when the beast "was not," they were only seduced into it by the craft of the false prophet. *And they lived* — Their souls and bodies being re-united. *And reigned with Christ* — Not on earth, but in heaven. The "reigning on earth" mentioned, Revelation 11:15, is quite different from this. *A thousand years* — It must be observed, that two distinct thousand years are mentioned throughout this whole passage. Each is mentioned thrice; the thousand wherein Satan is bound, verses 2, 3, 7; the thousand wherein the saints shall reign, verses 4-6. The former ends before the end of the world; the latter reaches to the general resurrection. So that the beginning and end of the former thousand is before the beginning and end of the latter. Therefore as in the second verse, at the first mention of the former; so in the fourth verse, at the first mention of the latter, it is only said, a thousand years; in the other places, "the thousand," verses 3, 5, 7, that is, the

rest of the dead lived not again till the thousand years were <u>ended</u>. This *is* the first resurrection. ⁶ <u>Happy</u> and holy *is* he that hath a part in the first resurrection; over these the second death hath no power, but they shall be priests of God and of Christ, and shall reign with him a thousand years.

⁷ And when the thousand years are <u>fulfilled</u>, Satan shall be loosed out of his prison, ⁸ and shall go <u>forth</u> to deceive the nations, which are in the four quarters of the earth, Gog and Magog, to gather them together to battle; whose number is as the sand of the sea. ⁹ And they went up on the breadth of

---

thousand mentioned before. During the former, the promises concerning the flourishing state of the church, Revelation 10:7, shall be fulfilled; during the latter, while the saints reign with Christ in heaven, men on earth will be careless and secure.

5. AV finished. *The rest of the dead lived not till the thousand years — Mentioned, verse* 4. *Were ended* — The thousand years during which Satan is bound both begin and end much sooner. The small time, and the second thousand years, begin at the same point, immediately after the first thousand. But neither the beginning of the first nor of the second thousand will be known to the men upon earth, as both the imprisonment of Satan and his loosing are transacted in the invisible world. By observing these two distinct thousand years, many difficulties are avoided. There is room enough for the fulfilling of all the prophecies, and those which before seemed to clash are reconciled; particularly those which speak, on the one hand, of a most flourishing state of the church as yet to come; and, on the other, of the fatal security of men in the last days of the world.

6. AV Blessed. *They shall be priests of God and of Christ* — Therefore Christ is God. *And shall reign with him* — With Christ, a thousand years.

7. AV expired. *And when the former thousand years are fulfilled, Satan shall be loosed out of his prison* — At the same time that the first resurrection begins. There is a great resemblance between this passage and Revelation 12:12. At the casting out of the dragon, there was joy in heaven, but there was woe upon earth: so at the loosing of Satan, the saints begin to reign with Christ; but the nations on earth are deceived.

8. AV out. *And shall go forth to deceive the nations in the four corners of the earth* — (That is, in all the earth)-the more diligently, as he hath been so long restrained, and knoweth he hath but a small time. *Gog and Magog* — Magog, the second son of Japhet, is the father of the innumerable northern nations toward the east. The prince of these nations, of which the bulk of that army will consist, is termed Gog by Ezekiel also, Ezekiel 38:2. Both Gog and Magog signify high or lifted up; a name well suiting both the prince and people. When that fierce leader of many nations shall appear, then will his

the earth, and surrounded the camp of the saints, and the beloved city; and fire came down from God out of heaven, and devoured them. ¹⁰ And the devil that deceived them was cast into the lake of fire and brimstone, where both the <u>wild beast</u> and the false prophet *are;* and they shall be tormented day and night for ever and ever.

¹¹ And I saw a great white throne, and him that sat thereon, from whose face the earth and the heaven fled away; and there was found no place for them. ¹² And I saw the dead, <u>great and small</u>, standing before the throne; and the books were opened; and another book was opened, which is *the book* of life; and the dead were judged out of the things that were written in the books, according to their works. ¹³ And the sea gave up the dead that were

---

own name be known. *To gather them* — Both Gog and his armies. Of Gog, little more is said, as being soon mingled with the rest in the common slaughter. The Revelation speaks of this the more briefly, because it had been so particularly described by Ezekiel. *Whose number is as the sand of the sea* — Immensely numerous: a proverbial expression.

9. *And they went up on the breadth of the earth, or the land* — Filling the whole breadth of it. *And surrounded the camp of the saints* — Perhaps the gentile church, dwelling round about Jerusalem. *And the beloved city* — So termed, likewise, Ecclesiasticus xxiv. 11.

10. AV **beast**. *And they* — All these. *Shall be tormented day and night* — That is, without any intermission. Strictly speaking, there is only night there: no day, no sun, no hope!

11. *And I saw* — A representation of that great day of the Lord. *A great white throne* — How great, who can say? White with the glory of God, of him that sat upon it, — Jesus Christ. The apostle does not attempt to describe him here; only adds that circumstance, far above all description, *From whose face the earth and the heaven fled away* — Probably both the aerial and the starry heaven; which "shall pass away with a great noise." *And there was found no place for them* — But they were wholly dissolved, the very "elements melting with fervent heat." It is not said, they were thrown into great commotions, but they fled entirely away; not, they started from their foundations, but they " fell into dissolution;" not, they removed to a distant place, but there was found no place for them; they ceased to exist; they were no more. And all this, not at the strict command of the Lord Jesus; not at his awful presence, or before his fiery indignation; but at the bare presence of his Majesty, sitting with severe but adorable dignity on his throne.

12. AV **small and great**. *And I saw the dead, great and small* — Of every age and condition. This includes, also, those who undergo a change equivalent to death, 1 Corinthians 15:51. *And the books* — Human judges

therein; and death and Hades gave up the dead that were in them; and they were judged every one according to their works. ¹⁴ And death and Hades were cast into the lake of fire. This is the second death. ¹⁵ And whosoever was not found written in the book of life was cast into the lake of fire.

Chapter 21

¹ And I saw a new heaven and a new earth; for the first heaven and the first earth were passed away; and there was no more sea. ² And I saw the

---

have their books written with pen and ink: *how different is the nature of these books! Were opened* — O how many hidden things will then come to light; and how many will have quite another appearance than they had before in the sight of men! With the book of God's omniscience, that of conscience will then exactly tally. The book of natural law, as well as of revealed, will then also be displayed. It is not said, The books will be read: the light of that day will make them visible to all. Then, particularly, shall every man know himself, and that with the last exactness This will be the first true, full, impartial, universal history. *And another book* — Wherein are enrolled all that are accepted through the Beloved; all who lived and died in the faith that worketh by love. Which is the book of life, *was opened* — What manner of expectation will then be, with regard to the issue of the whole! Malachi 3:16, etc.

13. AV Hell. *Death and Hades gave up the dead that were in them* — Death gave up all the bodies of men; and Hades, the receptacle of separate souls, gave them up, to be re-united to their bodies.

14. *And death and Hades were cast into the lake of fire* — That is, were abolished for ever; for neither the righteous nor the wicked were to die any more: their souls and bodies were no more to be separated. Consequently, neither death nor Hades could any more have a being.

Ch 21. 1. *And I saw* — So it runs, Revelation 19:11, 20:1, 4, 11, in a succession. All these several representations follow one another in order: so the vision reaches into eternity. *A new heaven and a new earth* — After the resurrection and general judgment. St. John is not now describing a flourishing state of the church, but a new and eternal state of all things. *For the first heaven and the first earth* — Not only the lowest part of heaven, not only the solar system, but the whole ethereal heaven, with all its host, whether of planets or fixed stars, Isaiah 34:4 Matthew 24:29. All the former things will be done away, that all may become new, verses 4, 5, 2 Peter 3:10, 12. *Are passed away* — But in the fourth verse it is said, "are gone away."

holy city, the new Jerusalem, coming down from God out of heaven, prepared as a bride adorned for her husband. ³ And I heard a loud voice out of heaven, saying, Behold, the tabernacle of God with men, and he will <u>pitch his tent</u> with them, and they shall be his people, and God himself *shall be* with them, *and be* their God. ⁴ And he shall wipe away all tears from their eyes; and death shall be no more, neither shall sorrow, or crying, or pain be any more; because the former things are <u>gone</u> away. ⁵ And he that sat upon the throne said, Behold, I make all things new. And he saith to me, Write; these sayings are faithful and true. ⁶ And he said to me, It is done. I am the Alpha and the Omega, the beginning and the end. I will give to him that thirsteth of the fountain of the water of life freely. ⁷ He that overcometh shall

---

There the stronger word is used; for death, mourning, and sorrow go away all together: the former heaven and earth only pass away, giving place to the new heaven and the new earth.

2. AV | John saw. *And I saw the holy city* — The new heaven, the new earth, and the new Jerusalem, are closely connected. This city is wholly new, belonging not to this world, not to the millennium, but to eternity. This appears from the series of the vision, the magnificence of the description, and the opposition of this city to the second death, Revelation 20:11, 12; 21:1, 2, 5, 8, 9; 22:5. *Coming down* — In the very act of descending.

3. AV dwell. *They shall be his people, and God himself shall be with them, and be their God* — So shall the covenant between God and his people be executed in the most glorious manner.

4. AV passed. *And death shall be no more* — This is a full proof that this whole description belongs not to time, but eternity. Neither shall sorrow, or crying, or pain, be any more: *for the former things are gone away* — Under the former heaven, and upon the former earth, there was death and sorrow, crying and pain; all which occasioned many tears: but now pain and sorrow are fled away, and the saints have everlasting life and joy.

5. *And he that sat upon the throne said* — Not to St. John only. From the first mention of "him that sat upon the throne," Revelation 4:2, this is the first speech which is expressly ascribed to him. *And he* — The angel. *Saith to me Write* — As follows. *These sayings are faithful and true* — This includes all that went before. The apostle seems again to have ceased writing, being overcome with ecstasy at the voice of him that spake.

6. *And he* — That sat upon the throne. Said to me, *It is done* — All that the prophets had spoken; all that was spoken, Revelation 4:1. We read this expression twice in this prophecy: first, Revelation 16:17, at the fulfilling of the wrath of God; and here, at the making all things new. I am the Alpha and

inherit these things; and I will be to him a God, and he shall be to me a son. ⁸ But the fearful, and unbelieving, and abominable, and murderers, and whoremongers, and sorcerers, and idolaters, and all liars, their part *is* in the lake that burneth with fire and brimstone; which is the second death.

⁹ And there came one of the seven angels that had the seven <u>phials</u> full of the seven last plagues, and talked with me, saying, Come hither, I will show thee the bride, the Lamb's wife. ¹⁰ And he carried me away in the spirit to a great and high mountain, and showed me the <u>holy Jerusalem</u>, descending out of heaven from God, ¹¹ having the glory of God; her <u>window</u> was like the

---

the Omega, *the beginning and the end* — The latter explains the former: the Everlasting. *I will give to him that thirsteth* — The Lamb saith the same, Revelation 22:17.

7. *He that overcometh* — Which is more than, "he that thirsteth." *Shall inherit these things* — Which I have made new. I will be his God, *and he shall be my son* — Both in the Hebrews and Greek language, in which the scriptures were written, what we translate shall and will are one and the same word. The only difference consists in an English translation, or in the want of knowledge in him that interprets what he does not understand.

8. *But the fearful and unbelieving* — Who, through want of courage and faith, do not overcome. *And abominable* — That is, sodomites. And whoremongers, and sorcerers, *and idolaters* — These three sins generally went together; their part is in the lake.

9. AV vials. *And there came one of the seven angels that had the seven phials* — Whereby room had been made for the kingdom of God. Saying, Come, *I will show thee the bride* — The same angel had before showed him Babylon, Revelation 17:1, which is directly opposed to the new Jerusalem.

10. AV great city, the holy Jerusalem. *And he carried me away in the spirit* — The same expression as before, Revelation 17:3. *And showed me the holy city Jerusalem* — The old city is now forgotten, so that this is no longer termed the new, but absolutely Jerusalem. O how did St. John long to enter in! but the time was not yet come. Ezekiel also describes "the holy city," and what pertains thereto, xl.-xlviii. Ezekiel 40:1- Ezekiel 48:35 but a city quite different from the old Jerusalem, as it was either before or after the Babylonish captivity. The descriptions of the prophet and of the apostle agree in many particulars; but in many more they differ. Ezekiel expressly describes the temple, and the worship of God therein, closely alluding to the Levitical service. But St. John saw no temple, and describes the city far more large, glorious, and heavenly than the prophet. Yet that which he describes is the same city; but as it subsisted soon after the destruction of the beast. This

most precious stone, like a jasper stone, clear as crystal. ¹² Having a wall great and high, having twelve gates, and at the gates twelve angels, and the names written thereon, which are *the names* of the twelve tribes of the children of Israel. ¹³ On the east three gates; and on the north three gates; and on the south three gates; and on the west three gates. ¹⁴ And the wall of the city had twelve foundations, and upon them the names of the twelve apostles of the Lamb. ¹⁵ And he that talked with me had a measure, a golden reed, to measure the city, and the gates thereof, and the wall thereof. ¹⁶ And the city

---

being observed, both the prophecies agree together and one may explain the other.

11. AV light. *Having the glory of God* — For her light, verse 23, Revelation 21:23, Isaiah 40:1, 2, Zechariah 2:5. *Her window* — There was only one, which ran all round the city. The light did not come in from without through this for the glory of God is within the city. But it shines out from within to a great distance, verses 23, 24. Revelation 21:23, 24.

12. *Twelve angels* — Still waiting upon the heirs of salvation.

14. *And the wall of the city had twelve foundations, and on them the names of the twelve apostles of the Lamb* — Figuratively showing that the inhabitants of the city had built only on that faith which the apostles once delivered to the saints.

15. *And he measured the city, twelve thousand furlongs* — Not in circumference, but on each of the four sides. Jerusalem was thirty-three furlongs in circumference; Alexandria thirty in length, ten in breadth. Nineveh is reported to have been four hundred furlongs round; Babylon four hundred and eighty. But what inconsiderable villages were all these compared to the new Jerusalem! By this measure is understood the greatness of the city, with the exact order and just proportion of every part of it; to show, figuratively, that this city was prepared for a great number of inhabitants, how small so ever the number of real Christians may sometimes appear to be; and that everything relating to the happiness of that state was prepared with the greatest order and exactness. The city is twelve thousand furlongs high; the wall, an hundred and forty-four reeds. This is exactly the same height, only expressed in a different manner. The twelve thousand furlongs, being spoken absolutely, without any explanation, are common, human furlongs: the hundred forty-four reeds are not of common human length, but of angelic, abundantly larger than human. It is said, the measure of a man that is, of an angel because St. John saw the measuring angel in an human shape. The reed therefore was as great as was the stature of that human form in which the angel appeared. In treating of all these things a deep reverence is necessary; and so is a measure of spiritual wisdom; that we may

lieth foursquare, and the length is as large as the breadth; and he measured the city with the reed, twelve thousand furlongs. The length and the breadth and the height of it are equal. ¹⁷ And he measured the wall thereof, an hundred *and* forty-four <u>reeds,</u> the measure of a man, that is, of an angel. ¹⁸ And the building of the wall thereof was jasper; and the city *was* of pure gold, like clear glass. ¹⁹ And the foundations of the wall of the city were <u>adorned</u> with all manner of precious stones. The first foundation *was* a jasper; the second, a sapphire; the third, a chalcedony; the fourth, an emerald; ²⁰ the fifth, a sardonyx; the sixth, a sardius; the seventh, a chrysolite; the eighth, a beryl; the ninth, a topaz; the tenth, a chrysoprase; the eleventh, a jacinth; the twelfth, an amethyst. ²¹ And the twelve gates *were* twelve pearls; <u>each of the gates</u> was of one pearl; and the street of the city *was* pure gold, transparent as

---

neither understand them too literally and grossly, nor go too far from the natural force of the words. The gold, the pearls, the precious stones, the walls, foundations, gates, are undoubtedly figurative expressions; seeing the city itself is in glory, and the inhabitants of it have spiritual bodies: yet these spiritual bodies are also real bodies, and the city is an abode distinct from its inhabitants, and proportioned to them who take up a finite and a determinate space. The measures, therefore, above mentioned are real and determinate.

17. AV cubits.

18. *And the building of the wall was jasper* — That is, the wall was built of jasper. *And the city* — The houses, was of pure gold.

19. AV garnished. *And the foundations were adorned with precious stones* — That is, beautifully made of them. The precious stones on the high priest's breastplate of judgment were a proper emblem to express the happiness of God's church in his presence with them, and in the blessing of his protection. The like ornaments on the foundations of the walls of this city may express the perfect glory and happiness of all the inhabitants of it from the most glorious presence and protection of God. Each precious stone was not the ornament of the foundation, but the foundation itself. The colors of these are remarkably mixed. A jasper is of the color of white marble, with a light shade of green and of red; a sapphire is of a sky-blue, speckled with gold; a chalcedony, or carbuncle, of the color of red-hot iron; an emerald, of a grass green.

20. *A sardonyx is red streaked with white; a sardius, of a deep red; a chrysolite, of a deep yellow; a beryl, sea-green; a topaz, pale yellow; a chrysoprase is greenish and transparent, with gold specks; a jacinth, of a red purple; an amethyst, violet purple.*

glass. ²² And I saw no temple therein; for the Lord God Almighty and the Lamb are the temple of it. ²³ And the city hath no need of the sun, neither of the moon, to shine on it; for the glory of God hath enlightened it, and the Lamb *is* the lamp thereof. ²⁴ And the nations shall walk by the light thereof; and the kings of the earth bring their glory into it. ²⁵ And the gates of it shall not be shut by day; and there shall be no night there. ²⁶ And they shall bring the glory and honour of the nations into it. ²⁷ But there shall in no wise enter into it any thing common, or that worketh abomination, or *maketh* a lie; but they who are written in the Lamb's book of life.

Chapter 22

¹ And he showed me a river of the water of life, clear as crystal, proceeding out of the throne of God and of the Lamb. ² In the midst of the

---

21. AV every several gate.

22. *The Lord God and the Lamb are the temple of it* — He fills the new heaven and the new earth. He surrounds the city and sanctifies it, and all that are therein. He is "all in all."

23. AV light. *The glory of God* — Infinitely brighter than the shining of the sun.

24. AV nations of them which are saved; glory and honour. *And the nations* — The whole verse is taken from Isaiah 60:3. *Shall walk by the light thereof* — Which throws itself outward from the city far and near. *And the kings of the earth* — Those of them who have a part there. *Bring their glory into it* — Not their old glory, which is now abolished; but such as becomes the new earth, and receives an immense addition by their entrance into the city.

26. *And they shall bring the glory of the nations into it* — It seems, a select part of each nation; that is, all which can contribute to make this city honorable and glorious shall be found in it; as if all that was rich and precious throughout the world was brought into one city.

27. AV that defileth. *Common* — That is. unholy. *But those who are written in the Lamb's book of life* — True, holy, persevering believers. This blessedness is enjoyed by those only; and, as such, they are registered among them who are to inherit eternal life.

Ch 22. 1. AV pure river. *And he showed me a river of the water of life* — The ever fresh and fruitful effluence of the Holy Ghost. See Ezekiel 47:1-12; where also the trees are mentioned which "bear fruit every month," that is,

street of it, and on each side of the river, *is* the tree of life, bearing twelve sorts of fruits, yielding its fruit every month; and the leaves of the tree *are* for the healing of the nations. ³ And there shall be no more curse; but the throne of God and of the Lamb shall be in it; and his servants shall worship him, ⁴ and shall see his face; and his name *shall be* on their foreheads. ⁵ And there shall be no night there; neither is there need of a lamp, or of the light of the sun; for the Lord God will enlighten them; and they shall reign for ever.

---

perpetually. Proceeding out of the throne of God, *and of the Lamb* — "All that the Father hath," saith the Son of God, "is mine;" even the throne of his glory.

2. AV *was*; *yielded*; *were*. *In the midst of the street* — Here is the paradise of God, mentioned, Revelation 2:7. *Is the tree of life* — Not one tree only, but many. *Every month* — That is, in inexpressible abundance. The variety, likewise, as well as the abundance of the fruits of the Spirit, may be intimated thereby. *And the leaves are for the healing of the nations* — For the continuing their health, not the restoring it; for no sickness is there.

3. AV **serve**. *And there shall be no more curse* — But pure life and blessing; every effect of the displeasure of God for sin being now totally removed. *But the throne of God and the Lamb shall be in it* — That is, the glorious presence and reign of God. *And his servants* — The highest honor in the universe. *Shalt worship him* — The noblest employment.

4. *And shall see his face* — Which was not granted to Moses. They shall have the nearest access to, and thence the highest resemblance of, him. This is the highest expression in the language of scripture to denote the most perfect happiness of the heavenly state, 1 John 3:2. *And his name shall be on their foreheads* — Each of them shall be openly acknowledged as God's own property, and his glorious nature most visibly shine forth in them. *And they shall reign* — But who are the subjects of these kings? The other inhabitants of the new earth. For there must needs be an everlasting difference between those who when on earth excelled in virtue, and those comparatively slothful and unprofitable servants, who were just saved as by fire. The kingdom of God is taken by force; but the prize is worth all the labor. Whatever of high, lovely, or excellent is in all the monarchies of the earth is all together not a grain of dust, compared to the glory of the children of God. God "is not ashamed to be called their God, for whom he hath prepared this city." But who shall come up into his holy place? "They who keep his commandments," verse 14. Revelation 22:14.

5. AV **candle; ever and ever**. *And they shall reign for ever and ever* — What encouragement is this to the patience and faithfulness of the saints, that, whatever their sufferings are, they will work out for them "an eternal weight

⁶ And he said to me, These sayings *are* faithful and true; the Lord, the God of the spirits of the prophets hath sent his angel to show his servants the things which must be done shortly. ⁷ Behold, I come quickly; happy *is* he that keepeth the words of the prophecy of this book. ⁸ And *it was* I, John, who heard and saw these things. And when I had heard and seen, I fell down to worship at the feet of the angel who showed me these things. ⁹ But he saith to me, See *thou do it* not. I am thy fellow servant, and of thy brethren the prophets, and of them who keep the sayings of this book; worship God. ¹⁰ And he saith to me, Seal not the sayings of the prophecy of this book; the time is nigh. ¹¹ He that is unrighteous, let him be unrighteous still; and he that is filthy, let him be filthy still; and he that is righteous, let him be

---

of glory!" Thus ends the doctrine of this Revelation, in the everlasting happiness of all the faithful. The mysterious ways of Providence are cleared up, and all things issue in an eternal Sabbath, an everlasting state of perfect peace and happiness, reserved for all who endure to the end.

6. AV **Lord God of the holy prophets sent.** *And he said to me* — Here begins the conclusion of the book, exactly agreeing with the introduction, (particularly verses 6, 7, 10, Revelation 22:6, 7, 10 with chap. 1:1, 3,) Revelation 1:1, 3 and giving light to the whole book, as this book does to the whole scripture. *These sayings are faithful and true* — All the things which you have heard and seen shall be faithfully accomplished in their order, and are infallibly true. The Lord, *the God of the holy prophets* — Who inspired and authorized them of old. Hath now sent me his angel, *to show his servants* — By thee. *The things which must be done shortly* — Which will begin to be performed immediately.

7. AV **Blessed.** *Behold, I come quickly* — Saith our Lord himself, to accomplish these things. *Happy is he that keepeth* — Without adding or diminishing, verses 18, 19, Revelation 22:18, 19 the words of this book.

8. AV **omitted (JW added).** *I fell down to worship at the feet of the angel* — The very same words which occur, Revelation 19:10. The reproof of the angel, likewise, See thou do it not, for I am thy fellow servant, is expressed in the very same terms as before. May it not be the very same incident which is here related again? Is not this far more probable, than that the apostle would commit a fault again, of which he had been so solemnly warned before?

9. *See thou do it not* — The expression in the original is short and elliptical, as is usual in showing vehement aversion.

10. AV **at hand.** *And he saith to me* — After a little pause. *Seal not the sayings of this book* — Conceal them not, like the things that are sealed up. *The time is nigh* — Wherein they shall begin to take place.

righteous still; and he that is holy, let him be holy still. ¹² Behold, I come quickly; and my reward *is* with me, to render to every one as his work shall be. ¹³ I am the Alpha and the Omega, the first and the last, the beginning and the end.

¹⁴ Happy *are* they that do his commandments, that they may have right to the tree of life, and may enter in by the gates into the city. ¹⁵ Without *are* dogs, and sorcerers, and whoremongers, and murderers, and idolaters, and every one that loveth and maketh a lie.

¹⁶ I, Jesus, have sent my angel to testify to you, to the churches, these things. I am the root and the offspring of David, the bright, the morning-star. ¹⁷ And the Spirit and the bride say, Come. And let him that heareth say,

---

11. AV unjust. *He that is unrighteous* — As if he had said, The final judgment is at hand; after which the condition of all mankind will admit of no change for ever. *Unrighteous* — Unjustified. *Filthy* — Unsanctified, unholy.

12. AV give. *I* — Jesus Christ. *Come quickly* — To judge the world. *And my reward is with me* — The rewards which I assign both to the righteous and the wicked are given at my coming. *To give to every man according as his work* — His whole inward and outward behavior shall be.

13. *I am the Alpha and the Omega, the first and the last* — Who exist from everlasting to everlasting. How clear, incontestable a proof, does our Lord here give of his divine glory!

14. *Happy are they that do his commandments* — His, who saith, *I come* — He speaks of himself. *That they may have right* — Through his gracious covenant. *To the tree of life* — To all the blessings signified by it. When Adam broke his commandment, he was driven from the tree of life. They who keep his commandments" shall eat thereof.

15. *Without are dogs* — The sentence in the original is abrupt, as expressing abhorrence. The gates are ever open; but not for dogs; fierce and rapacious men.

16. AV you these things in the churches. *I Jesus have sent my angel to testify these things* — Primarily. *To you* — The seven angels of the churches; *then to those churches* — and afterwards to all other churches in succeeding ages. *I* — as God. *Am the root* — And source of David's family and kingdom; as man, an descended from his loins. "I am the star out of Jacob," Numbers 24:17; like the bright morning star, who put an end to the night of ignorance, sin, and sorrow, and usher in an eternal day of light, purity, and joy.

Come. And let him that is thirsteth, come. And let him that willeth, take the water of life freely.

¹⁸ I testify to every one that heareth the words of the prophecy of this book. If any man add to them, God shall add to him the plagues that are written in this book. ¹⁹ And if any man shall take away from the words of the book of this prophecy, God shall take away his part <u>of the</u> book of life, and the holy city, which are written in this book.

²⁰ He that testifieth these things saith, <u>Yea</u>, I come quickly. Amen. Come, Lord Jesus!

²¹ The grace of the Lord Jesus Christ *be* with <u>all</u>.

---

17. *The Spirit and the bride* — The Spirit of adoption in the bride, in the heart of every true believer. *Say* — With earnest desire and expectation. *Come* — And accomplish all the words of this prophecy. And let him that thirsteth, *come* — Here they also who are farther off are invited. And whosoever will, *let him take the water of life* — He may partake of my spiritual and unspeakable blessings, as freely as he makes use of the most common refreshments; as freely as he drinks of the running stream.

18, 19. *I testify to every one, etc.* — From the fullness of his heart, the apostle utters this testimony, this weighty admonition, not only to the churches of Asia, but to all who should ever hear this book. He that adds, all the plagues shall be added to him; he that takes from it, all the blessings shall be taken from him; and, doubtless, this guilt is incurred by all those who lay hindrances in the way of the faithful, which prevent them from hearing their Lord's "I come," and answering, "Come, Lord Jesus." This may likewise be considered as an awful sanction, given to the whole New Testament; in like manner as Moses guarded the law, Deuteronomy 4:2, and Deuteronomy 12:32; and as God himself did, Malachi 4:4, in closing the canon of the Old Testament.

19. AV out of the. See note on "Revelation 22:18."

20. AV Surely. *He that testifieth these things* — Even all that is contained in this book. *Saith* — For the encouragement of the church in all her afflictions. *Yea* — Answering the call of the Spirit and the bride. *I come quickly* — To destroy all her enemies, and establish her in a state of perfect and everlasting happiness. The apostle expresses his earnest desire and hope of this, by answering, Amen. Come, Lord Jesus!

21. AV adds Amen. *The grace* — The free love. *Of the Lord Jesus* — And all its fruits. *Be with all* — Who thus long for his appearing!

The Book of Daniel
1765

For centuries Christians have recognized a kinship between the Books of Daniel and Revelation. This kinship explains why Wesley's comments on the pertinent chapters of Daniel are included in this Reader. There is little of surprise regarding Wesley's insights. He follows conventional Protestant interpretation that identifies the four kingdoms with Babylon, Persia, Greece, and Rome. Wesley's postmillennialism is evident in his comments on the stone and great mountain (ch. 2). Antiochus Epiphanies is the great villain who turns out to be a type of the future papal Antichrist (11:36). The 'time of trouble' looks ahead to the destruction of Jerusalem in AD 70, followed by the church age and the final eschatological struggle and the conversion of the Jews (12:1ff.). Wesley envisions a dual fulfillment of prophecy at this point, with the sack of Jerusalem serving as a foreshadow of the final siege before the end. The approach of the 'Son of man' to the Ancient of Days is Christ's ascension and investiture to destroy God's enemies and to protect his people. This parallels the Apostle John's vision of the same event in Revelation 5. Last, Wesley offers an interpretation of 9:24-27 that was widely accepted by Protestants in his day (and by some today). In his first coming Christ confirmed a (new) covenant with 'many' and in the middle of the week (after 3 1/2 years) put an end to the Jewish sacrificial system on the cross. Many contemporary readers might object to this interpretation, but this was a widely held view—including Wesley's primary source: Matthew Henry. Wesley states in the introduction of his Old Testament commentary that his primary goal was to improve on Henry's well respected but lengthy Commentary on the Whole Bible. *Wesley's introduction can be found in* Works *(Jackson) 14:246-53. Regarding the scripture text, Wesley utilized the Authorized Version for his Old Testament commentary.*

Chapter 2

[24] Therefore Daniel went in unto Arioch, whom the king had ordained to destroy the wise *men* of Babylon; he went and said thus unto him; Destroy not the wise *men* of Babylon; bring me in before the king, and I will show unto the king the interpretation. [25] Then Arioch brought in Daniel before the king in haste, and said thus unto him, I have found a man of the captives of

Judah, that will make known unto the king the interpretation. ²⁶ The king answered and said to Daniel, whose name *was* Belteshazzar, Art thou able to make known unto me the dream which I have seen, and the interpretation thereof? ²⁷ Daniel answered in the presence of the king, and said, The secret which the king hath demanded cannot the wise *men*, the astrologers, the magicians, the soothsayers, show unto the king; ²⁸ But there is a God in heaven that revealeth secrets, and maketh known to the king Nebuchadnezzar what shall be in the latter days. Thy dream, and the visions of thy head upon thy bed, are these; ²⁹ As for thee, O king, thy thoughts came *into thy mind* upon thy bed, what should come to pass hereafter: and he that revealeth secrets maketh known to thee what shall come to pass. ³⁰ But as for me, this secret is not revealed to me for *any* wisdom that I have more than any living, but for *their* sakes that shall make known the interpretation to the king, and that thou mightest know the thoughts of thy heart.

³¹ Thou, O king, sawest, and behold a great image. This great image, whose brightness *was* excellent, stood before thee; and the form thereof *was* terrible. ³² This image's head *was* of fine gold, his breast and his arms of silver, his belly and his thighs of brass, ³³ His legs of iron, his feet part of iron and part of clay. ³⁴ Thou sawest till that a stone was cut out without hands, which smote the image upon his feet *that were* of iron and clay, and brake them to pieces. ³⁵ Then was the iron, the clay, the brass, the silver, and the gold, broken to pieces together, and became like the chaff of the summer threshingfloors; and the wind carried them away, that no place was found for them: and the stone that smote the image became a great mountain, and filled the whole earth.

³⁶ This *is* the dream; and we will tell the interpretation thereof before the king. ³⁷ Thou, O king, *art* a king of kings; for the God of heaven hath given thee a kingdom, power, and strength, and glory. ³⁸ And wheresoever the

---

26. *Belteshazzar* — By this name of Belteshazzar he had given Daniel, he took courage as if he might expect some great thing from him: for the word signifies the keeper of secret treasure.

28. *What shall be* — Observe the prophet's wisdom, he does not fall abruptly upon the dream, but first prepares this lofty king for it, and by degrees labors to win him to the knowledge of the true God.

30. *But* — But that the interpretation may be manifest to the king, and that thou mayest be better instructed and satisfied in thy mind.

36. *And we* — By this word we appears Daniel's piety and modesty, or he declares by it, that he and his companions had begged this skill from God, and therefore he did not arrogate it to himself.

children of men dwell, the beasts of the field and the fowls of the heaven hath he given into thine hand, and hath made thee ruler over them all. Thou *art* this head of gold. ³⁹ And after thee shall arise another kingdom inferior to thee, and another third kingdom of brass, which shall bear rule over all the earth. ⁴⁰ And the fourth kingdom shall be strong as iron; forasmuch as iron breaketh in pieces and subdueth all *things*; and as iron that breaketh all these, shall it break in pieces and bruise. ⁴¹ And whereas thou sawest the feet and toes, part of potters' clay, and part of iron, the kingdom shall be divided; but there shall be in it of the strength of the iron, forasmuch as thou sawest the iron mixed with miry clay. ⁴² And *as* the toes of the feet *were* part of iron, and part of clay, *so* the kingdom shall be partly strong, and partly broken. ⁴³ And whereas thou sawest iron mixed with miry clay, they shall mingle themselves with the seed of men; but they shall not cleave one to another, even as iron is not mixed with clay. ⁴⁴ And in the days of these kings shall

---

38. *Made thee ruler* — He hath given thee absolute dominion of all creatures, men and beasts within the bounds of thy vast kingdom. *Thou* — He was first in order, as the head is before the other parts, and the vision began in him, and descended downwards to the other three monarchies. He was the head of gold, because of the vast riches wherein this monarchy abounded, and because it stood longest, five hundred years, and was fortunate and flourishing to the last.

39. *Another kingdom* — This was that of the Medes and Persians, inferior in time for it lasted not half so long as the Assyrian in prosperity and tranquility; yet, was this wonderful, rich and large for a time. *Third kingdom* — This was the Grecian monarchy under Alexander the great, called brass, because coarser than the other. *Over all the earth* — Alexander marched even to the Indies, and was said to conquer the world.

40. *Fourth kingdom* — This is the kingdom of the Romans, and was to last not only to Christ's first coming, but under antichrist, to his second coming. This did break in pieces all other kingdoms, being too strong for them, and brought all into subjection to it, 'till the stone fell upon it.

41. *Divided* — Partly strong, and partly weak; the Roman kingdom was divided, partly by their civil wars, partly when conquered provinces and kingdoms cast off the Roman yoke, and set up king's of their own, and so the empire was divided into ten kingdoms or toes.

42. *Broken* — This was plain in the civil wars of the Romans, and the falling off of some countries, especially towards the end of it.

43. *Mingle themselves* — By marriage, but they shall never knit well together, because ambition is stronger than affinity.

the God of heaven set up a kingdom, which shall never be destroyed: and the kingdom shall not be left to other people, *but* it shall break in pieces and consume all these kingdoms, and it shall stand for ever. [45] Forasmuch as thou sawest that the stone was cut out of the mountain without hands, and that it brake in pieces the iron, the brass, the clay, the silver, and the gold; the great God hath made known to the king what shall come to pass hereafter; and the dream *is* certain, and the interpretation thereof sure.

Chapter 7

[1] In the first year of Belshazzar king of Babylon Daniel had a dream and visions of his head upon his bed; then he wrote the dream, *and* told the sum of the matters. [2] Daniel spake and said, I saw in my vision by night, and, behold, the four winds of the heaven strove upon the great sea. [3] And four

---

44. *In the days of these kings* — While the iron kingdom stood, for Christ was born in the reign of Augustus Caesar. And this kingdom is not bounded by any limits, as worldly empires are, but is truly universal. And it shall be for ever, never destroyed or given to others, as the rest were.

45. *And the gold* — This denotes the small beginning of Christ's visible kingdom, and the different rise of Christ from all other; his conception by the Holy Ghost, without father and mother, respectively as to his two natures. This stone, falling from the mountain, brake the image in pieces; for Christ is a stone that grinds to powder those it falls on; and he is a growing stone even to a mountain, and therefore will fill the earth.

Ch 7. We come now to the prophetical part of Daniel, in which are many things hard to be understood. In this chapter we have, The vision of the four beasts, ver. 1-8. The vision of God's throne of government and judgment, ver. 9-14. The interpretation of those visions, ver. 15-28.

1. *In the first year of Belshazzar* — This prophecy is written in Chaldee, to be a monument to him, of the reverence his father and grandfather shewed towards God, who had done such mighty works for them. *Then he wrote* — These visions were recorded for the benefit of the church, to rectify their mistake: for they thought all things would succeed prosperously after they returned out of their captivity.

2. *The four winds* — Probably by the four winds of the great sea is signified commotions of contrary nations, striving together by wars, and producing these four beasts successively.

great beasts came up from the sea, diverse one from another. ⁴ The first *was* like a lion, and had eagle's wings; I beheld till the wings thereof were plucked, and it was lifted up from the earth, and made stand upon the feet as a man, and a man's heart was given to it. ⁵ And behold another beast, a second, like to a bear, and it raised up itself on one side, and *it had* three ribs in the mouth of it between the teeth of it; and they said thus unto it, Arise, devour much flesh. ⁶ After this I beheld, and lo another, like a leopard, which had upon the back of it four wings of a fowl; the beast had also four heads; and dominion was given to it. ⁷ After this I saw in the night visions, and behold a fourth beast, dreadful and terrible, and strong exceedingly; and it had great iron teeth; it devoured and brake in pieces, and stamped the residue with the feet of it; and it *was* diverse from all the beasts that *were* before it; and it had ten horns. ⁸ I considered the horns, and, behold, there came up among them another little horn, before whom there were three of the first horns plucked up by the roots; and, behold, in this horn *were* eyes like the eyes of man, and a mouth speaking great things.

---

3. *Four great beasts* — That is, four great monarchies, great, in comparison of particular kingdoms; beasts for their tyrannical oppressions.

4. *The first* — This was the Chaldean, or Assyrian; whose seat was first at Babylon, afterwards at Nineveh, and then at Babylon again. *Eagle's wings* — They were swift, over-running many countries, and brought their monarchy to a prodigious height in a short time. *The wings were plucked* — Which was first done in stopping the career of their victories, and afterwards in casting them out of their kingdom. *A man's heart* — They lost their lion-like courage, and became faint and cowardly like other men.

5. *Another beast* — The Mede's and Persians, a fierce, ravenous creature. *On one side* — The north side; for the Mede first arose and sent to Cyrus the Persian to come and assist him against the Assyrian. *Three ribs* — Several of the Babylonian subjects revolted, and all these made the three ribs.

6. *Like a leopard* — This leopard was the Grecian monarchy; a leopard is less than a lion, so was this monarchy at first, but yet durst fight with a lion; so did Alexander encounter Darius with an inferior force. A leopard also for his swiftness; therefore described with four wings on his back. *Four heads* — He was succeeded by four of his chief commanders, who divided that empire into four parts.

7. *A fourth beast* — The Roman empire.

8. *Another little horn* — Probably either the Turk or the Romish antichrist.

⁹ I beheld till the thrones were cast down, and the Ancient of days did sit, whose garment *was* white as snow, and the hair of his head like the pure wool; his throne *was like* the fiery flame, *and* his wheels *as* burning fire. ¹⁰ A fiery stream issued and came forth from before him; thousand thousands ministered unto him, and ten thousand times ten thousand stood before him; the judgment was set, and the books were opened. ¹¹ I beheld then because of the voice of the great words which the horn spake; I beheld *even* till the beast was slain, and his body destroyed, and given to the burning flame. ¹² As concerning the rest of the beasts, they had their dominion taken away; yet their lives were prolonged for a season and time. ¹³ I saw in the night visions, and, behold, *one* like the Son of man came with the clouds of heaven, and came to the Ancient of days, and they brought him near before him. ¹⁴ And there was given him dominion, and glory, and a kingdom, that all people, nations, and languages, should serve him; his dominion *is* an everlasting dominion, which shall not pass away, and his kingdom *that* which shall not be destroyed.

¹⁵ I Daniel was grieved in my spirit in the midst of *my* body, and the visions of my head troubled me. ¹⁶ I came near unto one of them that stood by, and asked him the truth of all this. So he told me, and made me know the interpretation of the things. ¹⁷ These great beasts, which are four, *are* four kings, *which* shall arise out of the earth. ¹⁸ But the saints of the most High shall take the kingdom, and possess the kingdom for ever, even for ever and ever. ¹⁹ Then I would know the truth of the fourth beast, which was diverse from all the others, exceeding dreadful, whose teeth *were of* iron, and his nails *of* brass; *which* devoured, brake in pieces, and stamped the residue with his feet; ²⁰ And of the ten horns that *were* in his head, and *of* the other which came up, and before whom three fell; even *of* that horn that had eyes, and a

---

9. *The thrones* — The kingdoms of this world were destroyed by God the king, and judge of all, called the Ancient of days, because of his eternal deity.

11. *Destroyed* — This cannot but be meant of the ruin and judgment of antichrist.

13. *A son of man* — That is, the Messiah, he came with the clouds of heaven, gloriously, swiftly and terribly. *And came* — This relates to his ascension, at which time, he received his royal investiture, for the protection of his church, and curbing of their enemies.

16. *Unto one* — That is, to an angel, that ministered. *The truth* — The true meaning of this vision.

18. *But the saints* — Jesus Christ being their king, they shall reign with him, and possess the kingdom for ever.

mouth that spake very great things, whose look *was* more stout than his fellows. ²¹ I beheld, and the same horn made war with the saints, and prevailed against them; ²² Until the Ancient of days came, and judgment was given to the saints of the most High; and the time came that the saints possessed the kingdom. ²³ Thus he said, The fourth beast shall be the fourth kingdom upon earth, which shall be diverse from all kingdoms, and shall devour the whole earth, and shall tread it down, and break it in pieces. ²⁴ And the ten horns out of this kingdom *are* ten kings *that* shall arise; and another shall rise after them; and he shall be diverse from the first, and he shall subdue three kings. ²⁵ And he shall speak *great* words against the most High, and shall wear out the saints of the most High, and think to change times and laws; and they shall be given into his hand until a time and times and the dividing of time. ²⁶ But the judgment shall sit, and they shall take away his dominion, to consume and to destroy *it* unto the end. ²⁷ And the kingdom and dominion, and the greatness of the kingdom under the whole heaven, shall be given to the people of the saints of the most High, whose kingdom *is* an everlasting kingdom, and all dominions shall serve and obey him. ²⁸ Hitherto *is* the end of the matter. As for me Daniel, my cogitations much troubled me, and my countenance changed in me: but I kept the matter in my heart.

Chapter 8

¹ In the third year of the reign of king Belshazzar a vision appeared unto me, *even unto* me Daniel, after that which appeared unto me at the first. ² And I saw in a vision; and it came to pass, when I saw, that I *was* at Shushan *in* the palace, which *is* in the province of Elam; and I saw in a vision, and I was by the river of Ulai. ³ Then I lifted up mine eyes, and saw, and, behold,

---

24. *And another* — This seems to mean the Romish antichrist.

25. *Until a time and times* — The numbers of Daniel and John seem to agree. Daniel was certainly prophetical in these things, and his prophecy reacheth to the end of times, even of antichrist's reign.

28. *Of the matter* — Of the vision, and the angel's interpretation.

Ch 8. This and the following chapters are not writ in Chaldee, but in Hebrew, for the benefit of the Jews. Here is the vision of the ram, and the he-goat, and the little horn, ver. 1-14. The interpretation of it, ver. 15-27.

1. *After that* — In the other vision he speaks of all the four monarchies; here only of the three first; this vision being a comment upon the first.

2. *The river of Ulai* — Which ran round the city.

there stood before the river a ram which had *two* horns: and the *two* horns *were* high; but one *was* higher than the other, and the higher came up last. ⁴ I saw the ram pushing westward, and northward, and southward; so that no beasts might stand before him, neither *was there any* that could deliver out of his hand; but he did according to his will, and became great. ⁵ And as I was considering, behold, an he goat came from the west on the face of the whole earth, and touched not the ground: and the goat *had* a notable horn between his eyes. ⁶ And he came to the ram that had *two* horns, which I had seen standing before the river, and ran unto him in the fury of his power. ⁷ And I saw him come close unto the ram, and he was moved with choler against him, and smote the ram, and brake his two horns: and there was no power in the ram to stand before him, but he cast him down to the ground, and stamped upon him: and there was none that could deliver the ram out of his hand. ⁸ Therefore the he goat waxed very great: and when he was strong, the great horn was broken; and for it came up four notable ones toward the four winds of heaven. ⁹ And out of one of them came forth a little horn, which waxed exceeding great, toward the south, and toward the east, and toward the

---

3. *Two horns* — The kingdom of Media and Persia. *And the higher* — The kingdom of Persia which rose last, in Cyrus, became more eminent than that of the Medes.

4. *West-ward* — Toward Babylon, Syria, Cappadocia, Asia the less, and Greece, all westward from Media and Persia. *North-ward* — Against the Armenians, Iberians, Lydians, Colchi Caspians. *South-ward* — Against Ethiopia, Arabia, Egypt.

5. *An he-goat* — The Grecian empire. *The whole earth* — The whole Persian empire. *Touched not the ground* — Went with incredible swiftness. *A horn* — This was Alexander the great.

6. *The ram* — The king of Media and Persia.

8. *Was broken* — When Alexander was greatest, then was he broken, and that to pieces, for he, his mother, son, brother, and all his kindred were destroyed. *The four winds* —

   1. Antipater got Greece.
   2. Asia was possessed by Antigonus.
   3. Ptolemy got Egypt.
   4. Seleucus had Babylon and Syria. All these were variously situated; to the east, Babylon and Syria; to the south, Egypt; to the north, Asia the less; to the west, Greece.

pleasant *land.* ¹⁰ And it waxed great, *even* to the host of heaven; and it cast down *some* of the host and of the stars to the ground, and stamped upon them. ¹¹ Yea, he magnified *himself* even to the prince of the host, and by him the daily *sacrifice* was taken away, and the place of his sanctuary was cast down. ¹² And an host was given *him* against the daily *sacrifice* by reason of transgression, and it cast down the truth to the ground; and it practised, and prospered.

¹³ Then I heard one saint speaking, and another saint said unto that certain *saint* which spake, How long *shall be* the vision *concerning* the daily *sacrifice,* and the transgression of desolation, to give both the sanctuary and the host to be trodden under foot? ¹⁴ And he said unto me, Unto two thousand and three hundred days; then shall the sanctuary be cleansed.

¹⁵ And it came to pass, when I, *even* I Daniel, had seen the vision, and sought for the meaning, then, behold, there stood before me as the appearance of a man. ¹⁶ And I heard a man's voice between *the banks of* Ulai, which called, and said, Gabriel, make this *man* to understand the vision. ¹⁷ So he came near where I stood: and when he came, I was afraid, and fell upon my

---

9. *A little horn* — This little horn was Antiochus Epiphanes. *The south* — Egypt where he besieged and took many places. *The east* — In Syria, Babylon, Armenia. *The pleasant land* — Judea, so called because of the temple and people of God in it, and the fruitfulness of it.

10. *The host of heaven* — The church of God militant, who worship the God of heaven, who are citizens of heaven, whose names are written in heaven; and among these the priests, and champions, who were as stars shining above the rest; these he profaned and slew cruelly.

11. *The prince* — Not only against the high-priest, but against God himself. *Was cast down* — He took away the use of the temple as to the holy service and sacrifices.

12. *By reason of transgression* — Both the transgression of the priests, and of the people.

13. *One saint* — That is, one holy angel. *How long* — How long shall Antiochus continue his vexations against the people and prevent the worship of God? This is, the treading down of the sanctuary, and the host.

14. *He* — That angel. *Then* — Just so long it was, from the defection of the people, procured by Menelaus, the high-priest, to the cleansing of the sanctuary, and the re-establishment of religion among them.

15. *The meaning* — A more clear discovery of those things. *The appearance of a man* — Probably Gabriel.

16. *A man's voice* — Of him before mentioned, namely, Christ.

face: but he said unto me, Understand, O son of man: for at the time of the end *shall be* the vision. ⁱ⁸ Now as he was speaking with me, I was in a deep sleep on my face toward the ground: but he touched me, and set me upright. ¹⁹ And he said, Behold, I will make thee know what shall be in the last end of the indignation; for at the time appointed the end *shall be*. ²⁰ The ram which thou sawest having *two* horns *are* the kings of Media and Persia. ²¹ And the rough goat *is* the king of Grecia; and the great horn that *is* between his eyes *is* the first king. ²² Now that being broken, whereas four stood up for it, four kingdoms shall stand up out of the nation, but not in his power. ²³ And in the latter time of their kingdom, when the transgressors are come to the full, a king of fierce countenance, and understanding dark sentences, shall stand up. ²⁴ And his power shall be mighty, but not by his own power; and he shall destroy wonderfully, and shall prosper, and practise, and shall destroy the mighty and the holy people. ²⁵ And through his policy also he shall cause craft to prosper in his hand; and he shall magnify *himself* in his heart, and by peace shall destroy many; he shall also stand up against the Prince of princes;

---

17. *He came near* — That he might speak more familiarly to him, yet Daniel could not bear the glory of it. How much less can we bear the glory of God, and how graciously hath the Lord dealt with us, to teach us by men, *and not by angels? O son of man* — He calls him son of man, to make him mind his frailty, and not to be lifted up with this great condescension of heaven. *At the time* — In God's appointed time, in the latter day, but not now in thy lifetime.

18. *Toward the ground* — Being terrified with the splendor and grandeur both of the messenger and message. *Set me upright* — By one touch only. The power of spirits is incomparably greater than that of the strongest of men.

19. *The indignation* — God will raise up Antiochus to execute his wrath against the Jews for their sins, yet there shall be an end of that indignation.

23. *In the latter time* — When they were come to the height, and beginning to decline. *When the transgressors* — When the Jews were grown to an excess of wickedness, then God suffered Antiochus to persecute them. *Dark sentences* — Full of subtilty: such all histories declare Antiochus to be.

24. *Not by his own power* — Not by any heroic deeds, but by making use of the Jewish factions, through the divine commission to punish a backsliding nation; and by means of Eumenes and Attalus, by whose help he got up to this height. *Shall destroy* — He shall by force, craft, and cruelty, destroy many of God's people.

but he shall be broken without hand. ²⁶ And the vision of the evening and the morning which was told *is* true; wherefore shut thou up the vision; for it *shall be* for many days. ²⁷ And I Daniel fainted, and was sick *certain* days; afterward I rose up, and did the king's business; and I was astonished at the vision, but none understood *it.*

Chapter 9

¹ In the first year of Darius the son of Ahasuerus, of the seed of the Medes, which was made king over the realm of the Chaldeans; ² In the first year of his reign I Daniel understood by books the number of the years, whereof the word of the LORD came to Jeremiah the prophet, that he would accomplish seventy years in the desolations of Jerusalem.

³ And I set my face unto the Lord God, to seek by prayer and supplications, with fasting, and sackcloth, and ashes. ⁴ And I prayed unto the LORD my God, and made my confession, and said, O Lord, the great and dreadful God, keeping the covenant and mercy to them that love him, and to them that keep his commandments; ⁵ We have sinned, and have committed iniquity, and have done wickedly, and have rebelled, even by departing from

---

25. *By peace* — Under color of kindness. *Against the prince of princes* — He fought against God, affronting God's laws, profaning God's worship, and temple, and setting up the image and worship of Jupiter there. *Without hand* — By a disease whereof he died, 1Macc 6:8.

26. *Shut thou up* — Lay it up in thy heart. *For many days* — Three hundred years after this; long after Daniel's days.

27. *Was sick* — Being overwhelmed by a sense of the calamity that should befall the people of God. *Did the king's business* — Having recovered strength, he minded his place, duty and trust, and concealed the whole, that they might not see it by his countenance.

Ch 9. Daniel's prayer for the restoration of Israel, ver. 1-23. The answer sent him by an angel, ver. 24-27. This is the clearest prophecy of the Messiah in all the Old Testament.

1. *In the first year of Darius* — That is, immediately after the overthrow of the kingdom of Babylon, which was the year of the Jews deliverance from captivity. *Of the Medes* — This Darius was not Darius the Persian, under whom the temple was built, as some have asserted, to invalidate the credibility of this book; but Darius the Mede, who lived in the time of Daniel.

2. *By books* — By the sacred books.

thy precepts and from thy judgments. ⁶ Neither have we hearkened unto thy servants the prophets, which spake in thy name to our kings, our princes, and our fathers, and to all the people of the land. ⁷ O Lord, righteousness *belongeth* unto thee, but unto us confusion of faces, as at this day; to the men of Judah, and to the inhabitants of Jerusalem, and unto all Israel, *that are* near, and *that are* far off, through all the countries whither thou hast driven them, because of their trespass that they have trespassed against thee. ⁸ O Lord, to us *belongeth* confusion of face, to our kings, to our princes, and to our fathers, because we have sinned against thee. ⁹ To the Lord our God *belong* mercies and forgivenesses, though we have rebelled against him; ¹⁰ Neither have we obeyed the voice of the LORD our God, to walk in his laws, which he set before us by his servants the prophets. ¹¹ Yea, all Israel have transgressed thy law, even by departing, that they might not obey thy voice; therefore the curse is poured upon us, and the oath that *is* written in the law of Moses the servant of God, because we have sinned against him. ¹² And he hath confirmed his words, which he spake against us, and against our judges that judged us, by bringing upon us a great evil; for under the whole heaven hath not been done as hath been done upon Jerusalem. ¹³ As *it is* written in the law of Moses, all this evil is come upon us: yet made we not our prayer before the LORD our God, that we might turn from our iniquities, and understand thy truth. ¹⁴ Therefore hath the LORD watched upon the evil, and brought it upon us; for the LORD our God *is* righteous in all his works which he doeth; for we obeyed not his voice. ¹⁵ And now, O Lord our God, that hast brought thy people forth out of the land of Egypt with a mighty hand, and hast gotten thee renown, as at this day; we have sinned, we have done wickedly.

¹⁶ O Lord, according to all thy righteousness, I beseech thee, let thine anger and thy fury be turned away from thy city Jerusalem, thy holy mountain; because for our sins, and for the iniquities of our fathers, Jerusalem and thy people *are become* a reproach to all *that are* about us. ¹⁷ Now therefore, O our God, hear the prayer of thy servant, and his supplications, and cause thy face to shine upon thy sanctuary that is desolate,

---

12. *Judged us* — Whose duty it was to govern the people, and to judge their causes; wherein if there was a failure, it was a sin, and judgment upon the people, and upon the rulers and judges themselves also. *Upon Jerusalem* — A place privileged many ways above all others, and punished above all others.

14. *The Lord watched* — God's watching denotes the fit ways that he always takes to punish sinners.

for the Lord's sake. ¹⁸ O my God, incline thine ear, and hear; open thine eyes, and behold our desolations, and the city which is called by thy name; for we do not present our supplications before thee for our righteousnesses, but for thy great mercies. ¹⁹ O Lord, hear; O Lord, forgive; O Lord, hearken and do; defer not, for thine own sake, O my God; for thy city and thy people are called by thy name.

²⁰ And whiles I *was* speaking, and praying, and confessing my sin and the sin of my people Israel, and presenting my supplication before the LORD my God for the holy mountain of my God; ²¹ Yea, whiles I *was* speaking in prayer, even the man Gabriel, whom I had seen in the vision at the beginning, being caused to fly swiftly, touched me about the time of the evening oblation. ²² And he informed *me,* and talked with me, and said, O Daniel, I am now come forth to give thee skill and understanding. ²³ At the beginning of thy supplications the commandment came forth, and I am come to show *thee;* for thou *art* greatly beloved; therefore understand the matter, and consider the vision. ²⁴ Seventy weeks are determined upon thy people and upon thy holy city, to finish the transgression, and to make an end of sins, and to make reconciliation for iniquity, and to bring in everlasting righteousness, and to seal up the vision and prophecy, and to anoint the most Holy. ²⁵ Know therefore and understand, *that* from the going forth of the

---

17. *For the Lord's sake* — For the sake of the Messiah: to whom the title Lord is frequently given in the Old Testament.

21. *About the time* — The time of the evening sacrifice was a solemn and set time of devotion. Tho' the altar was in ruins, and there was no oblation offered upon it, yet the pious Jews were daily thoughtful of the time when it should have been offered, and hoped that their prayer would be set forth before God as incense, and the lifting up of their hands, as the evening sacrifice. This was peculiarly a type of that great sacrifice, which Christ was to offer: and it was in virtue of that sacrifice, that Daniel's prayer was accepted, when he prayed for the Lord's sake.

24. *Seventy weeks* — These weeks are weeks of days, and these days are so many years. *To finish the transgression* — The angel discovers first the disease in three several words, which contain all sorts of sin, which the Messiah should free us from by his full redemption. He shews the cure of this disease in three words:

1. To finish transgression.
2. To make an end of sin.
3. To make reconciliation: all which words are very expressive in the original, and signify to pardon, to blot out, to destroy.

commandment to restore and to build Jerusalem unto the Messiah the Prince *shall be* seven weeks, and threescore and two weeks: the street shall be built again, and the wall, even in troublous times. ²⁶ And after threescore and two weeks shall Messiah be cut off, but not for himself; and the people of the prince that shall come shall destroy the city and the sanctuary; and the end thereof *shall be* with a flood, and unto the end of the war desolations are determined. ²⁷ And he shall confirm the covenant with many for one week: and in the midst of the week he shall cause the sacrifice and the oblation to cease, and for the overspreading of abominations he shall make *it* desolate, even until the consummation, and that determined shall be poured upon the desolate.

To bring in everlasting righteousness — To bring in justification by the free grace of God in Christ, and sanctification by his spirit: called everlasting, because Christ is eternal, and so are the acceptance and holiness purchased for us. Christ brings this in,

1. By his merit.
2. By his gospel declaring it.
3. By faith applying, and sealing it by the Holy Ghost.

To seal up — To abrogate the former dispensation of the law, and to ratify the gospel covenant. *To anoint* — This alludes to his name Messiah and Christ, both which signify anointed. Christ was anointed at his first conception, and personal union, Luke 1:35. In his baptism, Matthew 3:17, to his three offices by the Holy Ghost:

1. King, Matthew 2:2.
2. Prophet, Isaiah 61:1.
3. Priest, Psalm 110:4.

25. *From the going forth* — From the publication of the edict, whether of Cyrus or Darius, to restore and to build it.

26. *And after* — After the seven and the sixty two that followed them. *Not for himself* — But for our sakes, and for our salvation. *And the people* — The Romans under the conduct of Titus. *Determined* — God hath decreed to destroy that place and people, by the miseries and desolations of war.

27. *He shall confirm* — Christ confirmed the new covenant,

1. By the testimony of angels, of John Baptist, of the wise men, of the saints then living, of Moses and Elias.
2. By his preaching.
3. By signs and wonders.

Chapter 10

¹ In the third year of Cyrus king of Persia a thing was revealed unto Daniel, whose name was called Belteshazzar; and the thing *was* true, but the time appointed *was* long: and he understood the thing, and had understanding of the vision. ² In those days I Daniel was mourning three full weeks. ³ I ate no pleasant bread, neither came flesh nor wine in my mouth, neither did I anoint myself at all, till three whole weeks were fulfilled. ⁴ And in the four and twentieth day of the first month, as I was by the side of the great river, which *is* Hiddekel; ⁵ Then I lifted up mine eyes, and looked, and behold a certain man clothed in linen, whose loins *were* girded with fine gold of Uphaz: ⁶ His body also *was* like the beryl, and his face as the appearance of lightning, and his eyes as lamps of fire, and his arms and his feet like in colour to polished brass, and the voice of his words like the voice of a multitude. ⁷ And I Daniel alone saw the vision; for the men that were with me saw not the vision; but a great quaking fell upon them, so that they fled to hide themselves. ⁸ Therefore I was left alone, and saw this great vision, and there remained no strength in me; for my comeliness was turned in me into

---

    4. By his holy life.
    5. By his resurrection and ascension.
    6. By his death and blood shedding.

Shall cause the sacrifice to cease — All the Jewish rites, and Levitical worship. By his death he abrogated, and put an end to this laborious service, for ever. *And that determined* — That spirit of slumber, which God has determined to pour on the desolate nation, 'till the time draws near, when all Israel shall be saved'.

Ch 10. This chapter and the two next make one entire vision and prophecy, given Daniel about two years after the former. This chapter is introductory: the next has the prophecy itself, and the twelfth chapter, the conclusion of it. In this we have Daniel's solemn humiliation, ver. 1-3. A glorious appearance of the Son of God, ver. 4-9. The encouragement given him to expect a full discovery of future events, ver. 10-25.

    2. *Was mourning* — Because he foresaw the many calamities that would befall the Jews for their sins, especially for destroying the Messiah, and rejecting his gospel.

    4. *The first month* — Nisan, which is March. *Hiddekel* — Or Tigris.

    5. *A certain man* — Very probably Christ, who appeared to Daniel in royal and priestly robes, and in so great brightness and majesty.

corruption, and I retained no strength. ⁹ Yet heard I the voice of his words; and when I heard the voice of his words, then was I in a deep sleep on my face, and my face toward the ground.

¹⁰ And, behold, an hand touched me, which set me upon my knees and *upon* the palms of my hands. ¹¹ And he said unto me, O Daniel, a man greatly beloved, understand the words that I speak unto thee, and stand upright; for unto thee am I now sent. And when he had spoken this word unto me, I stood trembling. ¹² Then said he unto me, Fear not, Daniel; for from the first day that thou didst set thine heart to understand, and to chasten thyself before thy God, thy words were heard, and I am come for thy words. ¹³ But the prince of the kingdom of Persia withstood me one and twenty days; but, lo, Michael, one of the chief princes, came to help me; and I remained there with the kings of Persia. ¹⁴ Now I am come to make thee understand what shall befall thy people in the latter days; for yet the vision *is* for *many* days. ¹⁵ And when he had spoken such words unto me, I set my face toward the ground, and I became dumb. ¹⁶ And, behold, *one* like the similitude of the sons of men touched my lips; then I opened my mouth, and spake, and said unto him that stood before me, O my lord, by the vision my sorrows are turned upon me, and I have retained no strength. ¹⁷ For how can the servant of this my lord talk with this my lord? for as for me, straightway there remained no strength in me, neither is there breath left in me. ¹⁸ Then there came again and touched me *one* like the appearance of a man, and he strengthened me, ¹⁹ And said, O man greatly beloved, fear not: peace *be* unto thee, be strong, yea, be strong. And when he had spoken unto me, I was strengthened, and said, Let my lord speak; for thou hast strengthened me. ²⁰ Then said he, Knowest thou wherefore I come unto thee? and now will I return to fight with the prince of

---

12. *He* — Not Christ, but Gabriel.

13. *Withstood me* — God suffered the wicked counsels of Cambyses to take place awhile; but Daniel by his prayers, and the angel by his power, overcame him at last: and this very thing laid a foundation of the ruin of the Persian monarchies. *Michael* — Michael here is commonly supposed to mean Christ. *I remained* — To counter-work their designs against the people of God.

15. *I set my face* — I prostrated myself upon the earth. *And I became dumb* — Thro' astonishment.

16. *One like the sons of men* — This likewise seems to have been Gabriel. *I have retained no strength* — Tho' he appeared to him, and spake to him as a man, yet Daniel could not bear his presence, without some dread.

Persia: and when I am gone forth, lo, the prince of Grecia shall come. [21] But I will show thee that which is noted in the scripture of truth: and *there is* none that holdeth with me in these things, but Michael your prince.

Chapter 11

[1] Also I in the first year of Darius the Mede, *even* I, stood to confirm and to strengthen him. [2] And now will I show thee the truth. Behold, there shall stand up yet three kings in Persia; and the fourth shall be far richer than *they* all: and by his strength through his riches he shall stir up all against the realm of Grecia. [3] And a mighty king shall stand up, that shall rule with great dominion, and do according to his will. [4] And when he shall stand up, his kingdom shall be broken, and shall be divided toward the four winds of heaven; and not to his posterity, nor according to his dominion which he ruled: for his kingdom shall be plucked up, even for others beside those.

[5] And the king of the south shall be strong, and *one* of his princes; and he shall be strong above him, and have dominion; his dominion *shall be* a great dominion. [6] And in the end of years they shall join themselves together; for

---

20. *To fight* — To oppose his mischievous designs.

21. *Michael* — Christ alone is the protector of his church, when all the princes of the earth desert or oppose it.

Ch 11. A prediction of the setting up of the Grecian monarchy, ver. 1-4. Of the affairs of Egypt and Syria, ver. 5-20. The rise and success of Antiochus Epiphanes, ver. 21-29. The mischief he would do to the Jews, ver. 30-43. His fall, ver. 44, 45.

2. *He* — Xerxes was more potent than all the other three, because his father Darius had gathered an incredible mass for him, which he himself increased for six years together, before he made his expedition against Greece. There were more kings of Persia besides those four, but they had no concern with the people of God.

3. *A mighty king* — Alexander the great.

4. *When he shall stand up* — When he is come to his highest point. *Nor according to his dominion* — They did not reign as kings at first, but only as captains; and as to the extent of their dominion, it was far less than Alexander's, yea, all four fell short of his. *Even for others* — Some lesser commanders shared several parts of the empire.

5. *The king of the south* — This king was Ptolemy, the first king of Egypt after Alexander who is brought in, because he took Jerusalem by treachery;

the king's daughter of the south shall come to the king of the north to make an agreement; but she shall not retain the power of the arm; neither shall he stand, nor his arm; but she shall be given up, and they that brought her, and he that begat her, and he that strengthened her in *these* times. ⁷ But out of a branch of her roots shall *one* stand up in his estate, which shall come with an army, and shall enter into the fortress of the king of the north, and shall deal against them, and shall prevail. ⁸ And shall also carry captives into Egypt their gods, with their princes, *and* with their precious vessels of silver and of gold; and he shall continue *more* years than the king of the north. ⁹ So the king of the south shall come into *his* kingdom, and shall return into his own land. ¹⁰ But his sons shall be stirred up, and shall assemble a multitude of great forces; and *one* shall certainly come, and overflow, and pass through: then shall he return, and be stirred up, *even* to his fortress. ¹¹ And the king of the south shall be moved with choler, and shall come forth and fight with him, *even* with the king of the north; and he shall set forth a great multitude; but the multitude shall be given into his hand. ¹² *And* when he hath taken away the multitude, his heart shall be lifted up; and he shall cast down *many*

---

for the angel minds only those persons and things which related to the Jews. *One of his princes* — Seleucus Nicanor, who overcame Demetrius, and added Asia to his empire.

6. *They* — The successors of those first kings of Egypt and Syria. *Make an agreement* — Bernice shall come from Egypt and marry with Antiochus Theus, who was the son of Antiochus Soter, and nephew to Seleucus Nicanor; for her father brought her to Pelusium with an infinite sum of gold and silver for her dowry. *She shall not retain* — She continued not in favor and authority. *Nor his arm* — His power.

7. *Shall one stand up* — Of Bernice shall come Ptolemaeus Euergetes, who shall revenge the wrong done to his sister. *Shall enter into the fortress* — For he invaded Syria, and took many strong-holds.

8. *He shall continue more years* — He continued forty-six years.

9. *Return* — So he did with a booty of forty thousand talents of silver.

10. *But his sons* — He means the sons of the king of the north, shall be incensed with the deeds of Ptolemaeus Euergetes, and his son Ptolemaeus Philopator. *One shall come* — Antiochus the great, shall pass through Syria and recover what the king of Egypt took from his father. *Even to his fortress* — To Raphia, which was a strong fortress at the entrance of Egypt.

11. *His hand* — Into the hand of Ptolemy.

ten thousands; but he shall not be strengthened *by it.* ¹³ For the king of the north shall return, and shall set forth a multitude greater than the former, and shall certainly come after certain years with a great army and with much riches. ¹⁴ And in those times there shall many stand up against the king of the south: also the robbers of thy people shall exalt themselves to establish the vision; but they shall fall. ¹⁵ So the king of the north shall come, and cast up a mount, and take the most fenced cities: and the arms of the south shall not withstand, neither his chosen people, neither *shall there be any* strength to withstand. ¹⁶ But he that cometh against him shall do according to his own will, and none shall stand before him; and he shall stand in the glorious land, which by his hand shall be consumed. ¹⁷ He shall also set his face to enter with the strength of his whole kingdom, and upright ones with him; thus shall he do; and he shall give him the daughter of women, corrupting her; but she shall not stand *on his side,* neither be for him. ¹⁸ After this shall he turn his face unto the isles, and shall take many; but a prince for his own behalf shall cause the reproach offered by him to cease; without his own reproach he shall cause *it* to turn upon him. ¹⁹ Then he shall turn his face toward the fort of his own land; but he shall stumble and fall, and not be found. ²⁰ Then shall stand up in his estate a raiser of taxes *in* the glory of the kingdom: but within few

---

12. *His heart shall be lifted up* — He might have recovered all, but he grew proud of his victory, and returned again to his luxury.

16. *But he* — Antiochus, that comes against Ptolemy. *The glorious land* — Judea. Antiochus held all Judea, and with the provision and product of it, maintained his army.

17. *He shall also set his face* — He shall use all the force he can to master Egypt, and engross it to himself. *Upright ones* — Many of the religious Jews joined with him: the rest of his army was a profane rabble of rude Heathens. *He shall give* — Antiochus shall give Cleopatra his daughter to young Ptolemy, called the daughter of women, for her beauty. *Corrupting her* — Persuading her to betray her husband: but she stuck to her husband's interest, and not her father's.

18. *The isles* — The isles and sea-coasts of the Mediterranean and Aegean sea. *But a prince* — The Roman ambassador Scipio beat Antiochus at his own weapons of power and policy, and turned the reproach upon his own head.

19. *Then* — Then he turned his face home-ward, yet was he not in safety, but was quickly after killed.

days he shall be destroyed, neither in anger, nor in battle. [21] And in his estate shall stand up a vile person, to whom they shall not give the honour of the kingdom; but he shall come in peaceably, and obtain the kingdom by flatteries. [22] And with the arms of a flood shall they be overflown from before him, and shall be broken; yea, also the prince of the covenant. [23] And after the league *made* with him he shall work deceitfully; for he shall come up, and shall become strong with a small people. [24] He shall enter peaceably even upon the fattest places of the province; and he shall do *that* which his fathers have not done, nor his fathers' fathers; he shall scatter among them the prey, and spoil, and riches; *yea,* and he shall forecast his devices against the strong holds, even for a time. [25] And he shall stir up his power and his courage against the king of the south with a great army; and the king of the south shall be stirred up to battle with a very great and mighty army; but he

---

20. *A raiser of taxes* — Seleucus Philopator, who peeled his subjects, and spared not to rob the temple. *Within few days* — For he lived not out the third part of his father's reign. *Not in battle* — Not by open force, but by poison.

21. *A vile person* — Antiochus, called Epiphanes by his flatterers, but the people of God accounted him infamous, base, and treacherous. *They* — Neither peers nor people, nor was he the heir, but his nephew; but he crept in by flatteries.

22. *Overflown* — The Egyptian force near Pelusium, where they fell by the power of Antiochus, with a great slaughter, near the river Nile. *The prince* — The high-priest with his place and honor, for he put out Onias, and set up in his stead, Jason his brother.

23. *After the league* — For he made a league with Egypt, and came with a few, (but chosen men) and took the passes, and put all in subjection to him.

24. *He shall enter peaceably* — He shall come in upon the Egyptians under pretense of peace, in a plentiful and delicious country, and among a mass of treasures which the kings successively had heaped up; the greatest part of which Antiochus distributed among his confidants, whereby he obliged them the faster to him. He did herein what his fathers had not done; the kings of Syria before him, could never attain to this success over Egypt. *Against the strong-holds* — Having succeeded thus far, he shall proceed to the places of greatest strength in that kingdom. *For a time* — That is 'till God put a stop to his career, for the Egyptians found means to deliver themselves from his yoke.

shall not stand: for they shall forecast devices against him. ²⁶ Yea, they that feed of the portion of his meat shall destroy him, and his army shall overflow; and many shall fall down slain. ²⁷ And both these kings' hearts *shall be* to do mischief, and they shall speak lies at one table; but it shall not prosper: for yet the end *shall be* at the time appointed. ²⁸ Then shall he return into his land with great riches; and his heart *shall be* against the holy covenant; and he shall do *exploits,* and return to his own land. ²⁹ At the time appointed he shall return, and come toward the south; but it shall not be as the former, or as the latter.

³⁰ For the ships of Chittim shall come against him: therefore he shall be grieved, and return, and have indignation against the holy covenant; so shall he do; he shall even return, and have intelligence with them that forsake the holy covenant. ³¹ And arms shall stand on his part, and they shall pollute the sanctuary of strength, and shall take away the daily *sacrifice,* and they shall place the abomination that maketh desolate. ³² And such as do wickedly against the covenant shall he corrupt by flatteries; but the people that do know their God shall be strong, and do *exploits.* ³³ And they that understand

---

25. *But he shall not stand* — He might have prospered, if he had not been betrayed by Eulaius, Benaeus, and the rest of his nobles, corrupted by Antiochus.

26. *Yea* — His most familiar friends and confidants; for he shall be overthrown with a great slaughter, as when the Nile overflows the country.

27. *At one table* — They shall meet under pretense of peace. *But it shall not prosper* — For neither shall Antiochus gain Egypt by all his artifice, nor Ptolemy, Syria. *At the time appointed* — By the Lord, whose purpose and counsel shall stand.

28. *Then shall he return* — Antiochus shall depart with his booty gotten in Egypt. *Against the holy covenant* — Against the law of God, with the people that worshipped God according to his will.

29. *Toward the south* — Egypt, to fight against Ptolemy. *But* — This shall not be so prosperous as the two former expeditions, but shall fail both of his victory and booty.

30. *The ships of Chittim* — The Romans out of Italy, and the Archipelago. This made his heart boil with rancor, which he spit out against the Jews; especially being solicited to it by Jason first, and Menelaus after, who were apostates, and betrayers of their brethren.

31. *And arms* — Not only of his own army, but many Jews. *The sanctuary* — Even the holy of holies. *The abomination* — The statue of Jupiter placed in the temple.

among the people shall instruct many; yet they shall fall by the sword, and by flame, by captivity, and by spoil, *many* days. ³⁴ Now when they shall fall, they shall be helped with a little help; but many shall cleave to them with flatteries. ³⁵ And *some* of them of understanding shall fall, to try them, and to purge, and to make *them* white, *even* to the time of the end; because *it is* yet for a time appointed. ³⁶ And the king shall do according to his will; and he shall exalt himself, and magnify himself above every god, and shall speak marvellous things against the God of gods, and shall prosper till the indignation be accomplished; for that that is determined shall be done. ³⁷ Neither shall he regard the God of his fathers, nor the desire of women, nor regard any god: for he shall magnify himself above all. ³⁸ But in his estate shall he honour the God of forces; and a god whom his fathers knew not shall he honour with gold, and silver, and with precious stones, and pleasant things. ³⁹ Thus shall he do in the most strong holds with a strange god, whom he shall acknowledge *and* increase with glory; and he shall cause them to rule over many, and shall divide the land for gain. ⁴⁰ And at the time of the end shall the king of the south push at him; and the king of the north shall come against him like a whirlwind, with chariots, and with horsemen, and with many ships; and he shall enter into the countries, and shall overflow and pass over. ⁴¹ He shall enter also into the glorious land, and many *countries* shall be overthrown; but these shall escape out of his hand, *even* Edom, and Moab, and the chief of the children of Ammon. ⁴² He shall stretch forth his hand also upon the countries; and the land of Egypt shall not escape. ⁴³ But he shall have power over the treasures of gold and of silver, and over all the precious things of Egypt; and the Libyans and the Ethiopians *shall be* at his steps. ⁴⁴

---

36. *The king* — Antiochus was an eminent type of antichrist; to whom many things that follow may be applied by way of accommodation; altho' they principally refer to Antiochus, and had their primary accomplishment in him. *For that that is determined* — That which God hath decreed to be done by him shall be done; and that which God hath purposed to be done upon him.

38. *But in his estate* — In the room of his father's God. *The God of forces* — This seems to be Jupiter Olympius, never introduced among the Syrians, 'till Antiochus did it'.

39. *With a strange God* — Using all art and authority to propagate his worship.

41. *The children of Ammon* — He will not hurt them; because they helped him against the Jews.

43. *At his steps* — He had them at his foot, at his beck.

But tidings out of the east and out of the north shall trouble him; therefore he shall go forth with great fury to destroy, and utterly to make away many. ⁴⁵ And he shall plant the tabernacles of his palace between the seas in the glorious holy mountain; yet he shall come to his end, and none shall help him.

Chapter 12

¹ And at that time shall Michael stand up, the great prince which standeth for the children of thy people; and there shall be a time of trouble, such as never was since there was a nation *even* to that same time; and at that time thy people shall be delivered, every one that shall be found written in the book. ² And many of them that sleep in the dust of the earth shall awake, some to everlasting life, and some to shame *and* everlasting contempt. ³ And they that be wise shall shine as the brightness of the firmament; and they that turn many to righteousness as the stars for ever and ever. ⁴ But thou, O Daniel, shut up the words, and seal the book, *even* to the time of the end: many shall run to and fro, and knowledge shall be increased.

⁵ Then I Daniel looked, and, behold, there stood other two, the one on this side of the bank of the river, and the other on that side of the bank of the

---

45. *None shall help him* — God shall cut him off in the midst of his days. And when he destroys, who can help?

Ch 12. A promise of deliverance, and of a joyful resurrection, ver. 1-4. A conference concerning the time of these events, ver. 5-7. An answer to Daniel's enquiry, ver. 8-13.

1. *For the children* — The meaning seems to be, as after the death of Antiochus the Jews had some deliverance, so there will be yet a greater deliverance to the people of God, when Michael your prince, the Messiah shall appear for your salvation. *A time of trouble* — the siege of Jerusalem, before the final judgment. The phrase 'at that time', probably includes all the time of Christ, from his first, to his last coming.

4. *Seal the book* — The book was command to be sealed, because it would be long before the words would be fulfilled, whereas those that were shortly to be fulfilled, were forbidden to be sealed. *Shall run* — Shall diligently search these prophecies; and they shall know the signs of the times, and wait upon God in the way of his judgments. He means chiefly in gospel-times.

river. ⁶ And *one* said to the man clothed in linen, which *was* upon the waters of the river, How long *shall it be to* the end of these wonders? ⁷ And I heard the man clothed in linen, which *was* upon the waters of the river, when he held up his right hand and his left hand unto heaven, and sware by him that liveth for ever that *it shall be* for a time, times, and an half; and when he shall have accomplished to scatter the power of the holy people, all these *things* shall be finished. ⁸ And I heard, but I understood not; then said I, O my Lord, what *shall be* the end of these *things?* ⁹ And he said, Go thy way, Daniel: for the words *are* closed up and sealed till the time of the end. ¹⁰ Many shall be purified, and made white, and tried; but the wicked shall do wickedly; and none of the wicked shall understand; but the wise shall understand. ¹¹ And from the time *that* the daily *sacrifice* shall be taken away, and the abomination that maketh desolate set up, *there shall be* a thousand two hundred and ninety days.

¹² Blessed *is* he that waiteth, and cometh to the thousand three hundred and five and thirty days. ¹³ But go thou thy way till the end *be*; for thou shalt rest, and stand in thy lot at the end of the days.

---

5. *Other two* — Two angels waiting on Christ.

6. *To the man* — To Christ, who seemed to stand in the air above the waters, or upon them.

7. *He held up his right hand* — He held up both hands to heaven, for the more sure and solemn confirmation of it; and to denote the unchangeableness of God's decrees both for good to the church, and for evil to her enemies. *By him* — By God the Father, and by himself that liveth for ever, to shew the eternal God only knew that decreed it, and would bring it to pass. *And an half* — That is, a year, two years and half a year. We meet with this in the revelation, under the title, some times of three days and an half, put for three years and an half, sometimes, forty two months, sometimes, twelve hundred and sixty days. *Shall be finished* — Which reaches to the calling of the Jews upon the destruction of antichrist.

8. *What shall be the end* — What is the meaning of all this?

9. *And sealed* — They shall not be clearly understood, 'till the event make them good.

10. *And tried* — The afflictions of the church are to prepare them, by taking away their filth, for the bridegroom, as gold and silver are tried and refined.

13. *But go thou* — I have revealed to thee these things, that thou and thy people, might be prepared for sufferings, and yet not without hope of a glorious deliverance. *For thou shalt rest* — In which hope thou shalt die, and rest from trouble, 'till the resurrection of the just. It ought to be the great concern of every one of us, to secure a happy lot in the end of the days, and then we may well be content with our present lot, welcoming the will of God.

Bibliography

John Wesley:

Hildebrandt, Franz and Oliver E. Beckerlegge. eds. *The Works of John Wesley: A Collection of Hymns for the Use of The People Called Methodists.* Nashville: Abingdon Press, 1983.

Outler, Albert. Ed. *John Wesley.* New York: Oxford University Press, 1964.

_____ ed. *The Works of John Wesley: Sermons.* 4 vols. Nashville: Abingdon Press, 1984-1987.

Olson, Mark K. ed. *John Wesley's 'A Plain Account of Christian Perfection': The Annotated Edition.* Fenwick: Truth In Heart, 2005.

Telford, John. ed. *The Letters of John Wesley.* 8 vols. London: Epworth Press, 1931.

Wesley, John. *Explanatory Notes Upon the New Testament.* 2 vols. Grand Rapids: Baker Book House, 1984.

_____ *Explanatory Notes Upon the Old Testament.* Albany: Ages Software, 1996.

_____ *A Survey of the Wisdom of God in Creation.* 2 vols. abridgment of Charles Bonnet "The Contemplation of Nature." Third American Edition. New York: Bangs and Mason, 1823.

General Studies:

Bengel, Johann Albrecht. *Bengelius's Introduction to His Exposition of the Apocalypse.* London: J. Ryall and R. Withy, 1757.

Brightman, Thomas. *A Revelation of the Apocalypse.* Amsterdam: Iudocus Hondius & Hendrick Laurenss, 1611.

Brown, Kenneth O. 'John Wesley – Post or premillennialist?' Methodist History 28:1 (October 1989), 33-41.

Burnet, Thomas. *The Theory of the Earth.* Books I-II. London: R. N., 1697.

_____ *The Sacred Theory of the Earth.* Books I-IV. London: Kinnersley, 1816.

Clark, J. C. D. *English Society, 1660-1832: Religion, Ideology and Politics during the Ancien Régime.* Second Edition. Cambridge: Cambridge University Press, 2000.

Cohn, Norman. *The Pursuit of the Millennium.* Revised and Expanded Edition. New York: Oxford University Press, 1970.

Collins, Kenneth J. *The Theology of John Wesley: Holy Love and the Shape of Grace.* Nashville: Abingdon Press, 2007.

Doddridge, Philip. *The Family Expositor.* 6 vols. London: J. Waugh, 1736-56.

Dunning, H. Ray. ed. *The Second Coming: A Wesleyan Approach to the Doctrine of Last Things.* Kansas City: Beacon Hill Press, 1995.

Force, James E. and Richard H. Popkin. eds. *Millenarianism and Messianism in Early Modern European Culture: The Millennial Turn.* Dordrecht: Kluwer Academic Publishers, 2001.

Fraser, Rebecca. *The Story of Britain: From the Romans to the Present: A Narrative History.* New York: W. W. Norton & Company, 2003.

Goen, C. C. ed. *The Great Awakening, The Works of Jonathan Edwards,* vol. 4. New Haven: Yale University Press, 1972.

Goold, William H. ed. *The Works of John Owen,* 16 vols. Carlisle: The Banner of Truth Trust, 1965.

Guyse, John. *An Exposition of the New Testament in the Form of a Paraphrase.* 3 vols., 1739-52.

Hartley, Thomas. *Paradise Restored: Or, A Testimony of the Doctrine of the Blessed Millennium.* Leeds: Binn and Brown, 1799.

Heylyn, John. *Theological Lectures.* 2 vols. London: Tonson and Draper, 1749.

Hildrop, John. *Free Thoughts Upon the Brute Creation.* London: R. Minors, 1742.

Jue, Jeffrey K. *Heaven Upon Earth: Joseph Mede and the Legacy of Millenarianism.* Dordrecht: Springer, 2006.

Kaplan, Yoset, Richard H. Popkin, and Henry Mechoulan. eds. *Menasseh Ben Israel and His World.* Leiden: E. J. Brill, 1989.

Knox, Ronald A. *Enthusiasm: A Chapter in the History of Religion with Special Reference to the Seventeenth and Eighteenth Centuries.* New York: Oxford University Press, 1961.

Koester, Craig R. *Revelation and the End of All Things.* Grand Rapids: Eerdmans Publishing Company, 2001.

Lavington, George. *The Enthusiasm of Methodists and Papists Compared.* Three Parts. London: J. & P. Knapton, 1754.

Lindberg, Carter. ed. *The Pietist Theologians.* Malden: Blackwell Publishing, 2005.

Lovejoy, Arthur O. *The Great Chain of Being: A Study of the History of an Idea.* New York: Harper & Brothers, 1936.

Maddox, Randy L. *Responsible Grace: John Wesley's Practical Theology.* Nashville: Kingswood Press, 1994.

_____ and Jason E. Vickers. eds. *The Cambridge Companion to John Wesley.* Cambridge: Cambridge University Press, 2010.

McCalla, Arthur. *A Romantic Historiosophy: The Philosophy of History of Pierre-Simon Ballanche.* Boston: Brill, 1998.

McLoughlin, William G. *Revivals, Awakenings, and Reform.* Chicago: University of Chicago Press, 1978.

Mede, Joseph. *Clavis Apocalyptica, or A Key to the Revelation.* Translated by R. Bransby Cooper. London: J. G. & F. Rivington, 1833.

_____ *The Apostasy of the Latter Times.* London: W.H. Dalton, 1845.

Meeks, M. Douglas. ed. *Wesleyan Perspectives on the New Creation.* Nashville: Kingswood Press, 2004.

Milton, John. *Paradise Lost.* The Modern Library. New York: Random House, 2007.

Moorman, J. R. H. *A History of the Church of England.* Third Edition. Harrisburg: Morehouse Publishing, 1980.

Newport, Kenneth G. C. *Apocalypse & Millennium: Studies in Biblical Eisegesis.* Cambridge: Cambridge University Press, 2000.

_____ *Premillennialism in the Early Writings of Charles Wesley.* Wesleyan Theological Journal, vol. 32, num. 1, 1997, 85-106.

_____ *The Sermons of Charles Wesley: A Critical Edition with introduction and Notes.* Oxford: Oxford University Press, 2001.

Newton, Thomas. *Analysis of the Revelation.* New Edition. London: T & W Boone, 1845.

Oden, Thomas C. *John Wesley's Scriptural Christianity: A Plain Exposition of His Teaching on Christian Doctrine.* Grand Rapids: Zondervan, 1994.

Patrides, C. A. and Joseph Wittreich. eds. *The Apocalypse in English Renaissance Thought and Literature.* Manchester: Manchester University Press, 1984.

Popkin, Richard N. ed. *Millenarianism and Messianism in English Literature and Thought 1650-1800.* Leiden: E. J. Brill, 1988.

Porter, Roy. *English Society in the 18th Century.* Revised Edition. London: Penguin Books, 1990.

Ray, John. *The Wisdom of God Manifested in the Works of Creation.* Tenth Edition. London: Innys and Manby, 1735.

Roberts, Alexander and James Donaldson. eds. *The Ante-Nicene Fathers*, 10 vols. Grand Rapids: Eerdmans, 1985 Reprint.

Stein, Stephen J. ed. *Apocalyptic Writings, The Works of Jonathan Edwards, vol. 5.* New Haven: Yale University Press, 1977.

Thomas, Keith. *The Ends of Life: Roads to Fulfilment in Early Modern England.* New York: Oxford University Press, 2009.

Tillyard, E. M. W. *The Elizabethan World Picture.* New York: Vintage Books, 1959.

Tyerman, Luke. *The Life and Times of the Rev. John Wesley.* 3 vols. Staffs: Tentmaker Publications, 2003 Reprint.

Ward, W. R. *Early Evangelicalism: A Global Intellectual History, 1670-1789.* Cambridge: Cambridge University Press, 2006.

Wesley, Charles. *The Journal of Charles Wesley.* 2 vols. Grand Rapids: Baker Book House, 1980.

Whiston, William. *An Essay on the Revelation of St. John.* Second Edition. London: John Whiston, 1744.

_____ *A New Theory of the Earth.* Sixth Edition. London: J. Whiston and B. White, 1755.

Wilson, John F. ed. *A History of the Work of Redemption, The Works of Jonathan Edwards,* vol. 9. New Haven: Yale University Press, 1989.

Zakai, Avihu. *Exile and Kingdom: History and Apocalypse in the Puritan Migration to America.* Cambridge: Cambridge University Press, 1992.

www.ingramcontent.com/pod-product-compliance
Lightning Source LLC
Chambersburg PA
CBHW081837230426
43669CB00018B/2742